SLEEPY PRINCESS IN THE DEMON CASTLE

14

Story & Art by
KAGIJI KUMANOMATA

NIGHTS

170th Night: You Don't Make Friends, You Just Have Them

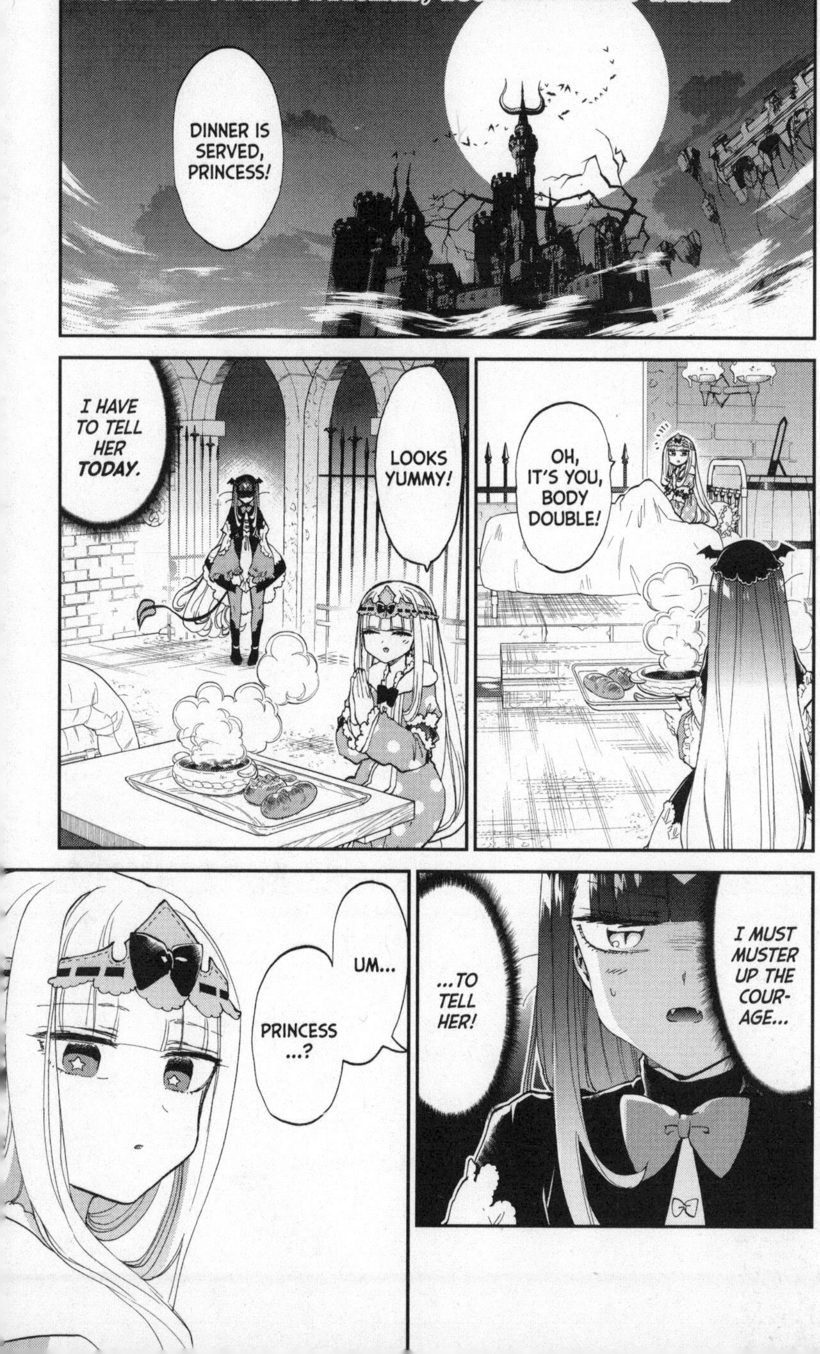
DINNER IS SERVED, PRINCESS!
OH, IT'S YOU, BODY DOUBLE!
LOOKS YUMMY!
I HAVE TO TELL HER TODAY.
I MUST MUSTER UP THE COUR-AGE...
...TO TELL HER!
UM...
PRINCESS ...?

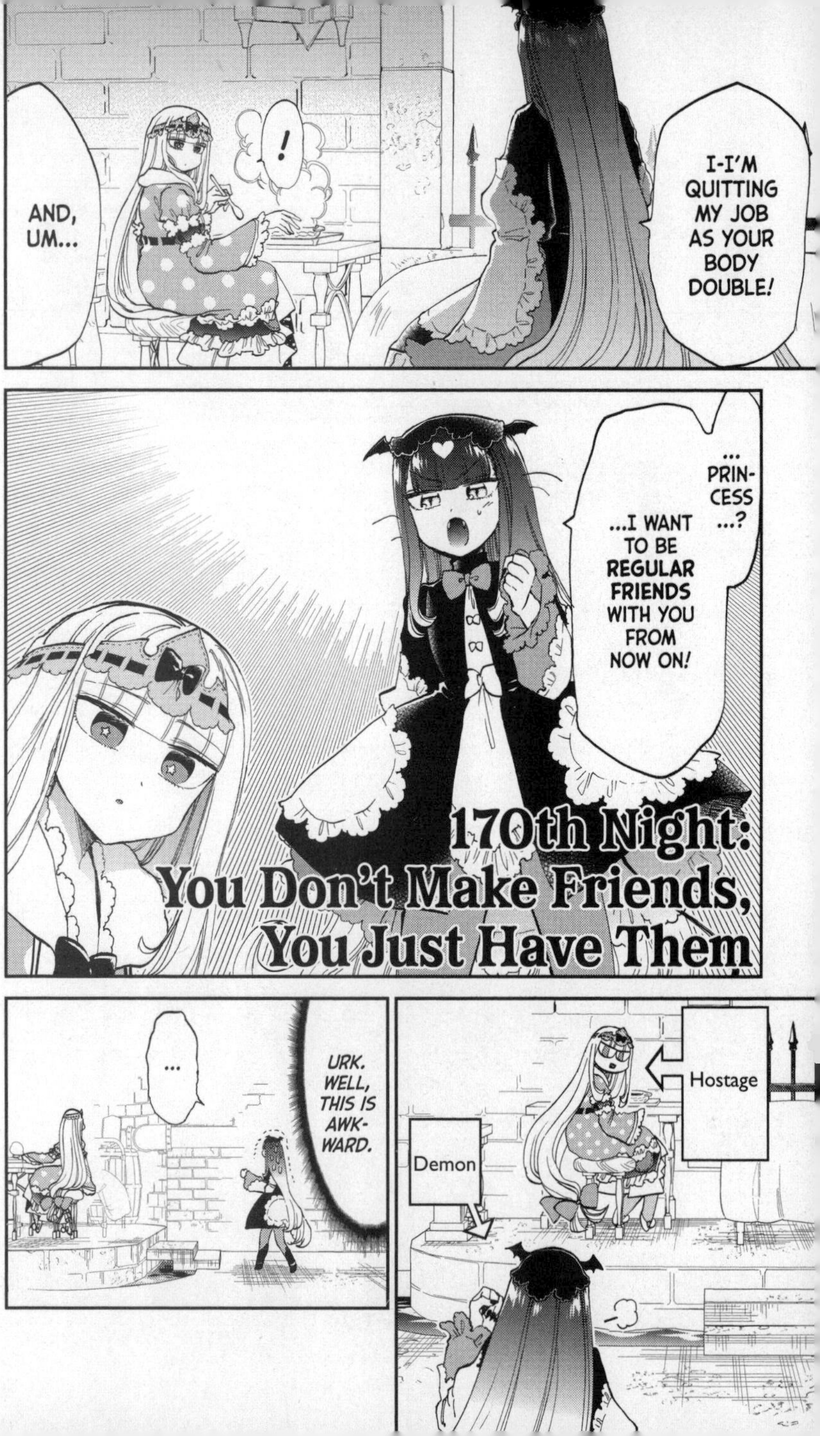
I-I'M QUITTING MY JOB AS YOUR BODY DOUBLE!
!
AND, UM...
... PRIN-CESS ...?
...I WANT TO BE REGULAR FRIENDS WITH YOU FROM NOW ON!
170th Night: You Don't Make Friends, You Just Have Them
Hostage
Demon
URK. WELL, THIS IS AWK-WARD.
...

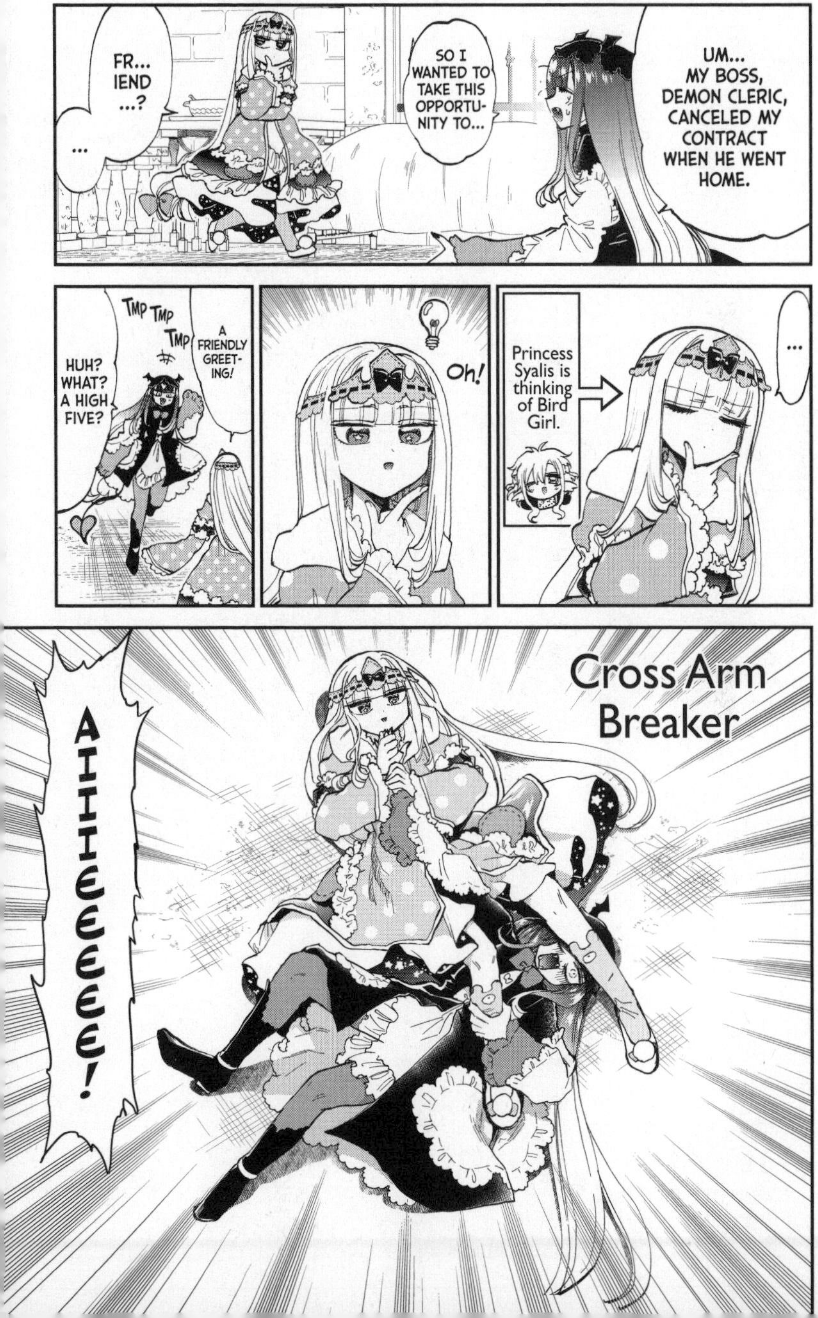

UM... MY BOSS, DEMON CLERIC, CANCELED MY CONTRACT WHEN HE WENT HOME.
SO I WANTED TO TAKE THIS OPPORTU-NITY TO...
FR... IEND ...?
...
...
Princess Syalis is thinking of Bird Girl.
Oh!
A FRIENDLY GREET-ING!
TMP TMP TMP
HUH? WHAT? A HIGH FIVE?
Cross Arm Breaker
AIIIIEEEEEEE!

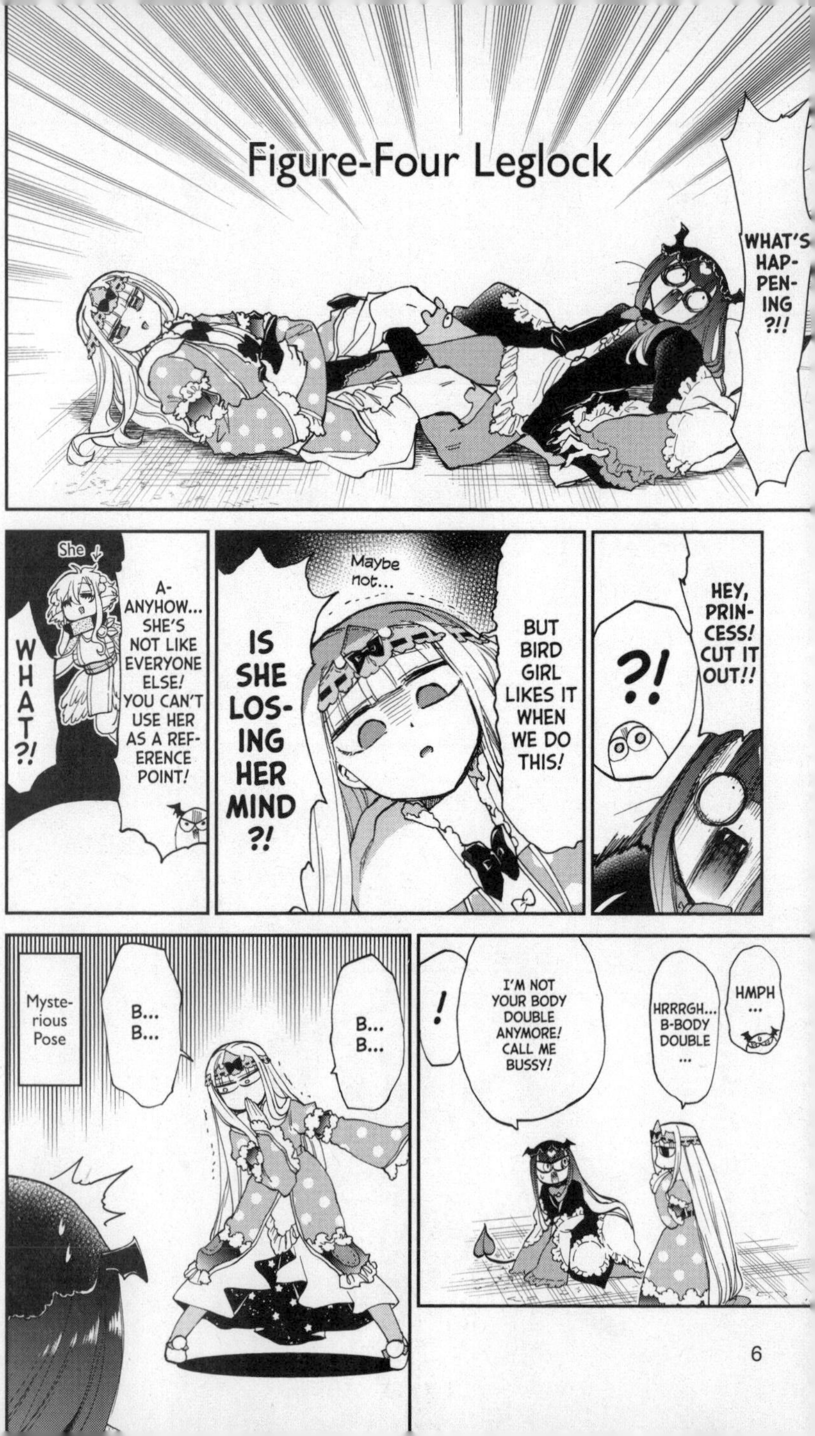

Figure-Four Leglock
WHAT'S HAPPENING?!!
HEY, PRINCESS! CUT IT OUT!!
?!
BUT BIRD GIRL LIKES IT WHEN WE DO THIS!
Maybe not...
IS SHE LOSING HER MIND?!
A-ANYHOW... SHE'S NOT LIKE EVERYONE ELSE! YOU CAN'T USE HER AS A REFERENCE POINT!
WHAT?!
She
HMPH...
HRRRGH... B-BODY DOUBLE...
I'M NOT YOUR BODY DOUBLE ANYMORE! CALL ME BUSSY!
!
B... B...
B... B...
Mysterious Pose

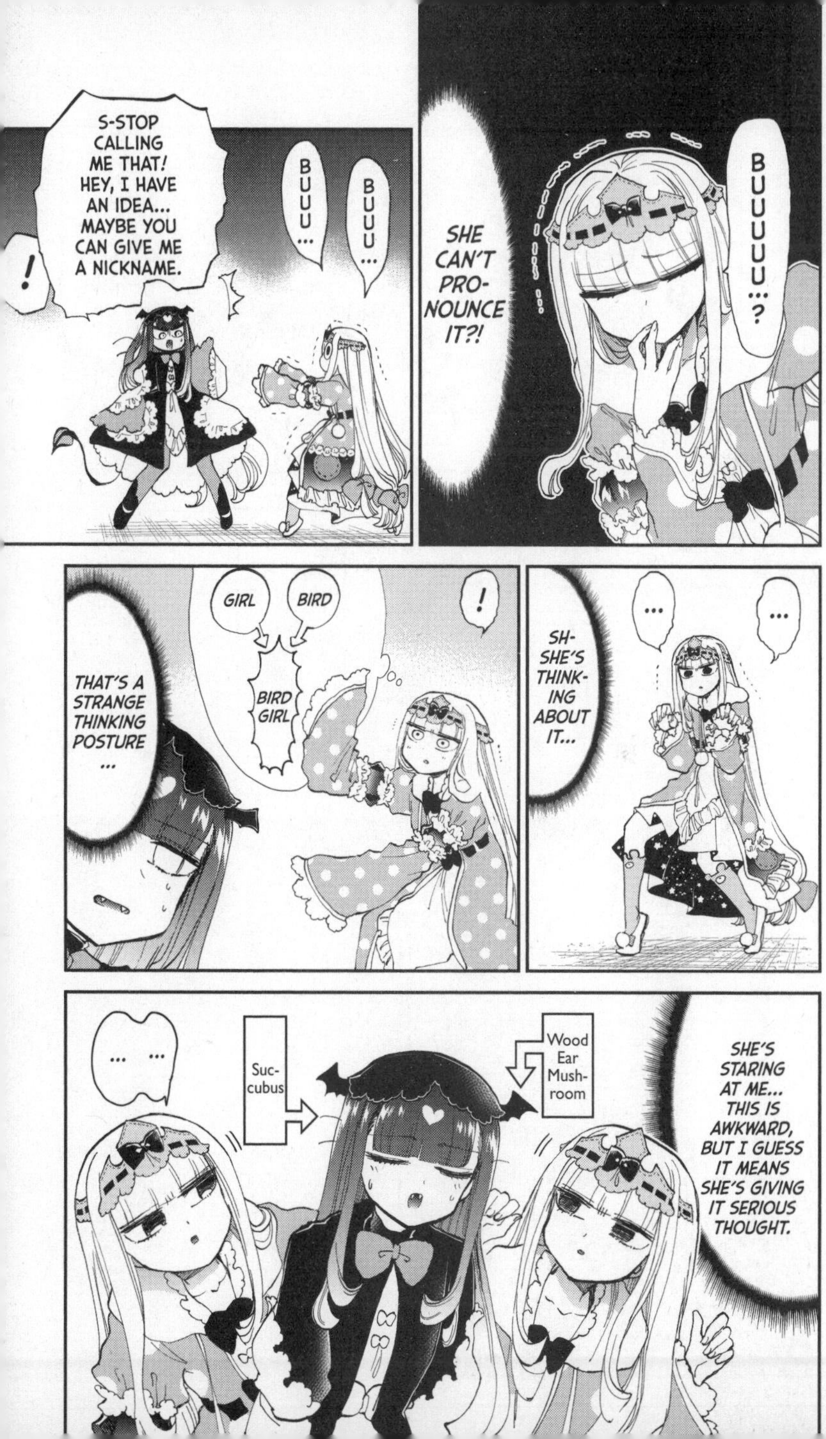
BUUUUU...?
SHE CAN'T PRO-NOUNCE IT?!
BUUU...
BUUU...
S-STOP CALLING ME THAT! HEY, I HAVE AN IDEA... MAYBE YOU CAN GIVE ME A NICKNAME.
!
...
...
SH-SHE'S THINKING ABOUT IT...
!
BIRD
GIRL
BIRD GIRL
THAT'S A STRANGE THINKING POSTURE...
SHE'S STARING AT ME... THIS IS AWKWARD, BUT I GUESS IT MEANS SHE'S GIVING IT SERIOUS THOUGHT.
Wood Ear Mush-room
Suc-cubus
... ...

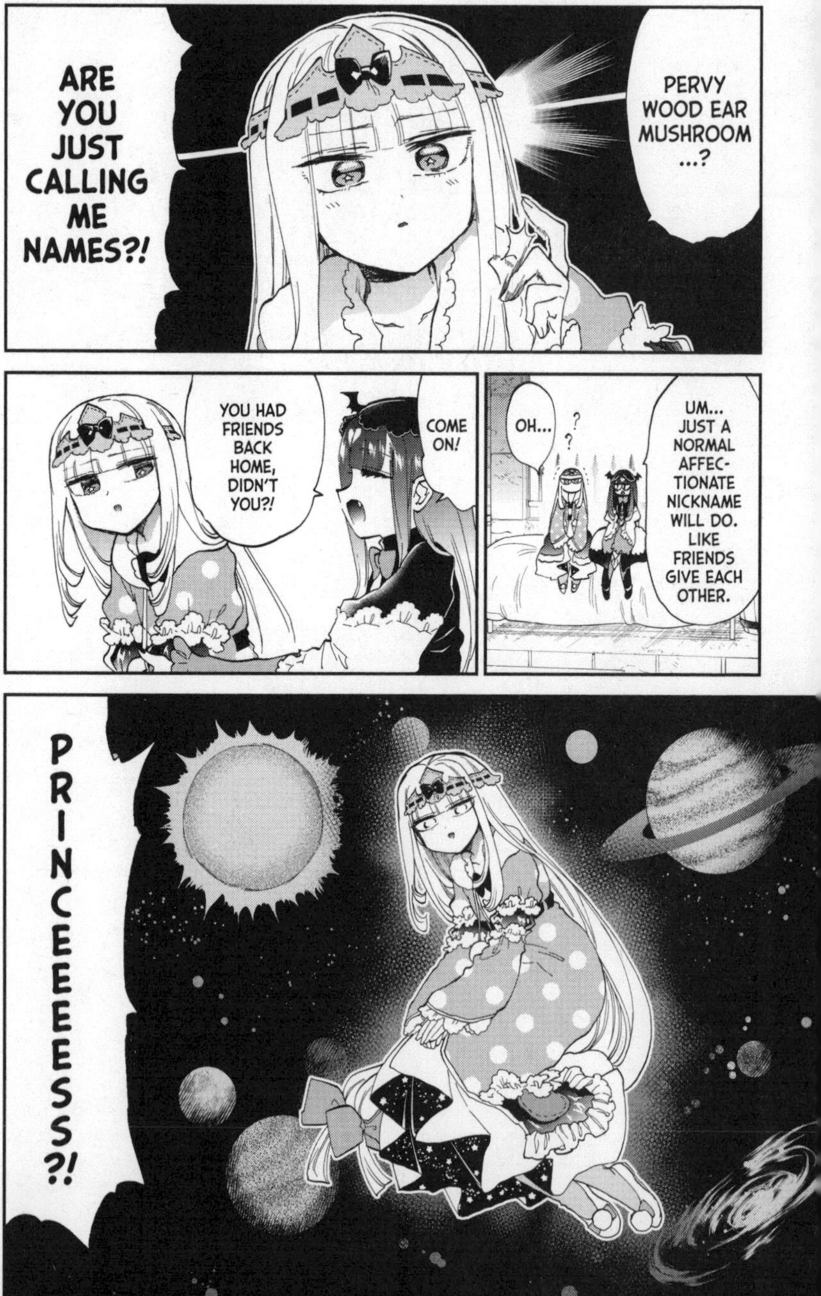
PERVY WOOD EAR MUSHROOM ...?
ARE YOU JUST CALLING ME NAMES?!
UM... JUST A NORMAL AFFEC-TIONATE NICKNAME WILL DO. LIKE FRIENDS GIVE EACH OTHER.
OH...
COME ON!
YOU HAD FRIENDS BACK HOME, DIDN'T YOU?!
PRINCEEEESS?!

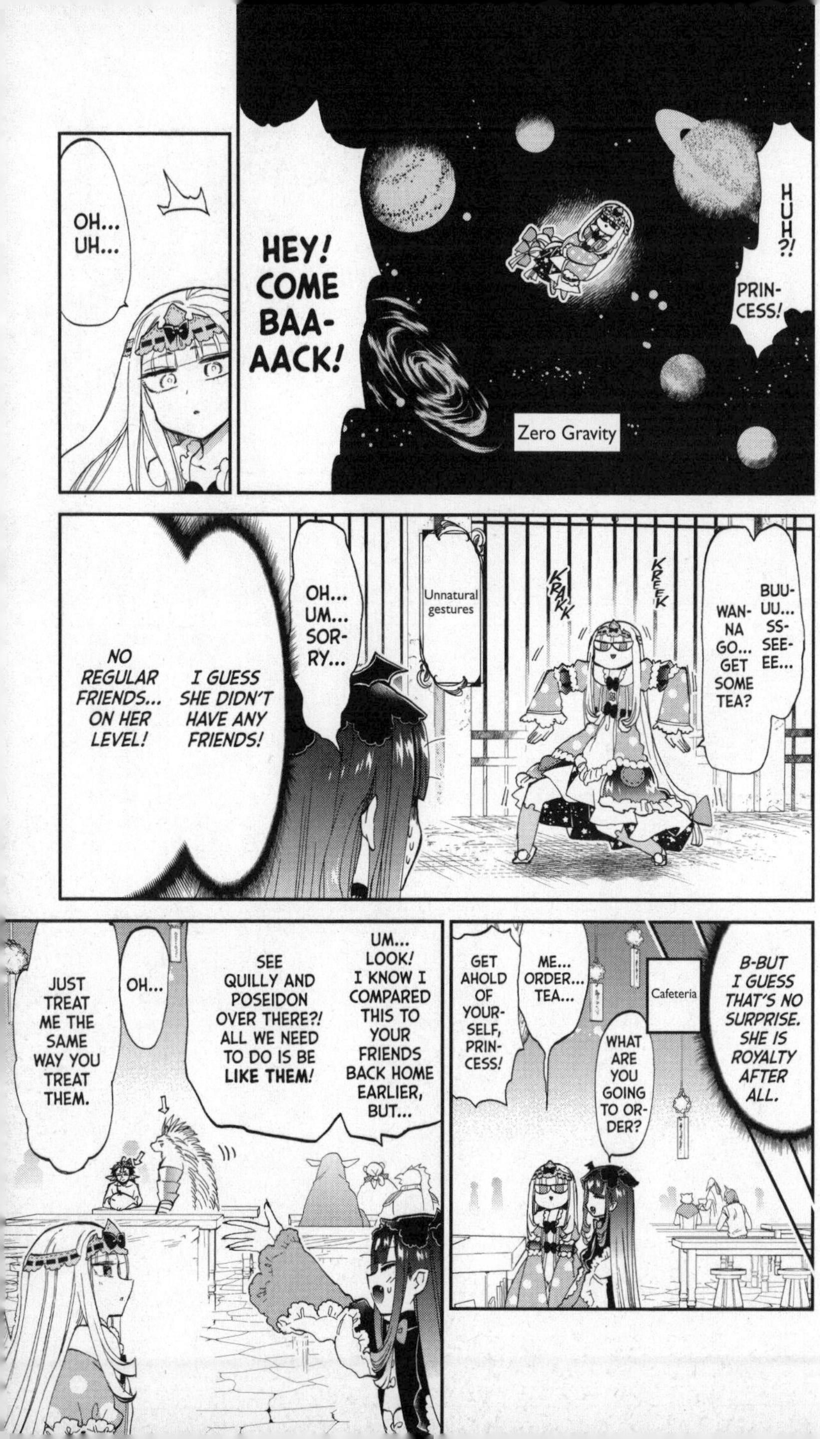
HUH?!
PRIN-CESS!
HEY! COME BAA-AACK!
Zero Gravity
OH... UH...
BUU-UU... SS-SEE-EE...
WAN-NA GO... GET SOME TEA?
KREEK
KRAKK
Unnatural gestures
OH... UM... SOR-RY...
I GUESS SHE DIDN'T HAVE ANY FRIENDS!
NO REGULAR FRIENDS... ON HER LEVEL!
B-BUT I GUESS THAT'S NO SURPRISE. SHE IS ROYALTY AFTER ALL.
Cafeteria
ME... ORDER... TEA...
GET AHOLD OF YOUR-SELF, PRIN-CESS!
WHAT ARE YOU GOING TO OR-DER?
UM... LOOK! I KNOW I COMPARED THIS TO YOUR FRIENDS BACK HOME EARLIER, BUT...
SEE QUILLY AND POSEIDON OVER THERE?! ALL WE NEED TO DO IS BE **LIKE THEM**!
OH...
JUST TREAT ME THE SAME WAY YOU TREAT THEM.

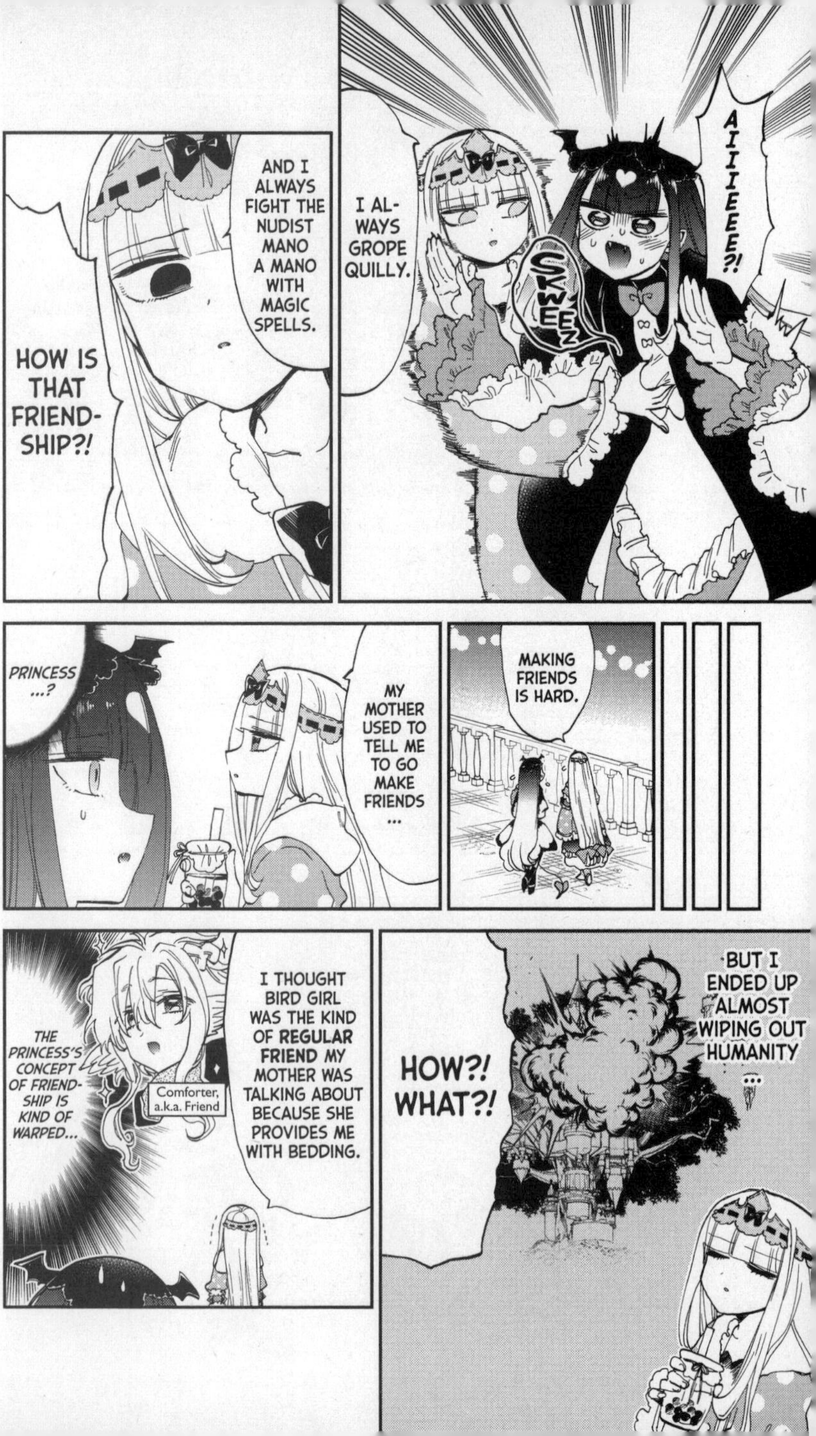
AIIIEEEE?!
SKWEEZ
I ALWAYS GROPE QUILLY.
AND I ALWAYS FIGHT THE NUDIST MANO A MANO WITH MAGIC SPELLS.
HOW IS THAT FRIENDSHIP?!
MAKING FRIENDS IS HARD.
MY MOTHER USED TO TELL ME TO GO MAKE FRIENDS...
PRINCESS...?
BUT I ENDED UP ALMOST WIPING OUT HUMANITY...
HOW?! WHAT?!
I THOUGHT BIRD GIRL WAS THE KIND OF REGULAR FRIEND MY MOTHER WAS TALKING ABOUT BECAUSE SHE PROVIDES ME WITH BEDDING.
Comforter, a.k.a. Friend
THE PRINCESS'S CONCEPT OF FRIENDSHIP IS KIND OF WARPED...

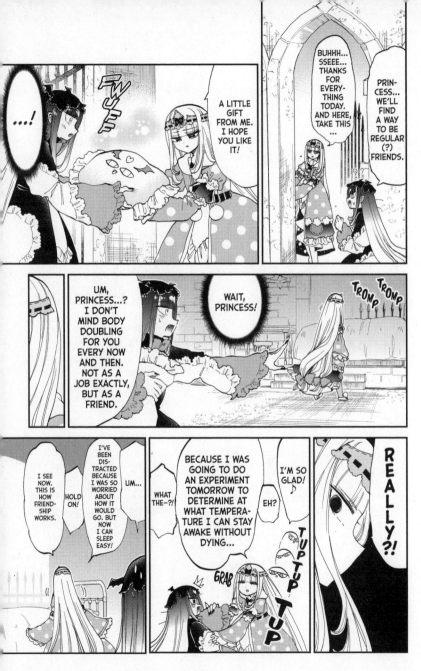

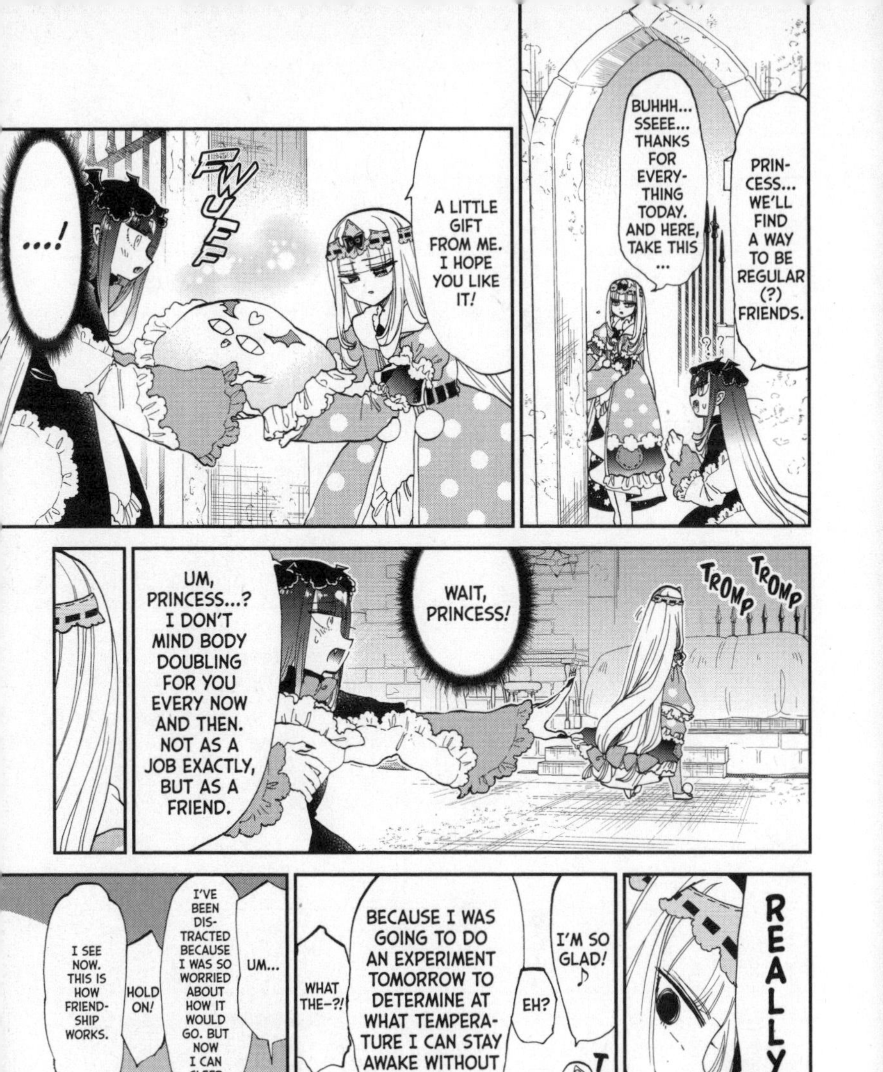
PRINCESS... WE'LL FIND A WAY TO BE REGULAR (?) FRIENDS.
BUHHH... SSEEE... THANKS FOR EVERYTHING TODAY. AND HERE, TAKE THIS ...
A LITTLE GIFT FROM ME. I HOPE YOU LIKE IT!
FWUFF
...!
TROMP TROMP
WAIT, PRINCESS!
UM, PRINCESS...? I DON'T MIND BODY DOUBLING FOR YOU EVERY NOW AND THEN. NOT AS A JOB EXACTLY, BUT AS A FRIEND.
REALLY?!
I'M SO GLAD! ♪
EH?
BECAUSE I WAS GOING TO DO AN EXPERIMENT TOMORROW TO DETERMINE AT WHAT TEMPERATURE I CAN STAY AWAKE WITHOUT DYING...
WHAT THE-?!
TUP TUP TUP TUP
GRAB
UM...
I'VE BEEN DISTRACTED BECAUSE I WAS SO WORRIED ABOUT HOW IT WOULD GO. BUT NOW I CAN SLEEP EASY!
HOLD ON!
I SEE NOW. THIS IS HOW FRIENDSHIP WORKS.

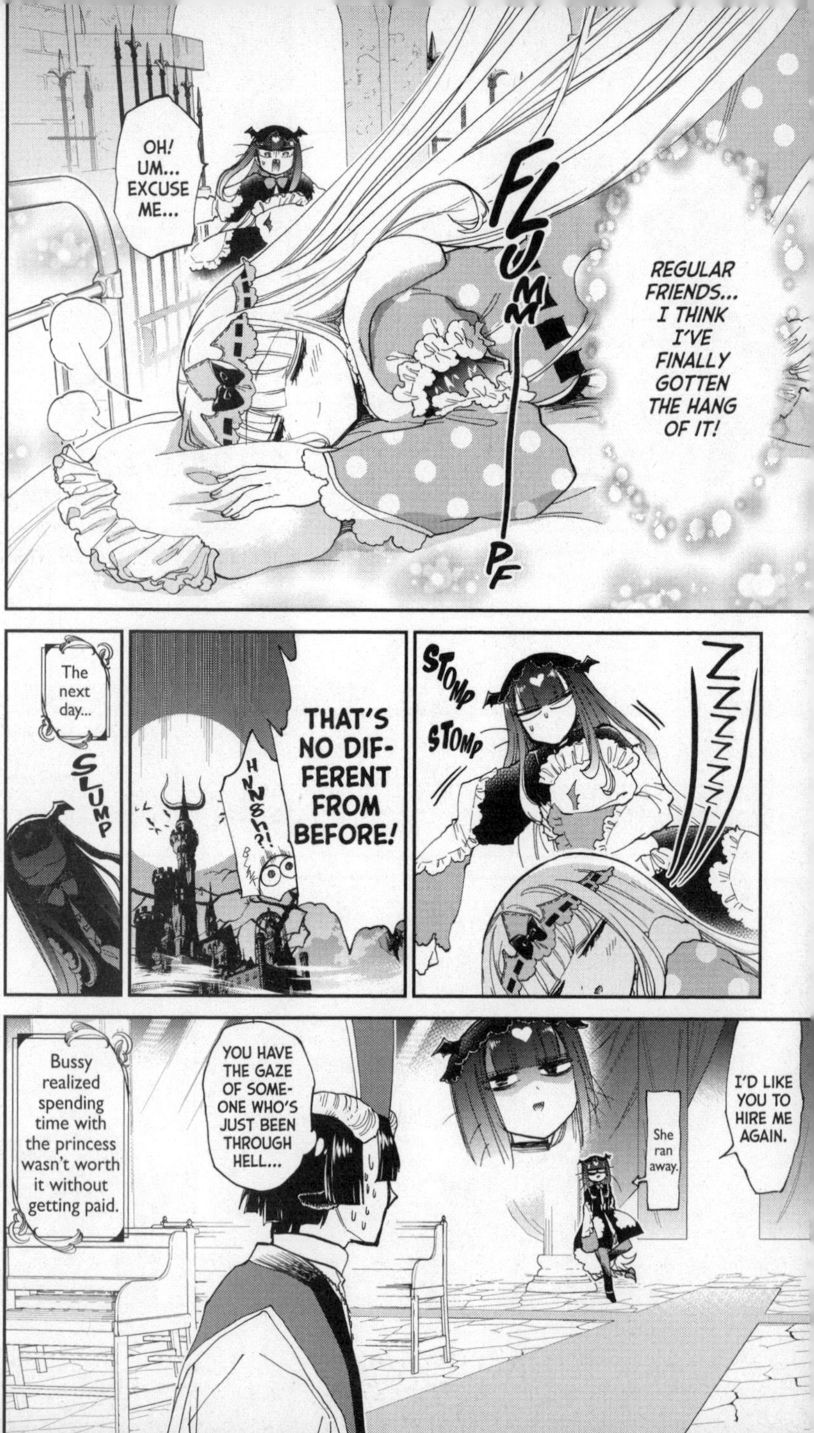
REGULAR FRIENDS... I THINK I'VE FINALLY GOTTEN THE HANG OF IT!
FLUMP
OH! UM... EXCUSE ME...
PF
ZZZZZZ
STOMP
STOMP
THAT'S NO DIF- FERENT FROM BEFORE!
HNNGH?!
BLINK
The next day...
SLUMP
I'D LIKE YOU TO HIRE ME AGAIN.
She ran away.
YOU HAVE THE GAZE OF SOME- ONE WHO'S JUST BEEN THROUGH HELL...
Bussy realized spending time with the princess wasn't worth it without getting paid.

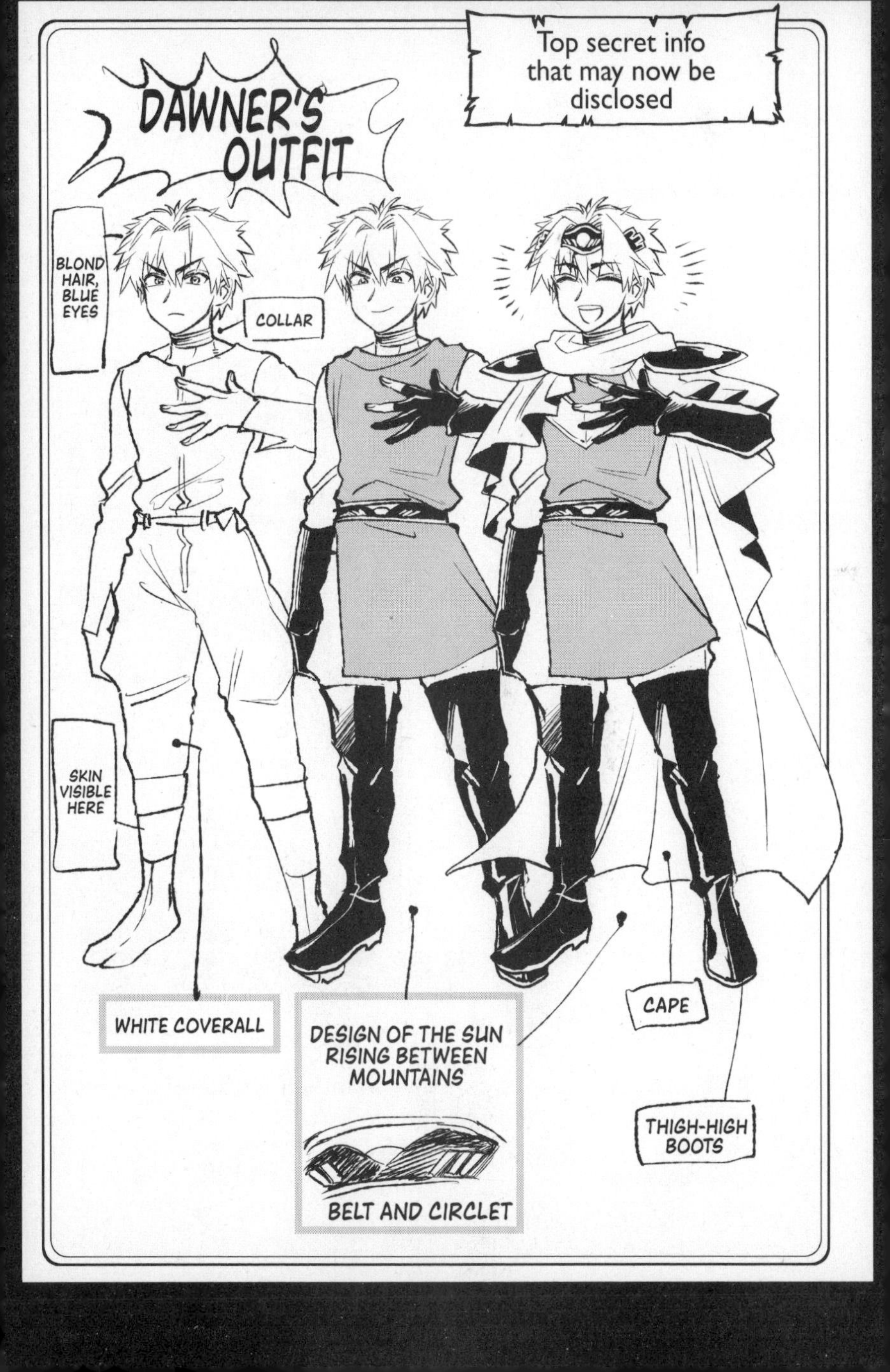
Top secret info that may now be disclosed
DAWNER'S OUTFIT
BLOND HAIR, BLUE EYES
COLLAR
SKIN VISIBLE HERE
WHITE COVERALL
DESIGN OF THE SUN RISING BETWEEN MOUNTAINS
BELT AND CIRCLET
CAPE
THIGH-HIGH BOOTS

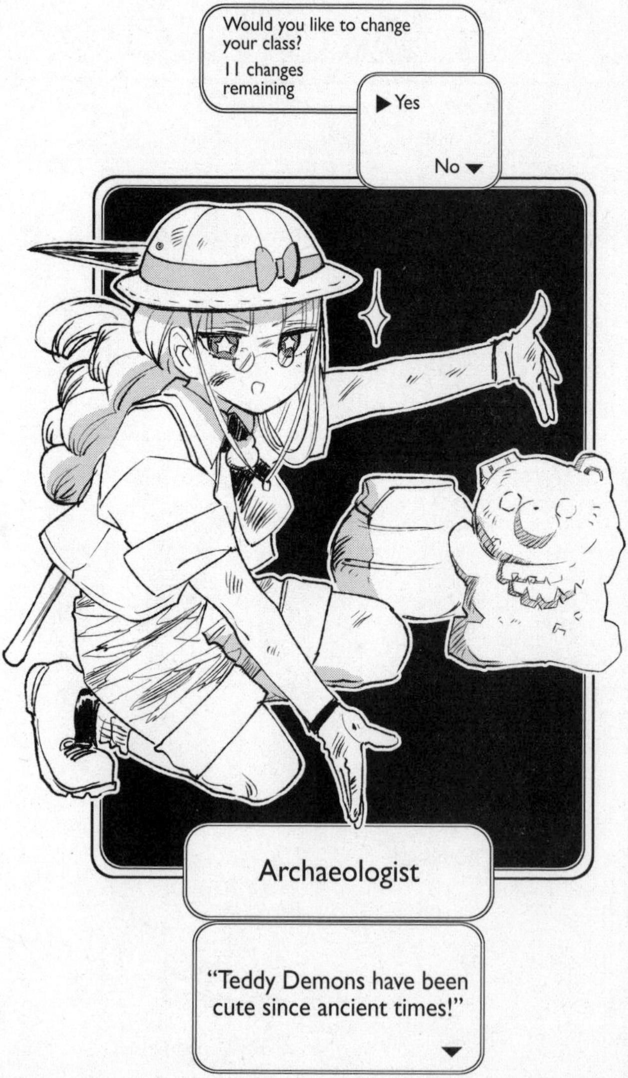
Would you like to change your class?
11 changes remaining
▶Yes
No
Archaeologist
"Teddy Demons have been cute since ancient times!"

171st Night: How Heavy Are the Slimes You Lift?

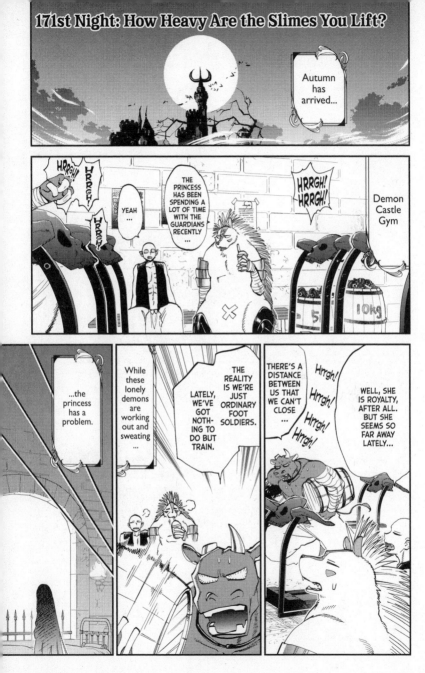

Autumn has arrived...
Demon Castle Gym
HRRGH! HRRGH!
THE PRINCESS HAS BEEN SPENDING A LOT OF TIME WITH THE GUARDIANS RECENTLY...
YEAH...
HRRGH!
HRRGH!
HRRGH!
WELL, SHE IS ROYALTY, AFTER ALL. BUT SHE SEEMS SO FAR AWAY LATELY...
Hrrgh!
Hrrgh!
Hrrgh!
Hrrgh!
THERE'S A DISTANCE BETWEEN US THAT WE CAN'T CLOSE...
THE REALITY IS WE'RE JUST ORDINARY FOOT SOLDIERS.
LATELY, WE'VE GOT NOTHING TO DO BUT TRAIN.
While these lonely demons are working out and sweating...
...the princess has a problem.

171st Night: How Heavy Are the Slimes You Lift?

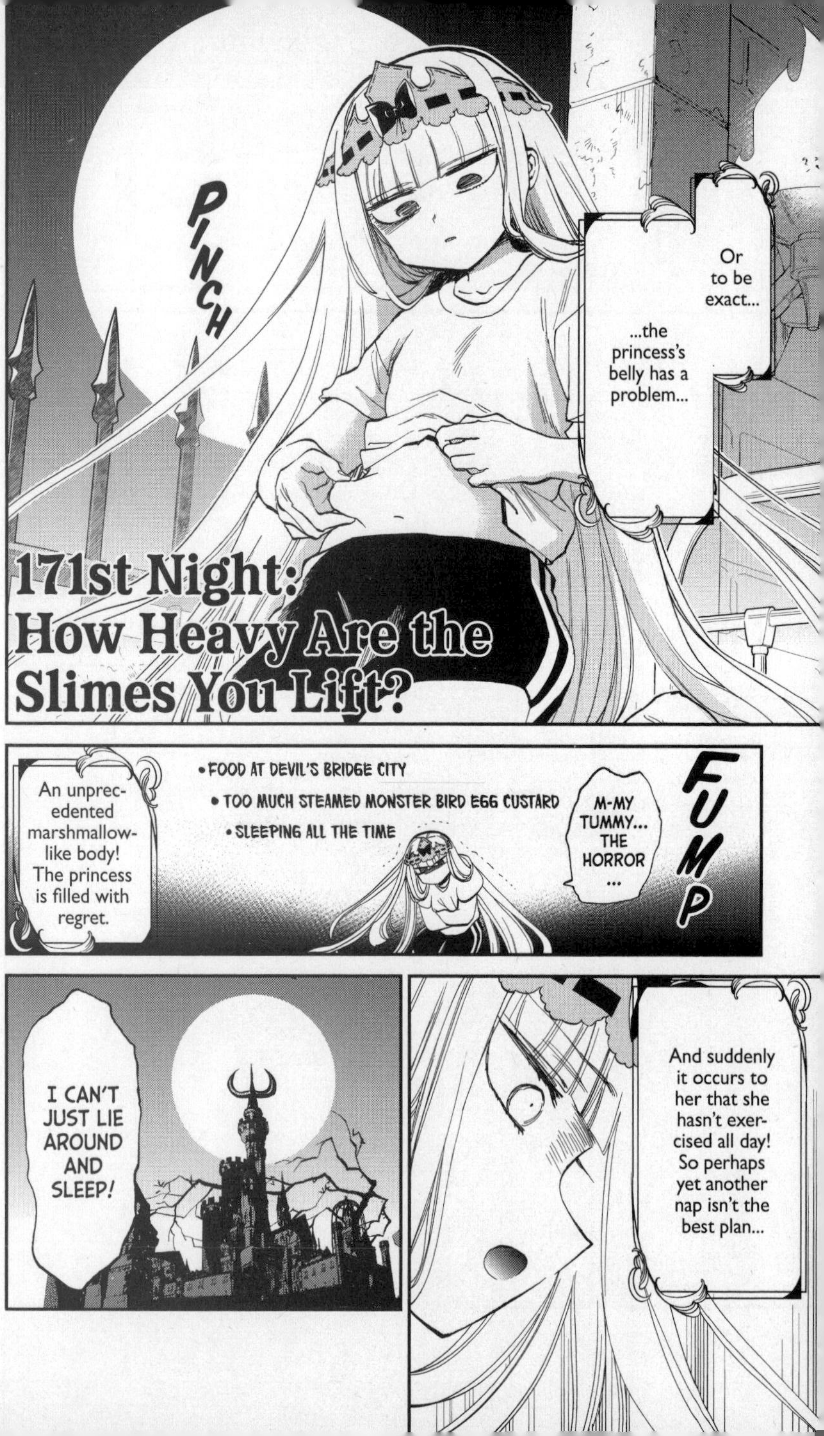

Or to be exact... ...the princess's belly has a problem...
PINCH
171st Night: How Heavy Are the Slimes You Lift?
FUMP
M-MY TUMMY... THE HORROR ...
• FOOD AT DEVIL'S BRIDGE CITY
• TOO MUCH STEAMED MONSTER BIRD EGG CUSTARD
• SLEEPING ALL THE TIME
An unprecedented marshmallow-like body! The princess is filled with regret.
And suddenly it occurs to her that she hasn't exercised all day! So perhaps yet another nap isn't the best plan...
I CAN'T JUST LIE AROUND AND SLEEP!

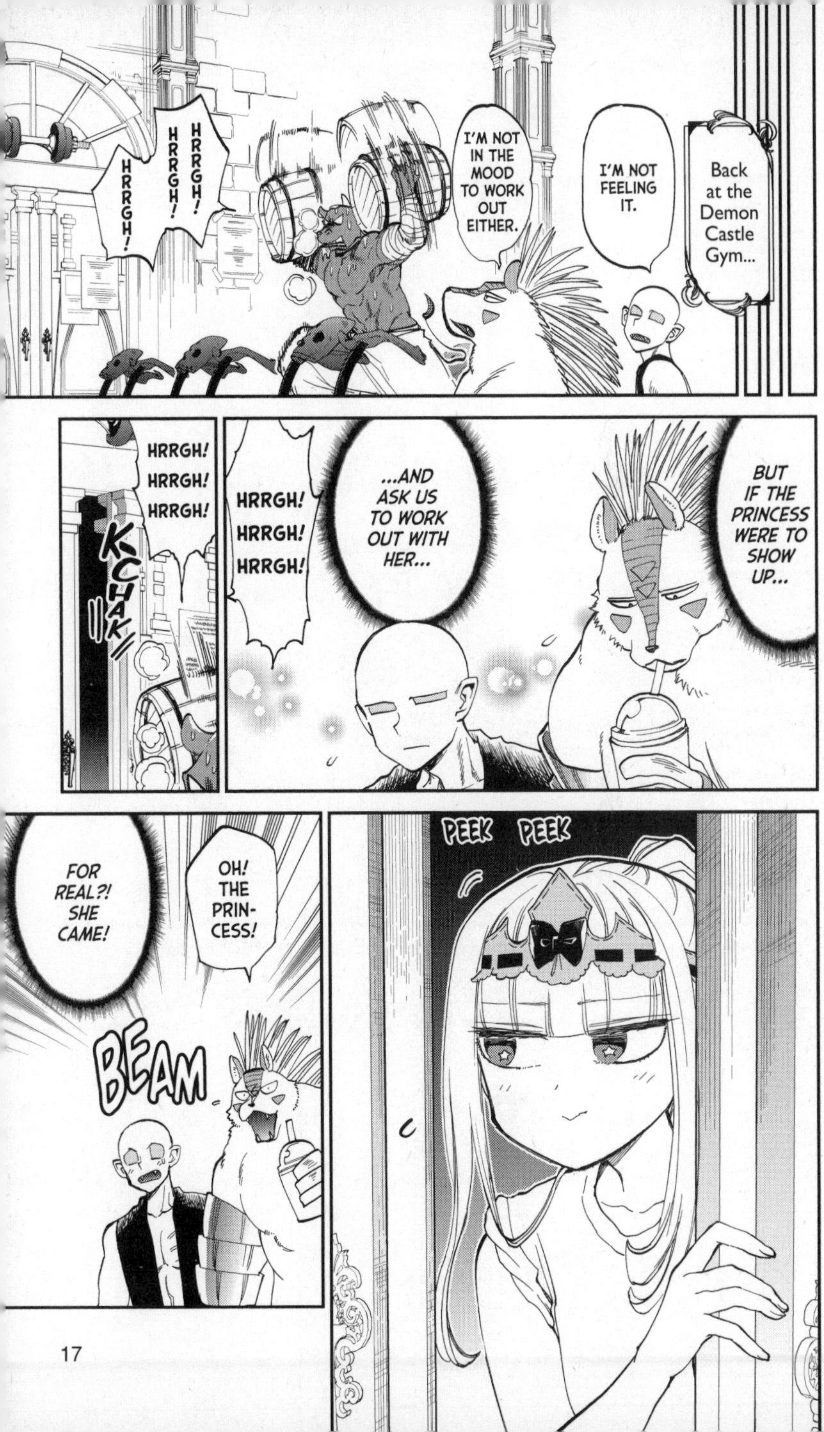
Back at the Demon Castle Gym...
I'M NOT FEELING IT.
I'M NOT IN THE MOOD TO WORK OUT EITHER.
HRRGH! HRRGH! HRRGH!
BUT IF THE PRINCESS WERE TO SHOW UP...
...AND ASK US TO WORK OUT WITH HER...
HRRGH! HRRGH! HRRGH!
HRRGH! HRRGH! HRRGH!
KCHAK
PEEK PEEK
OH! THE PRIN-CESS!
FOR REAL?! SHE CAME!
BEAM

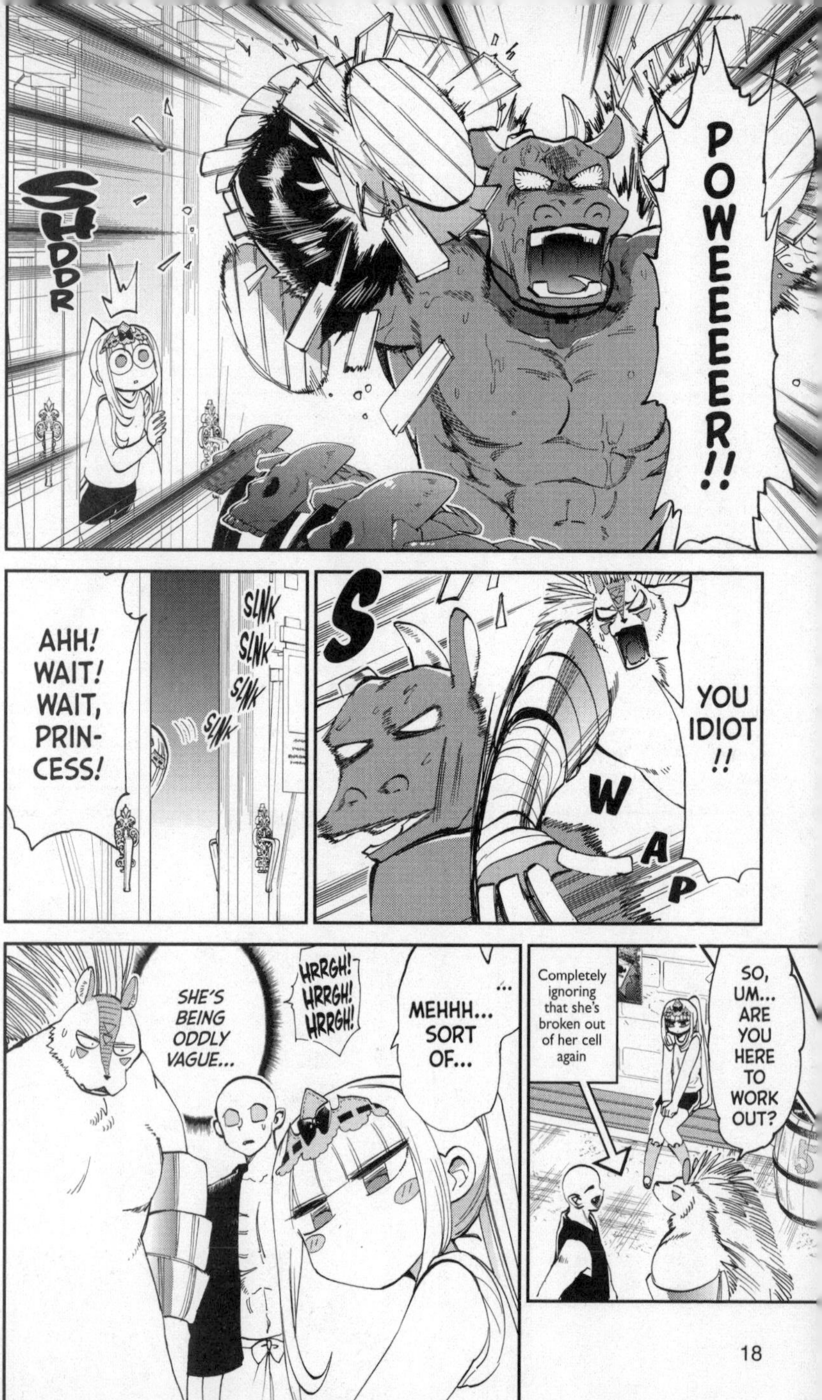
POWEEEEER!!
SHDDR
YOU IDIOT!!
S
WAP
SLNK SLNK SLNK SLNK
AHH! WAIT! WAIT, PRIN-CESS!
SO, UM... ARE YOU HERE TO WORK OUT?
Completely ignoring that she's broken out of her cell again
...
MEHHH... SORT OF...
HRRGH! HRRGH! HRRGH!
SHE'S BEING ODDLY VAGUE...

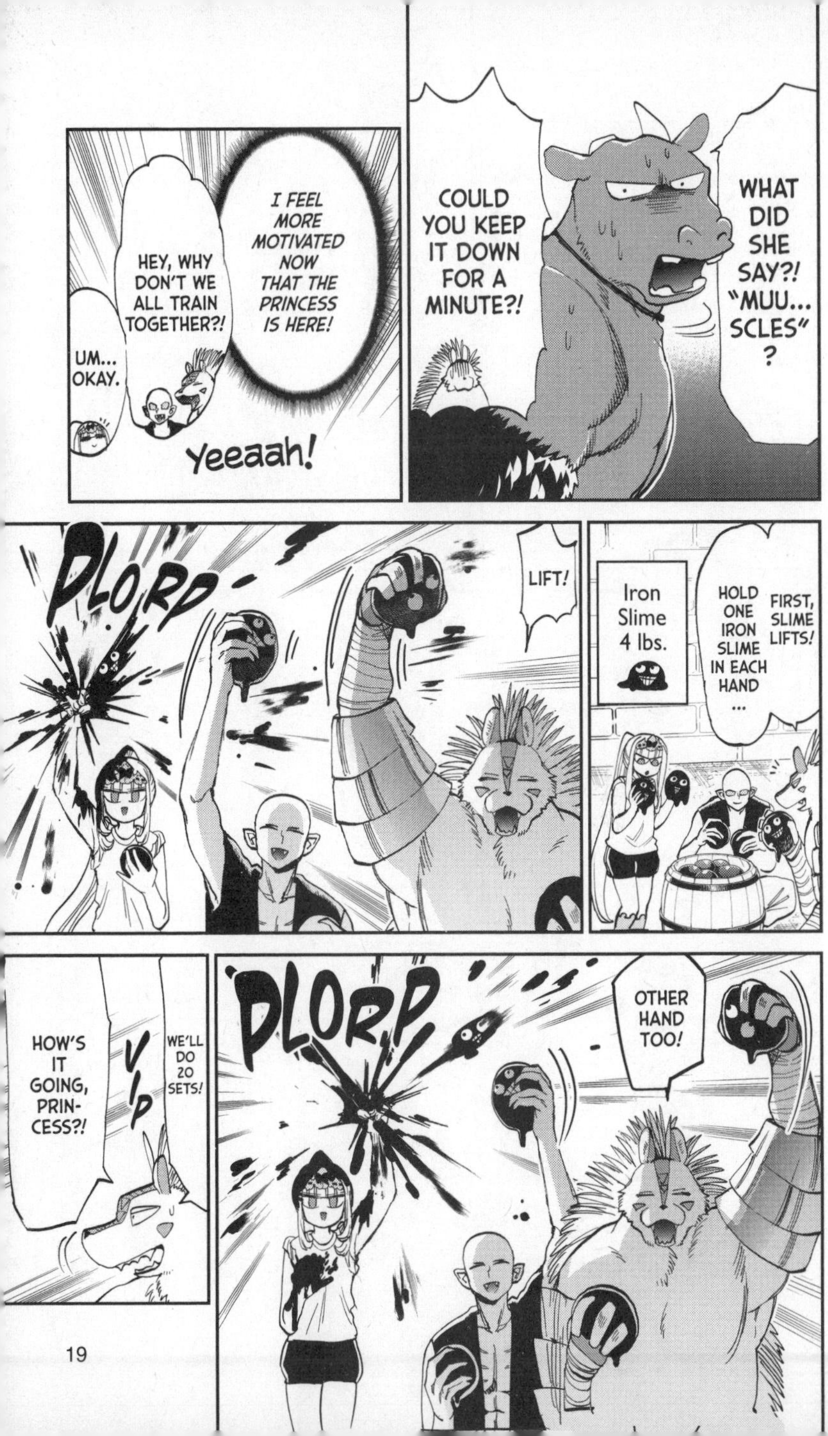
WHAT DID SHE SAY?! "MUU... SCLES"?
COULD YOU KEEP IT DOWN FOR A MINUTE?!
I FEEL MORE MOTIVATED NOW THAT THE PRINCESS IS HERE!
HEY, WHY DON'T WE ALL TRAIN TOGETHER?!
UM... OKAY.
Yeeaah!
FIRST, SLIME LIFTS!
HOLD ONE IRON SLIME IN EACH HAND ...
Iron Slime 4 lbs.
LIFT!
PLORP
OTHER HAND TOO!
PLORP
WE'LL DO 20 SETS!
VIP
HOW'S IT GOING, PRINCESS?!

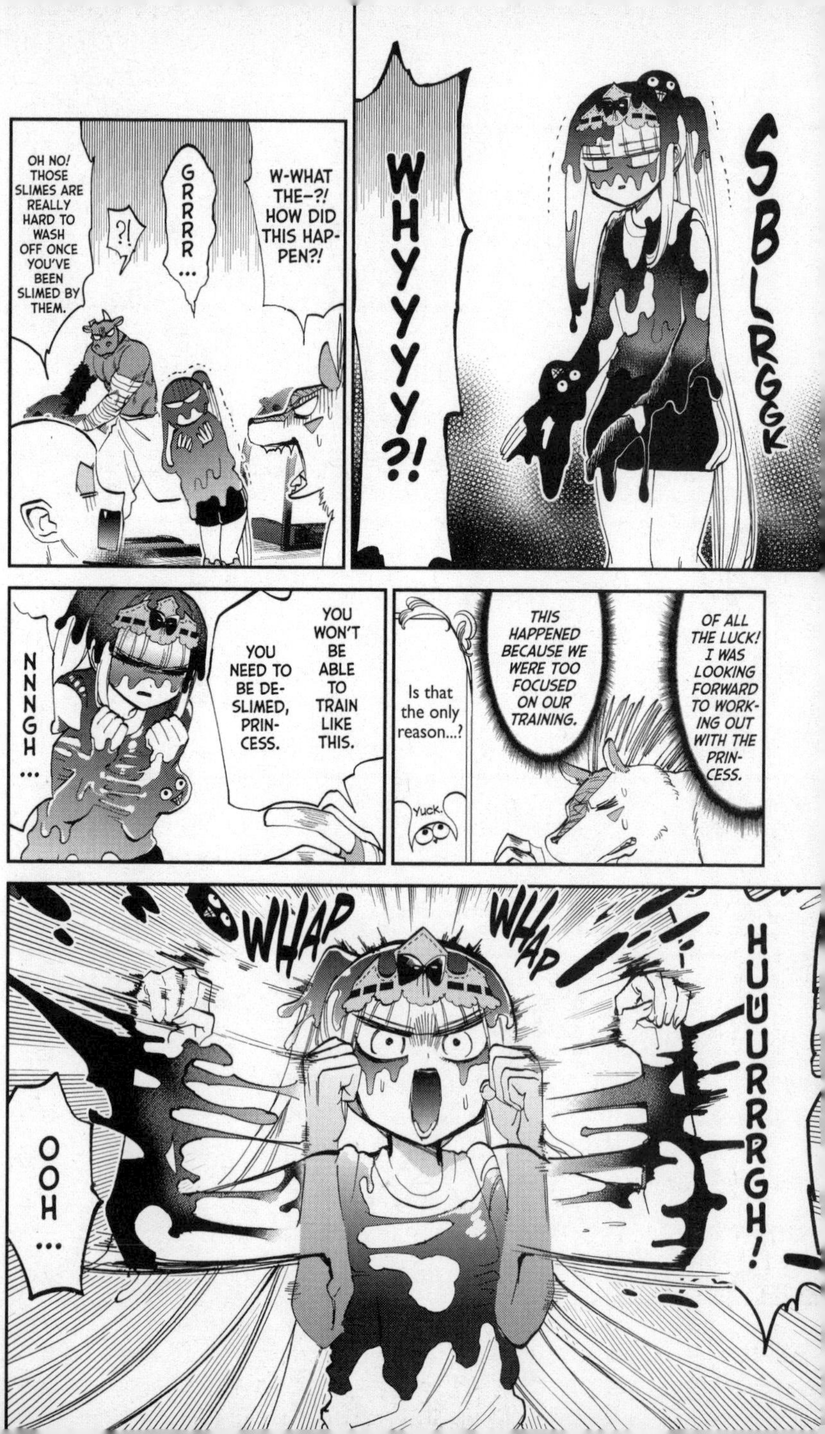
SBLRGGK
WHYYYYY?!
W-WHAT THE–?! HOW DID THIS HAP-PEN?!
GRRRR...
?!
OH NO! THOSE SLIMES ARE REALLY HARD TO WASH OFF ONCE YOU'VE BEEN SLIMED BY THEM.
OF ALL THE LUCK! I WAS LOOKING FORWARD TO WORK-ING OUT WITH THE PRIN-CESS.
THIS HAPPENED BECAUSE WE WERE TOO FOCUSED ON OUR TRAINING.
Is that the only reason...?
YUCK.
YOU WON'T BE ABLE TO TRAIN LIKE THIS.
YOU NEED TO BE DE-SLIMED, PRIN-CESS.
NNNGH...
HUUURRRGH!
WHAP
WHAP
OOH...

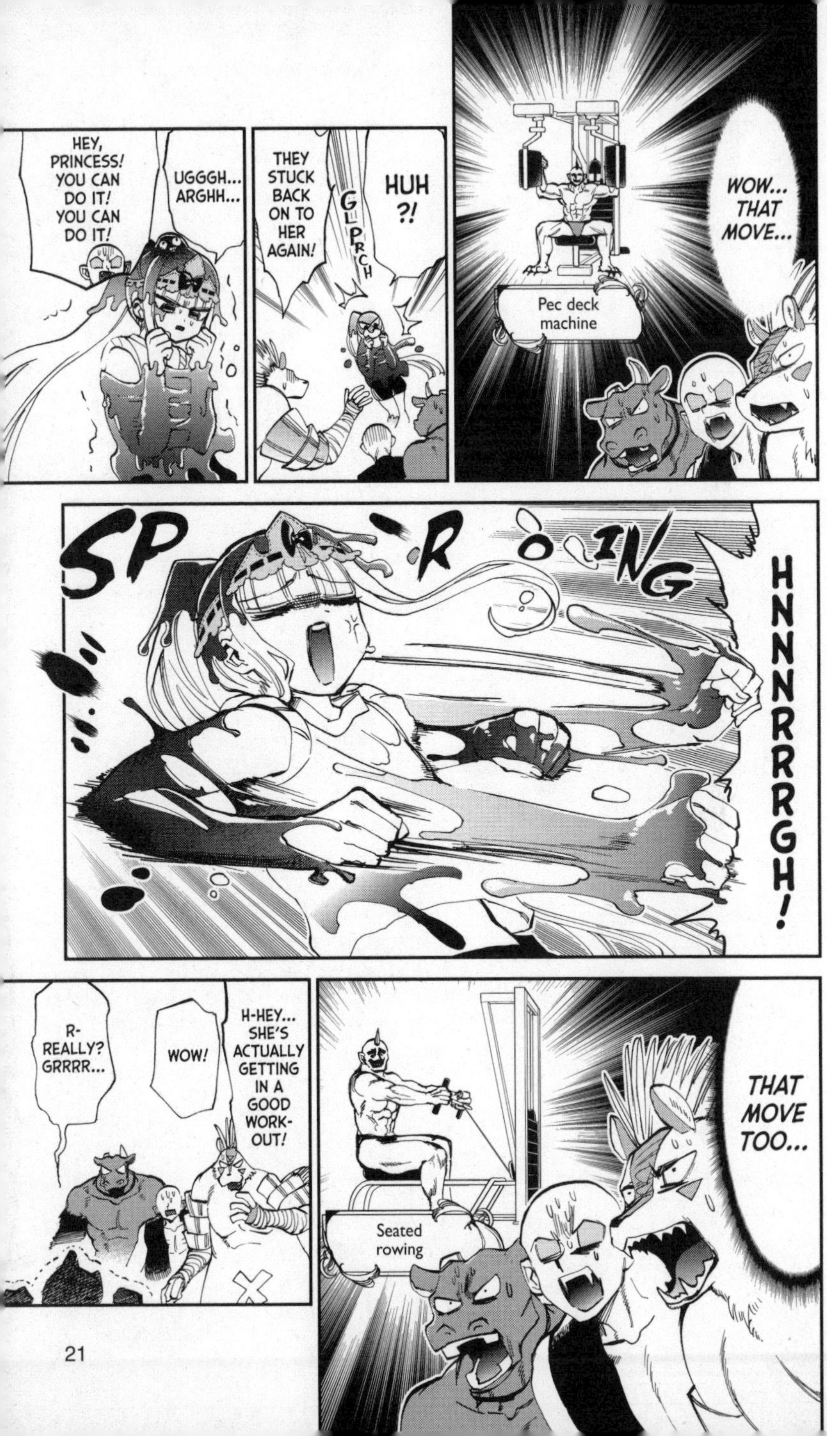
WOW... THAT MOVE...
Pec deck machine
HUH ?!
THEY STUCK BACK ON TO HER AGAIN!
GLPRCH
UGGGH... ARGHH...
HEY, PRINCESS! YOU CAN DO IT! YOU CAN DO IT!
HNNNRRRRGH!
SPROING
THAT MOVE TOO...
Seated rowing
H-HEY... SHE'S ACTUALLY GETTING IN A GOOD WORK-OUT!
WOW!
R-REALLY? GRRRR...

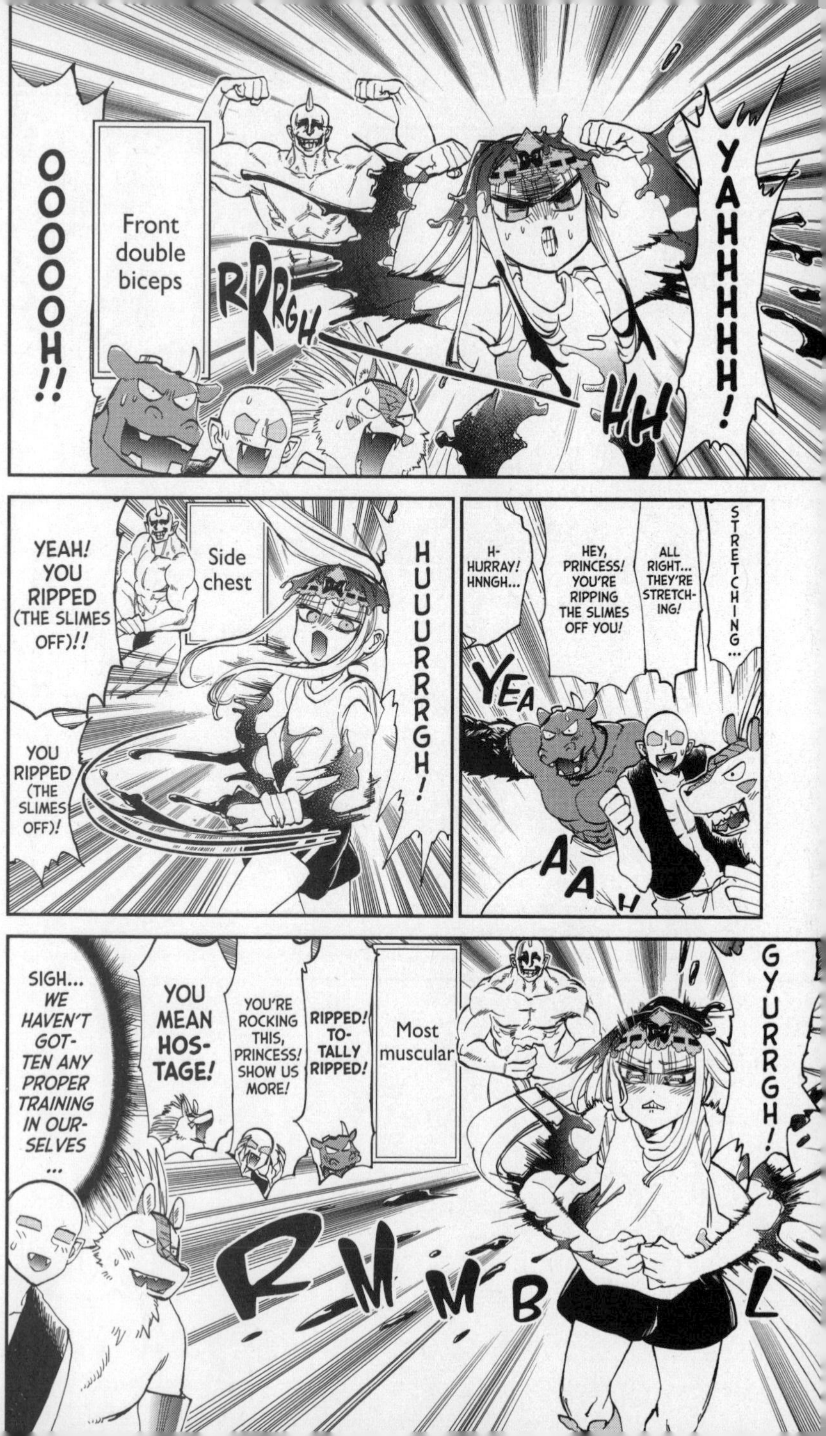
YAHHHHHHH!
HH
RRRGH
Front double biceps
OOOOOOH!!
STRETCHING...
ALL RIGHT... THEY'RE STRETCHING!
HEY, PRINCESS! YOU'RE RIPPING THE SLIMES OFF YOU!
H-HURRAY! HNNGH...
YEA
AAH
HUUURRRGH!
Side chest
YEAH! YOU RIPPED (THE SLIMES OFF)!!
YOU RIPPED (THE SLIMES OFF)!
GYURRGH!
Most muscular
RIPPED! TOTALLY RIPPED!
YOU'RE ROCKING THIS, PRINCESS! SHOW US MORE!
YOU MEAN HOSTAGE!
SIGH... WE HAVEN'T GOTTEN ANY PROPER TRAINING IN OURSELVES...
RMMBL

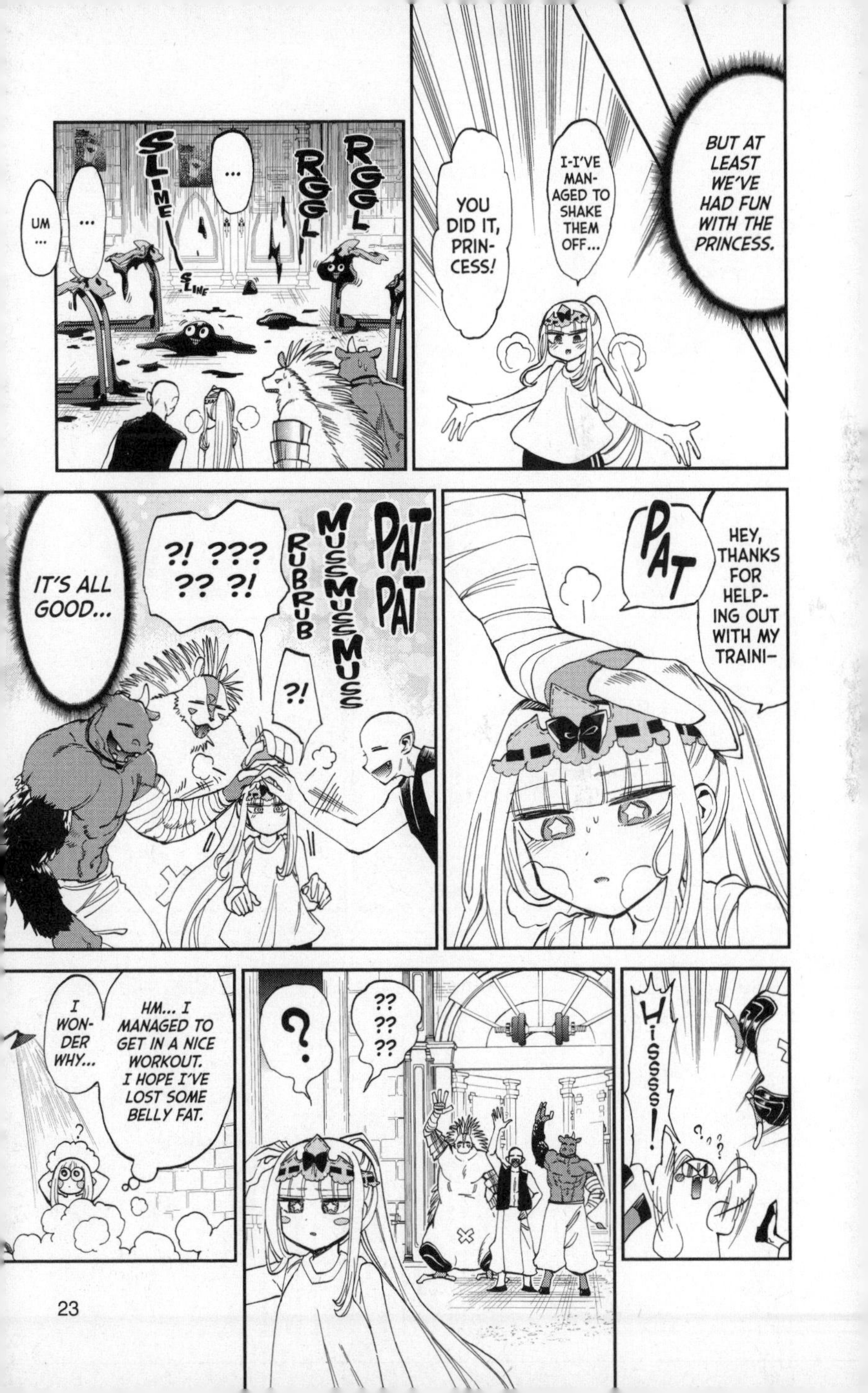
BUT AT LEAST WE'VE HAD FUN WITH THE PRINCESS.
I-I'VE MAN-AGED TO SHAKE THEM OFF...
YOU DID IT, PRIN-CESS!
RGGL RGGL
...
SLIME SLIME
...
UM ...
PAT
HEY, THANKS FOR HELP-ING OUT WITH MY TRAINI–
PAT PAT
MUSSMUSSMUSS
RUBRUB
?!
?! ??? ?? ?!
IT'S ALL GOOD...
HISSSS!
???
?? ?? ??
?
HM... I MANAGED TO GET IN A NICE WORKOUT. I HOPE I'VE LOST SOME BELLY FAT.
I WON-DER WHY...
?

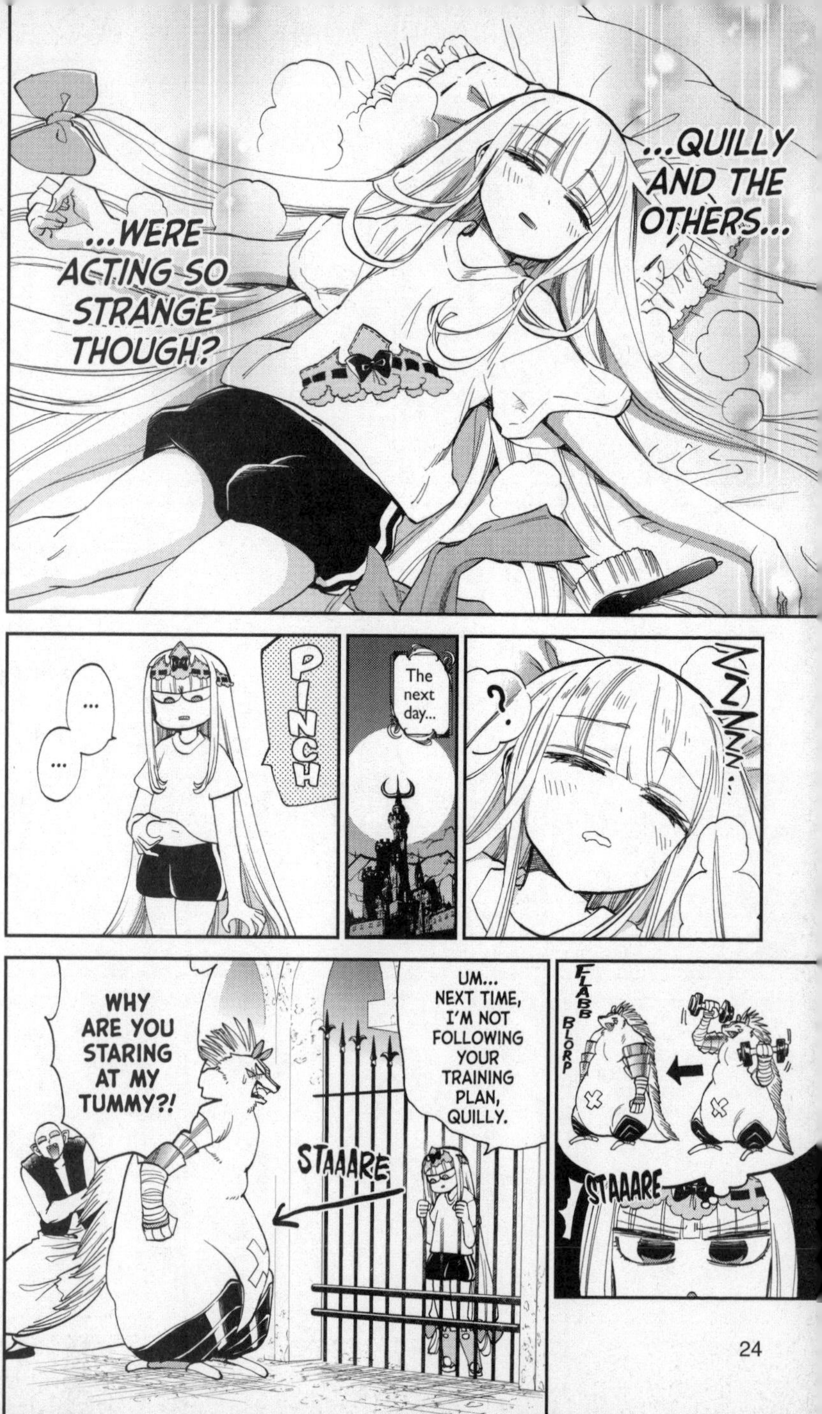
...QUILLY AND THE OTHERS...
...WERE ACTING SO STRANGE THOUGH?
?
ZZZZZ...
The next day...
PINCH
...
...
FLABB
BLORP
STAAARE
UM... NEXT TIME, I'M NOT FOLLOWING YOUR TRAINING PLAN, QUILLY.
WHY ARE YOU STARING AT MY TUMMY?!
STAAARE

DEMON KING BATTLE STYLE

The battle against Hades in vol. 4

Top secret info that may now be disclosed

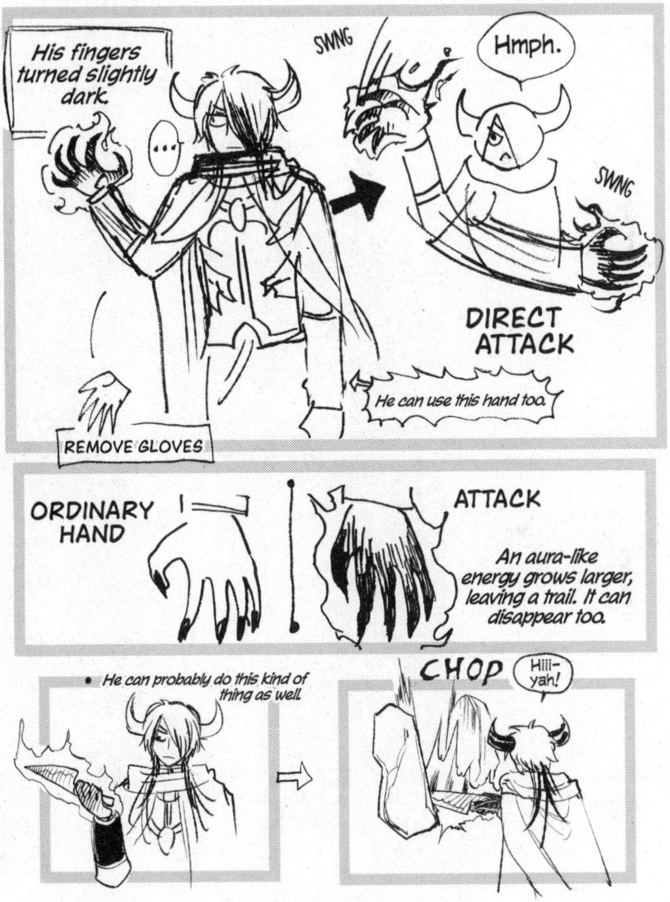
SWNG
Hmph.
SWNG
DIRECT ATTACK
His fingers turned slightly dark.
...
He can use this hand too.
REMOVE GLOVES
ATTACK
An aura-like energy grows larger, leaving a trail. It can disappear too.
ORDINARY HAND
CHOP
Hiii-yah!
• He can probably do this kind of thing as well.

*Not fighting all out

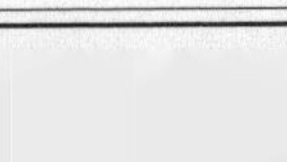

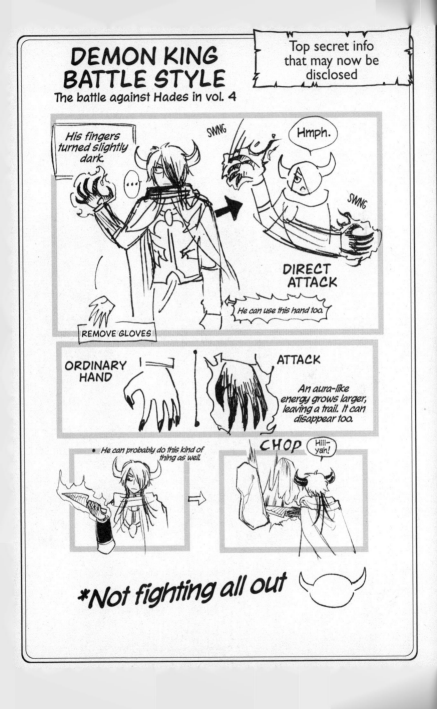

Would you like to change your class?
10 changes remaining
▶Yes
No
Cleaner
"I have to sweep up now."

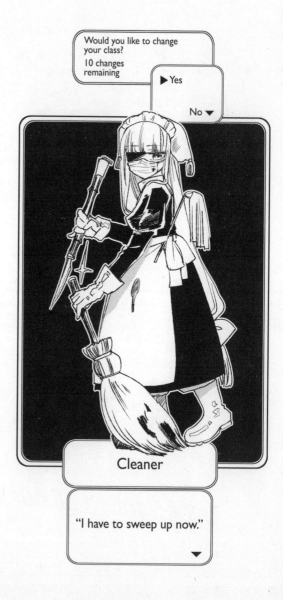

172nd Night: The Prison Cell Turned Confessional

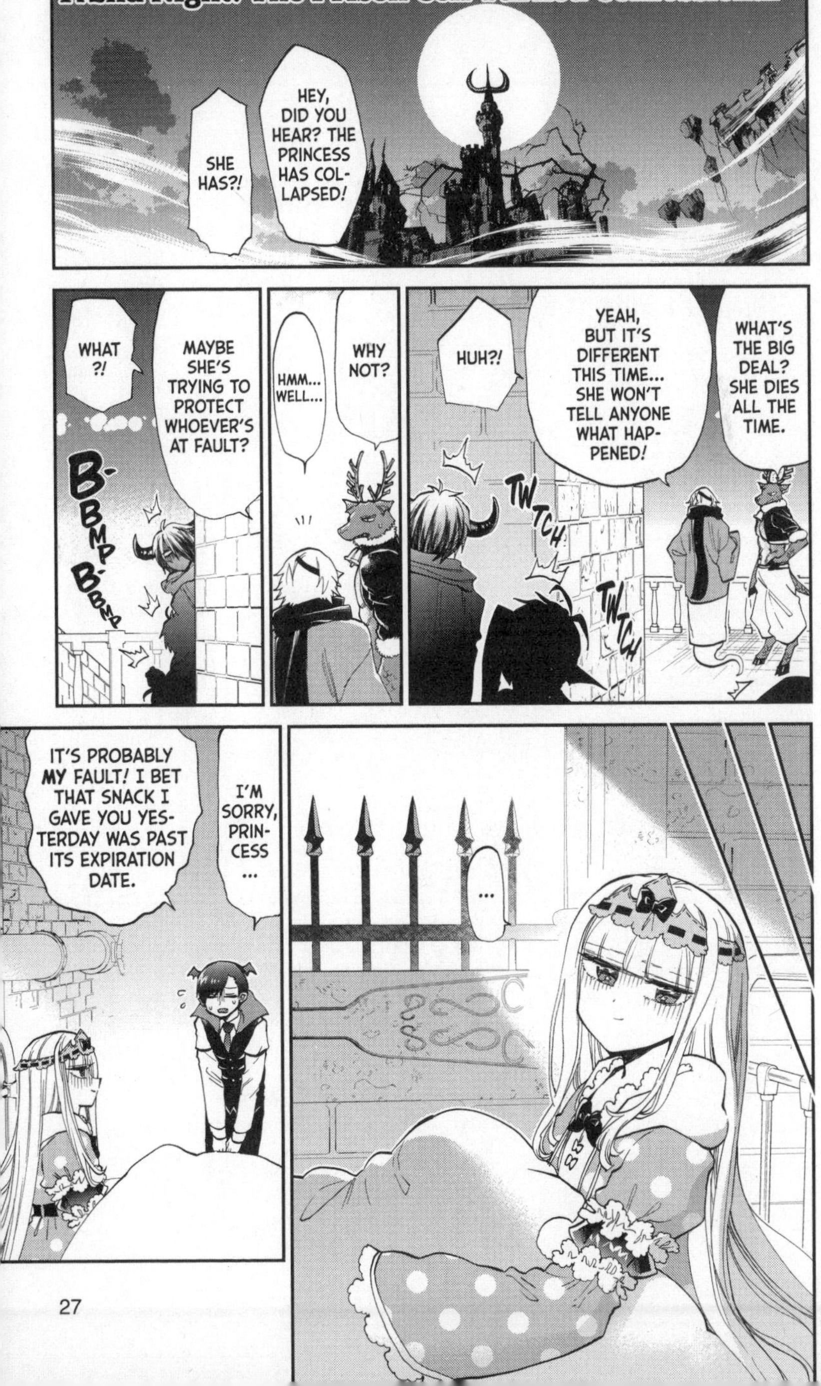

HEY, DID YOU HEAR? THE PRINCESS HAS COLLAPSED!
SHE HAS?!
WHAT'S THE BIG DEAL? SHE DIES ALL THE TIME.
YEAH, BUT IT'S DIFFERENT THIS TIME... SHE WON'T TELL ANYONE WHAT HAPPENED!
HUH?!
TWITCH
TWITCH
WHY NOT?
HMM... WELL...
MAYBE SHE'S TRYING TO PROTECT WHOEVER'S AT FAULT?
WHAT?!
B-BUMP
B-BUMP
...
I'M SORRY, PRINCESS...
IT'S PROBABLY MY FAULT! I BET THAT SNACK I GAVE YOU YESTERDAY WAS PAST ITS EXPIRATION DATE.

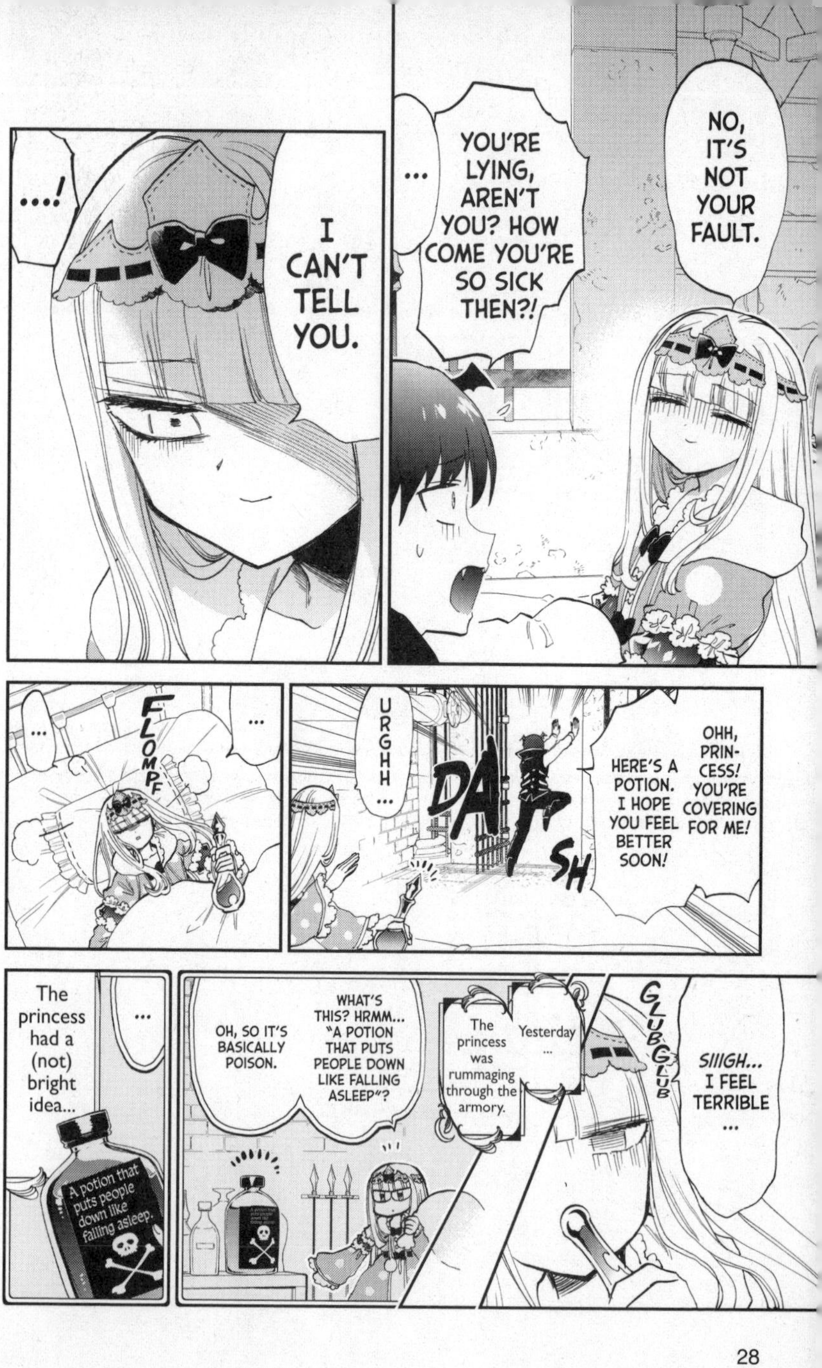
NO, IT'S NOT YOUR FAULT.
YOU'RE LYING, AREN'T YOU? HOW COME YOU'RE SO SICK THEN?!
...
I CAN'T TELL YOU.
...!
OHH, PRINCESS! YOU'RE COVERING FOR ME!
HERE'S A POTION. I HOPE YOU FEEL BETTER SOON!
DASH
URGHH...
...
FLOMPF
...
GLUBGLUB
SIIIGH... I FEEL TERRIBLE...
Yesterday...
The princess was rummaging through the armory.
WHAT'S THIS? HRMM... "A POTION THAT PUTS PEOPLE DOWN LIKE FALLING ASLEEP"?
OH, SO IT'S BASICALLY POISON.
...
The princess had a (not) bright idea...
A potion that puts people down like falling asleep.

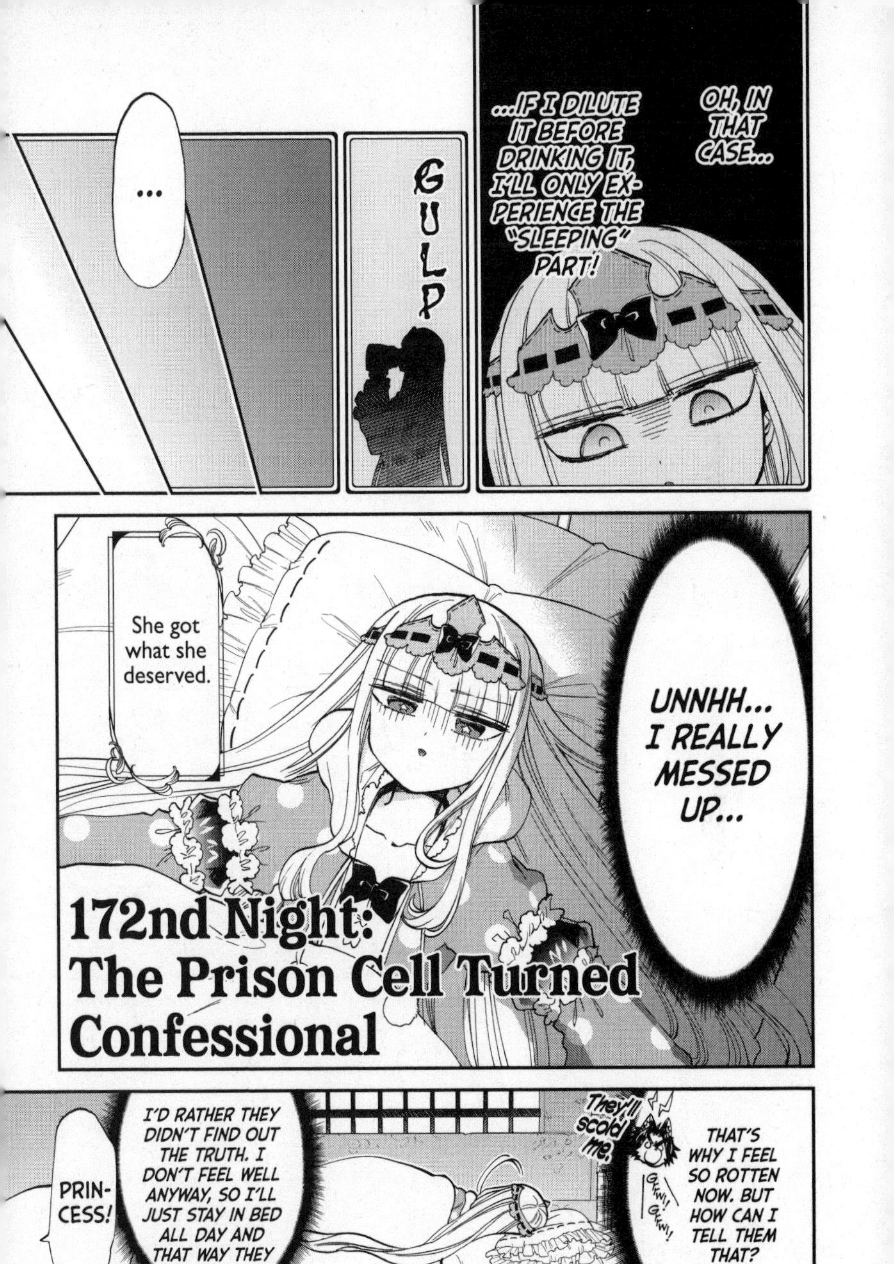
OH, IN THAT CASE...
...IF I DILUTE IT BEFORE DRINKING IT, I'LL ONLY EXPERIENCE THE "SLEEPING" PART!
GULP
...
UNNHH... I REALLY MESSED UP...
She got what she deserved.
172nd Night: The Prison Cell Turned Confessional
THAT'S WHY I FEEL SO ROTTEN NOW. BUT HOW CAN I TELL THEM THAT?
They'll scold me.
I'D RATHER THEY DIDN'T FIND OUT THE TRUTH. I DON'T FEEL WELL ANYWAY, SO I'LL JUST STAY IN BED ALL DAY AND THAT WAY THEY WON'T–
PRIN-CESS!

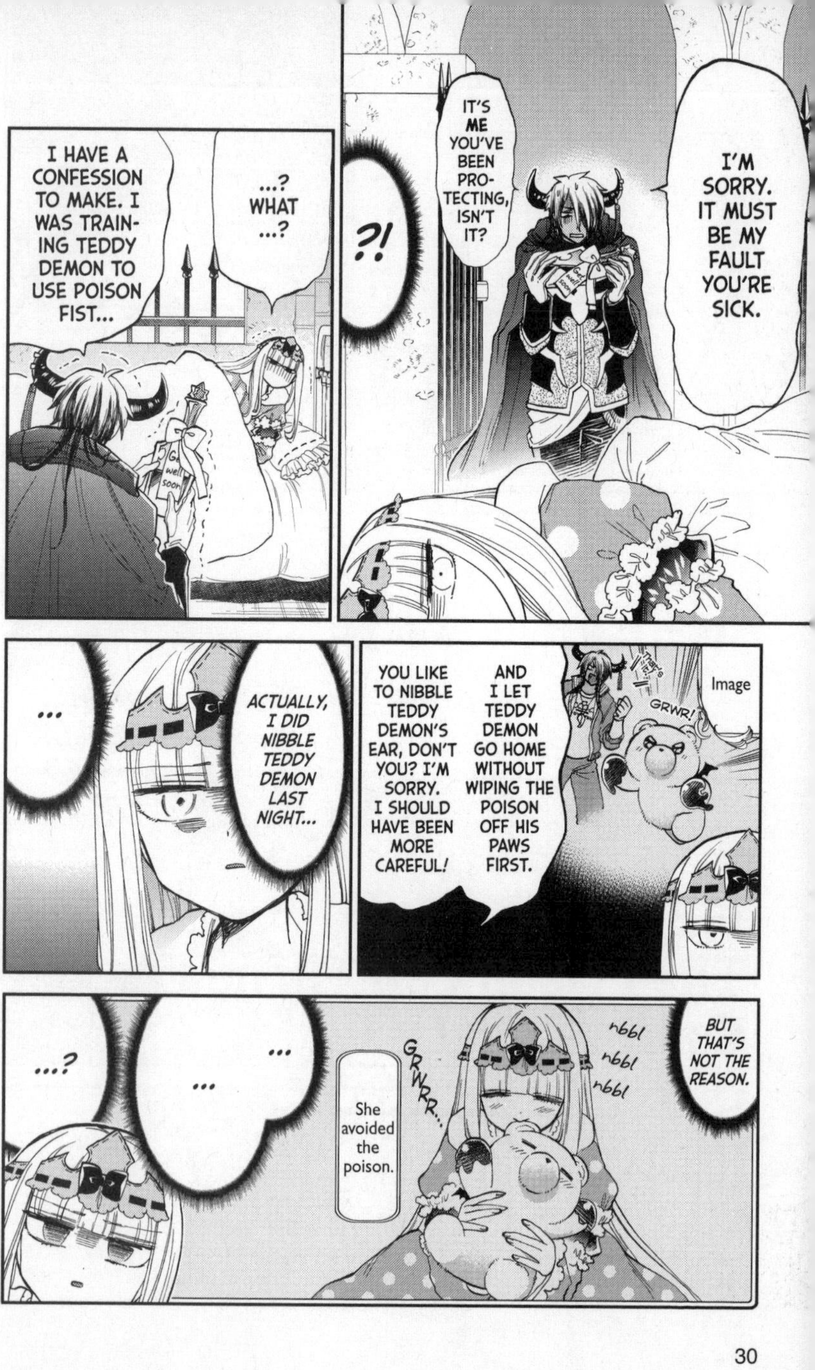
I'M SORRY. IT MUST BE MY FAULT YOU'RE SICK.
IT'S ME YOU'VE BEEN PRO-TECTING, ISN'T IT?
Get well soon
?!
...? WHAT ...?
I HAVE A CONFESSION TO MAKE. I WAS TRAIN-ING TEDDY DEMON TO USE POISON FIST...
Get well soon
Image
That's it!
GRWR!
YOU LIKE TO NIBBLE TEDDY DEMON'S EAR, DON'T YOU? I'M SORRY. I SHOULD HAVE BEEN MORE CAREFUL! AND I LET TEDDY DEMON GO HOME WITHOUT WIPING THE POISON OFF HIS PAWS FIRST.
ACTUALLY, I DID NIBBLE TEDDY DEMON LAST NIGHT...
...
BUT THAT'S NOT THE REASON.
nbbl
nbbl
nbbl
GRWRR...
She avoided the poison.
...
...
...?

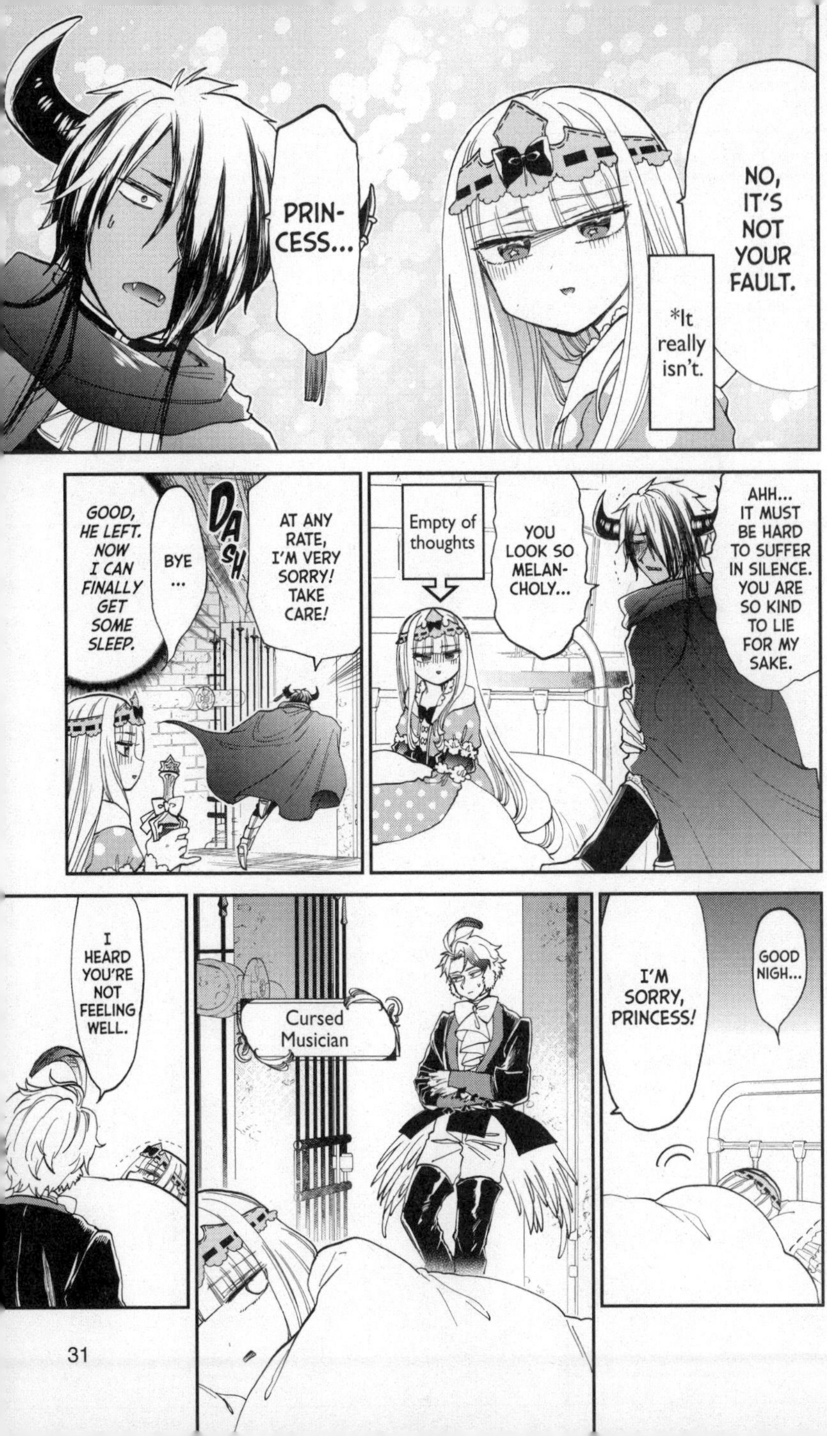
NO, IT'S NOT YOUR FAULT.
*It really isn't.
PRIN-CESS...
AHH... IT MUST BE HARD TO SUFFER IN SILENCE. YOU ARE SO KIND TO LIE FOR MY SAKE.
YOU LOOK SO MELAN-CHOLY...
Empty of thoughts
AT ANY RATE, I'M VERY SORRY! TAKE CARE!
DASH
BYE ...
GOOD, HE LEFT. NOW I CAN FINALLY GET SOME SLEEP.
GOOD NIGH...
I'M SORRY, PRINCESS!
Cursed Musician
I HEARD YOU'RE NOT FEELING WELL.

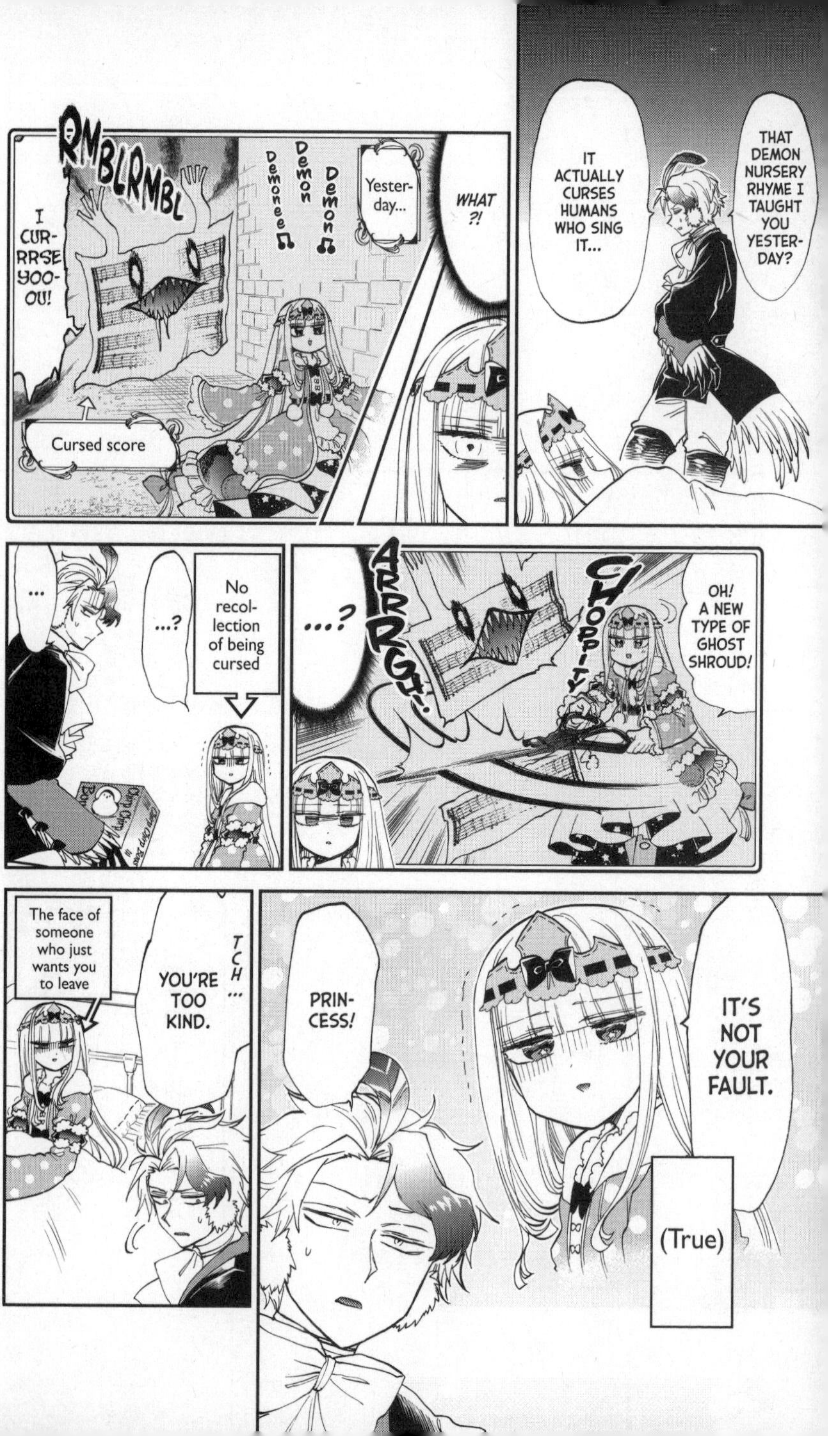
THAT DEMON NURSERY RHYME I TAUGHT YOU YESTERDAY?
IT ACTUALLY CURSES HUMANS WHO SING IT...
WHAT?!
Yesterday...
Demon Demon♫
Demon Demonee♫
RMBLRMBL
I CURRRSE YOOOU!
Cursed score
OH! A NEW TYPE OF GHOST SHROUD!
CHOPPITY
ARRRGH!
...?
No recollection of being cursed
...?
...
IT'S NOT YOUR FAULT.
(True)
PRINCESS!
TCH...
YOU'RE TOO KIND.
The face of someone who just wants you to leave

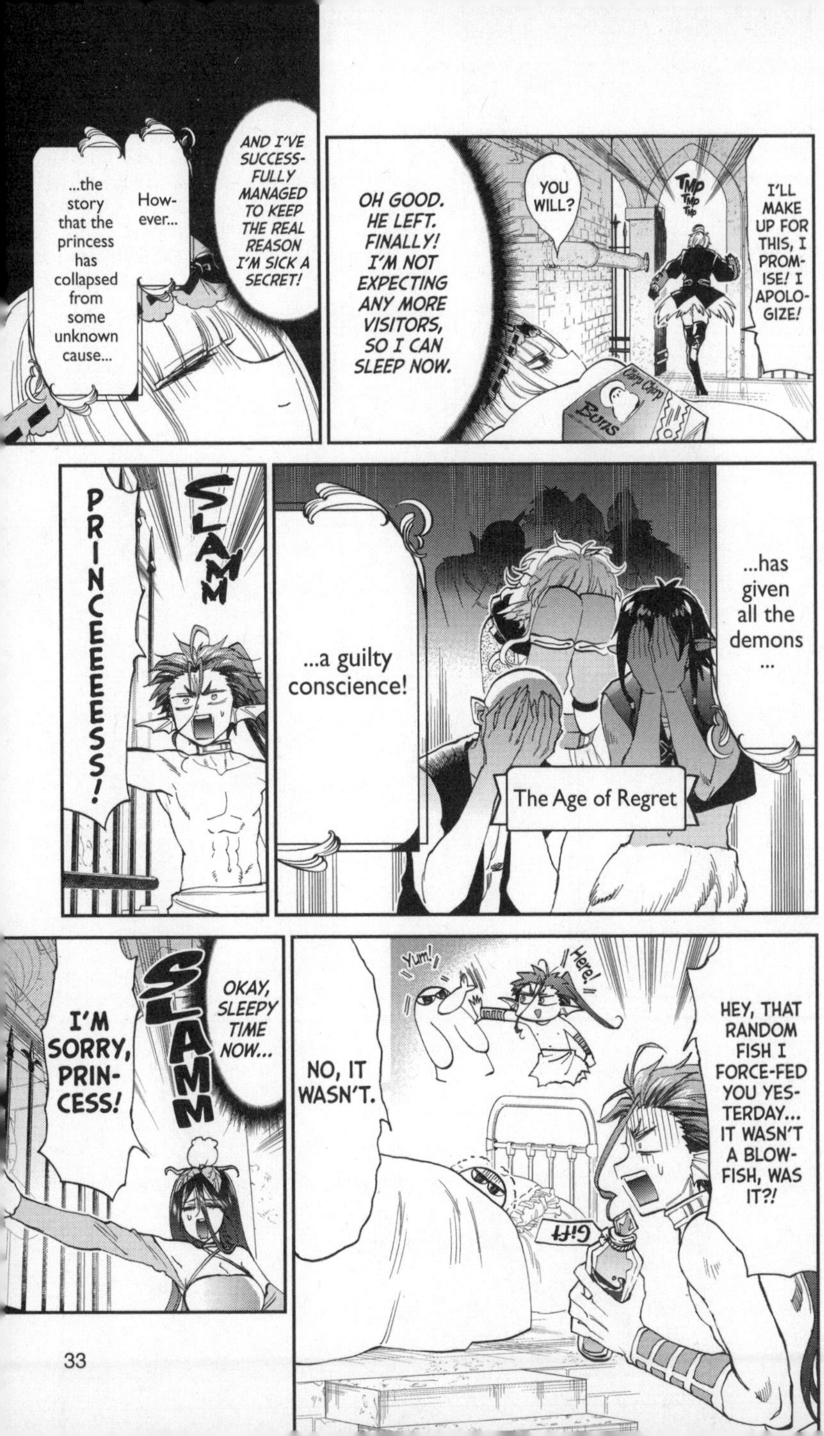

I'LL MAKE UP FOR THIS, I PROMISE! I APOLOGIZE!
TMP TMP TMP
YOU WILL?
OH GOOD. HE LEFT. FINALLY! I'M NOT EXPECTING ANY MORE VISITORS, SO I CAN SLEEP NOW.
Chirp Chirp Buns
AND I'VE SUCCESSFULLY MANAGED TO KEEP THE REAL REASON I'M SICK A SECRET!
However...
...the story that the princess has collapsed from some unknown cause...
...has given all the demons ...
...a guilty conscience!
The Age of Regret
SLAMM
PRINCEEEEESS!
HEY, THAT RANDOM FISH I FORCE-FED YOU YESTERDAY... IT WASN'T A BLOWFISH, WAS IT?!
Here!
Yum!
NO, IT WASN'T.
Gift
OKAY, SLEEPY TIME NOW...
SLAMM
I'M SORRY, PRINCESS!

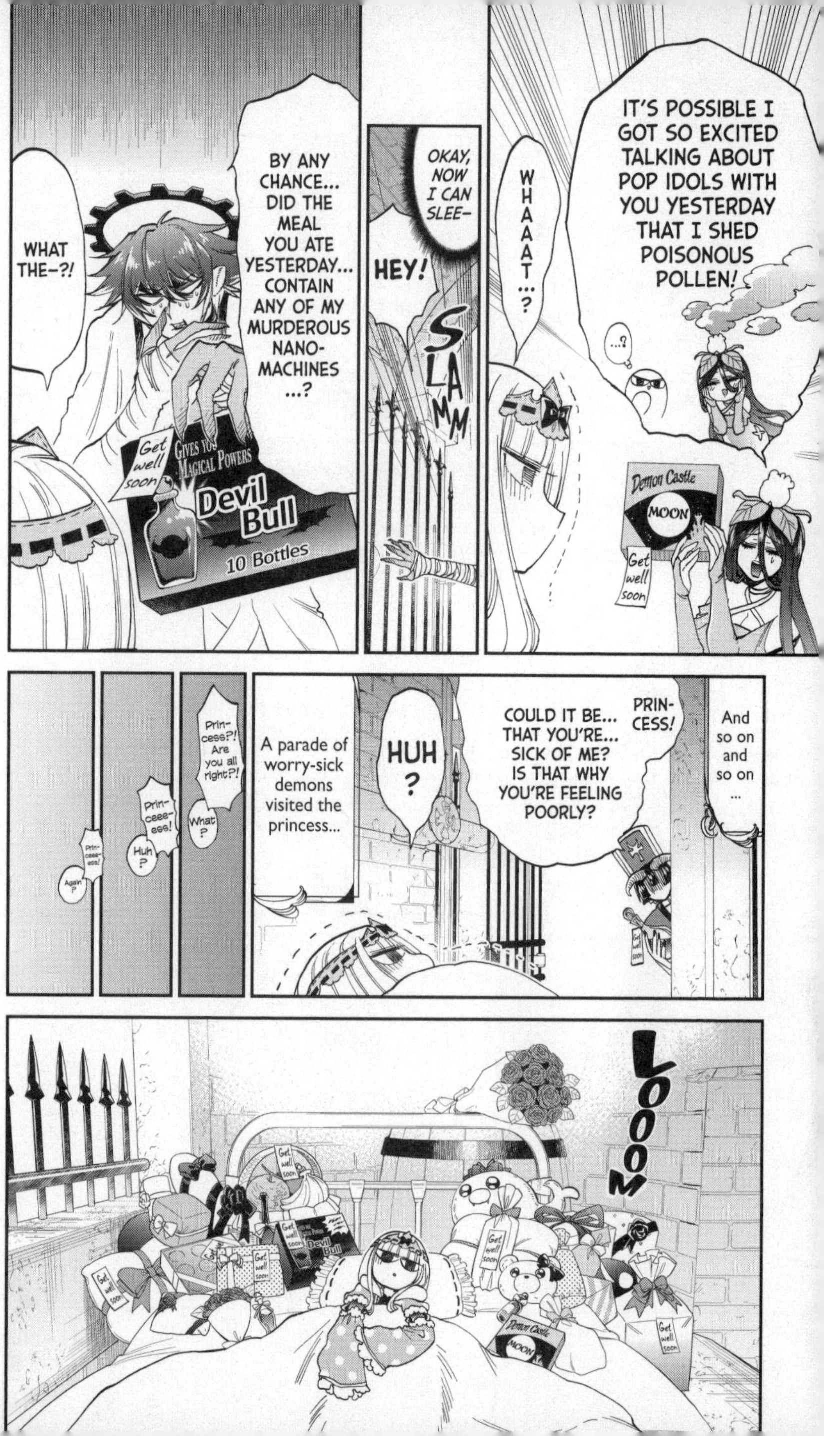
IT'S POSSIBLE I GOT SO EXCITED TALKING ABOUT POP IDOLS WITH YOU YESTERDAY THAT I SHED POISONOUS POLLEN!
WHAAAT...?
...?
Demon Castle
MOON
Get well soon
OKAY, NOW I CAN SLEE–
HEY!
SLAMM
BY ANY CHANCE... DID THE MEAL YOU ATE YESTERDAY... CONTAIN ANY OF MY MURDEROUS NANO-MACHINES ...?
WHAT THE–?!
Get well soon
GIVES YOU MAGICAL POWERS
Devil Bull
10 Bottles
And so on and so on ...
PRIN-CESS!
COULD IT BE... THAT YOU'RE... SICK OF ME? IS THAT WHY YOU'RE FEELING POORLY?
HUH ?
A parade of worry-sick demons visited the princess...
Prin-cess?! Are you all right?!
What ?
Prin-ceee-ees!
Huh ?
Prin-ceeeees!
Again ?
LOOOOM
Get well soon
Devil Bull
Get well soon
Get well soon
Demon Castle
MOON
Get well soon

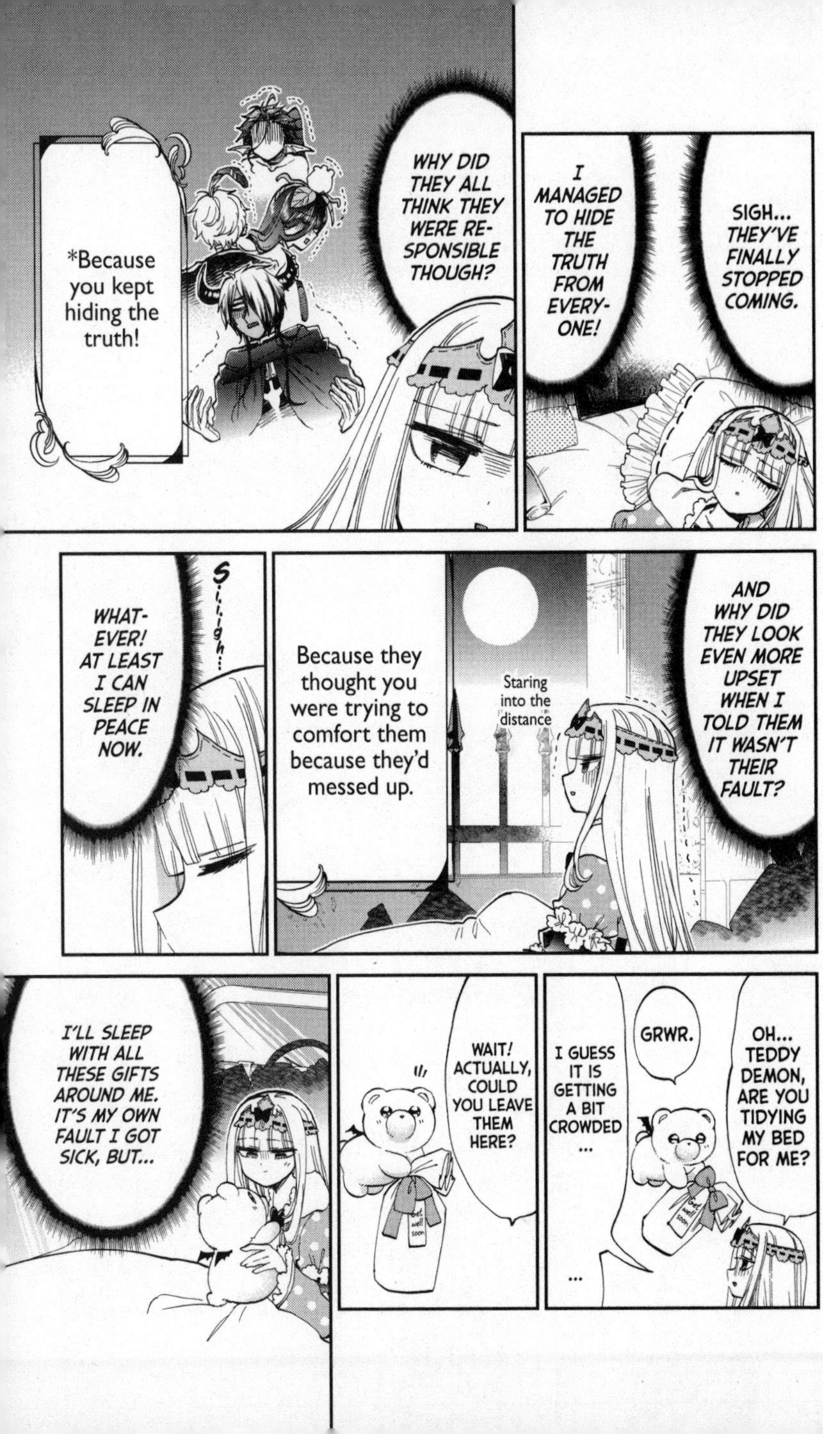
SIGH... THEY'VE FINALLY STOPPED COMING.
I MANAGED TO HIDE THE TRUTH FROM EVERYONE!
WHY DID THEY ALL THINK THEY WERE RESPONSIBLE THOUGH?
*Because you kept hiding the truth!
AND WHY DID THEY LOOK EVEN MORE UPSET WHEN I TOLD THEM IT WASN'T THEIR FAULT?
Staring into the distance
Because they thought you were trying to comfort them because they'd messed up.
Siiigh...
WHATEVER! AT LEAST I CAN SLEEP IN PEACE NOW.
OH... TEDDY DEMON, ARE YOU TIDYING MY BED FOR ME?
GRWR.
I GUESS IT IS GETTING A BIT CROWDED...
...
Get well soon
WAIT! ACTUALLY, COULD YOU LEAVE THEM HERE?
Get well soon
I'LL SLEEP WITH ALL THESE GIFTS AROUND ME. IT'S MY OWN FAULT I GOT SICK, BUT...

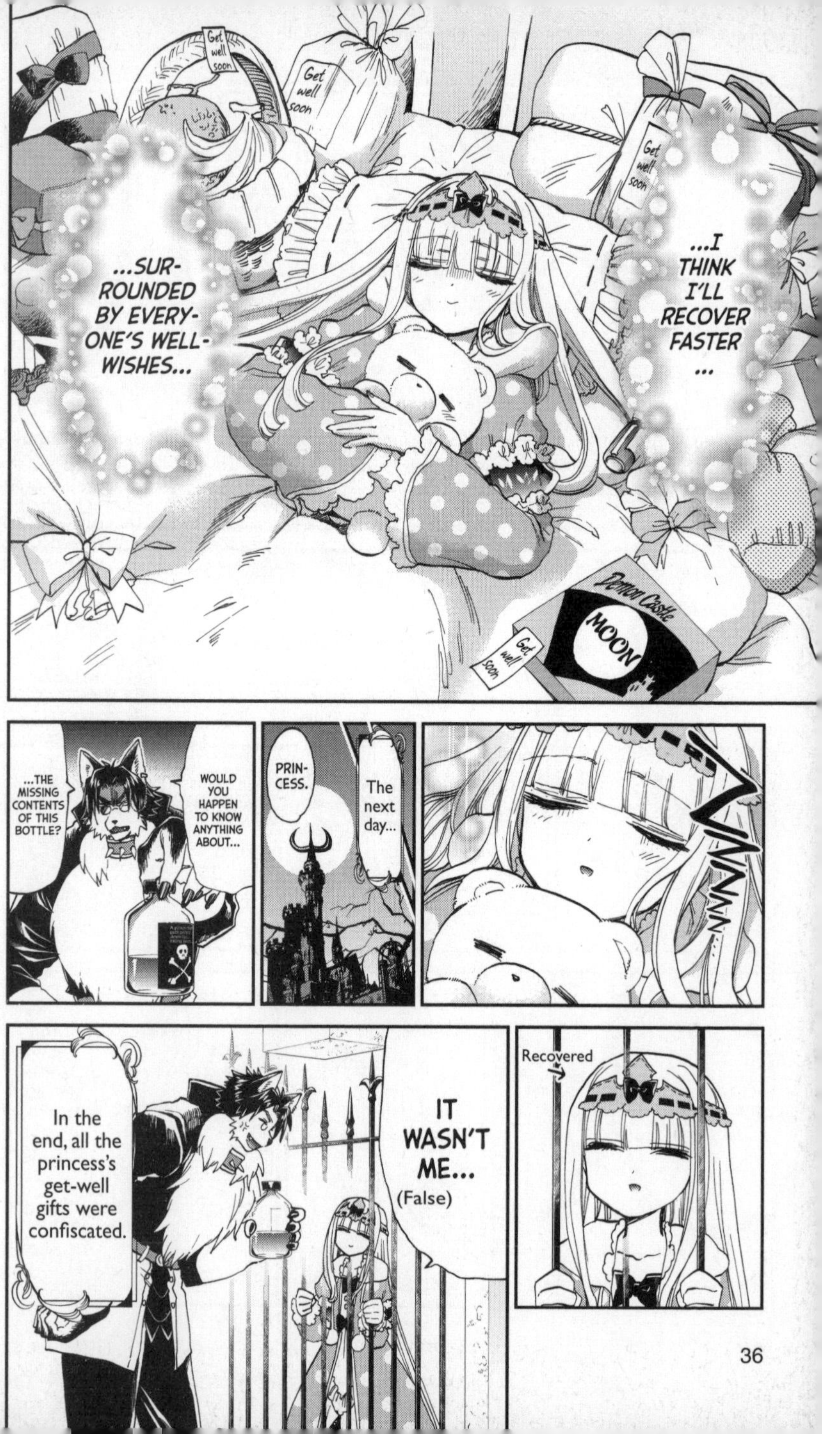
Get well soon
Get well soon
Get well soon
...I THINK I'LL RECOVER FASTER ...
...SUR-ROUNDED BY EVERY-ONE'S WELL-WISHES...
Demon Castle MOON
Get well soon
The next day...
PRIN-CESS.
WOULD YOU HAPPEN TO KNOW ANYTHING ABOUT...
...THE MISSING CONTENTS OF THIS BOTTLE?
Recovered
IT WASN'T ME...
(False)
In the end, all the princess's get-well gifts were confiscated.

DATA ON HOW THE DOG BATTLES

Top secret info that may now be disclosed

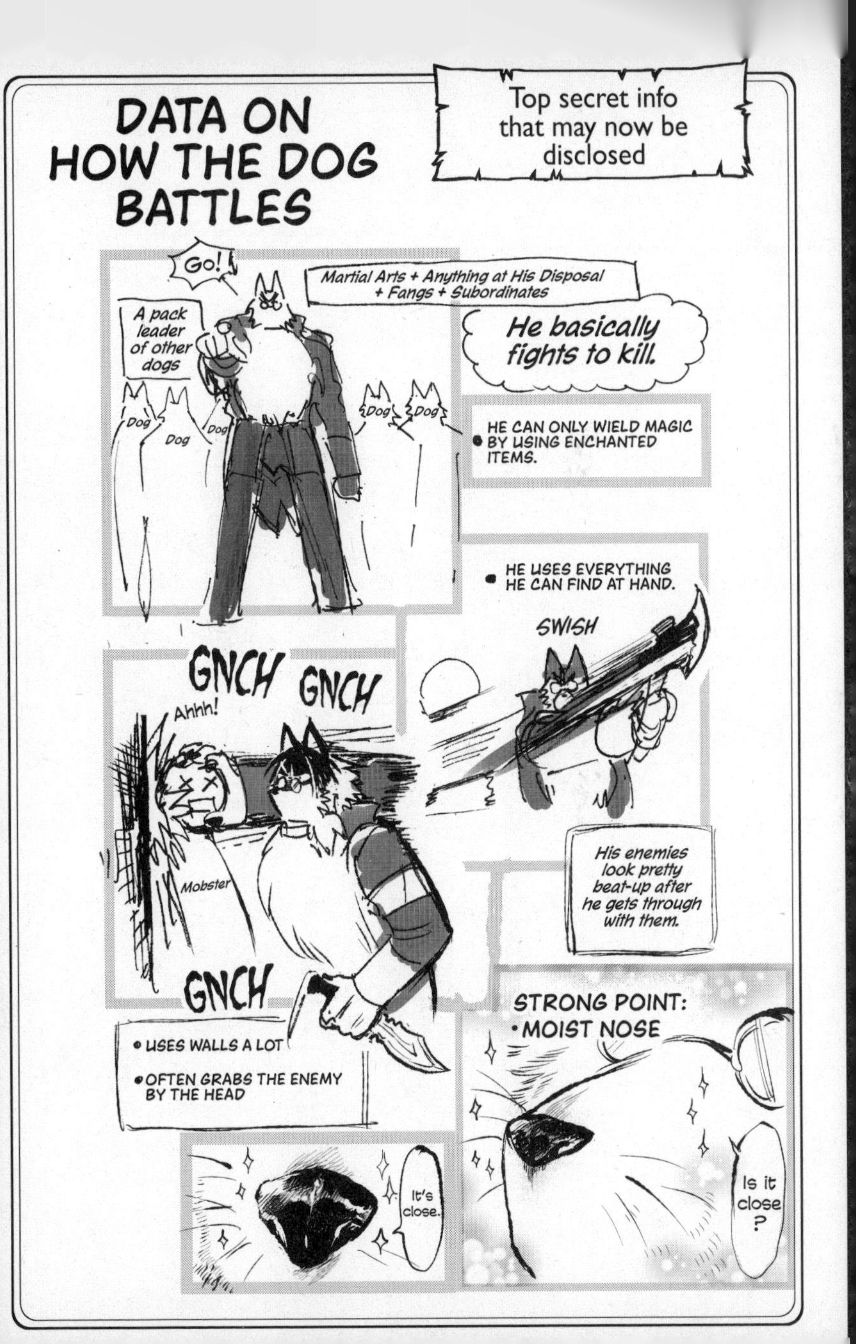
Martial Arts + Anything at His Disposal + Fangs + Subordinates
He basically fights to kill.
HE CAN ONLY WIELD MAGIC BY USING ENCHANTED ITEMS.
Go!
A pack leader of other dogs
Dog
Dog
Dog
Dog
Dog
HE USES EVERYTHING HE CAN FIND AT HAND.
SWISH
His enemies look pretty beat-up after he gets through with them.
GNCH
GNCH
Ahhh!
Mobster
GNCH
USES WALLS A LOT
OFTEN GRABS THE ENEMY BY THE HEAD
STRONG POINT:
MOIST NOSE
Is it close?
It's close.

Would you like to change
your class?
9 changes
remaining

▶ Yes

No ▼

Cupid

"Do I have to shoot?"

▼

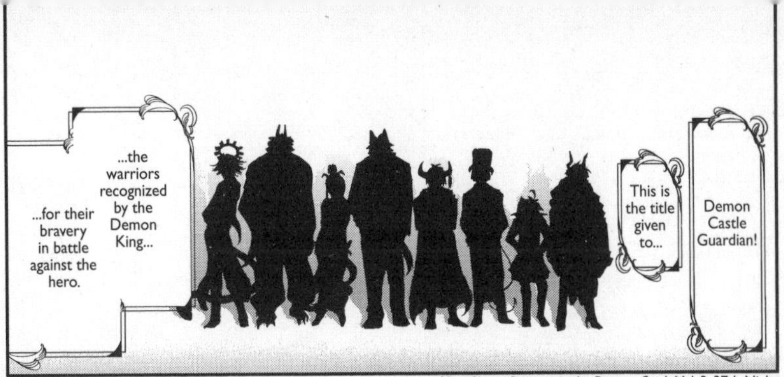
Demon Castle Guardian!
This is the title given to...
...the warriors recognized by the Demon King...
...for their bravery in battle against the hero.

*See *Sleepy Princess in the Demon Castle* Vol. 3, 37th Night

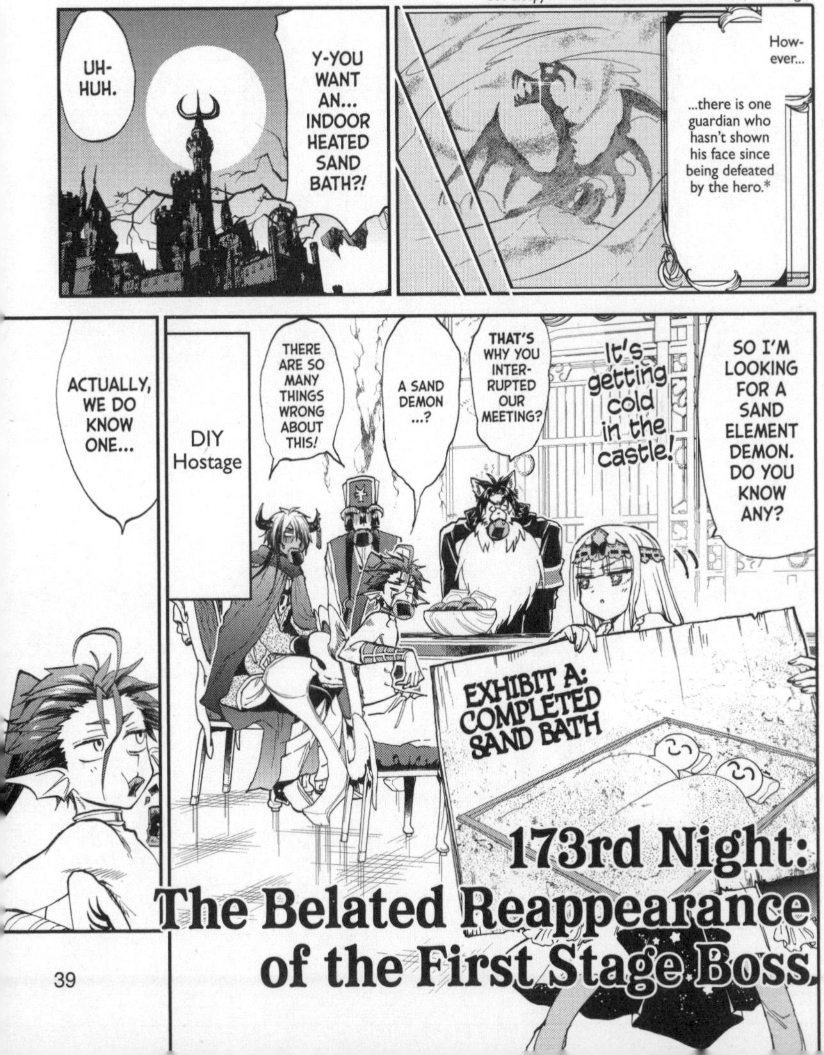
However...
...there is one guardian who hasn't shown his face since being defeated by the hero.*
Y-YOU WANT AN... INDOOR HEATED SAND BATH?!
UH-HUH.
SO I'M LOOKING FOR A SAND ELEMENT DEMON. DO YOU KNOW ANY?
It's getting cold in the castle!
THAT'S WHY YOU INTERRUPTED OUR MEETING?
A SAND DEMON ...?
THERE ARE SO MANY THINGS WRONG ABOUT THIS!
EXHIBIT A: COMPLETED SAND BATH
DIY Hostage
ACTUALLY, WE DO KNOW ONE...
173rd Night:
The Belated Reappearance of the First Stage Boss

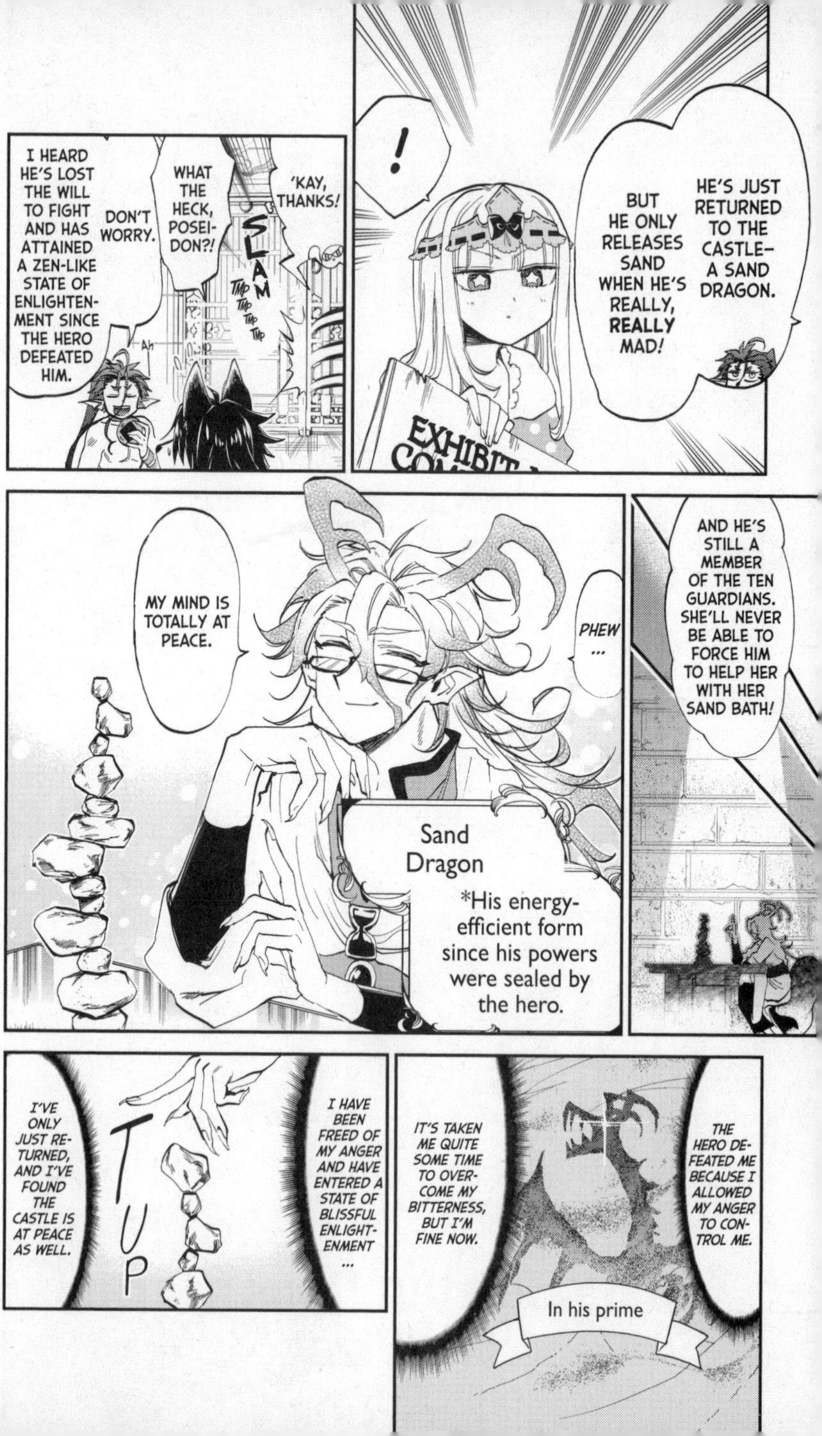
HE'S JUST RETURNED TO THE CASTLE— A SAND DRAGON.
BUT HE ONLY RELEASES SAND WHEN HE'S REALLY, **REALLY** MAD!
!
EXHIBIT
'KAY, THANKS!
SLAM
TMP TMP TMP TMP
WHAT THE HECK, POSEI-DON?!
DON'T WORRY.
Ah
I HEARD HE'S LOST THE WILL TO FIGHT AND HAS ATTAINED A ZEN-LIKE STATE OF ENLIGHTEN-MENT SINCE THE HERO DEFEATED HIM.
AND HE'S STILL A MEMBER OF THE TEN GUARDIANS. SHE'LL NEVER BE ABLE TO FORCE HIM TO HELP HER WITH HER SAND BATH!
PHEW...
MY MIND IS TOTALLY AT PEACE.
Sand Dragon
*His energy-efficient form since his powers were sealed by the hero.
THE HERO DE-FEATED ME BECAUSE I ALLOWED MY ANGER TO CON-TROL ME.
IT'S TAKEN ME QUITE SOME TIME TO OVER-COME MY BITTERNESS, BUT I'M FINE NOW.
In his prime
I HAVE BEEN FREED OF MY ANGER AND HAVE ENTERED A STATE OF BLISSFUL ENLIGHT-ENMENT...
TUP
I'VE ONLY JUST RE-TURNED, AND I'VE FOUND THE CASTLE IS AT PEACE AS WELL.

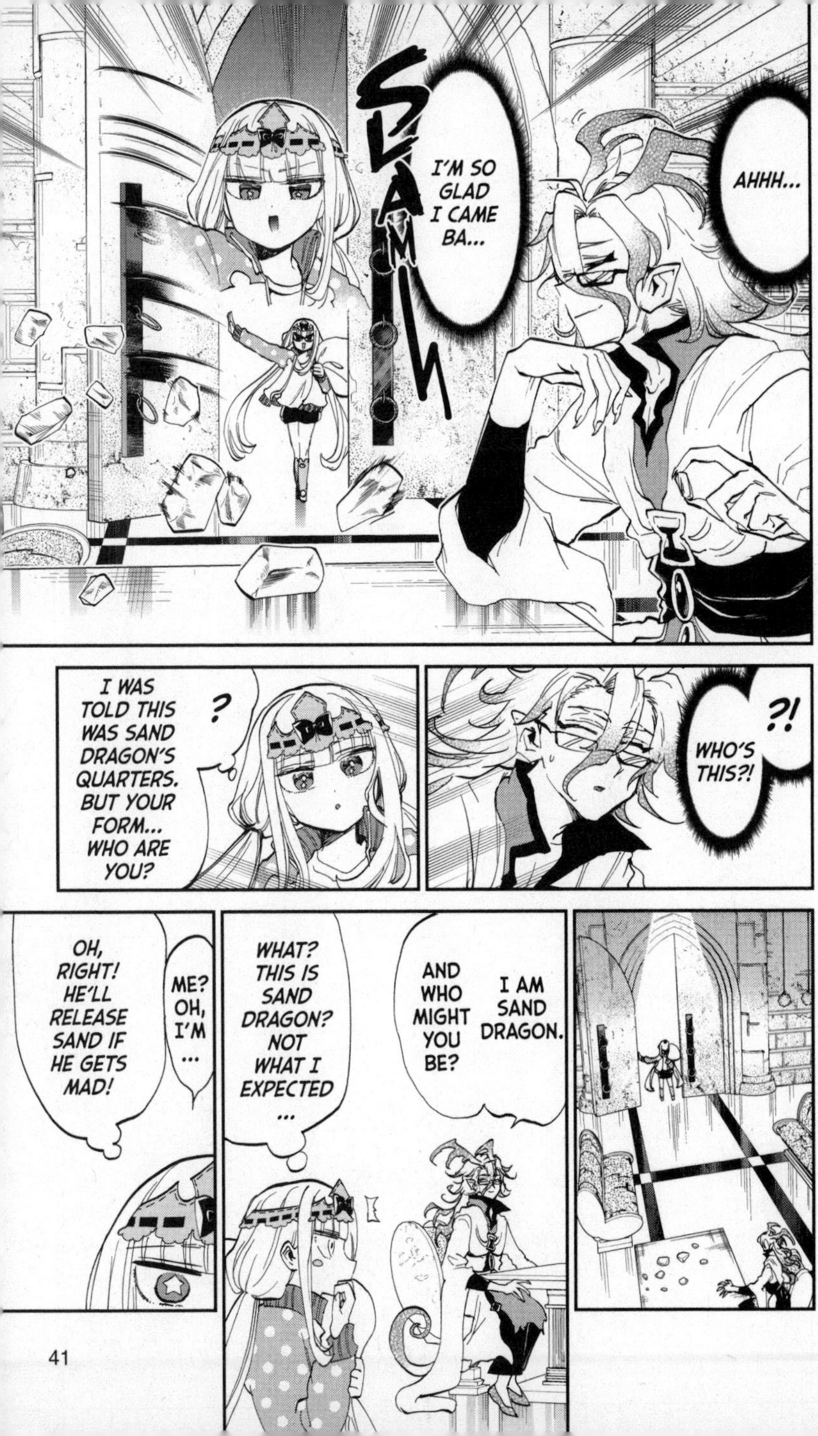
AHHH...
I'M SO GLAD I CAME BA...
SLAM
?!
WHO'S THIS?!
?
I WAS TOLD THIS WAS SAND DRAGON'S QUARTERS. BUT YOUR FORM... WHO ARE YOU?
I AM SAND DRAGON.
AND WHO MIGHT YOU BE?
WHAT? THIS IS SAND DRAGON? NOT WHAT I EXPECTED...
ME? OH, I'M...
OH, RIGHT! HE'LL RELEASE SAND IF HE GETS MAD!

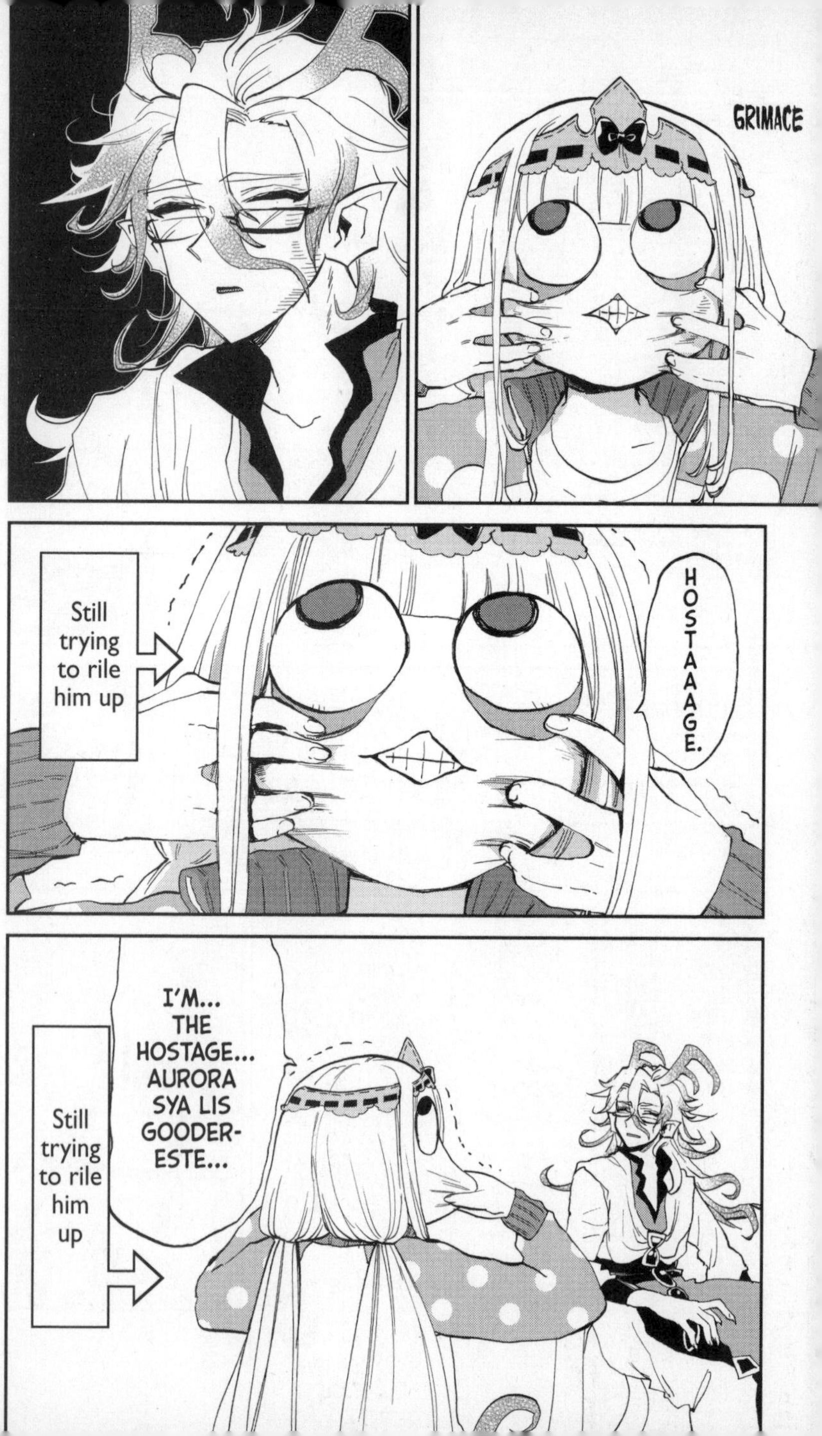
GRIMACE
HOSTAAAGE.
Still trying to rile him up
I'M... THE HOSTAGE... AURORA SYA LIS GOODER-ESTE...
Still trying to rile him up

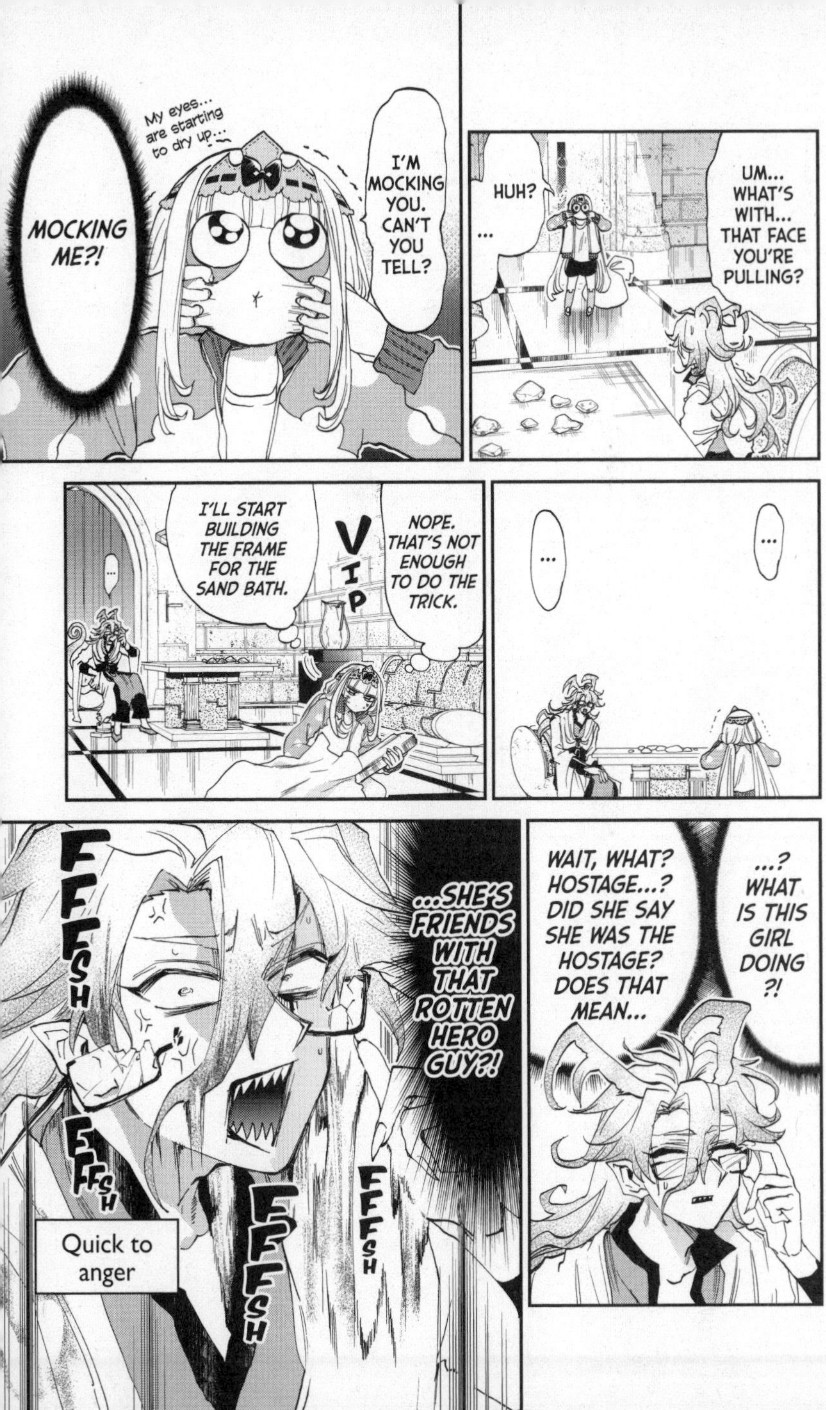
UM... WHAT'S WITH... THAT FACE YOU'RE PULLING?
HUH?
...
I'M MOCKING YOU. CAN'T YOU TELL?
My eyes... are starting to dry up...
MOCKING ME?!
...
...
NOPE. THAT'S NOT ENOUGH TO DO THE TRICK.
VIP
I'LL START BUILDING THE FRAME FOR THE SAND BATH.
...
...? WHAT IS THIS GIRL DOING?!
WAIT, WHAT? HOSTAGE...? DID SHE SAY SHE WAS THE HOSTAGE? DOES THAT MEAN...
...SHE'S FRIENDS WITH THAT ROTTEN HERO GUY?!
FFFSH
FFFSH
FFFSH
FFFSH
FFFSH
Quick to anger

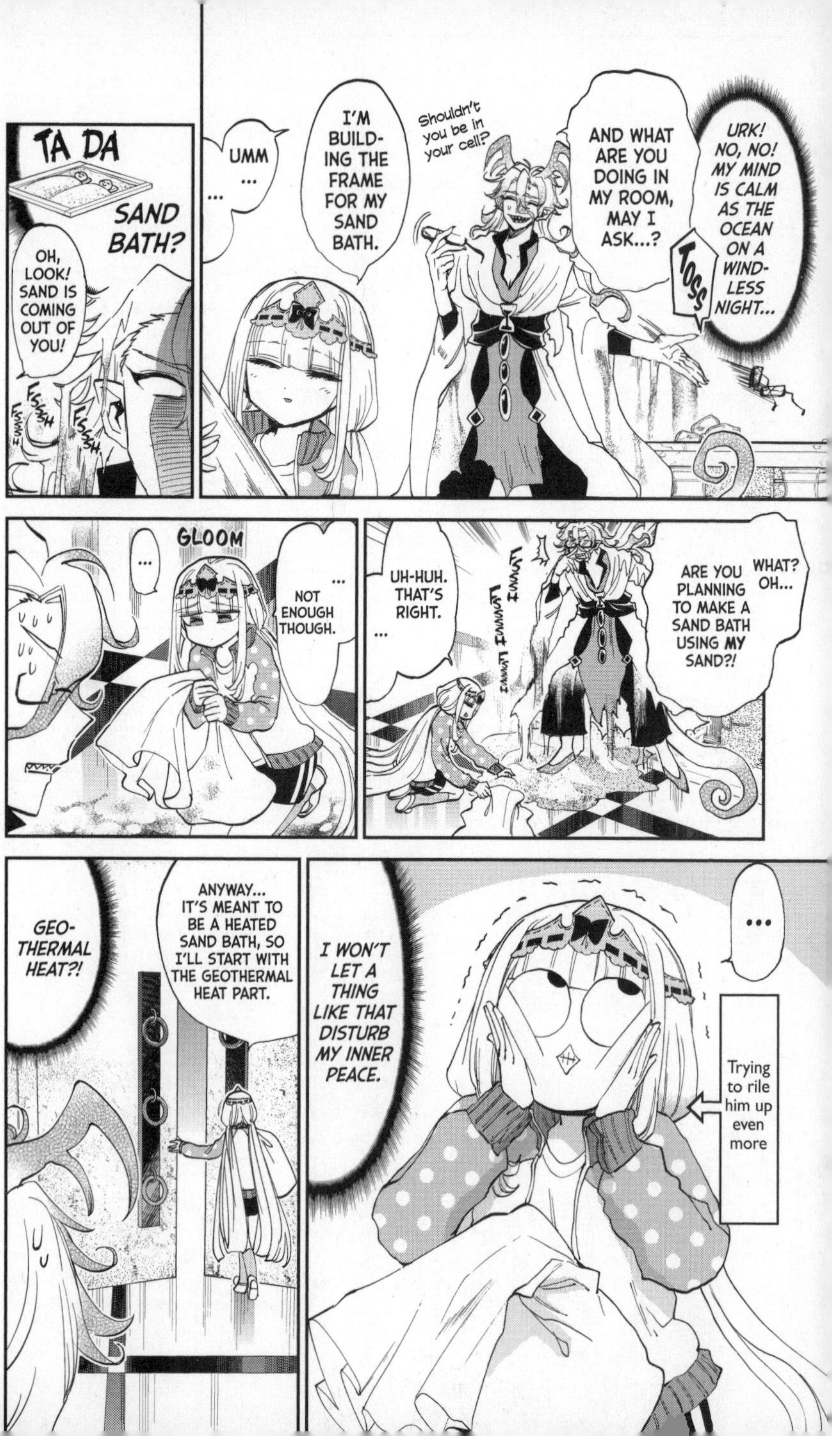
URK! NO, NO! MY MIND IS CALM AS THE OCEAN ON A WINDLESS NIGHT...
AND WHAT ARE YOU DOING IN MY ROOM, MAY I ASK...?
TOSS
Shouldn't you be in your cell?
I'M BUILDING THE FRAME FOR MY SAND BATH.
UMM ...
...
TA DA
SAND BATH?
OH, LOOK! SAND IS COMING OUT OF YOU!
FSSSH
FSSSH
WHAT? OH...
ARE YOU PLANNING TO MAKE A SAND BATH USING MY SAND?!
UH-HUH. THAT'S RIGHT. ...
... NOT ENOUGH THOUGH.
GLOOM
...
...
Trying to rile him up even more
I WON'T LET A THING LIKE THAT DISTURB MY INNER PEACE.
ANYWAY... IT'S MEANT TO BE A HEATED SAND BATH, SO I'LL START WITH THE GEOTHERMAL HEAT PART.
GEO-THERMAL HEAT?!

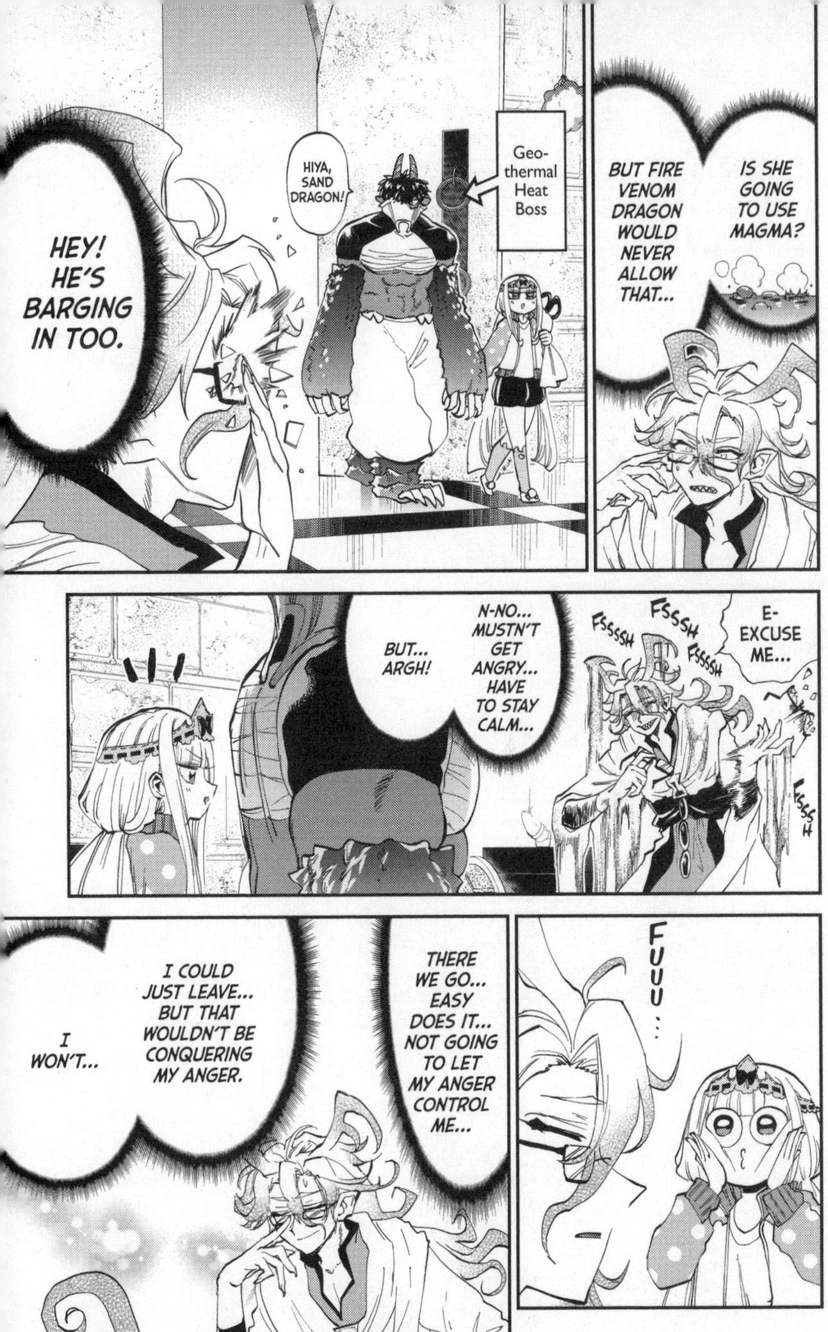
IS SHE GOING TO USE MAGMA?
BUT FIRE VENOM DRAGON WOULD NEVER ALLOW THAT...
Geo-thermal Heat Boss
HIYA, SAND DRAGON!
HEY! HE'S BARGING IN TOO.
E- EXCUSE ME...
FSSSSH
FSSSH
FSSSSH
FSSSSH
FSSSH
N-NO... MUSTN'T GET ANGRY... HAVE TO STAY CALM...
BUT... ARGH!
FUUU...
THERE WE GO... EASY DOES IT... NOT GOING TO LET MY ANGER CONTROL ME...
I COULD JUST LEAVE... BUT THAT WOULDN'T BE CONQUERING MY ANGER.
I WON'T...

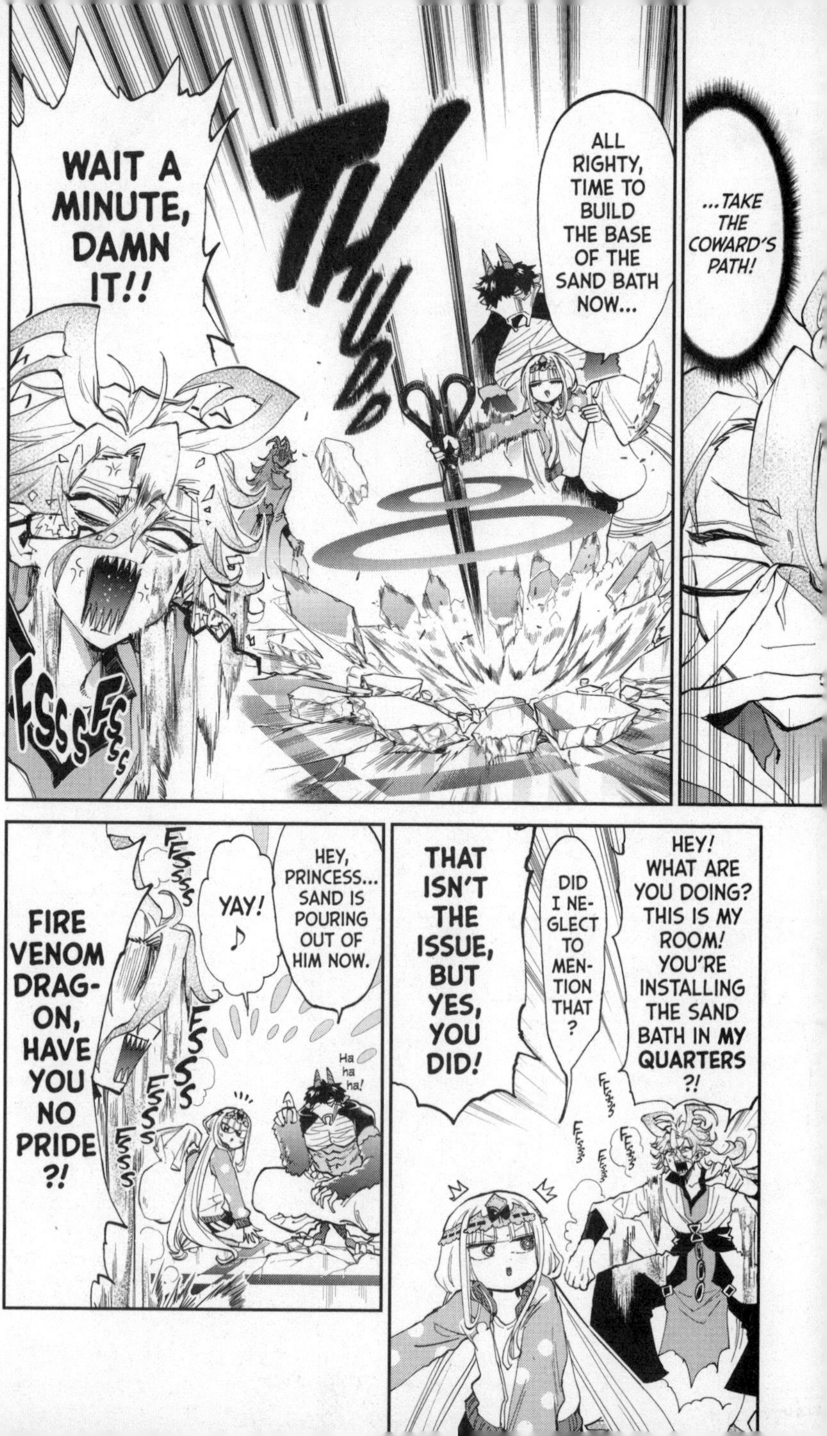
...TAKE THE COWARD'S PATH!
ALL RIGHTY, TIME TO BUILD THE BASE OF THE SAND BATH NOW...
WAIT A MINUTE, DAMN IT!!
FSSS FSSS
HEY! WHAT ARE YOU DOING? THIS IS MY ROOM! YOU'RE INSTALLING THE SAND BATH IN MY QUARTERS?!
DID I NEGLECT TO MENTION THAT?
THAT ISN'T THE ISSUE, BUT YES, YOU DID!
HEY, PRINCESS... SAND IS POURING OUT OF HIM NOW.
YAY! ♪
Ha ha ha!
FIRE VENOM DRAGON, HAVE YOU NO PRIDE?!

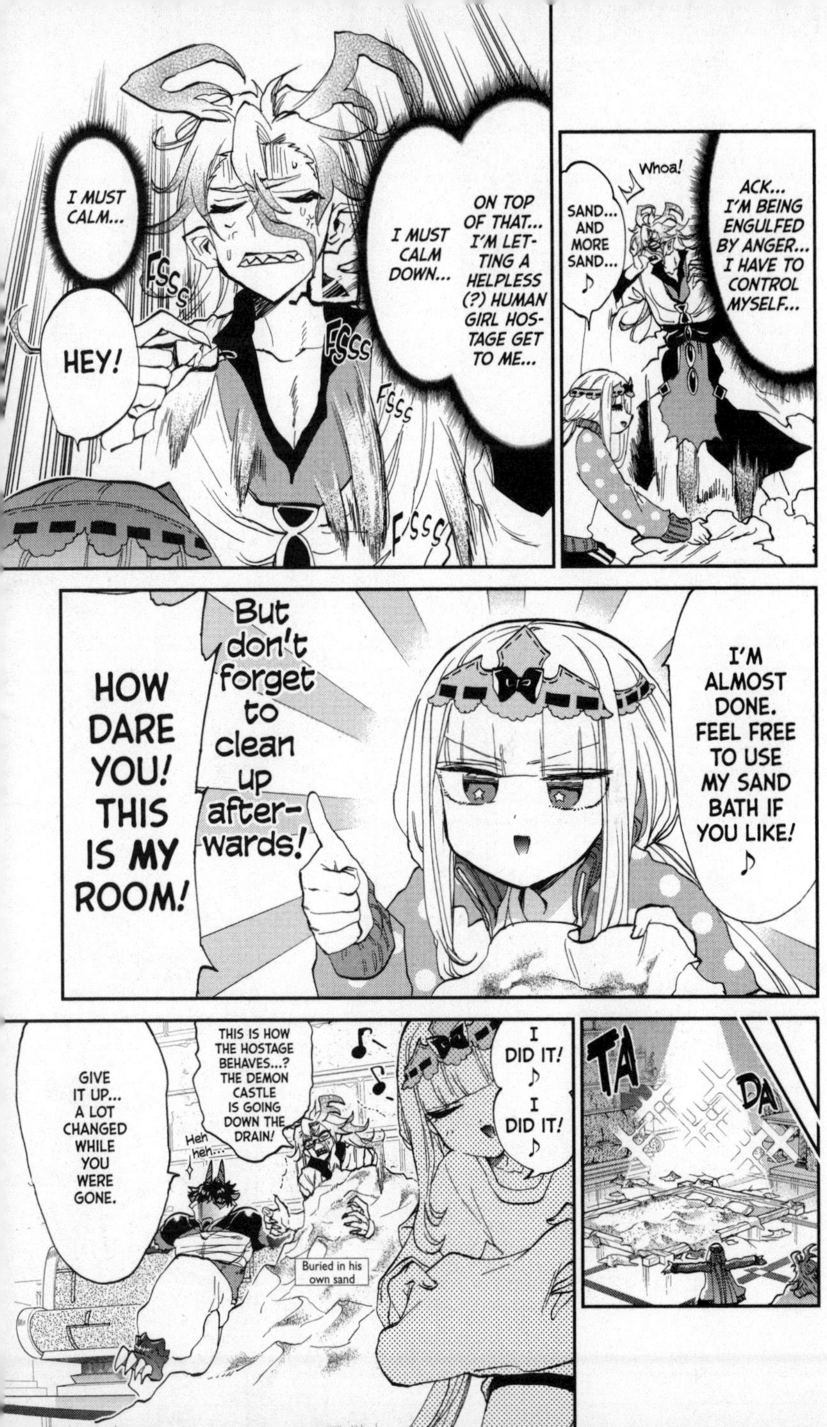
ACK... I'M BEING ENGULFED BY ANGER... I HAVE TO CONTROL MYSELF...
Whoa!
SAND... AND MORE SAND... ♪
ON TOP OF THAT... I'M LET-TING A HELPLESS (?) HUMAN GIRL HOS-TAGE GET TO ME...
I MUST CALM DOWN...
I MUST CALM...
FSSS
FSSS
FSSS
FSSS
HEY!
I'M ALMOST DONE. FEEL FREE TO USE MY SAND BATH IF YOU LIKE! ♪
But don't forget to clean up after-wards!
HOW DARE YOU! THIS IS MY ROOM!
TA
DA
I DID IT! ♪
I DID IT! ♪
THIS IS HOW THE HOSTAGE BEHAVES...? THE DEMON CASTLE IS GOING DOWN THE DRAIN!
Heh heh...
GIVE IT UP... A LOT CHANGED WHILE YOU WERE GONE.
Buried in his own sand

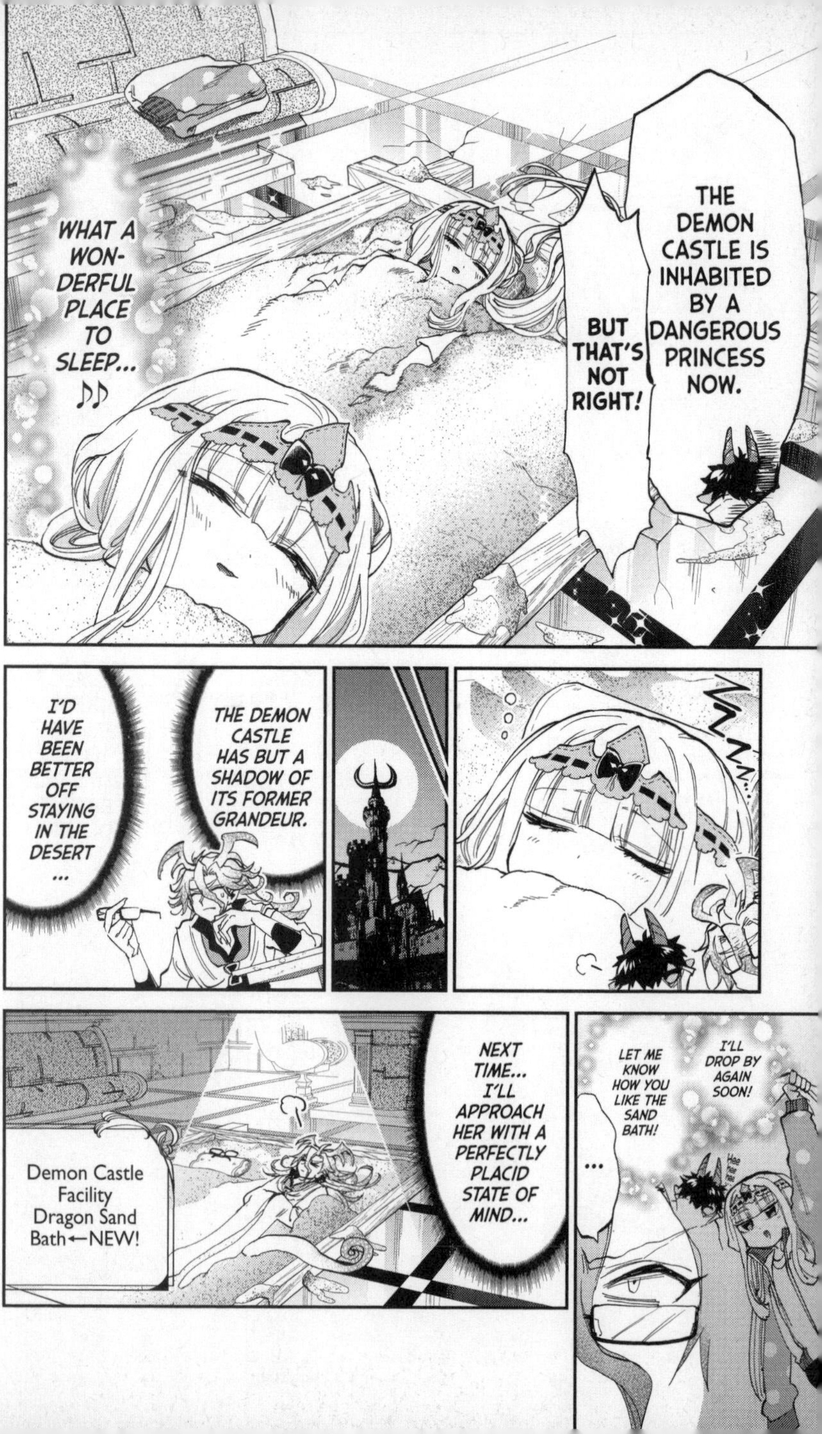
THE DEMON CASTLE IS INHABITED BY A DANGEROUS PRINCESS NOW.
BUT THAT'S NOT RIGHT!
WHAT A WON-DERFUL PLACE TO SLEEP... ♪♪
ZZZ...
THE DEMON CASTLE HAS BUT A SHADOW OF ITS FORMER GRANDEUR.
I'D HAVE BEEN BETTER OFF STAYING IN THE DESERT ...
I'LL DROP BY AGAIN SOON!
LET ME KNOW HOW YOU LIKE THE SAND BATH!
...
NEXT TIME... I'LL APPROACH HER WITH A PERFECTLY PLACID STATE OF MIND...
Demon Castle Facility Dragon Sand Bath←NEW!

The return of the first stage boss.

Sand Dragon

Short-Temperedness: ☆☆☆☆☆☆☆☆
Glasses: ∞

A demon of the dragon species and one of the Ten Guardians. He is the first area boss who fought the hero, Dawner. After being defeated, he locked himself up near the Fortress of the Desert.

He was just starting to get over his humiliation when he returned to the Demon Castle in his new energy-efficient form. Unfortunately for him, Princess Syalis was in residence.

He always has a supply of fake glasses to make himself look calm and composed.

Former problem:
"I was defeated by the hero..."

Current problem:
"This sand bath...
I should get rid of it, but...
I kind of enjoy using it..."

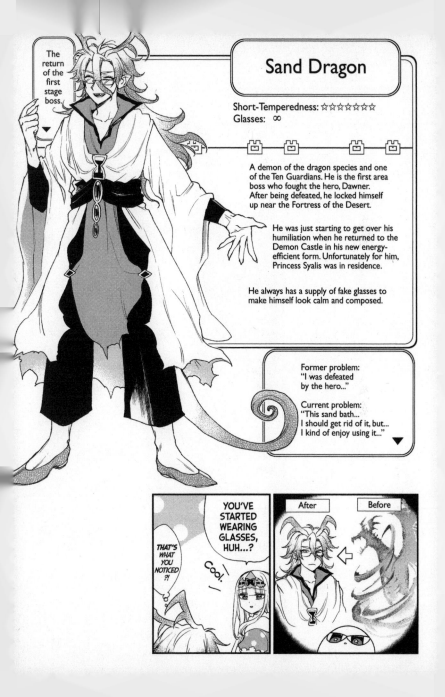

Before
After
YOU'VE STARTED WEARING GLASSES, HUH...?
Cool!
THAT'S WHAT YOU NOTICED?!

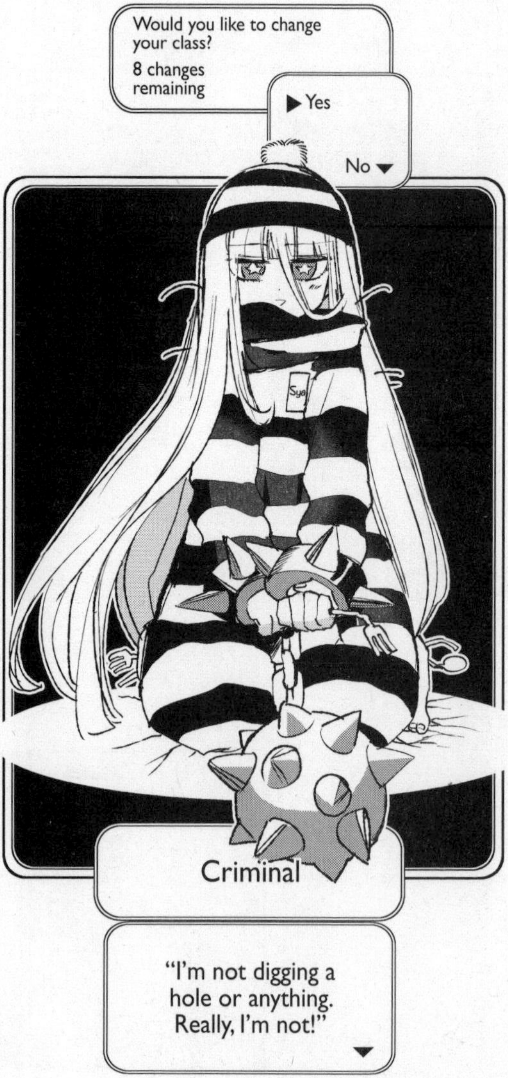

Would you like to change your class?
8 changes remaining
▶ Yes
No
Syu
Criminal
"I'm not digging a hole or anything. Really, I'm not!"

174th Night: Teddy Demons Are the Cutest Demons in the World

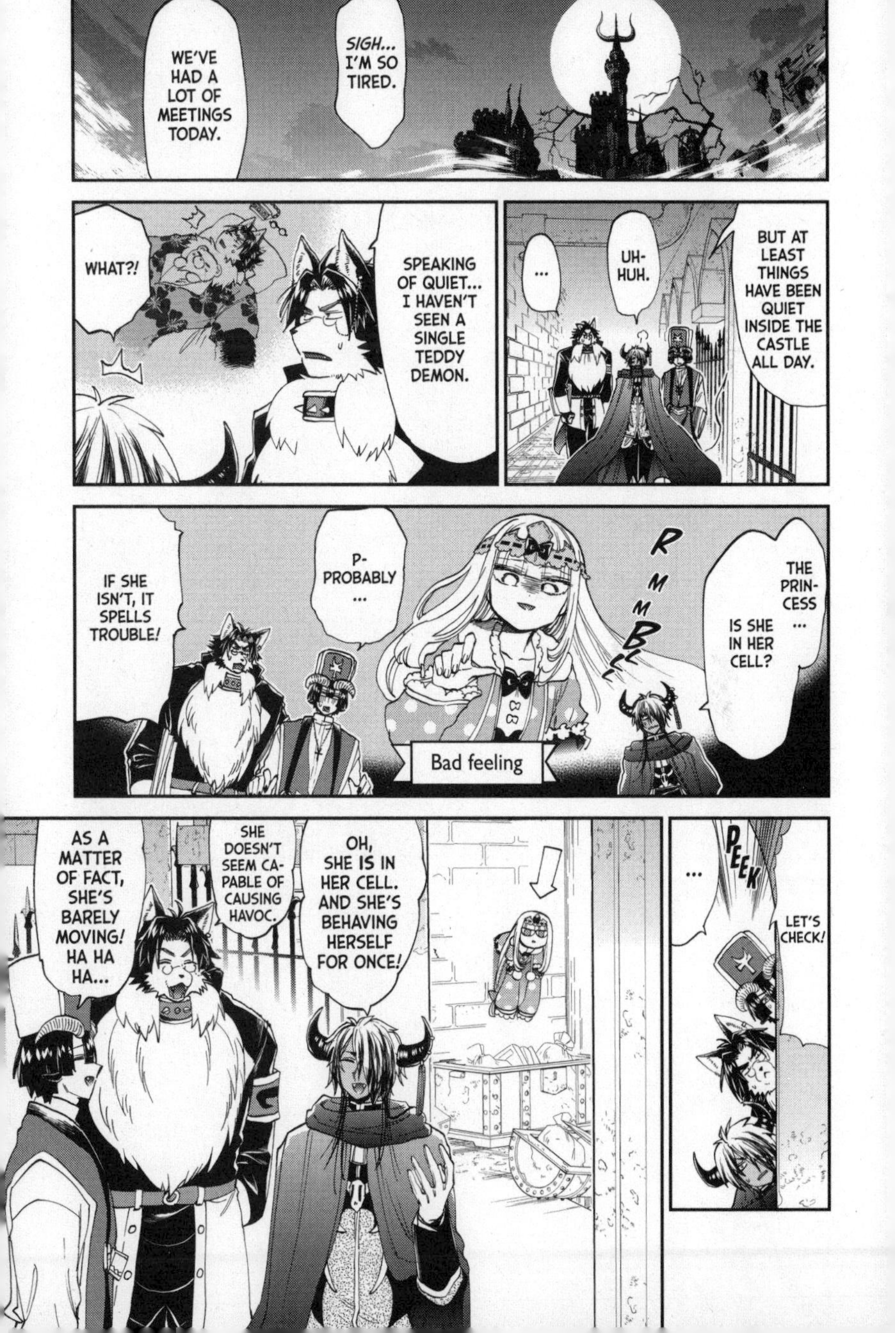
SIGH... I'M SO TIRED.
WE'VE HAD A LOT OF MEETINGS TODAY.
BUT AT LEAST THINGS HAVE BEEN QUIET INSIDE THE CASTLE ALL DAY.
UH-HUH.
...
SPEAKING OF QUIET... I HAVEN'T SEEN A SINGLE TEDDY DEMON.
WHAT?!
THE PRINCESS... IS SHE IN HER CELL?
RMMBLE
P-PROBABLY...
IF SHE ISN'T, IT SPELLS TROUBLE!
Bad feeling
PEEK
...
LET'S CHECK!
OH, SHE IS IN HER CELL. AND SHE'S BEHAVING HERSELF FOR ONCE!
SHE DOESN'T SEEM CAPABLE OF CAUSING HAVOC.
AS A MATTER OF FACT, SHE'S BARELY MOVING! HA HA HA...

174th Night: Teddy Demons Are the Cutest Demons in the World

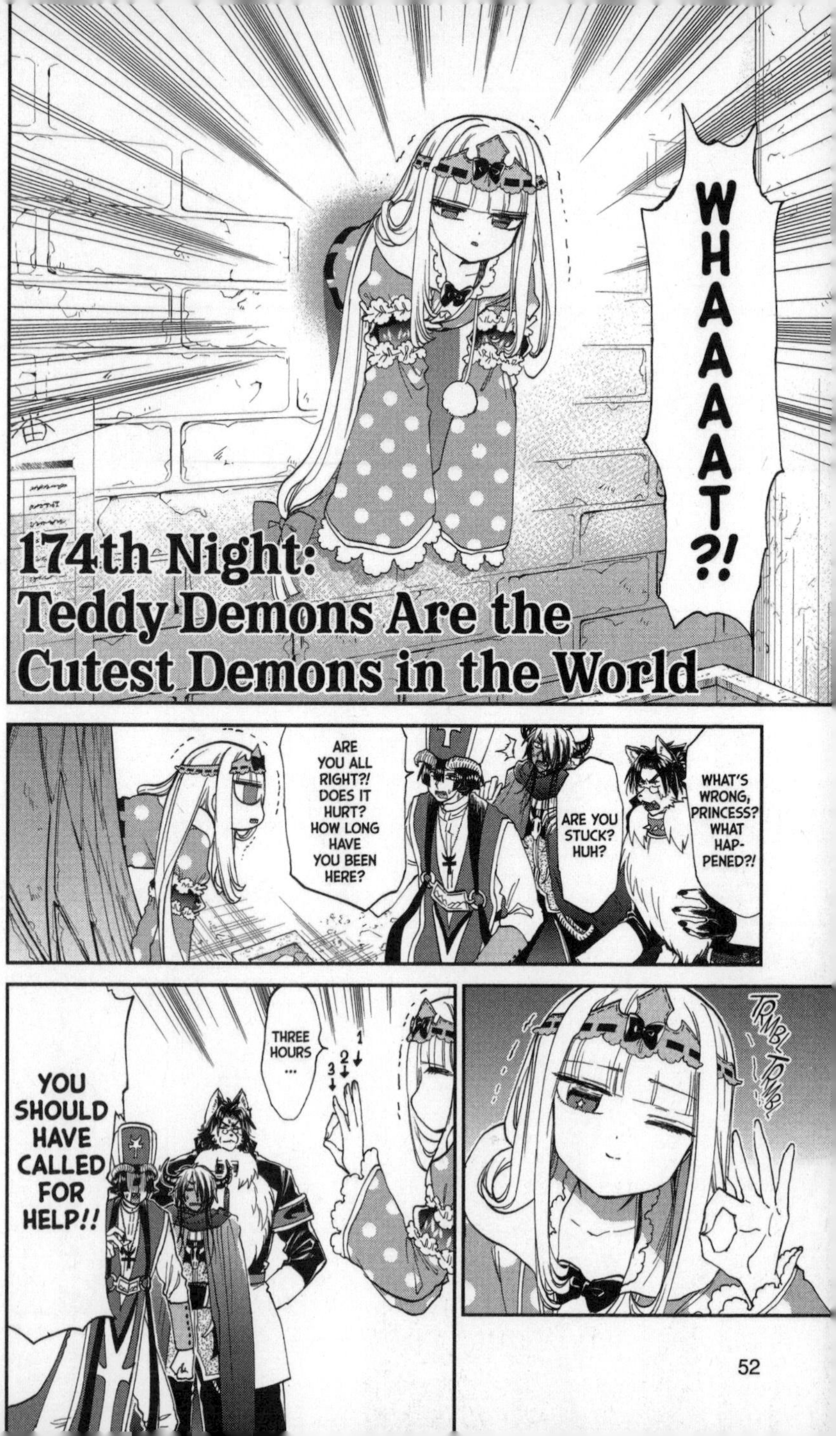
WHAAAAT?!
WHAT'S WRONG, PRINCESS? WHAT HAP-PENED?!
ARE YOU STUCK? HUH?
ARE YOU ALL RIGHT?! DOES IT HURT? HOW LONG HAVE YOU BEEN HERE?
TRMBL TRMBL
1 2 3
THREE HOURS ...
YOU SHOULD HAVE CALLED FOR HELP!!

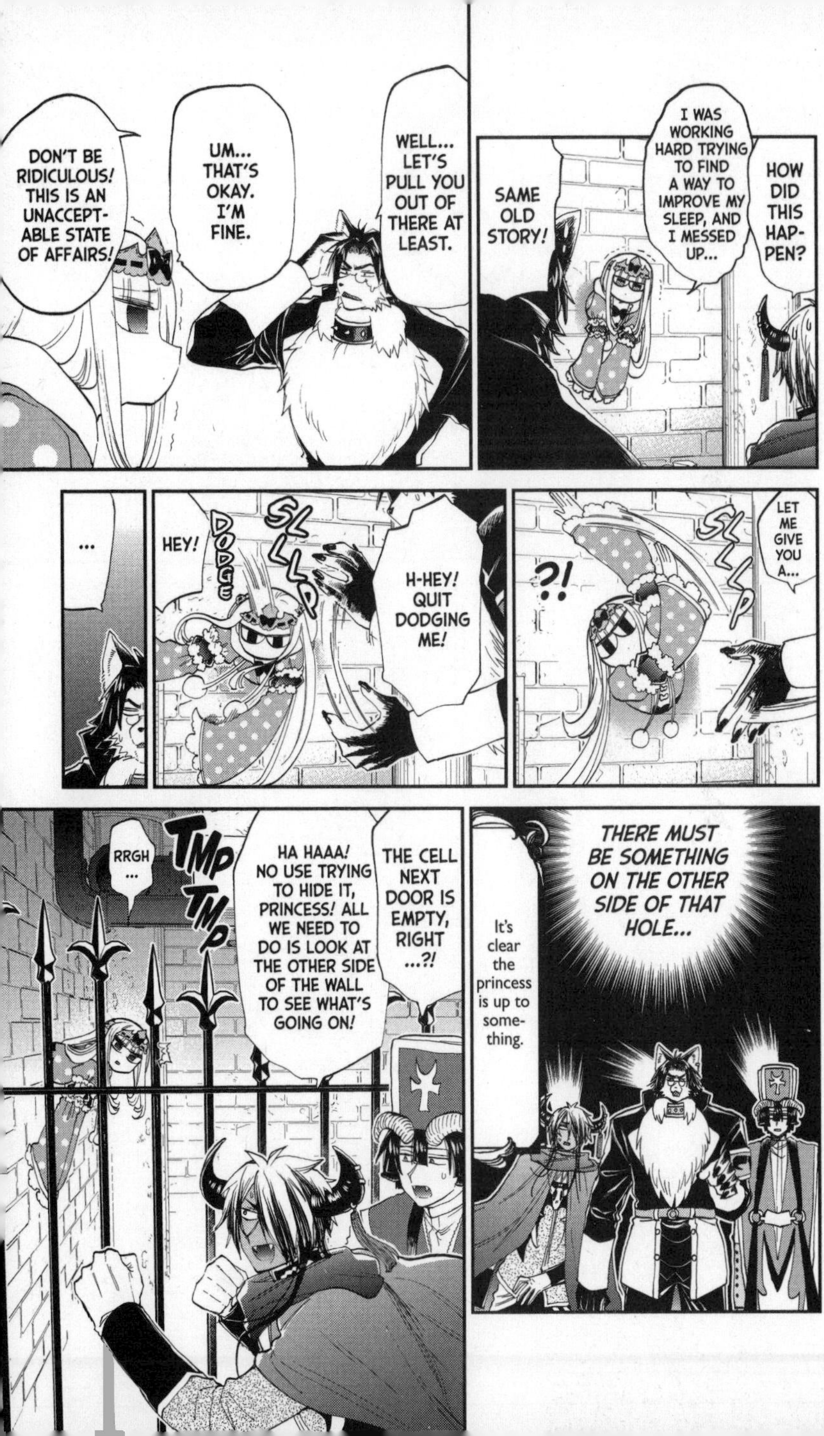
HOW DID THIS HAP-PEN?
I WAS WORKING HARD TRYING TO FIND A WAY TO IMPROVE MY SLEEP, AND I MESSED UP...
SAME OLD STORY!
WELL... LET'S PULL YOU OUT OF THERE AT LEAST.
UM... THAT'S OKAY. I'M FINE.
DON'T BE RIDICULOUS! THIS IS AN UNACCEPT-ABLE STATE OF AFFAIRS!
LET ME GIVE YOU A...
SLLLP
?!
H-HEY! QUIT DODGING ME!
SLLLP
DODGE
HEY!
...
THERE MUST BE SOMETHING ON THE OTHER SIDE OF THAT HOLE...
It's clear the princess is up to some-thing.
THE CELL NEXT DOOR IS EMPTY, RIGHT ...?!
HA HAAA! NO USE TRYING TO HIDE IT, PRINCESS! ALL WE NEED TO DO IS LOOK AT THE OTHER SIDE OF THE WALL TO SEE WHAT'S GOING ON!
TMP TMP TMP
RRGH ...

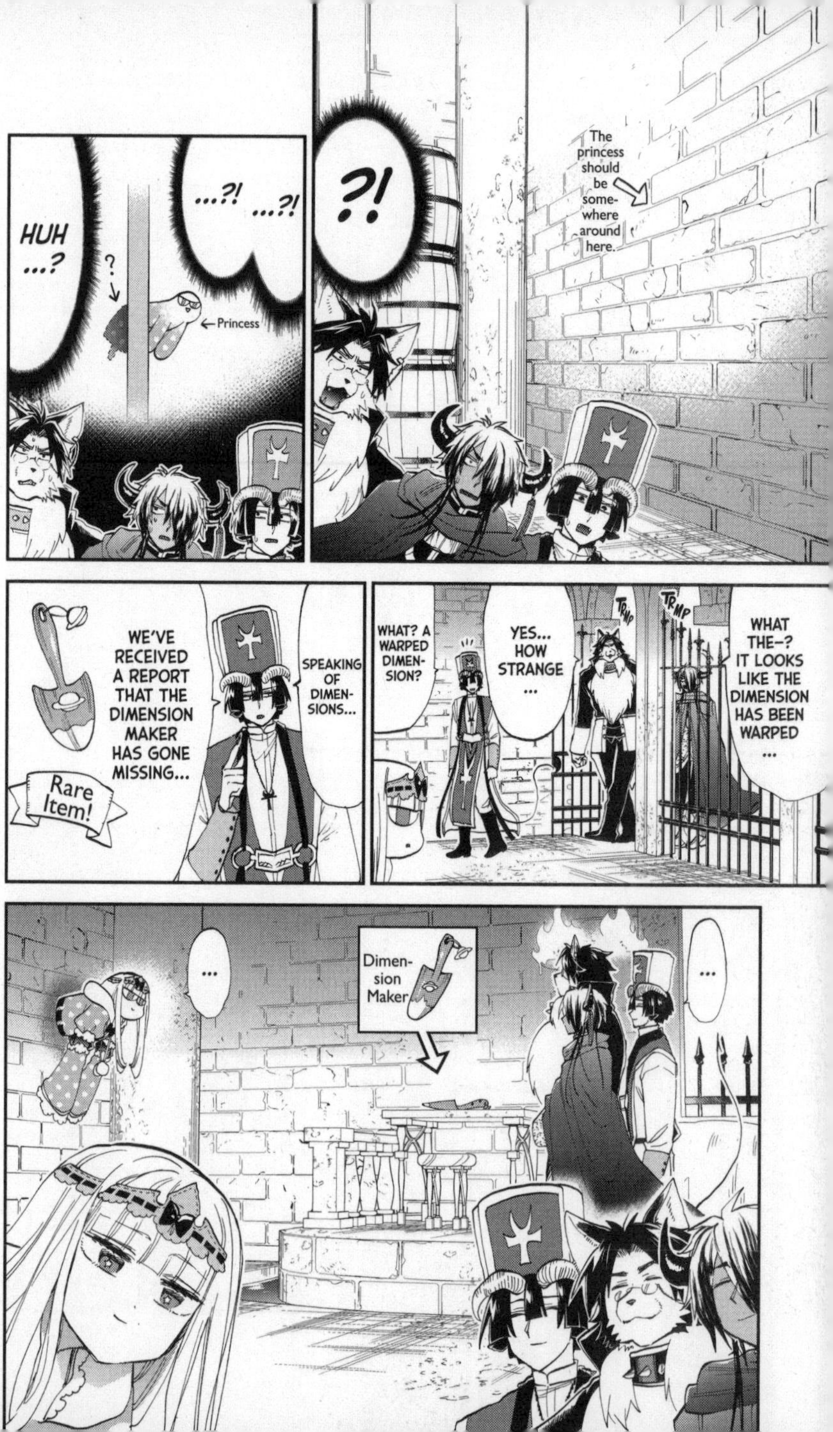
The princess should be somewhere around here.
?!
...?!
...?!
HUH ...?
?
Princess
TRMP
TRMP
WHAT THE–? IT LOOKS LIKE THE DIMENSION HAS BEEN WARPED ...
YES... HOW STRANGE ...
WHAT? A WARPED DIMENSION?
SPEAKING OF DIMENSIONS...
WE'VE RECEIVED A REPORT THAT THE DIMENSION MAKER HAS GONE MISSING...
Rare Item!
...
Dimension Maker
...

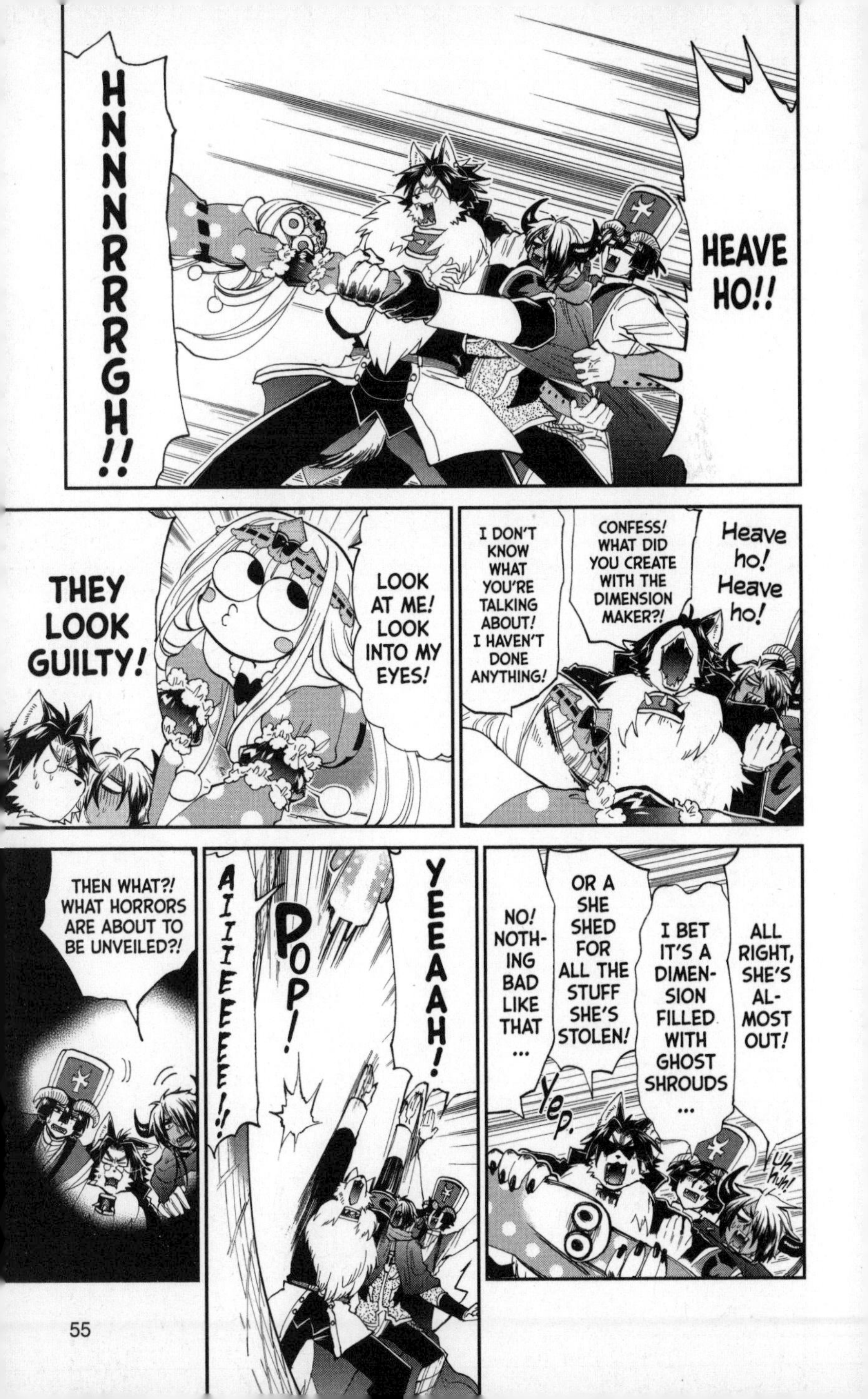
HEAVE HO!!
HNNNRRRRGH!!
Heave ho! Heave ho!
CONFESS! WHAT DID YOU CREATE WITH THE DIMENSION MAKER?!
I DON'T KNOW WHAT YOU'RE TALKING ABOUT! I HAVEN'T DONE ANYTHING!
LOOK AT ME! LOOK INTO MY EYES!
THEY LOOK GUILTY!
ALL RIGHT, SHE'S AL-MOST OUT!
I BET IT'S A DIMEN-SION FILLED WITH GHOST SHROUDS...
OR A SHE SHED FOR ALL THE STUFF SHE'S STOLEN!
NO! NOTH-ING BAD LIKE THAT...
Yep.
Uh huh!
YEEAAH!
POP!
AIIIEEEEE!!
THEN WHAT?! WHAT HORRORS ARE ABOUT TO BE UNVEILED?!

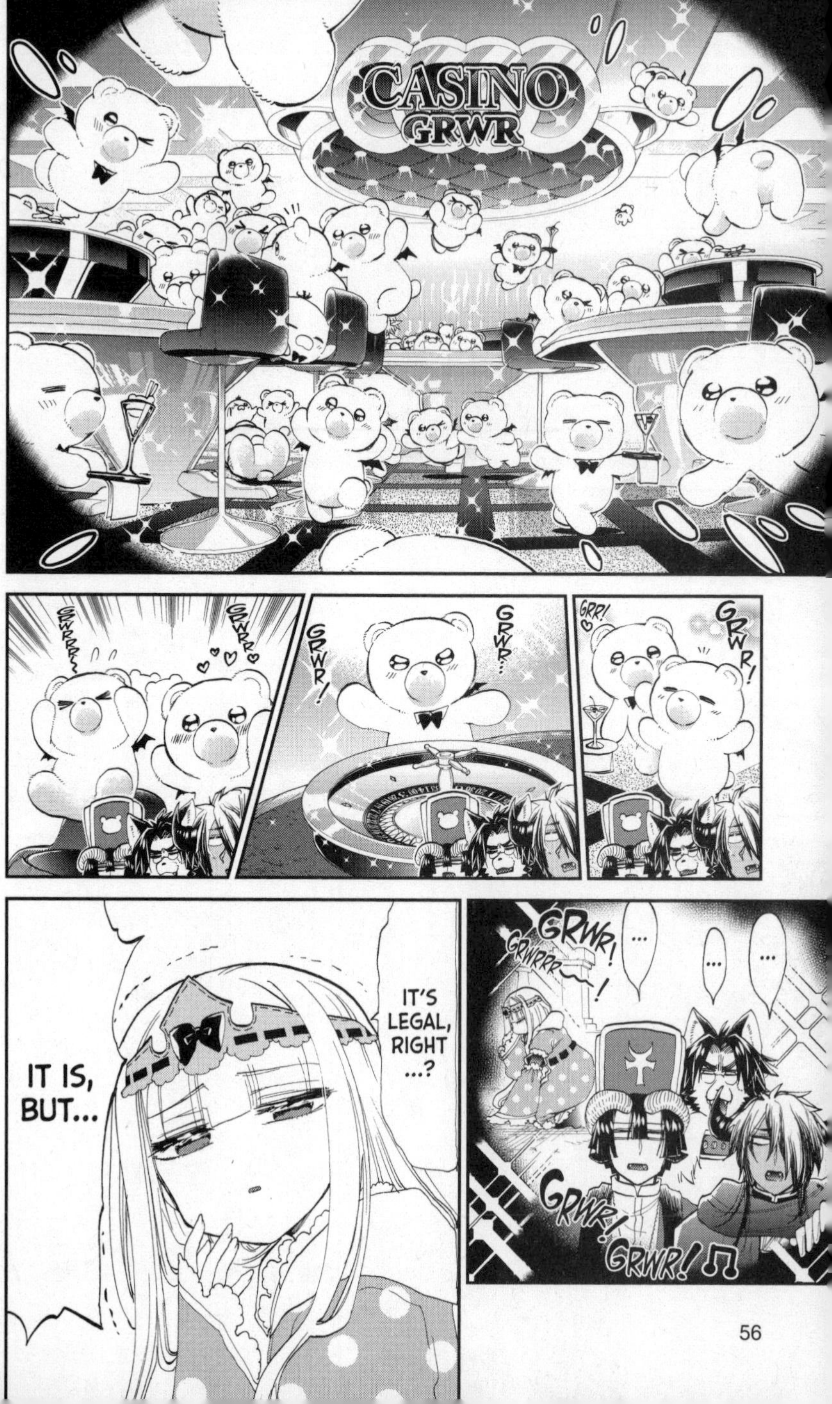
CASINO GRWR
GRR! ♡
GRWR!
GRWR!
GRWR...
GRWRRR~
GRWRR
GRWR!
GRWRRR~!
...
...
...
GRWR!
GRWR! ♫
IT'S LEGAL, RIGHT...?
IT IS, BUT...

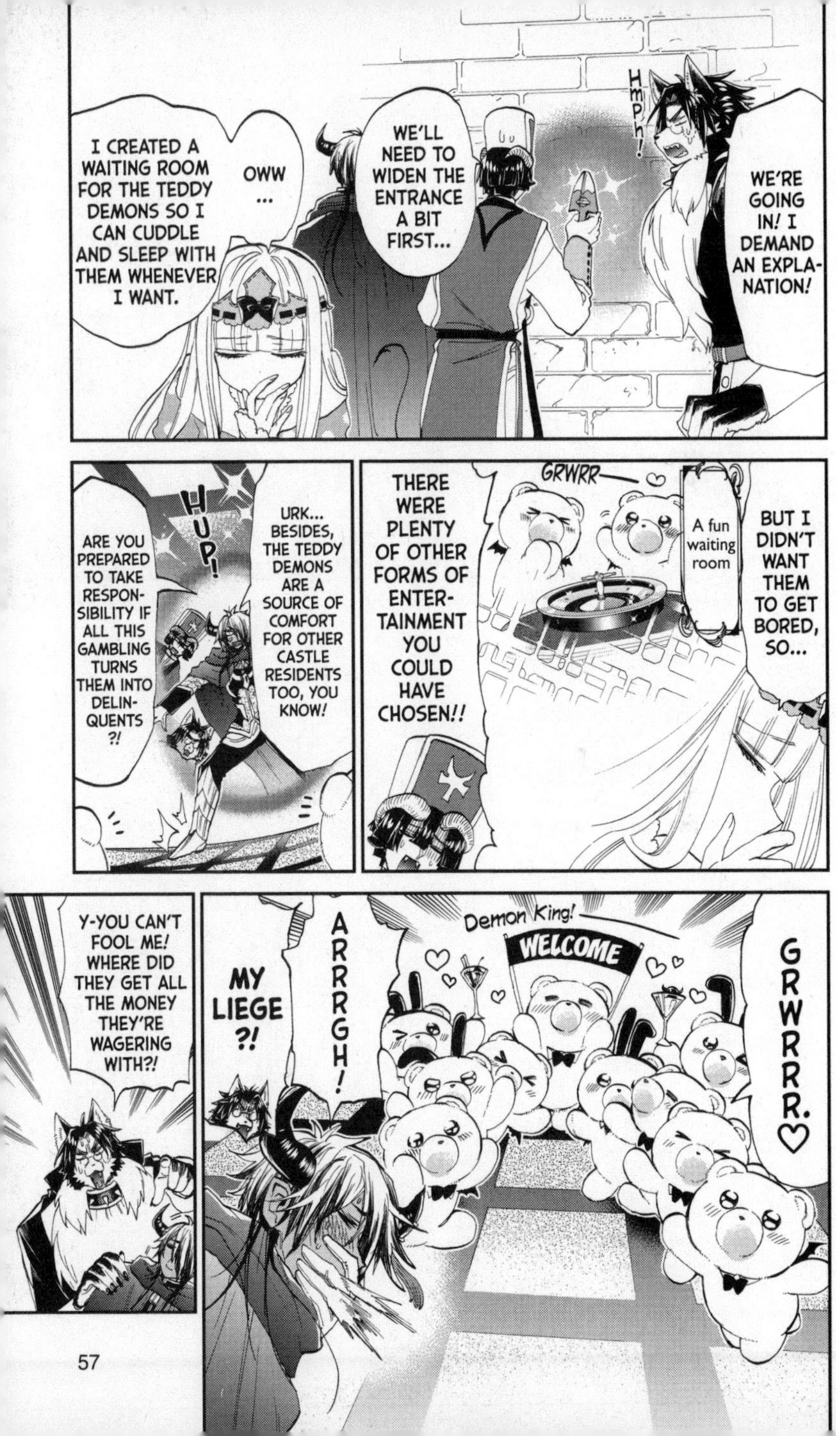
Hmph!
WE'RE GOING IN! I DEMAND AN EXPLANATION!
WE'LL NEED TO WIDEN THE ENTRANCE A BIT FIRST...
OWW ...
I CREATED A WAITING ROOM FOR THE TEDDY DEMONS SO I CAN CUDDLE AND SLEEP WITH THEM WHENEVER I WANT.
BUT I DIDN'T WANT THEM TO GET BORED, SO...
GRWRR—♡
A fun waiting room
THERE WERE PLENTY OF OTHER FORMS OF ENTERTAINMENT YOU COULD HAVE CHOSEN!!
URK... BESIDES, THE TEDDY DEMONS ARE A SOURCE OF COMFORT FOR OTHER CASTLE RESIDENTS TOO, YOU KNOW!
HUP!
ARE YOU PREPARED TO TAKE RESPONSIBILITY IF ALL THIS GAMBLING TURNS THEM INTO DELINQUENTS?!
GRWRRR.♡
Demon King!
WELCOME
ARRRGH!
MY LIEGE?!
Y-YOU CAN'T FOOL ME! WHERE DID THEY GET ALL THE MONEY THEY'RE WAGERING WITH?!

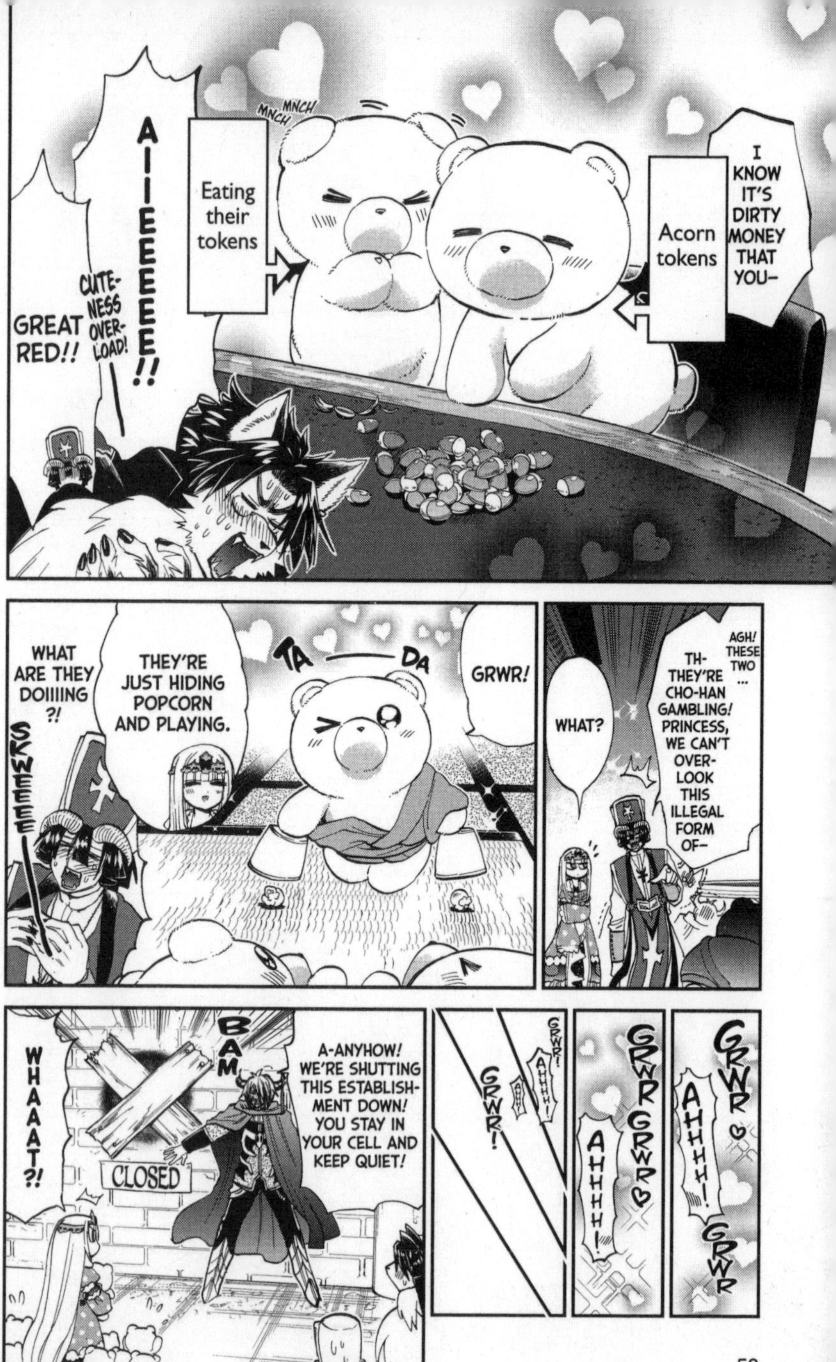
I KNOW IT'S DIRTY MONEY THAT YOU-
Acorn tokens
MNCH MNCH
Eating their tokens
AIIEEEEEE!!
CUTENESS OVERLOAD!
GREAT RED!!
AGH! THESE TWO ...
TH- THEY'RE CHO-HAN GAMBLING! PRINCESS, WE CAN'T OVERLOOK THIS ILLEGAL FORM OF-
WHAT?
GRWR!
TA DA
THEY'RE JUST HIDING POPCORN AND PLAYING.
WHAT ARE THEY DOIIIING?!
SKWEEEE
GRWR ♡
AHHHH!
GRWR
GRWR GRWR ♡
AHHHH!
GRWR!
AHHHHH!
AHH!
GRWR!
BAM
A-ANYHOW! WE'RE SHUTTING THIS ESTABLISHMENT DOWN! YOU STAY IN YOUR CELL AND KEEP QUIET!
CLOSED
WHAAAAT?!

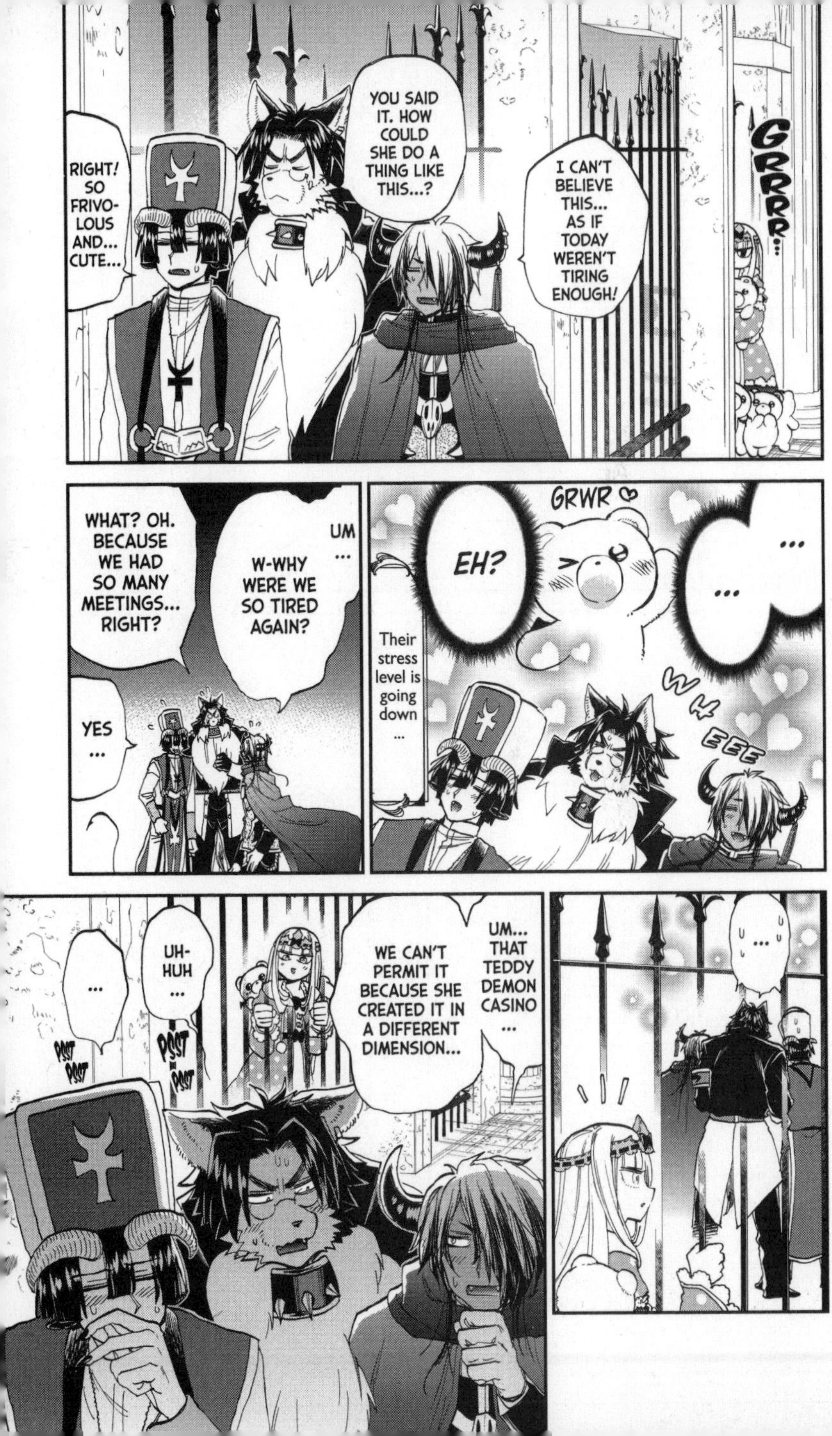
GRRRR...
I CAN'T BELIEVE THIS... AS IF TODAY WEREN'T TIRING ENOUGH!
YOU SAID IT. HOW COULD SHE DO A THING LIKE THIS...?
RIGHT! SO FRIVOLOUS AND... CUTE...
...
...
GRWR
EH?
WHEEE
Their stress level is going down ...
UM ...
W-WHY WERE WE SO TIRED AGAIN?
WHAT? OH. BECAUSE WE HAD SO MANY MEETINGS... RIGHT?
YES ...
...
UM... THAT TEDDY DEMON CASINO ...
WE CAN'T PERMIT IT BECAUSE SHE CREATED IT IN A DIFFERENT DIMENSION...
UH-HUH ...
PSST PSST
...
PSST PSST

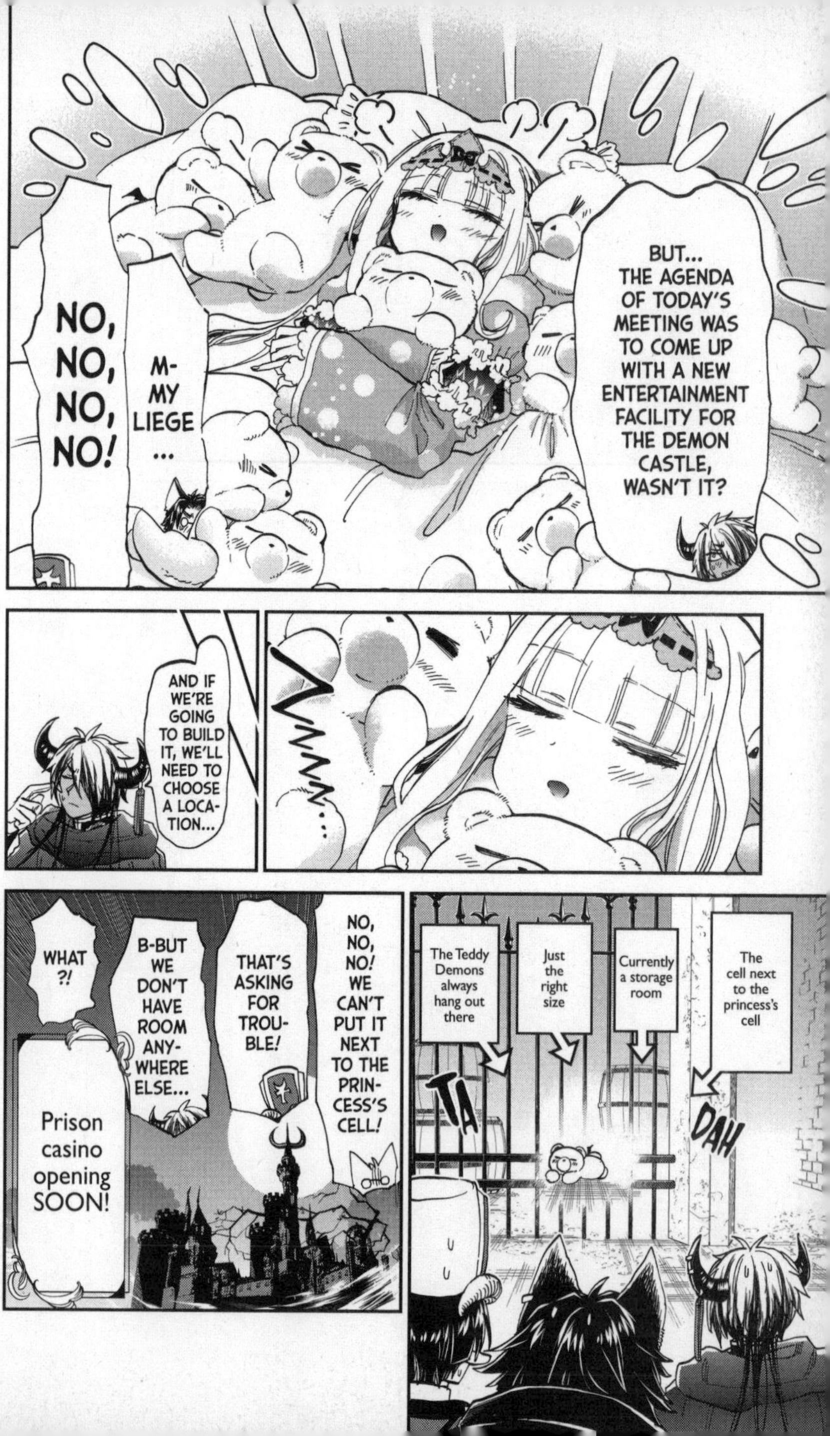
BUT... THE AGENDA OF TODAY'S MEETING WAS TO COME UP WITH A NEW ENTERTAINMENT FACILITY FOR THE DEMON CASTLE, WASN'T IT?
M-MY LIEGE...
NO, NO, NO, NO!
AND IF WE'RE GOING TO BUILD IT, WE'LL NEED TO CHOOSE A LOCATION...
The cell next to the princess's cell
Currently a storage room
Just the right size
The Teddy Demons always hang out there
TA
DAH
NO, NO, NO! WE CAN'T PUT IT NEXT TO THE PRINCESS'S CELL!
THAT'S ASKING FOR TROUBLE!
B-BUT WE DON'T HAVE ROOM ANYWHERE ELSE...
WHAT?!
Prison casino opening SOON!

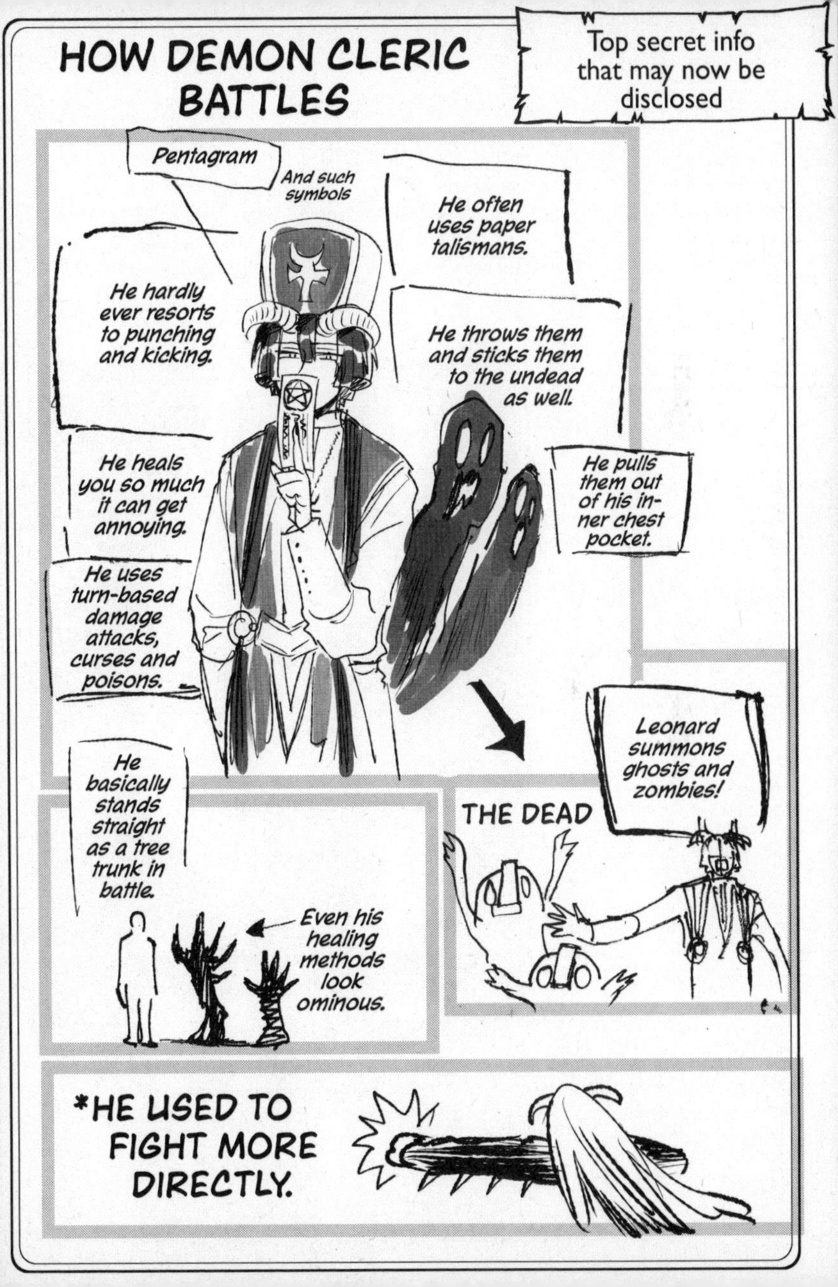
HOW DEMON CLERIC BATTLES
Top secret info that may now be disclosed
He often uses paper talismans.
He throws them and sticks them to the undead as well.
He pulls them out of his inner chest pocket.
Pentagram
And such symbols
He hardly ever resorts to punching and kicking.
He heals you so much it can get annoying.
He uses turn-based damage attacks, curses and poisons.
Leonard summons ghosts and zombies!
THE DEAD
He basically stands straight as a tree trunk in battle.
Even his healing methods look ominous.
*HE USED TO FIGHT MORE DIRECTLY.

Would you like to change your class?

7 changes remaining

▶ Yes

No ▼

Literary Figure

"I am a princess..."

▼

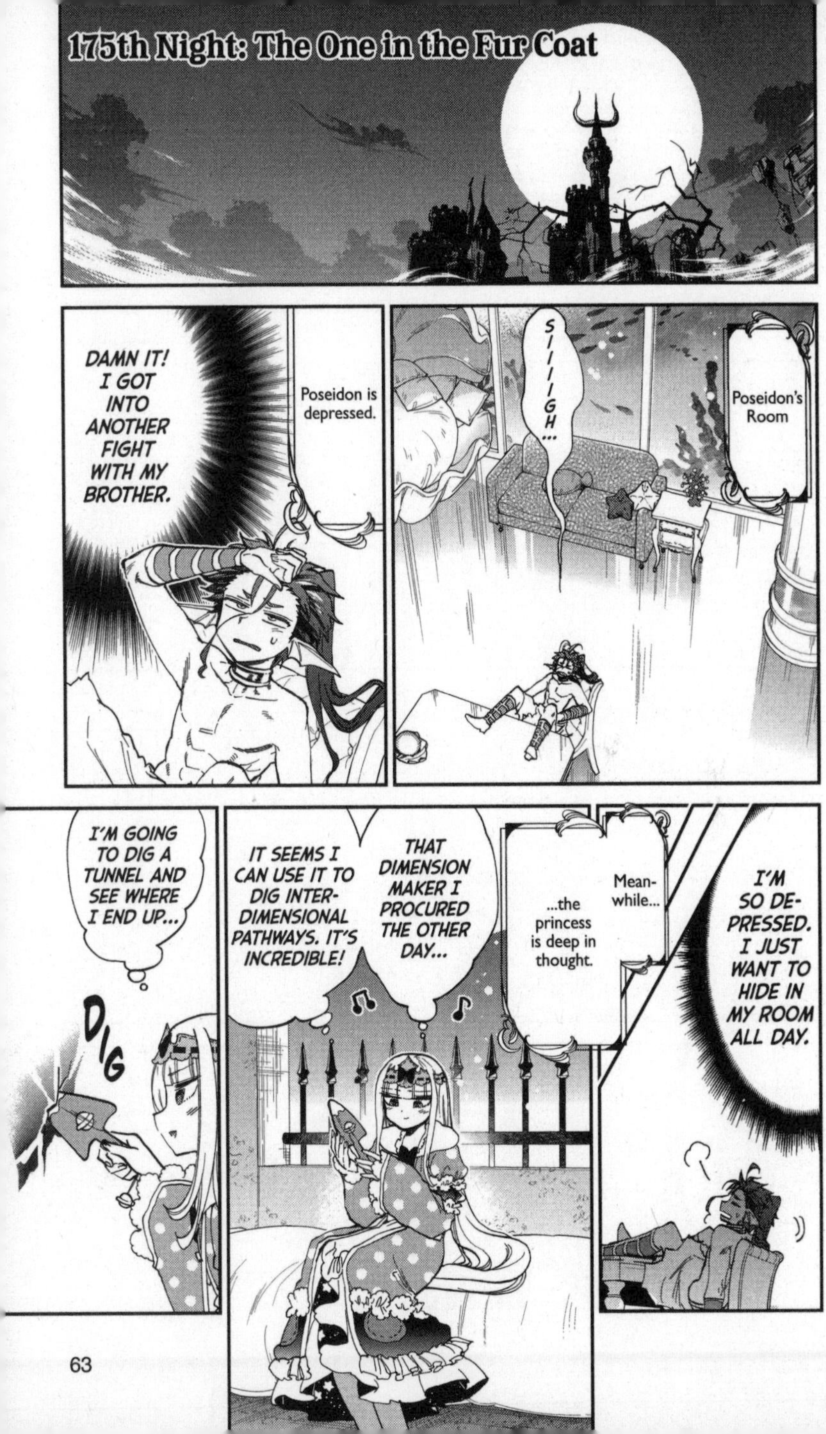
175th Night: The One in the Fur Coat
Poseidon's Room
SIIIIGH...
Poseidon is depressed.
DAMN IT! I GOT INTO ANOTHER FIGHT WITH MY BROTHER.
I'M SO DE-PRESSED. I JUST WANT TO HIDE IN MY ROOM ALL DAY.
Mean-while...
...the princess is deep in thought.
THAT DIMENSION MAKER I PROCURED THE OTHER DAY...
IT SEEMS I CAN USE IT TO DIG INTER-DIMENSIONAL PATHWAYS. IT'S INCREDIBLE!
I'M GOING TO DIG A TUNNEL AND SEE WHERE I END UP...
DIG

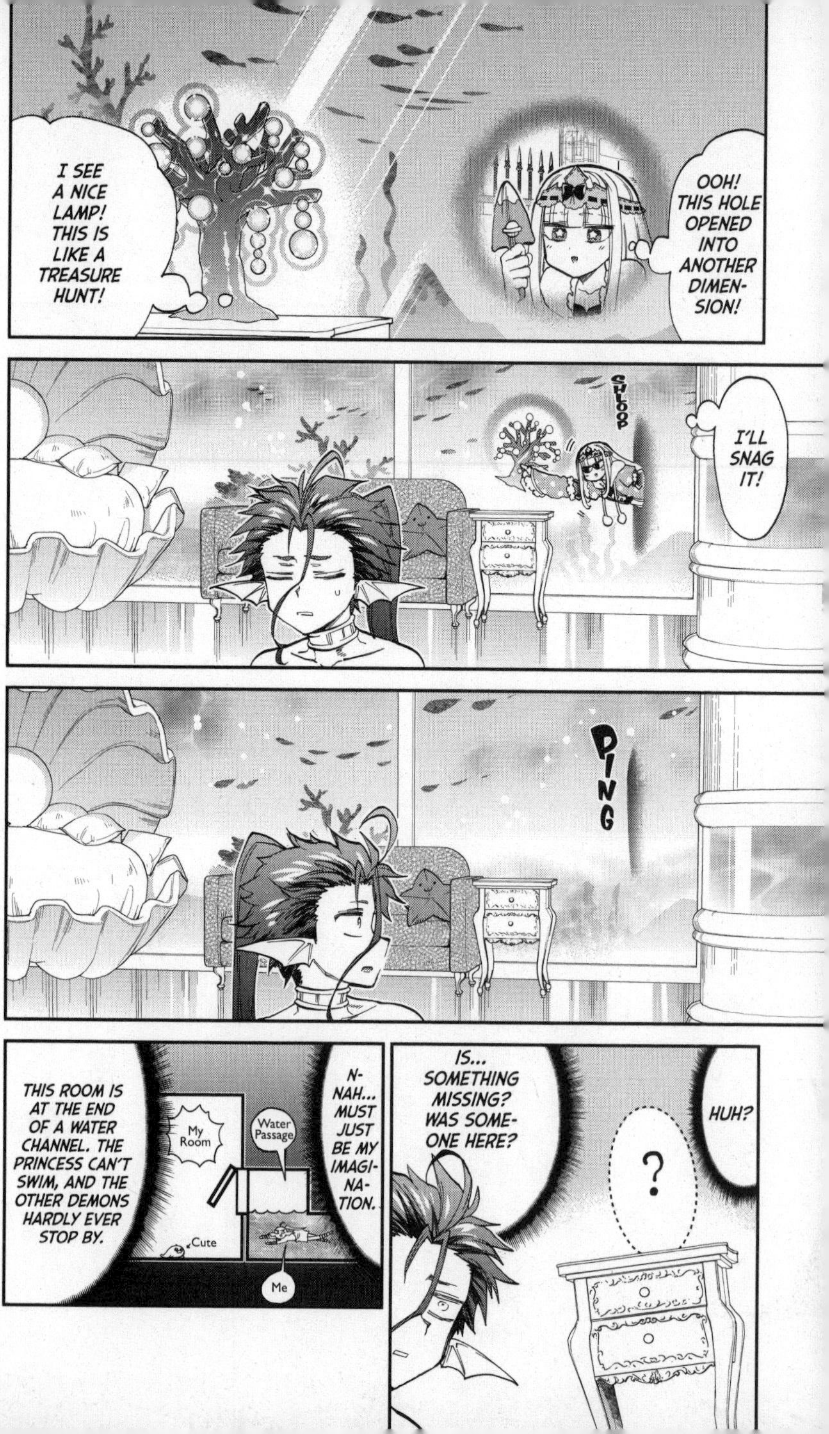
OOH! THIS HOLE OPENED INTO ANOTHER DIMENSION!
I SEE A NICE LAMP! THIS IS LIKE A TREASURE HUNT!
I'LL SNAG IT!
SHLOOP
PING
HUH?
?
IS... SOMETHING MISSING? WAS SOMEONE HERE?
N-NAH... MUST JUST BE MY IMAGINATION.
THIS ROOM IS AT THE END OF A WATER CHANNEL. THE PRINCESS CAN'T SWIM, AND THE OTHER DEMONS HARDLY EVER STOP BY.
Water Passage
My Room
Cute
Me

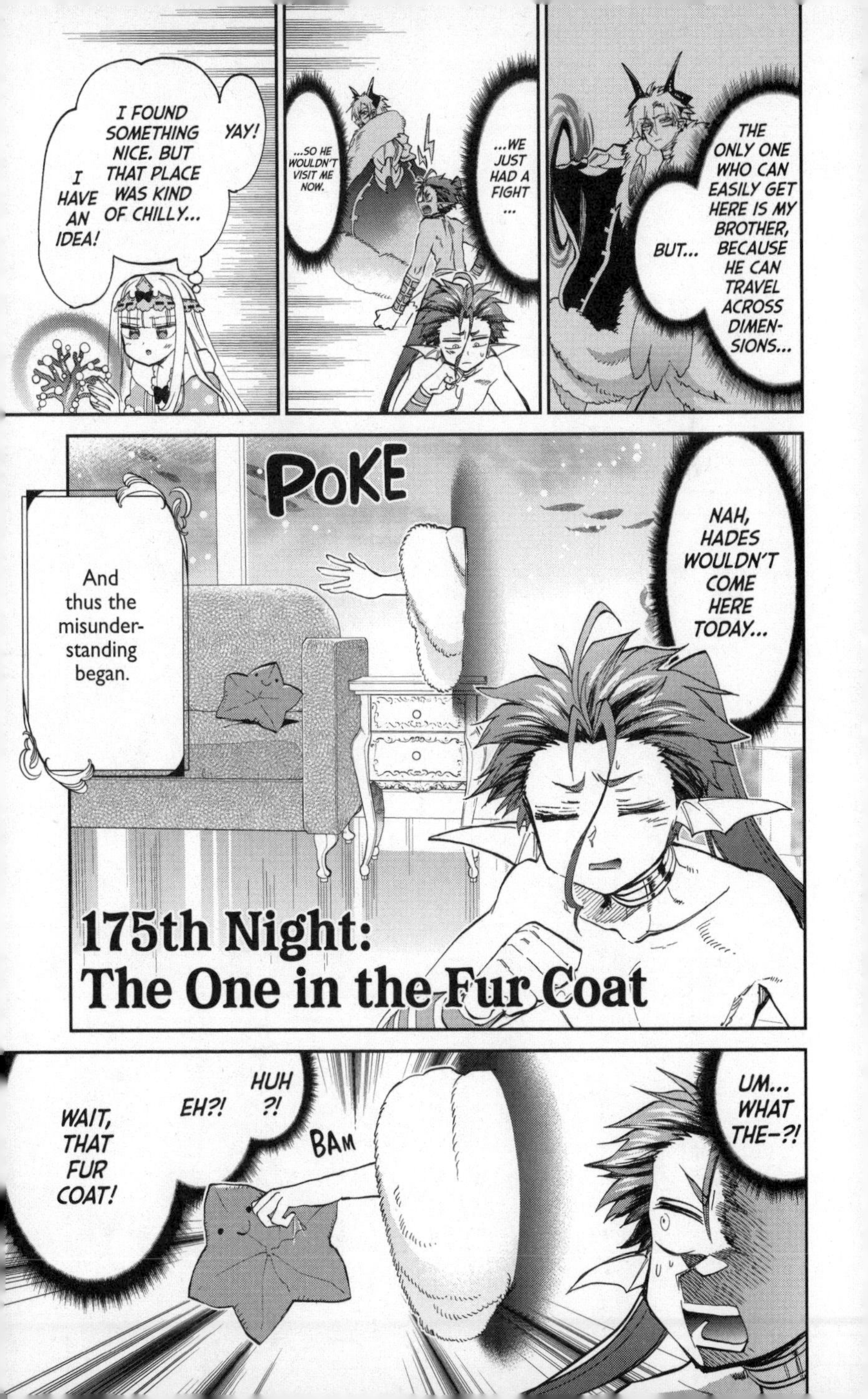
BUT... THE ONLY ONE WHO CAN EASILY GET HERE IS MY BROTHER, BECAUSE HE CAN TRAVEL ACROSS DIMENSIONS...
...WE JUST HAD A FIGHT...
...SO HE WOULDN'T VISIT ME NOW.
YAY!
I FOUND SOMETHING NICE. BUT THAT PLACE WAS KIND OF CHILLY...
I HAVE AN IDEA!
NAH, HADES WOULDN'T COME HERE TODAY...
POKE
And thus the misunderstanding began.
175th Night: The One in the Fur Coat
UM... WHAT THE-?!
HUH?!
BAM
EH?!
WAIT, THAT FUR COAT!

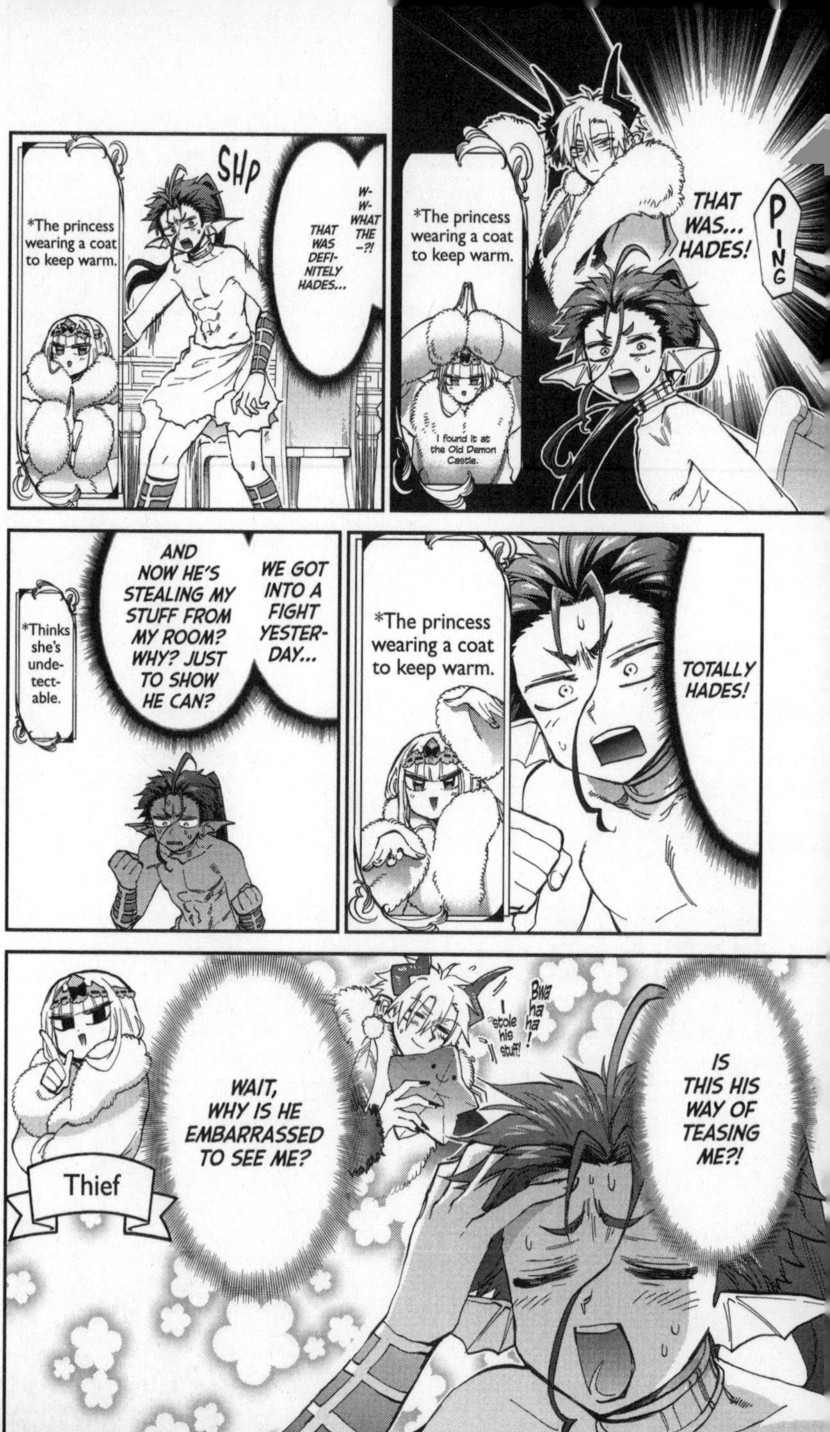
THAT WAS... HADES!
PING
*The princess wearing a coat to keep warm.
I found it at the Old Demon Castle.
W-W-WHAT THE—?!
THAT WAS DEFINITELY HADES...
SHP
*The princess wearing a coat to keep warm.
TOTALLY HADES!
*The princess wearing a coat to keep warm.
WE GOT INTO A FIGHT YESTERDAY...
AND NOW HE'S STEALING MY STUFF FROM MY ROOM? WHY? JUST TO SHOW HE CAN?
*Thinks she's undetectable.
IS THIS HIS WAY OF TEASING ME?!
Bwa ha ha!
I stole his stuff!
WAIT, WHY IS HE EMBARRASSED TO SEE ME?
Thief

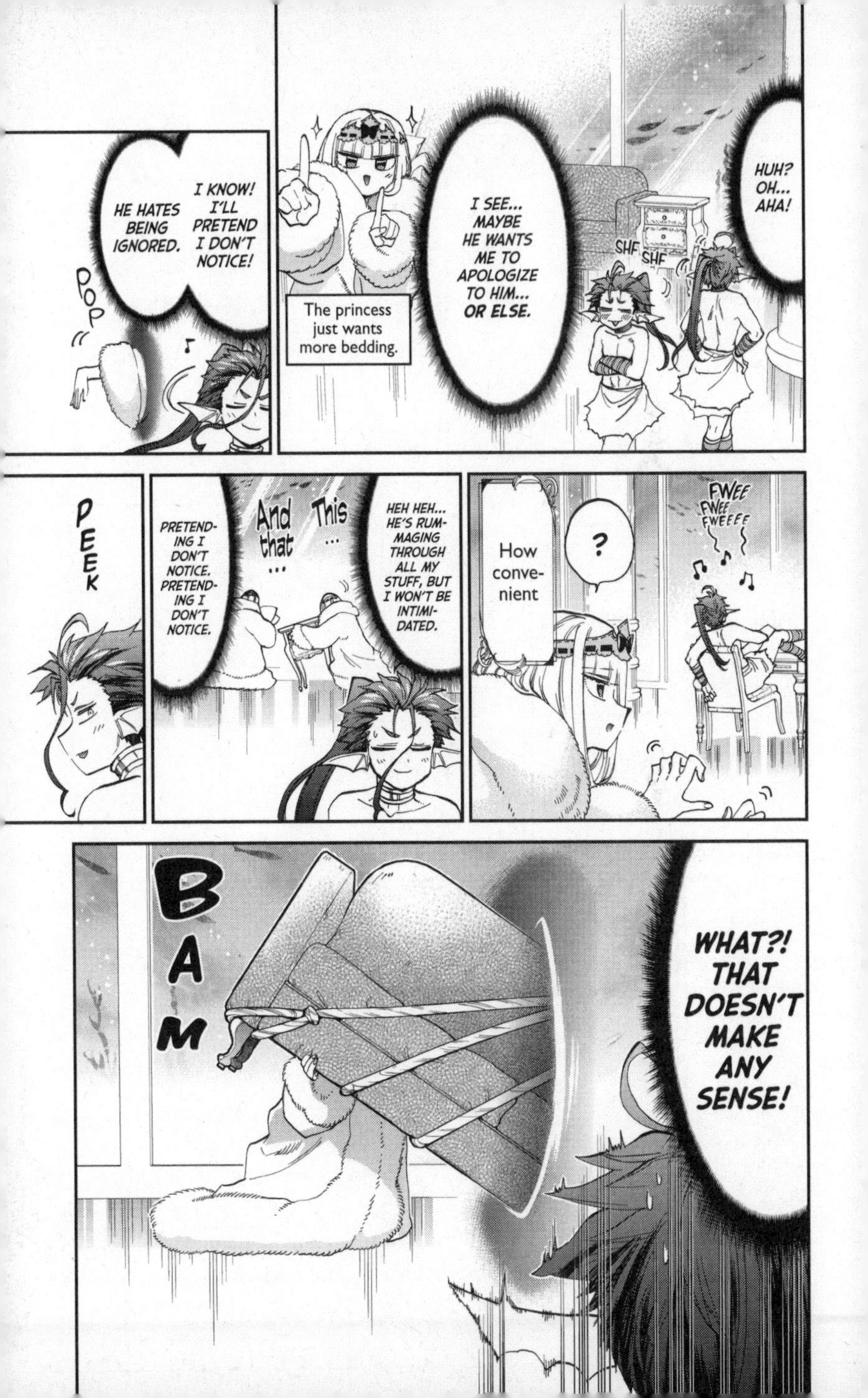

HUH? OH... AHA!
I SEE... MAYBE HE WANTS ME TO APOLOGIZE TO HIM... OR ELSE.
SHF SHF
The princess just wants more bedding.
I KNOW! I'LL PRETEND I DON'T NOTICE!
HE HATES BEING IGNORED.
POP
FWEE FWEE FWEEEE
?
How convenient
HEH HEH... HE'S RUMMAGING THROUGH ALL MY STUFF, BUT I WON'T BE INTIMIDATED.
This...
And that...
PRETENDING I DON'T NOTICE. PRETENDING I DON'T NOTICE.
PEEK
WHAT?! THAT DOESN'T MAKE ANY SENSE!
BAM

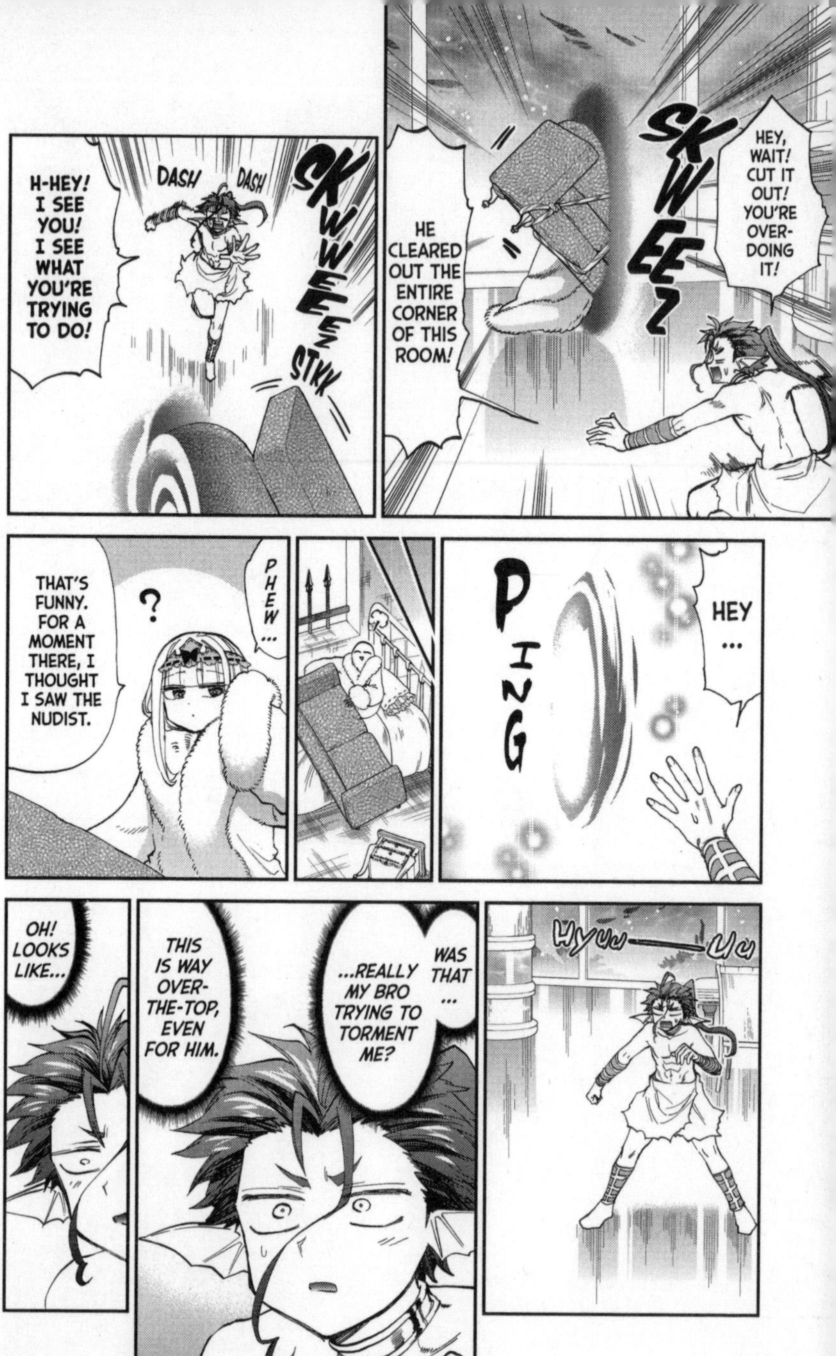
SKWEEZ
HEY, WAIT! CUT IT OUT! YOU'RE OVER-DOING IT!
HE CLEARED OUT THE ENTIRE CORNER OF THIS ROOM!
SKWWEEEEZ
STKK
DASH
DASH
H-HEY! I SEE YOU! I SEE WHAT YOU'RE TRYING TO DO!
HEY...
PING
PHEW...
?
THAT'S FUNNY. FOR A MOMENT THERE, I THOUGHT I SAW THE NUDIST.
HYUU—UU
WAS THAT...
...REALLY MY BRO TRYING TO TORMENT ME?
THIS IS WAY OVER-THE-TOP, EVEN FOR HIM.
OH! LOOKS LIKE...

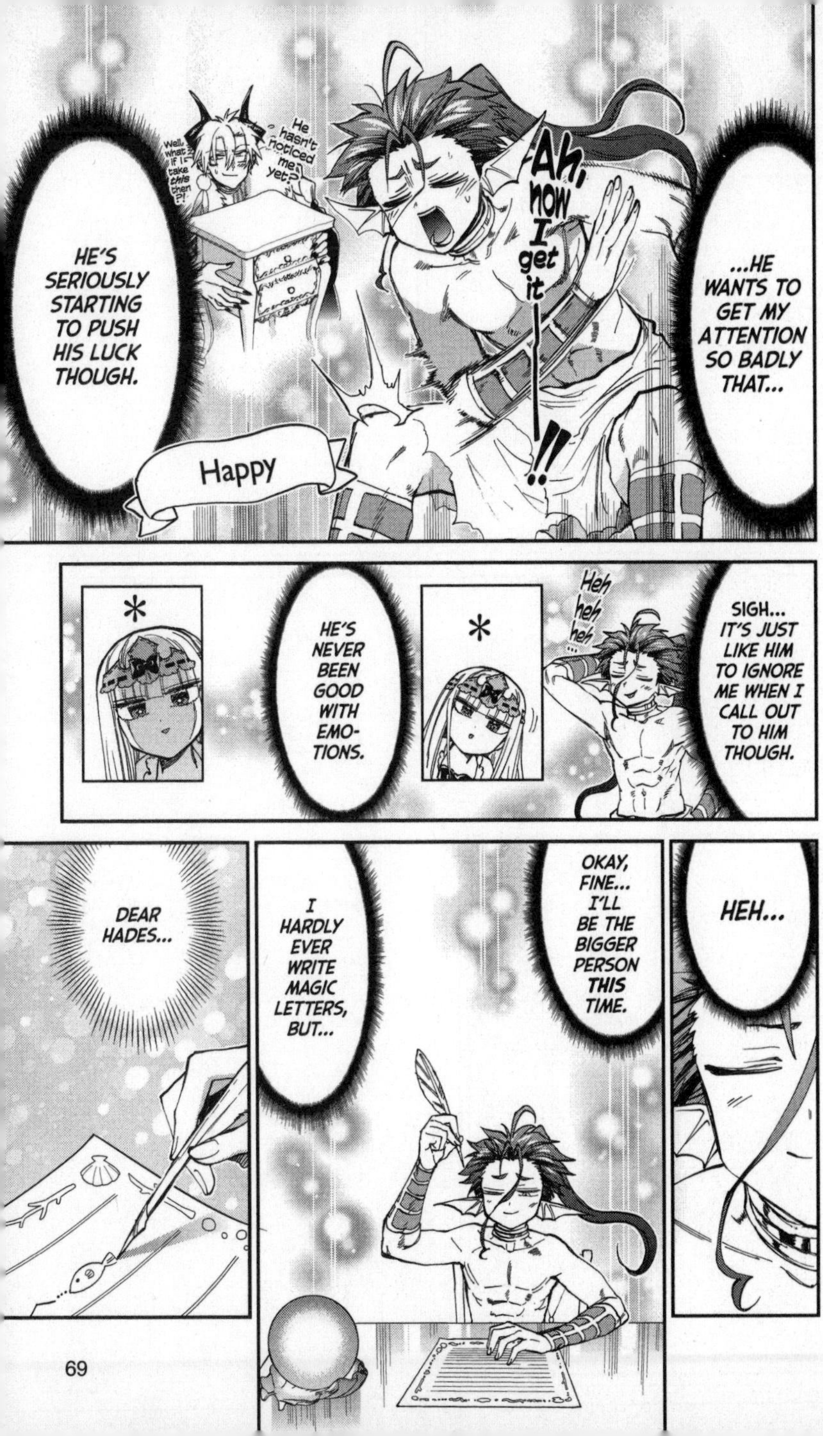
...HE WANTS TO GET MY ATTENTION SO BADLY THAT...
Ah, now I get it—!!
He hasn't noticed me yet?
Well, what if I take *this* then?!
HE'S SERIOUSLY STARTING TO PUSH HIS LUCK THOUGH.
Happy
SIGH... IT'S JUST LIKE HIM TO IGNORE ME WHEN I CALL OUT TO HIM THOUGH.
Heh heh heh...
*
HE'S NEVER BEEN GOOD WITH EMO-TIONS.
*
HEH...
OKAY, FINE... I'LL BE THE BIGGER PERSON THIS TIME.
I HARDLY EVER WRITE MAGIC LETTERS, BUT...
DEAR HADES...

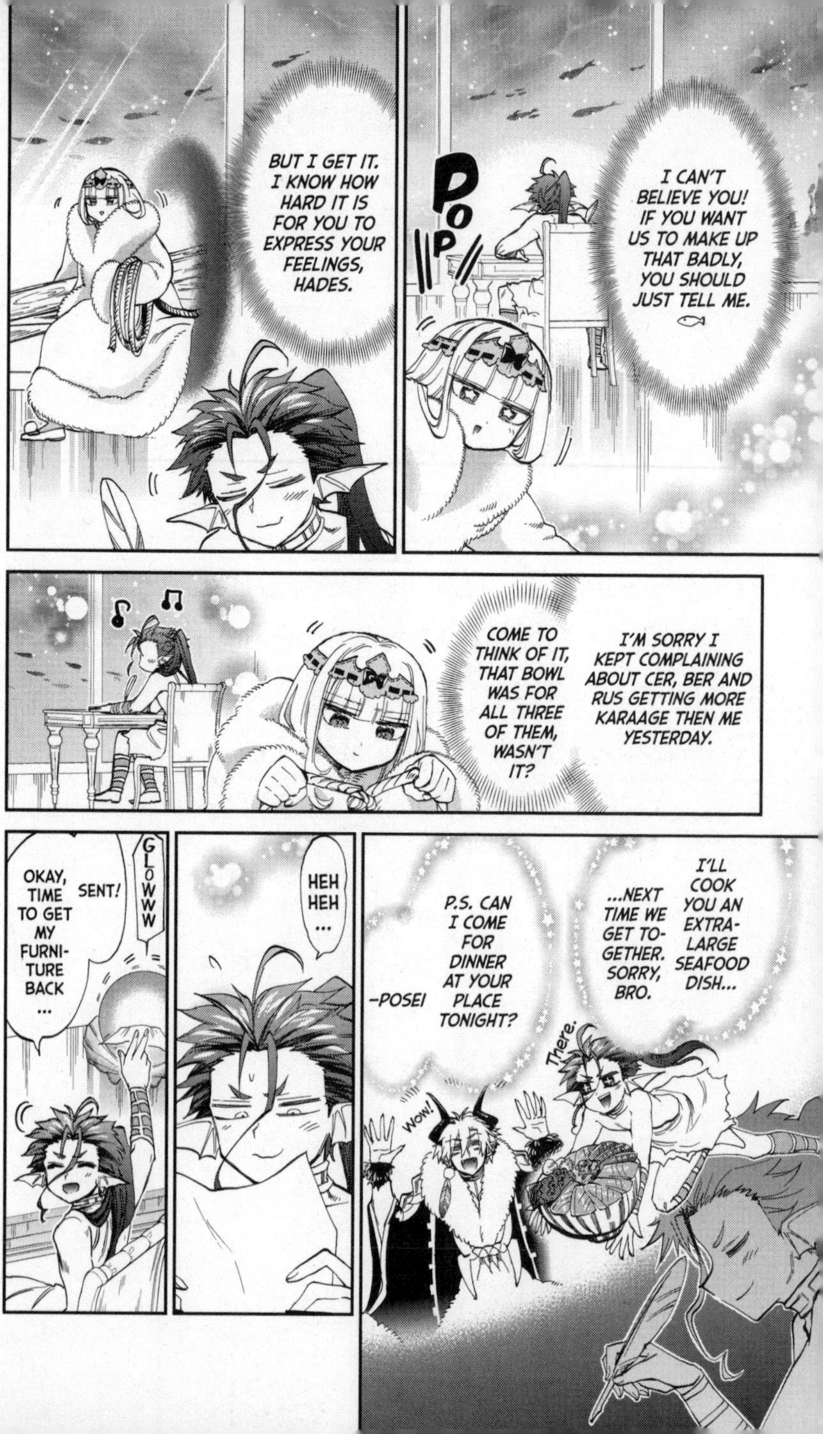
POP
I CAN'T BELIEVE YOU! IF YOU WANT US TO MAKE UP THAT BADLY, YOU SHOULD JUST TELL ME.
BUT I GET IT. I KNOW HOW HARD IT IS FOR YOU TO EXPRESS YOUR FEELINGS, HADES.
I'M SORRY I KEPT COMPLAINING ABOUT CER, BER AND RUS GETTING MORE KARAAGE THEN ME YESTERDAY.
COME TO THINK OF IT, THAT BOWL WAS FOR ALL THREE OF THEM, WASN'T IT?
I'LL COOK YOU AN EXTRA-LARGE SEAFOOD DISH...
...NEXT TIME WE GET TO-GETHER. SORRY, BRO.
P.S. CAN I COME FOR DINNER AT YOUR PLACE TONIGHT?
—POSEI
There.
Wow!
HEH HEH ...
GLOWWW
SENT!
OKAY, TIME TO GET MY FURNI-TURE BACK ...

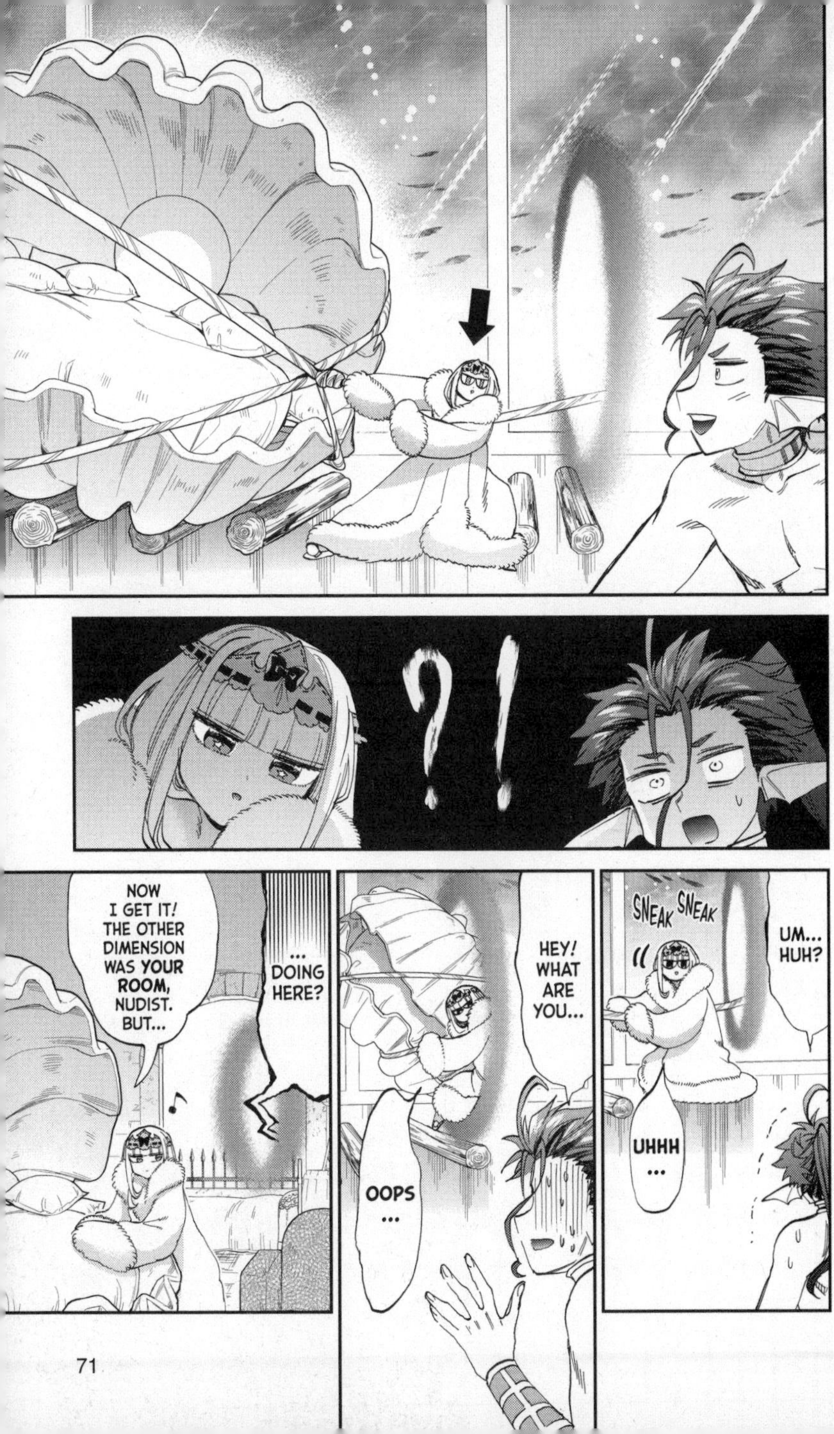
?!
UM... HUH?
SNEAK SNEAK
UHHH...
HEY! WHAT ARE YOU...
OOPS...
... DOING HERE?
NOW I GET IT! THE OTHER DIMENSION WAS YOUR ROOM, NUDIST. BUT...

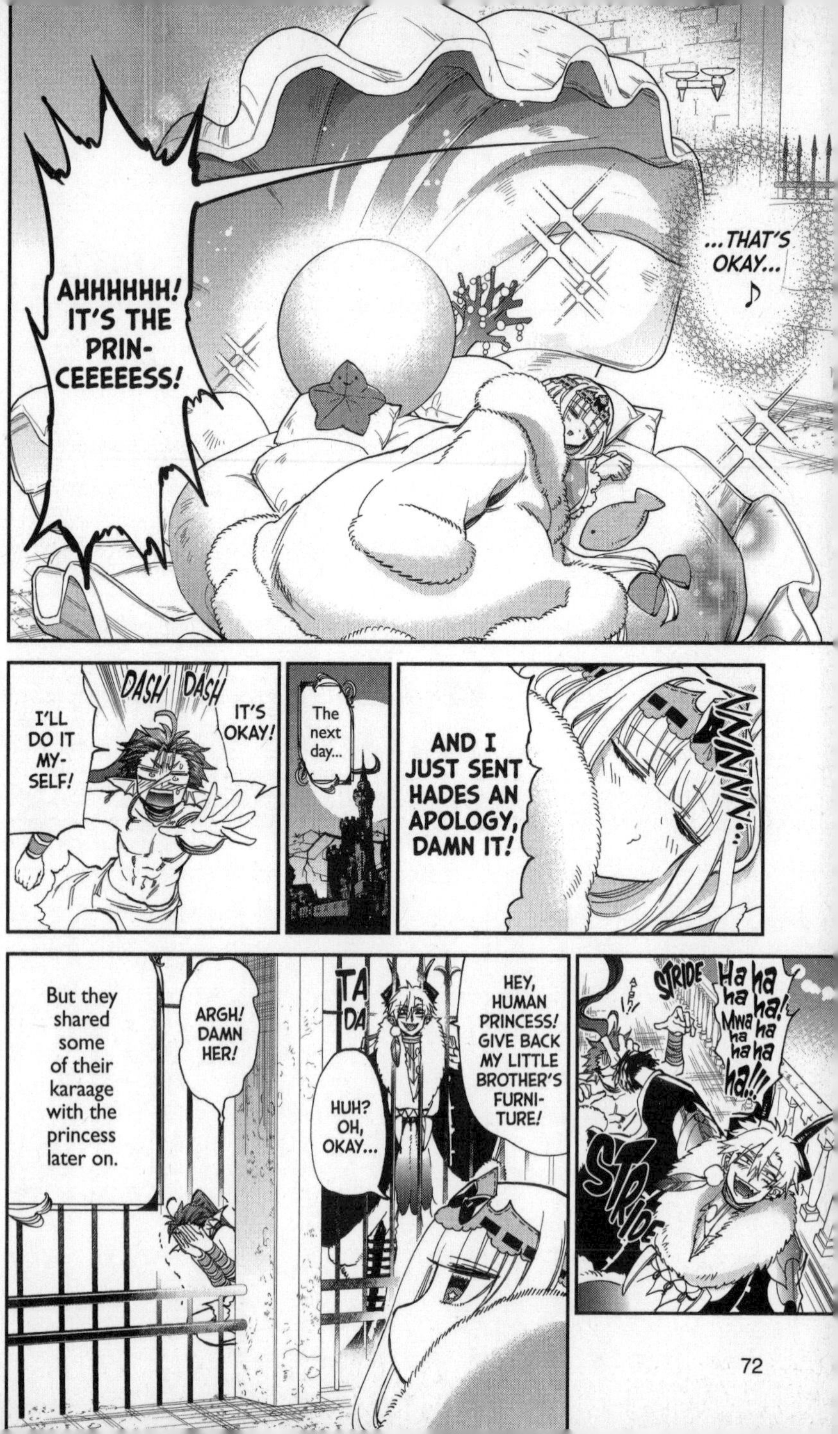
...THAT'S OKAY... ♪
AHHHHHH! IT'S THE PRIN-CEEEEEESS!
AND I JUST SENT HADES AN APOLOGY, DAMN IT!
The next day...
IT'S OKAY!
DASH DASH
I'LL DO IT MY-SELF!
Ha ha ha ha! Mwa ha ha ha ha ha ha!!!
STRIDE
STRIDE
HEY, HUMAN PRINCESS! GIVE BACK MY LITTLE BROTHER'S FURNI-TURE!
TA DA
HUH? OH, OKAY...
ARGH! DAMN HER!
But they shared some of their karaage with the princess later on.

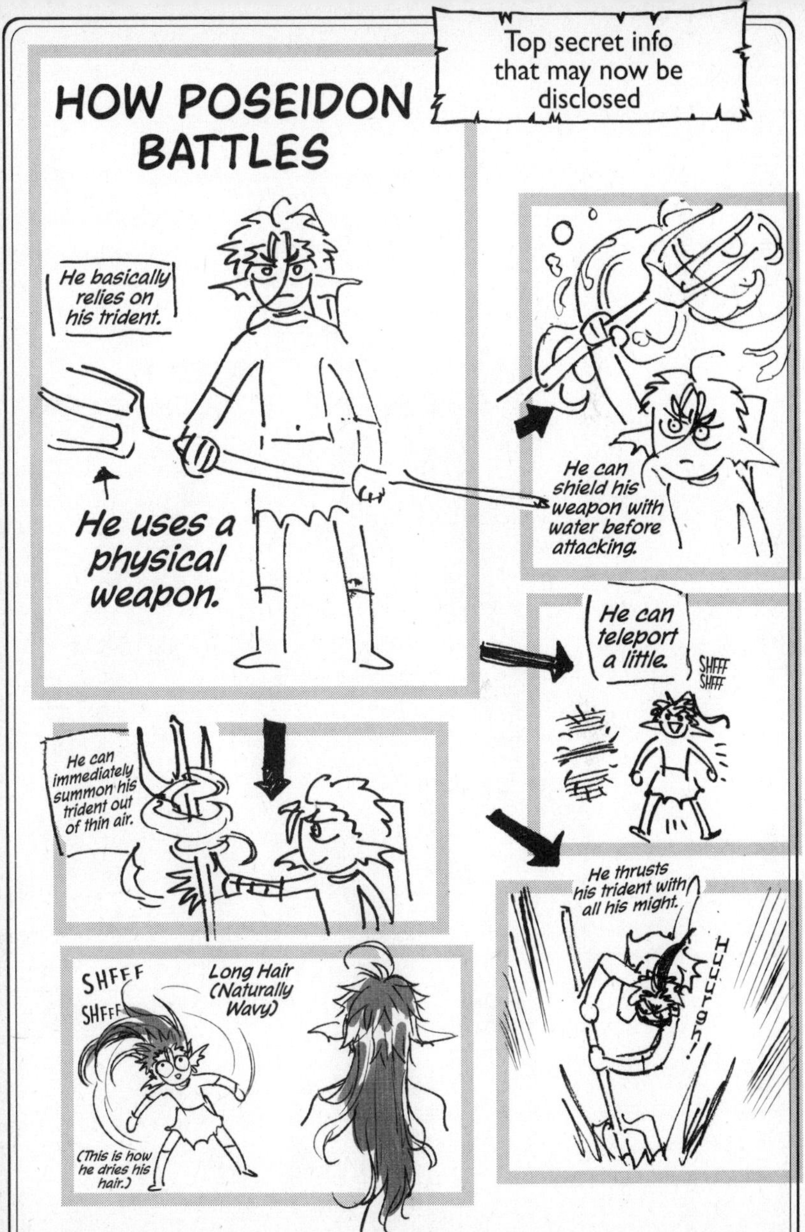
Top secret info that may now be disclosed
HOW POSEIDON BATTLES
He can shield his weapon with water before attacking.
He can teleport a little.
SHFFF SHFFF
He thrusts his trident with all his might.
Huuurgh!
He basically relies on his trident.
He uses a physical weapon.
He can immediately summon his trident out of thin air.
Long Hair (Naturally Wavy)
SHFFF
SHFFF
(This is how he dries his hair.)

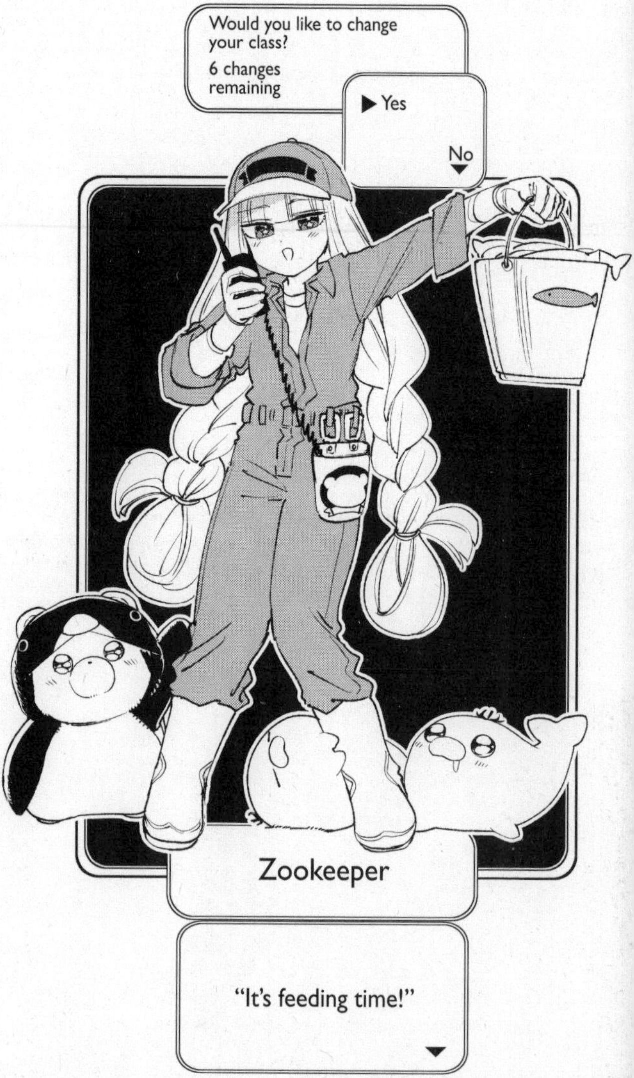
Would you like to change your class?
6 changes remaining
▶ Yes
No
Zookeeper
"It's feeding time!"

176th Night: Just an Ordinary Dog

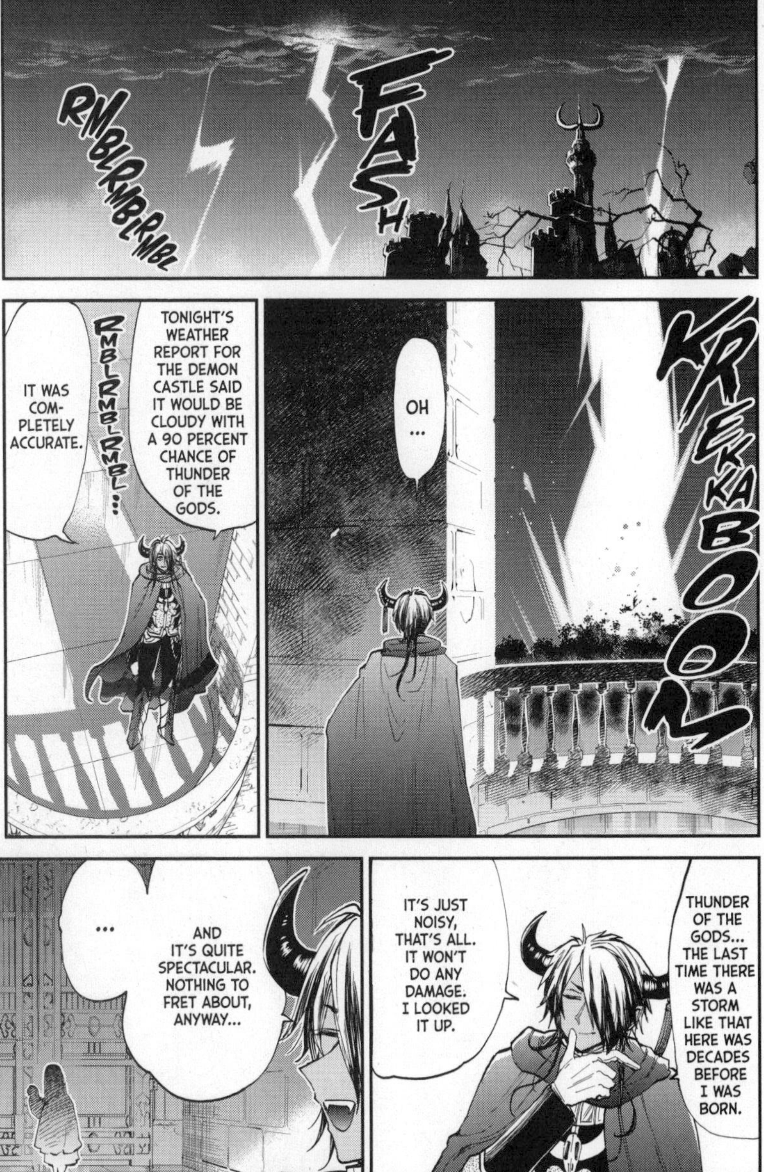
FASH
RMBLRMBLRMBLRMBL
KRAKABOOOM
OH ...
TONIGHT'S WEATHER REPORT FOR THE DEMON CASTLE SAID IT WOULD BE CLOUDY WITH A 90 PERCENT CHANCE OF THUNDER OF THE GODS.
RMBLRMBLRMBLRMBL...
IT WAS COMPLETELY ACCURATE.
THUNDER OF THE GODS... THE LAST TIME THERE WAS A STORM LIKE THAT HERE WAS DECADES BEFORE I WAS BORN.
IT'S JUST NOISY, THAT'S ALL. IT WON'T DO ANY DAMAGE. I LOOKED IT UP.
AND IT'S QUITE SPECTACULAR. NOTHING TO FRET ABOUT, ANYWAY...
...

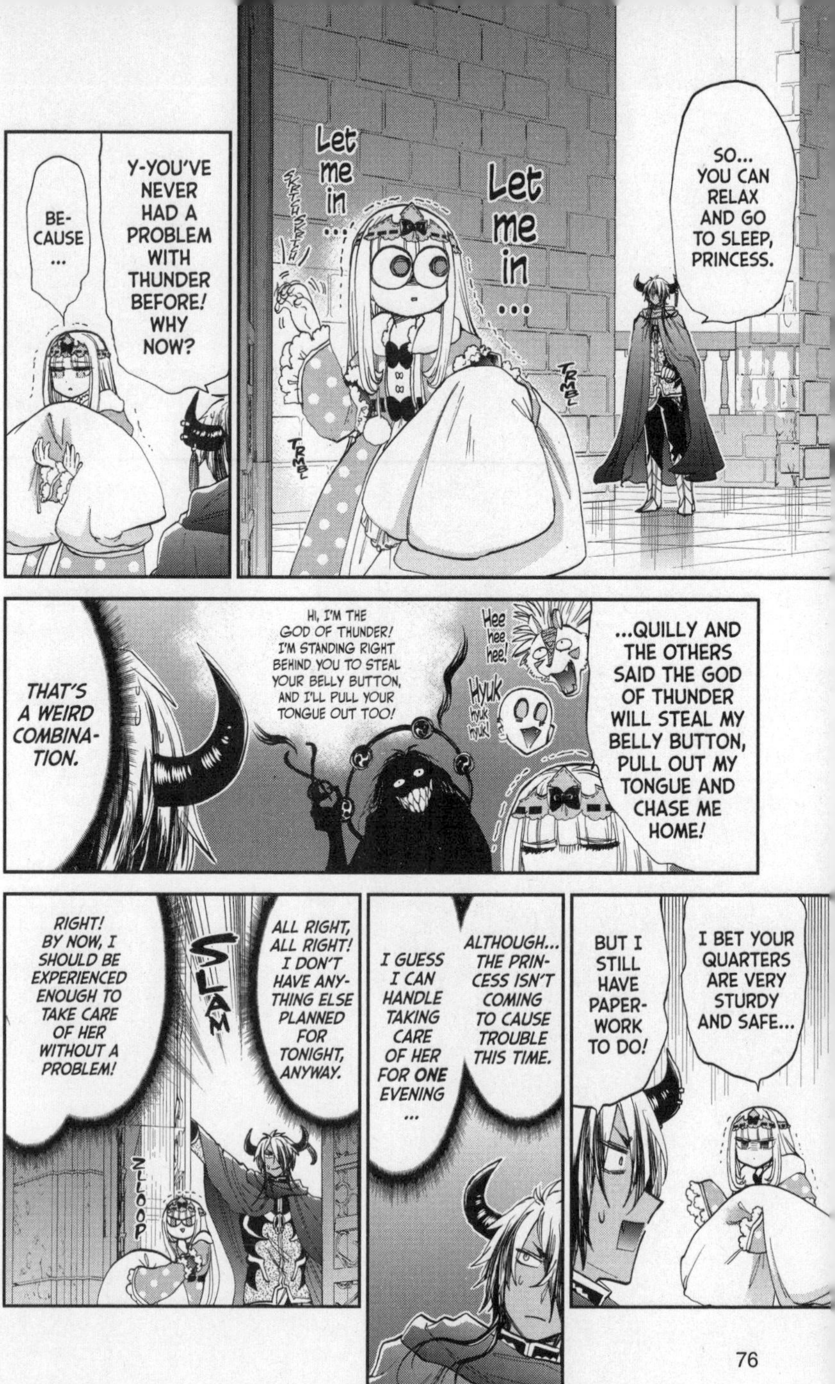
SO... YOU CAN RELAX AND GO TO SLEEP, PRINCESS.
TRMBL
Let me in...
Let me in...
SKRTCH SKRTCH
TRMBL
Y-YOU'VE NEVER HAD A PROBLEM WITH THUNDER BEFORE! WHY NOW?
BE-CAUSE...
...QUILLY AND THE OTHERS SAID THE GOD OF THUNDER WILL STEAL MY BELLY BUTTON, PULL OUT MY TONGUE AND CHASE ME HOME!
Hee hee hee!
Hyuk hyuk hyuk!
HI, I'M THE GOD OF THUNDER! I'M STANDING RIGHT BEHIND YOU TO STEAL YOUR BELLY BUTTON, AND I'LL PULL YOUR TONGUE OUT TOO!
THAT'S A WEIRD COMBINA-TION.
I BET YOUR QUARTERS ARE VERY STURDY AND SAFE...
BUT I STILL HAVE PAPER-WORK TO DO!
ALTHOUGH... THE PRIN-CESS ISN'T COMING TO CAUSE TROUBLE THIS TIME.
I GUESS I CAN HANDLE TAKING CARE OF HER FOR ONE EVENING...
ALL RIGHT, ALL RIGHT! I DON'T HAVE ANY-THING ELSE PLANNED FOR TONIGHT, ANYWAY.
SLAM
RIGHT! BY NOW, I SHOULD BE EXPERIENCED ENOUGH TO TAKE CARE OF HER WITHOUT A PROBLEM!
ZLLOOP

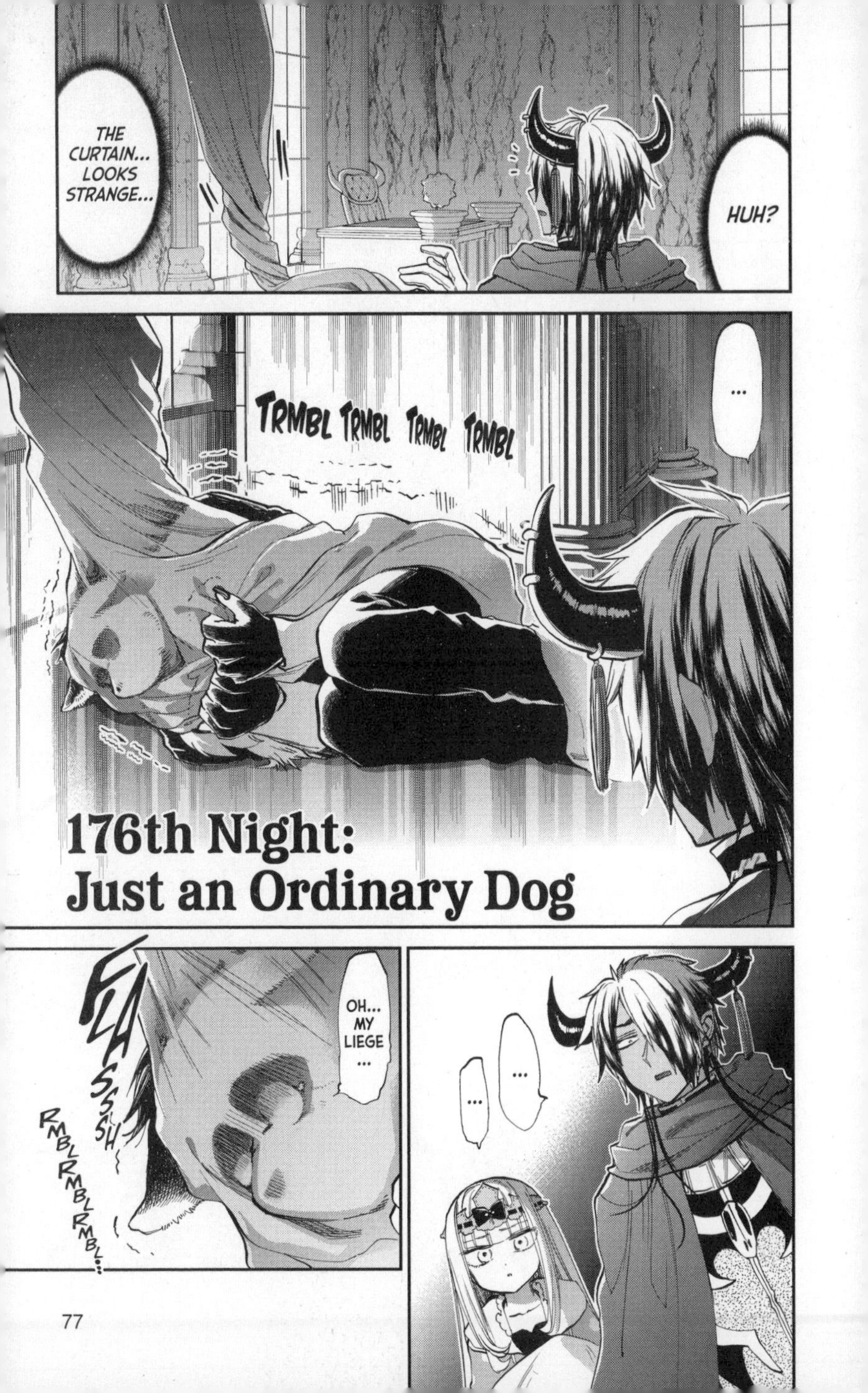
HUH?
THE CURTAIN... LOOKS STRANGE...
...
TRMBL TRMBL TRMBL TRMBL
...
...
OH... MY LIEGE...
FLASSSH
RMBLRMBLRMBL

176th Night: Just an Ordinary Dog

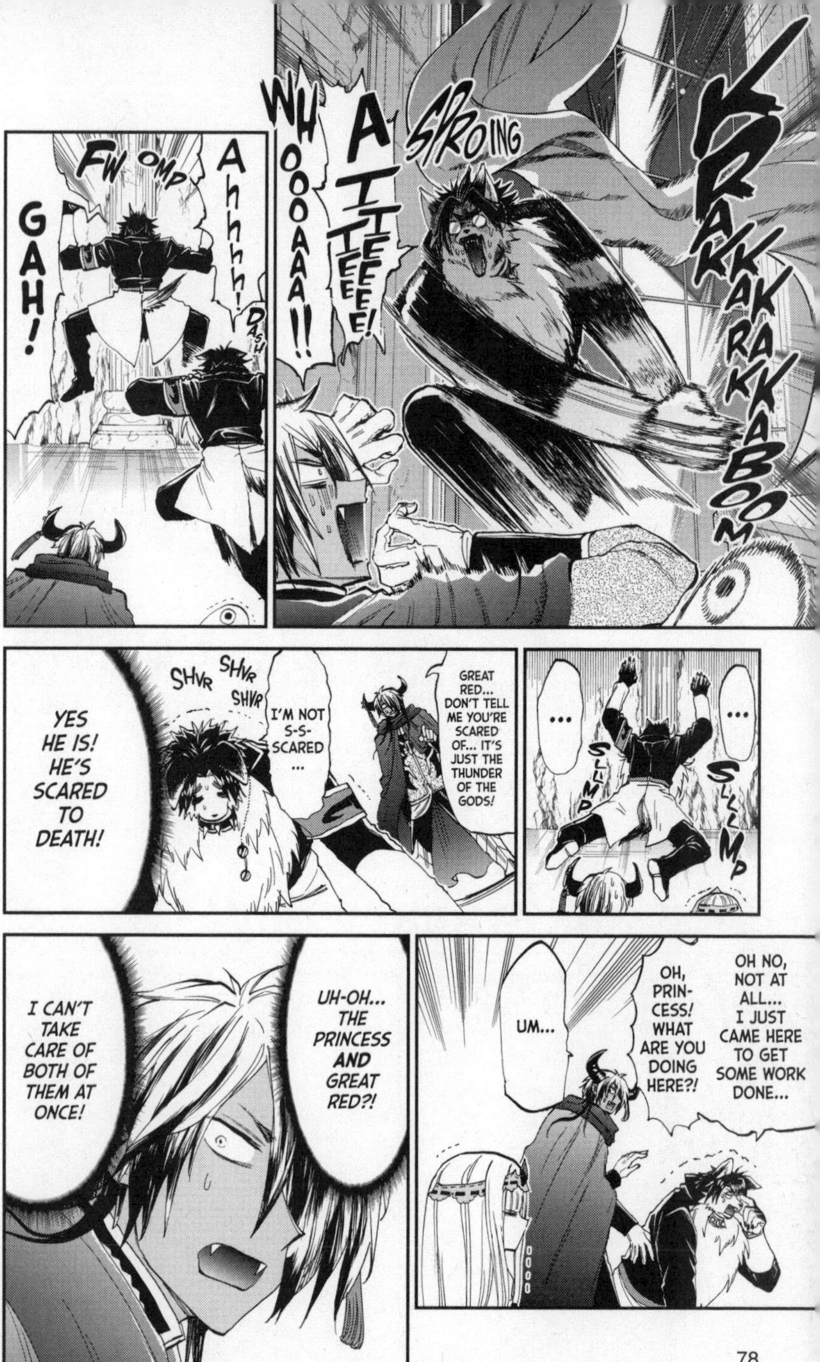
KRAKAKAKAKABOOM
SPROING
AIIIEEEEE!
WHOOOOAAAA!!
Ahhhh!
FWOMP
GAH!
DASH
...
...
SLLUMP
SLLUMP
GREAT RED... DON'T TELL ME YOU'RE SCARED OF... IT'S JUST THE THUNDER OF THE GODS!
I'M NOT S-S-SCARED...
SHVR SHVR SHVR
YES HE IS! HE'S SCARED TO DEATH!
OH NO, NOT AT ALL... I JUST CAME HERE TO GET SOME WORK DONE...
OH, PRINCESS! WHAT ARE YOU DOING HERE?!
UM...
UH-OH... THE PRINCESS AND GREAT RED?!
I CAN'T TAKE CARE OF BOTH OF THEM AT ONCE!

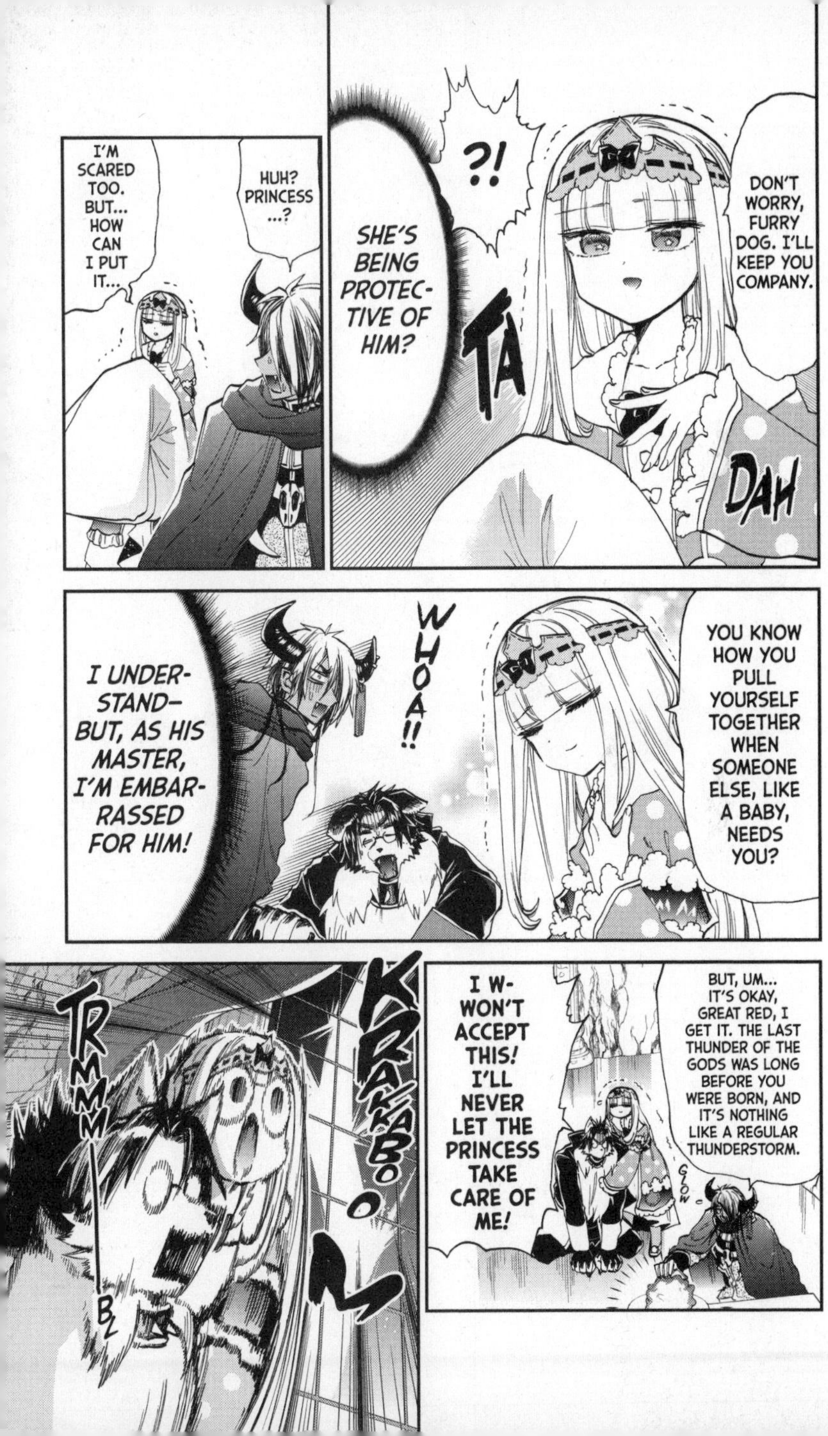
DON'T WORRY, FURRY DOG. I'LL KEEP YOU COMPANY.
?!
SHE'S BEING PROTEC-TIVE OF HIM?
TA
DAH
HUH? PRINCESS ...?
I'M SCARED TOO. BUT... HOW CAN I PUT IT...
YOU KNOW HOW YOU PULL YOURSELF TOGETHER WHEN SOMEONE ELSE, LIKE A BABY, NEEDS YOU?
WHOA!!
I UNDER-STAND—BUT, AS HIS MASTER, I'M EMBAR-RASSED FOR HIM!
BUT, UM... IT'S OKAY, GREAT RED, I GET IT. THE LAST THUNDER OF THE GODS WAS LONG BEFORE YOU WERE BORN, AND IT'S NOTHING LIKE A REGULAR THUNDERSTORM.
GLOW
I W-WON'T ACCEPT THIS! I'LL NEVER LET THE PRINCESS TAKE CARE OF ME!
KRAKABOOM
TRMMMM
BL

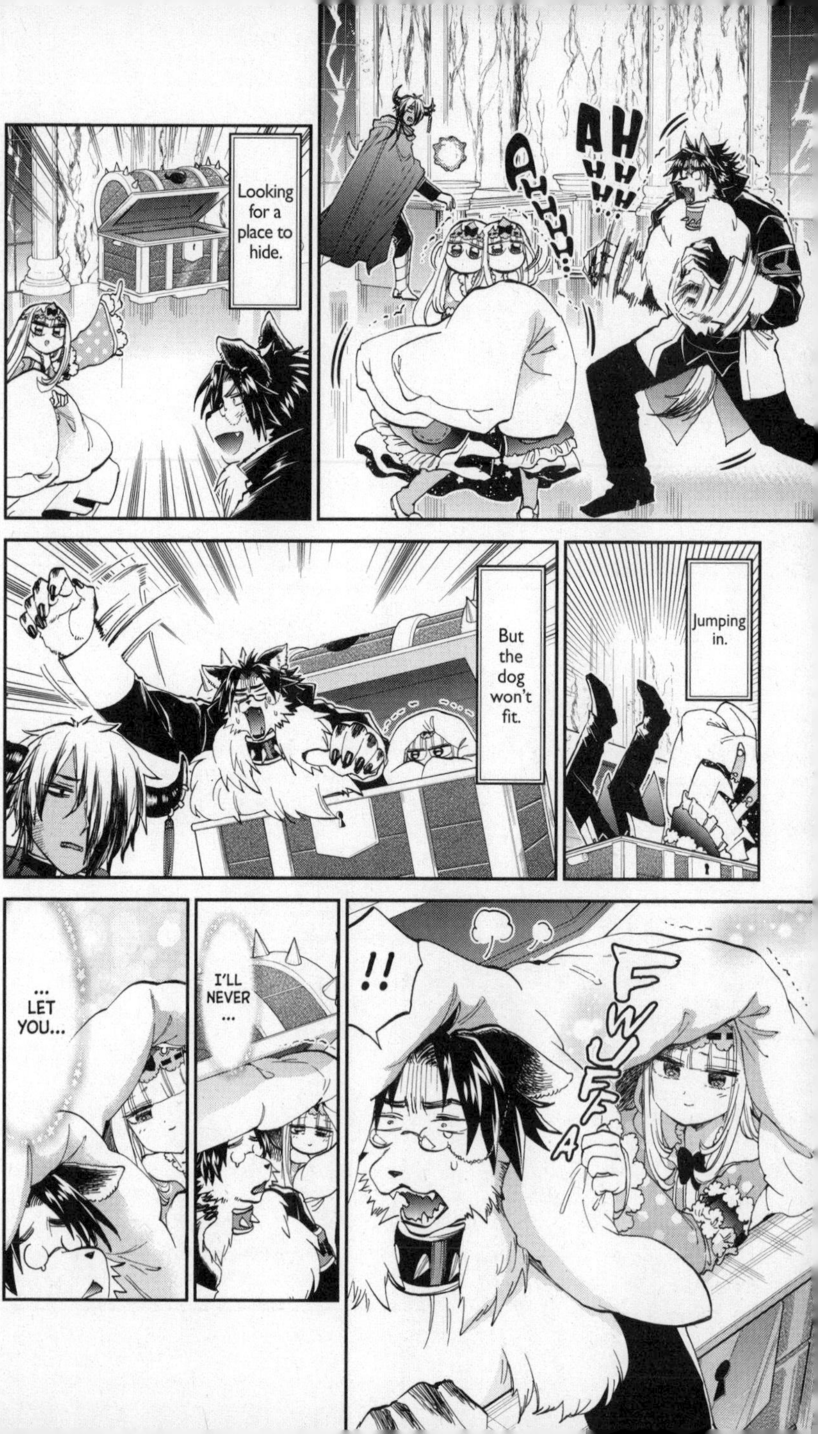
AHHHHH
AHHHH!!
Looking for a place to hide.
Jumping in.
But the dog won't fit.
!!
FWUFFA
I'LL NEVER ...
... LET YOU...

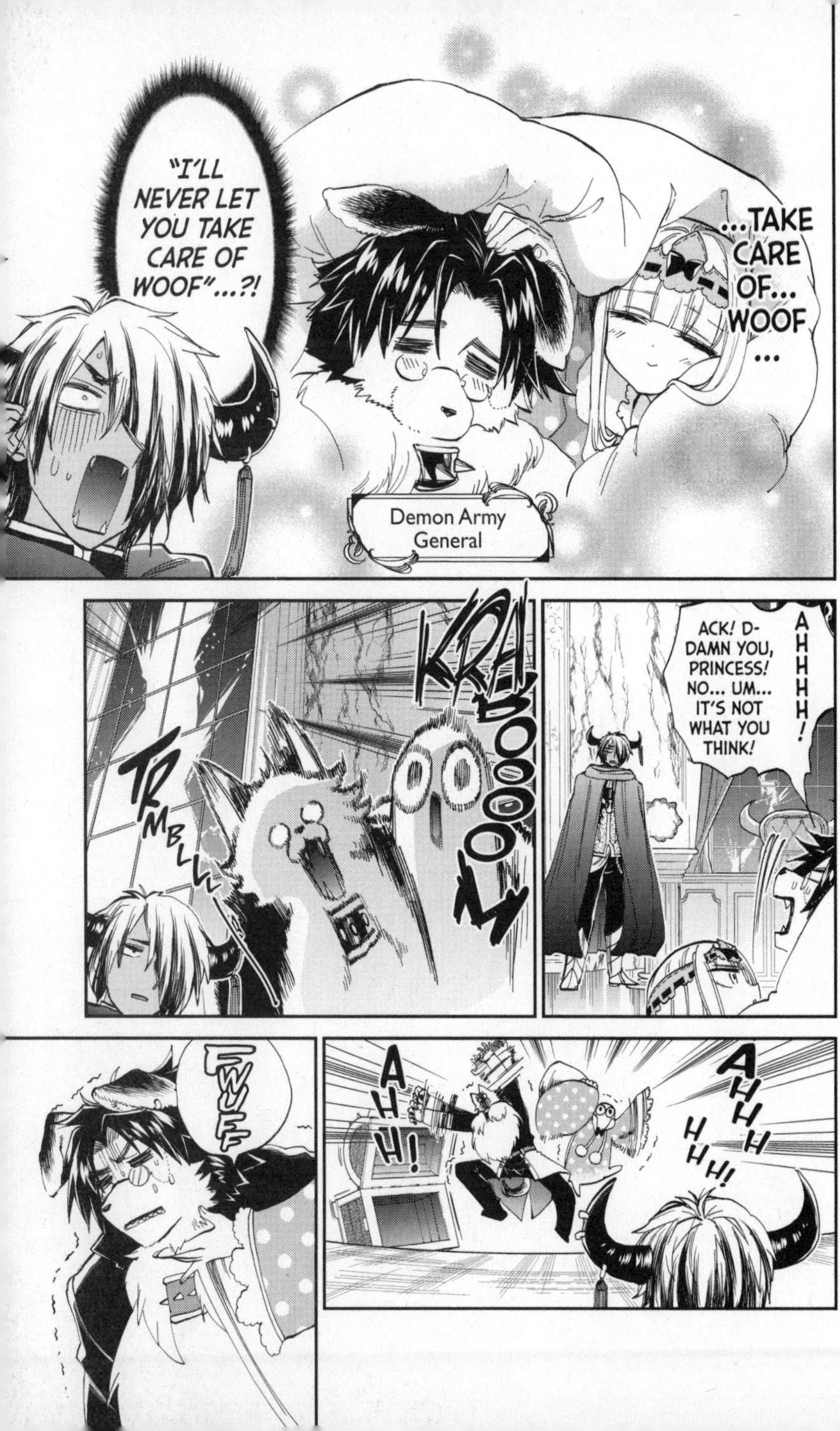
...TAKE CARE OF... WOOF ...
"I'LL NEVER LET YOU TAKE CARE OF WOOF"...?!
Demon Army General
AHHHHH!
ACK! D-DAMN YOU, PRINCESS! NO... UM... IT'S NOT WHAT YOU THINK!
KRA-BOOOOOOOM
TRMBLLLL
AHHHHHH!
AHHH!
FWUFF

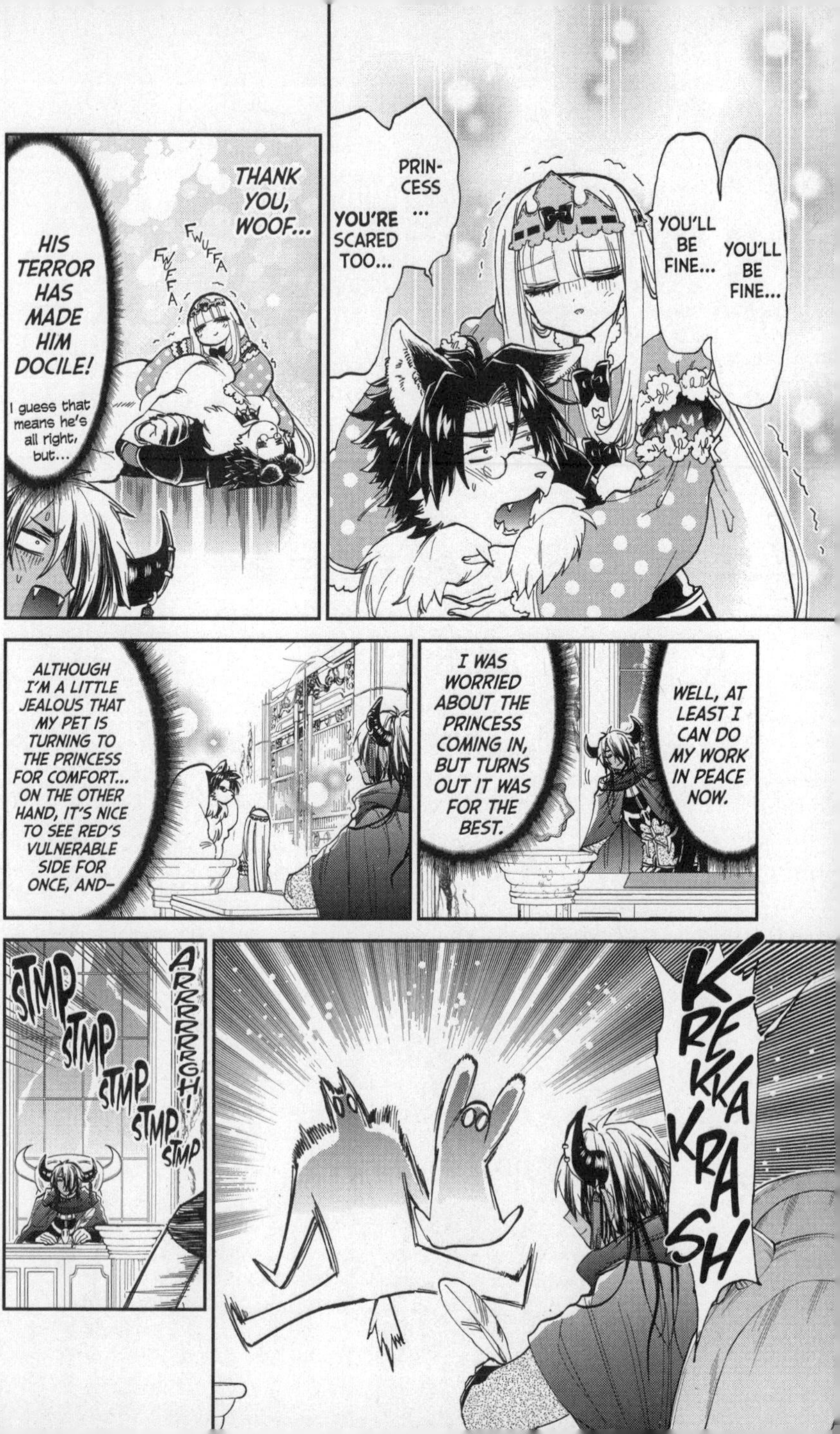
PRIN-CESS...
YOU'RE SCARED TOO...
YOU'LL BE FINE... YOU'LL BE FINE...
THANK YOU, WOOF...
FWUFFA FWUFFA
HIS TERROR HAS MADE HIM DOCILE!
I guess that means he's all right, but...
WELL, AT LEAST I CAN DO MY WORK IN PEACE NOW.
I WAS WORRIED ABOUT THE PRINCESS COMING IN, BUT TURNS OUT IT WAS FOR THE BEST.
ALTHOUGH I'M A LITTLE JEALOUS THAT MY PET IS TURNING TO THE PRINCESS FOR COMFORT... ON THE OTHER HAND, IT'S NICE TO SEE RED'S VULNERABLE SIDE FOR ONCE, AND–
KREKKA KRASH
ARRRRRGH!
STMP STMP STMP STMP STMP

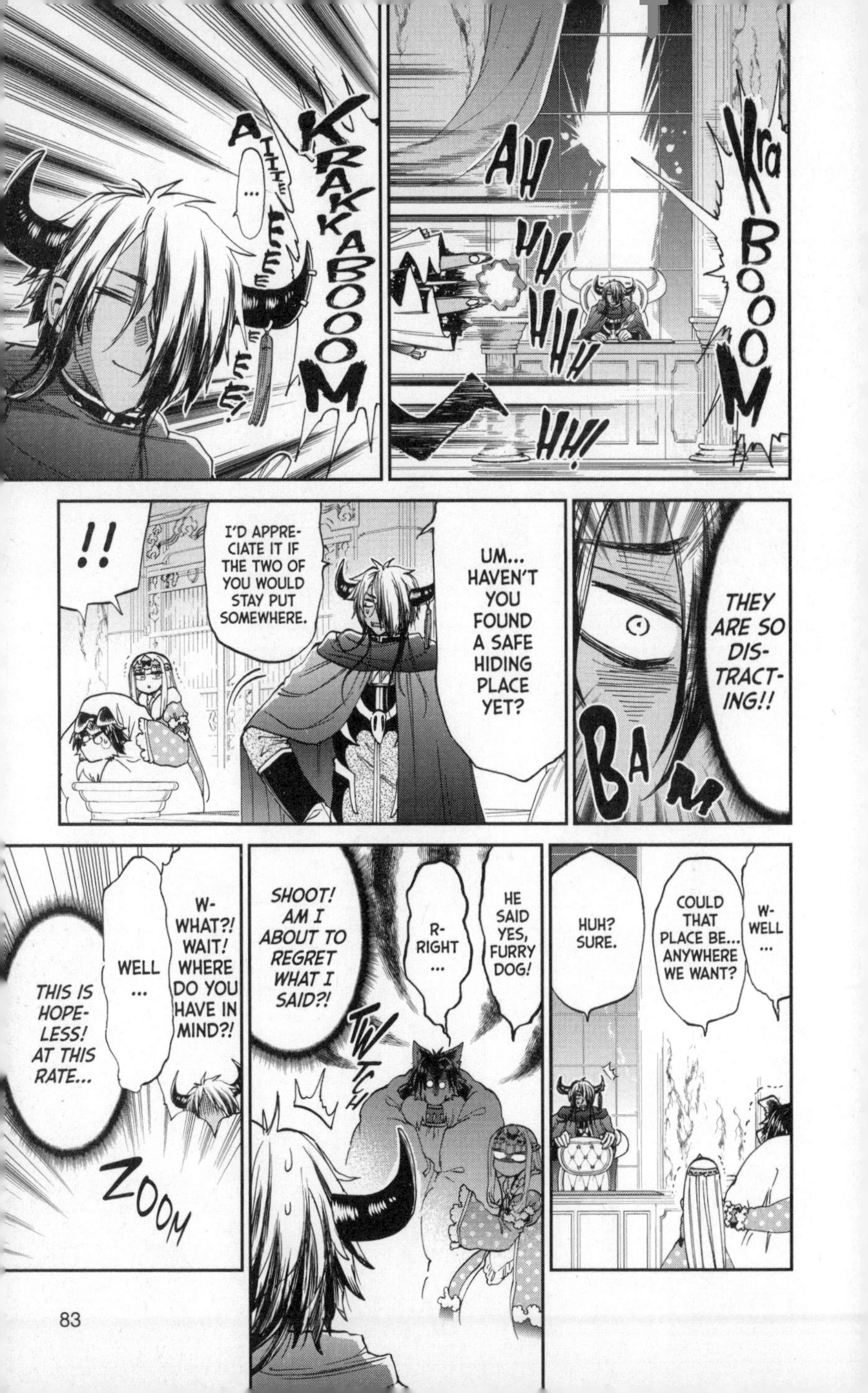
KRABOOOOM
AHHHHHHHHH!
KRAKKABOOOOM
AIIIEEEEEE!
...
THEY ARE SO DISTRACTING!!
BAM
UM... HAVEN'T YOU FOUND A SAFE HIDING PLACE YET?
I'D APPRECIATE IT IF THE TWO OF YOU WOULD STAY PUT SOMEWHERE.
!!
W-WELL...
COULD THAT PLACE BE... ANYWHERE WE WANT?
HUH? SURE.
HE SAID YES, FURRY DOG!
R-RIGHT...
TWITCH
SHOOT! AM I ABOUT TO REGRET WHAT I SAID?!
W-WHAT?! WAIT! WHERE DO YOU HAVE IN MIND?!
WELL...
THIS IS HOPELESS! AT THIS RATE...
ZOOM

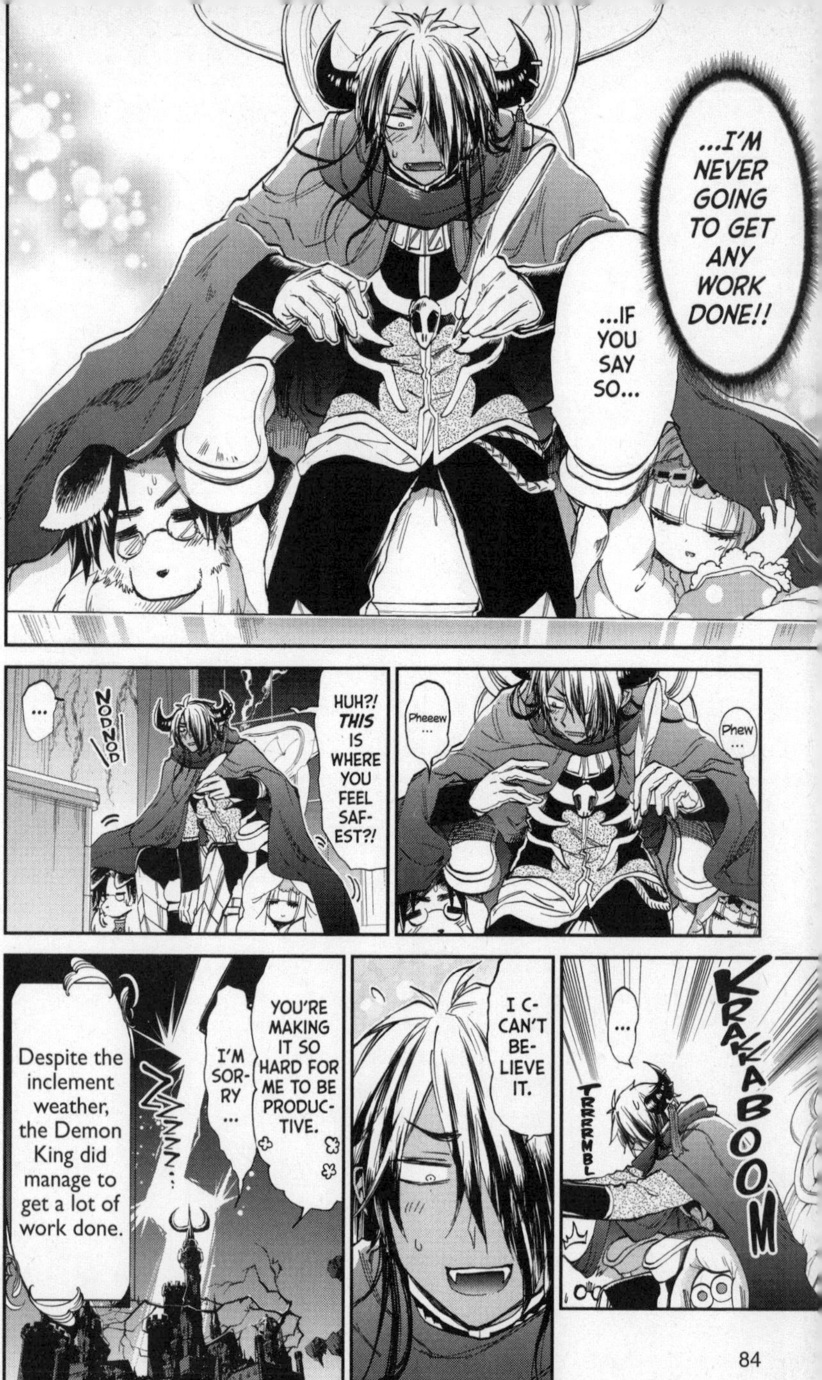
...I'M NEVER GOING TO GET ANY WORK DONE!!
...IF YOU SAY SO...
Phew...
Pheeew...
HUH?! *THIS* IS WHERE YOU FEEL SAFEST?!
...
NODNOD
KRAKKABOOM
...
TRRRRMBL
I C-CAN'T BELIEVE IT.
YOU'RE MAKING IT SO HARD FOR ME TO BE PRODUCTIVE.
I'M SORRY...
ZZZZZ...
Despite the inclement weather, the Demon King did manage to get a lot of work done.

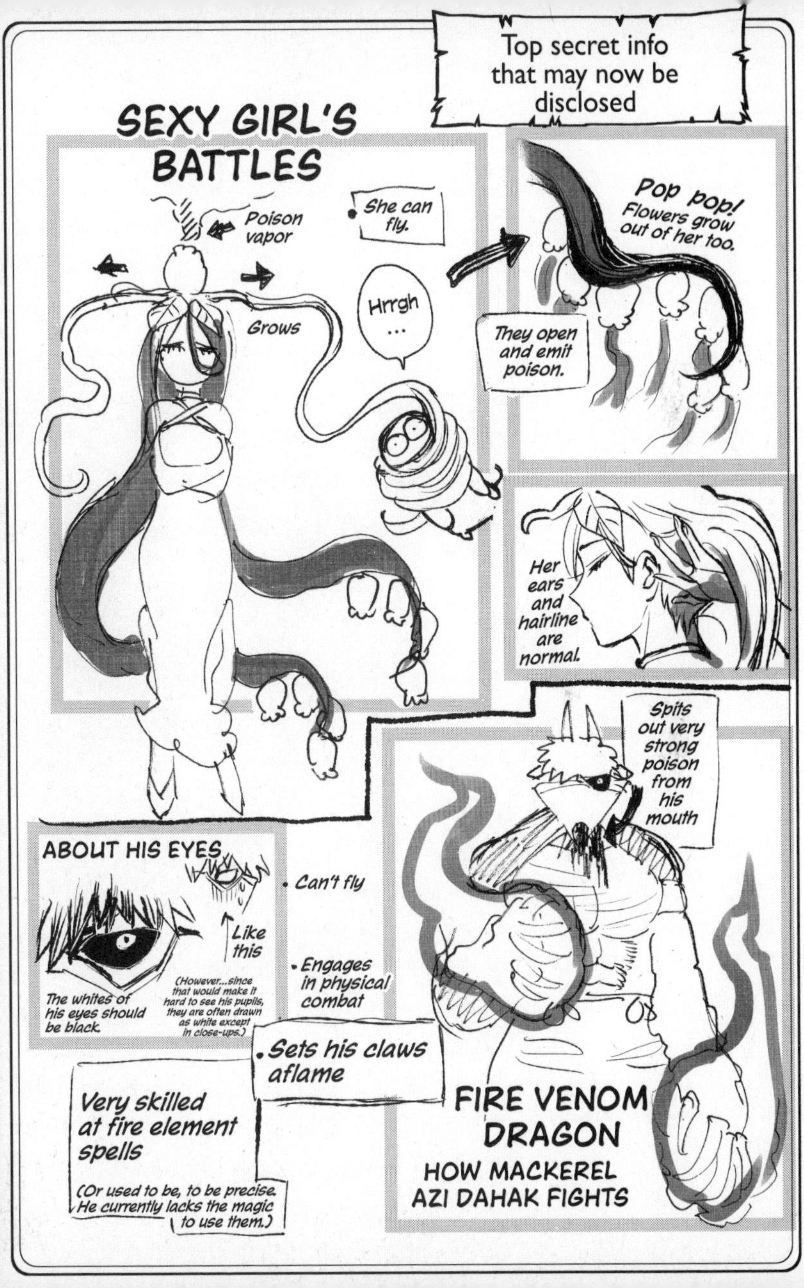
Top secret info that may now be disclosed
Pop pop!
Flowers grow out of her too.
They open and emit poison.
Her ears and hairline are normal.
SEXY GIRL'S BATTLES
• She can fly.
Poison vapor
Hrrgh …
Grows
Spits out very strong poison from his mouth
FIRE VENOM DRAGON
HOW MACKEREL AZI DAHAK FIGHTS
• Can't fly
• Engages in physical combat
• Sets his claws aflame
ABOUT HIS EYES
Like this
The whites of his eyes should be black.
(However…since that would make it hard to see his pupils, they are often drawn as white except in close-ups.)
Very skilled at fire element spells
(Or used to be, to be precise. He currently lacks the magic to use them.)

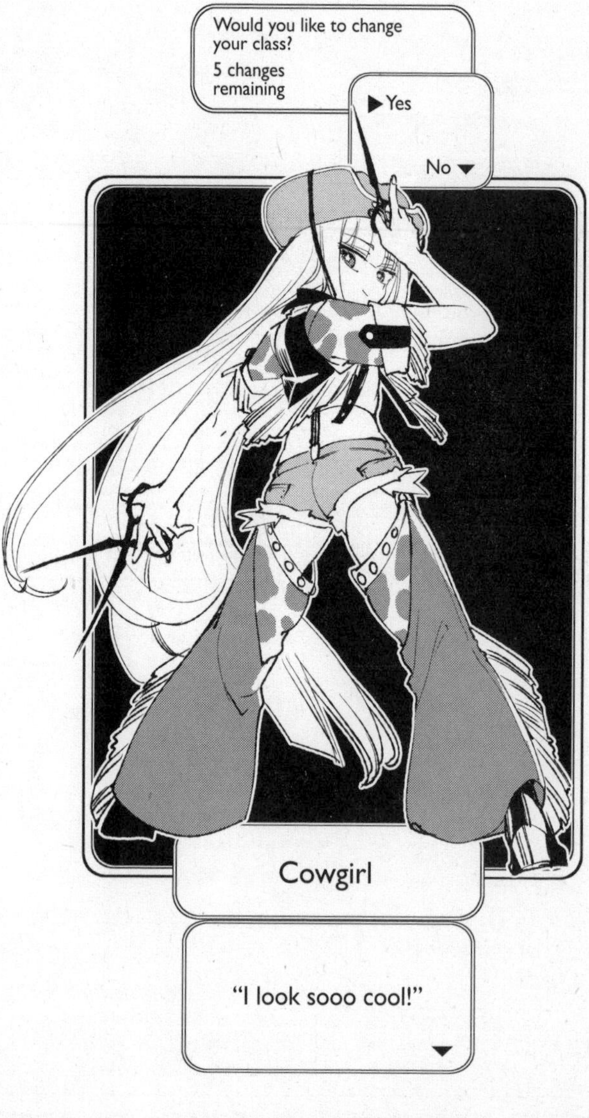
Would you like to change your class?
5 changes remaining
▶Yes
No ▼
Cowgirl
"I look sooo cool!"

177th Night: The Famed Casino Dealer Better Known as the Hostage

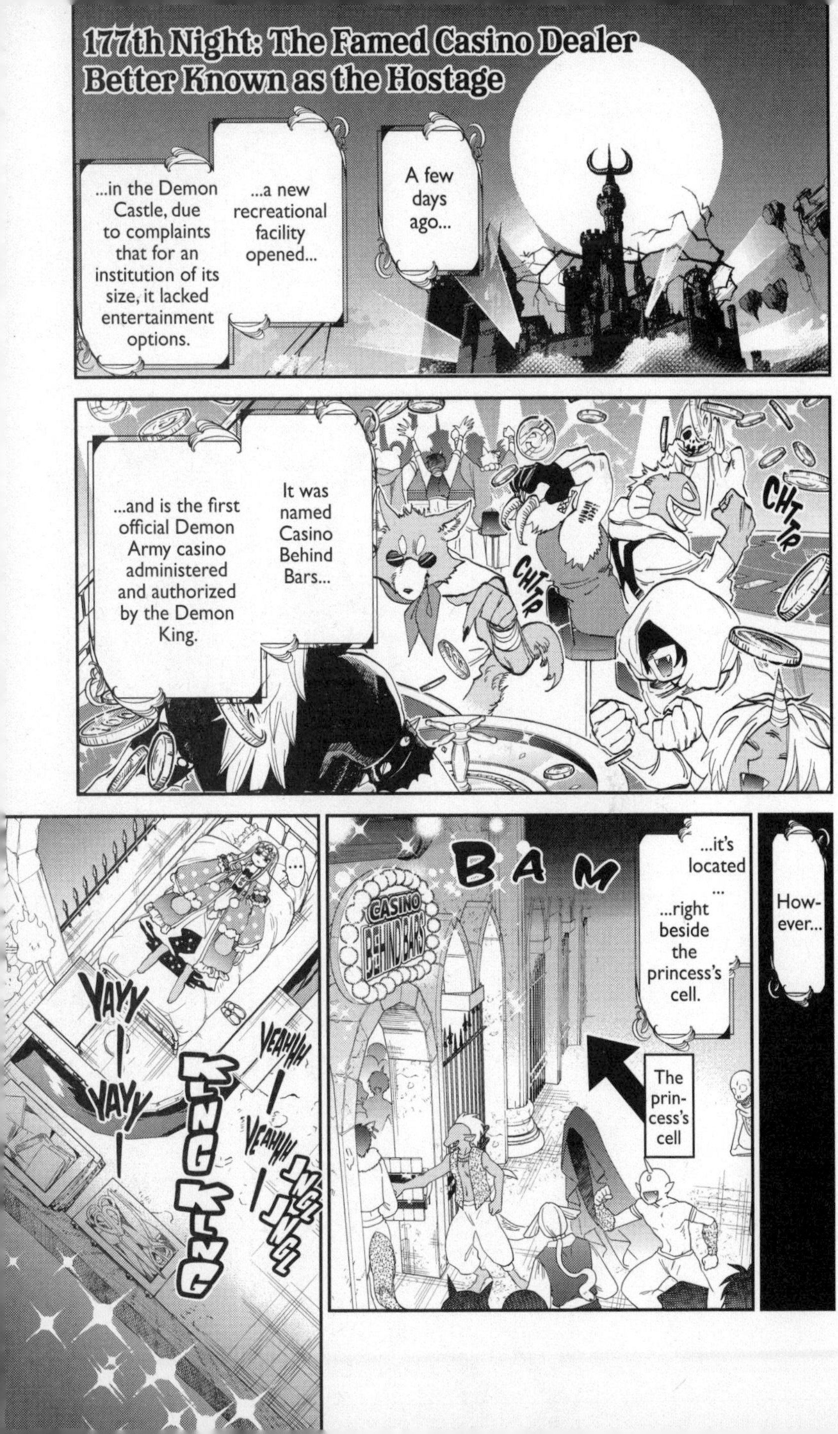

A few days ago...
...a new recreational facility opened...
...in the Demon Castle, due to complaints that for an institution of its size, it lacked entertainment options.
It was named Casino Behind Bars...
...and is the first official Demon Army casino administered and authorized by the Demon King.
CHT TR
CHT TR
However...
...it's located ... ...right beside the princess's cell.
BAM
CASINO BEHIND BARS
The princess's cell
...
YAYY YAYY
VEAHHH VEAHHH
KING KING
JINGL JINGL

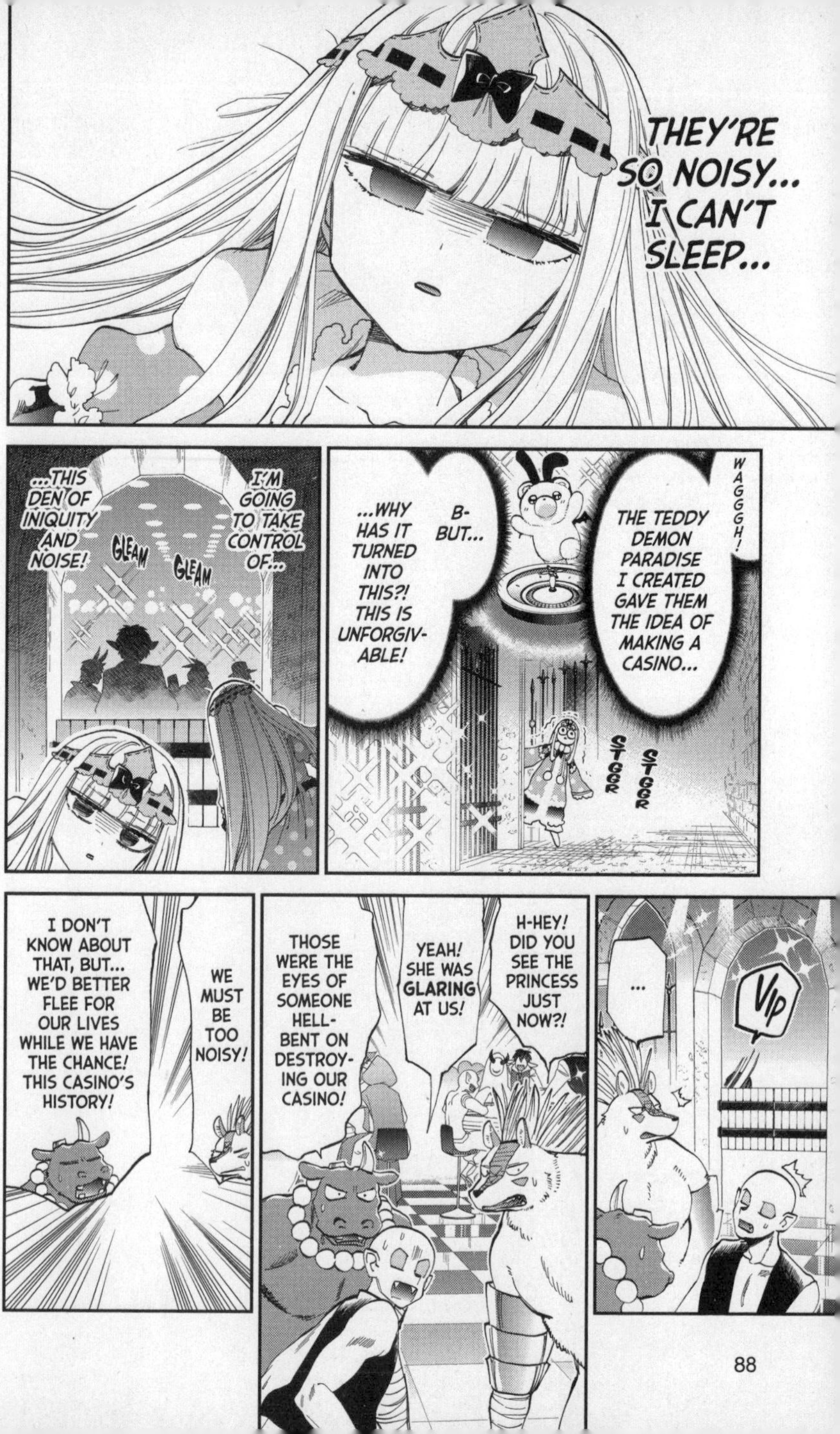
THEY'RE SO NOISY... I CAN'T SLEEP...
WAGGGH!
THE TEDDY DEMON PARADISE I CREATED GAVE THEM THE IDEA OF MAKING A CASINO...
STGGR
STGGR
B-BUT...
...WHY HAS IT TURNED INTO THIS?! THIS IS UNFORGIV-ABLE!
I'M GOING TO TAKE CONTROL OF...
GLEAM
GLEAM
...THIS DEN OF INIQUITY AND NOISE!
VIP
...
H-HEY! DID YOU SEE THE PRINCESS JUST NOW?!
YEAH! SHE WAS GLARING AT US!
THOSE WERE THE EYES OF SOMEONE HELL-BENT ON DESTROY-ING OUR CASINO!
WE MUST BE TOO NOISY!
I DON'T KNOW ABOUT THAT, BUT... WE'D BETTER FLEE FOR OUR LIVES WHILE WE HAVE THE CHANCE! THIS CASINO'S HISTORY!

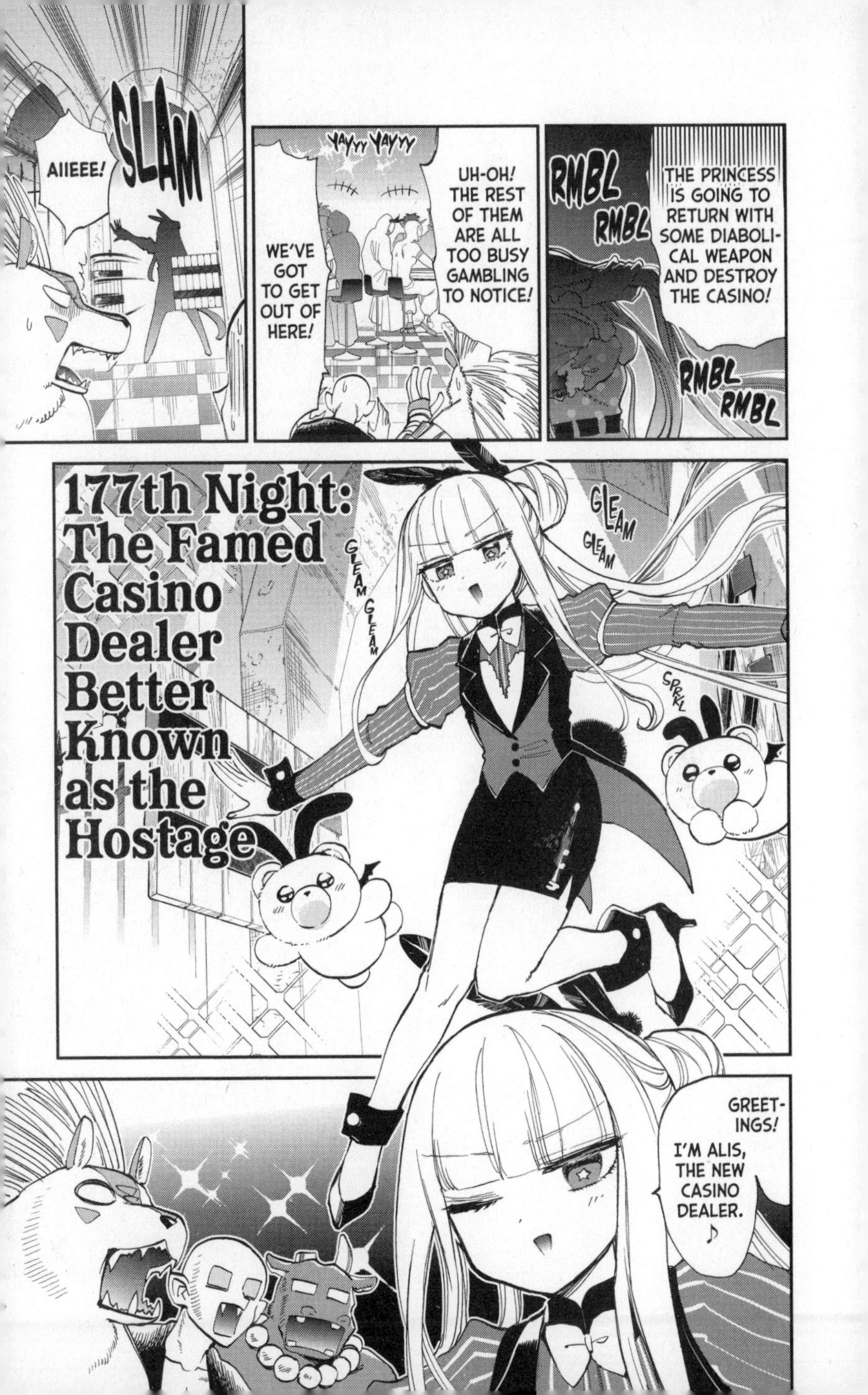
THE PRINCESS IS GOING TO RETURN WITH SOME DIABOLICAL WEAPON AND DESTROY THE CASINO!
RMBL RMBL
RMBL RMBL
YAYYY YAYYY
UH-OH! THE REST OF THEM ARE ALL TOO BUSY GAMBLING TO NOTICE!
WE'VE GOT TO GET OUT OF HERE!
SLAM
AIIEEE!
177th Night: The Famed Casino Dealer Better Known as the Hostage
GLEAM GLEAM
GLEAM GLEAM
SPRKL
GREETINGS! I'M ALIS, THE NEW CASINO DEALER. ♪

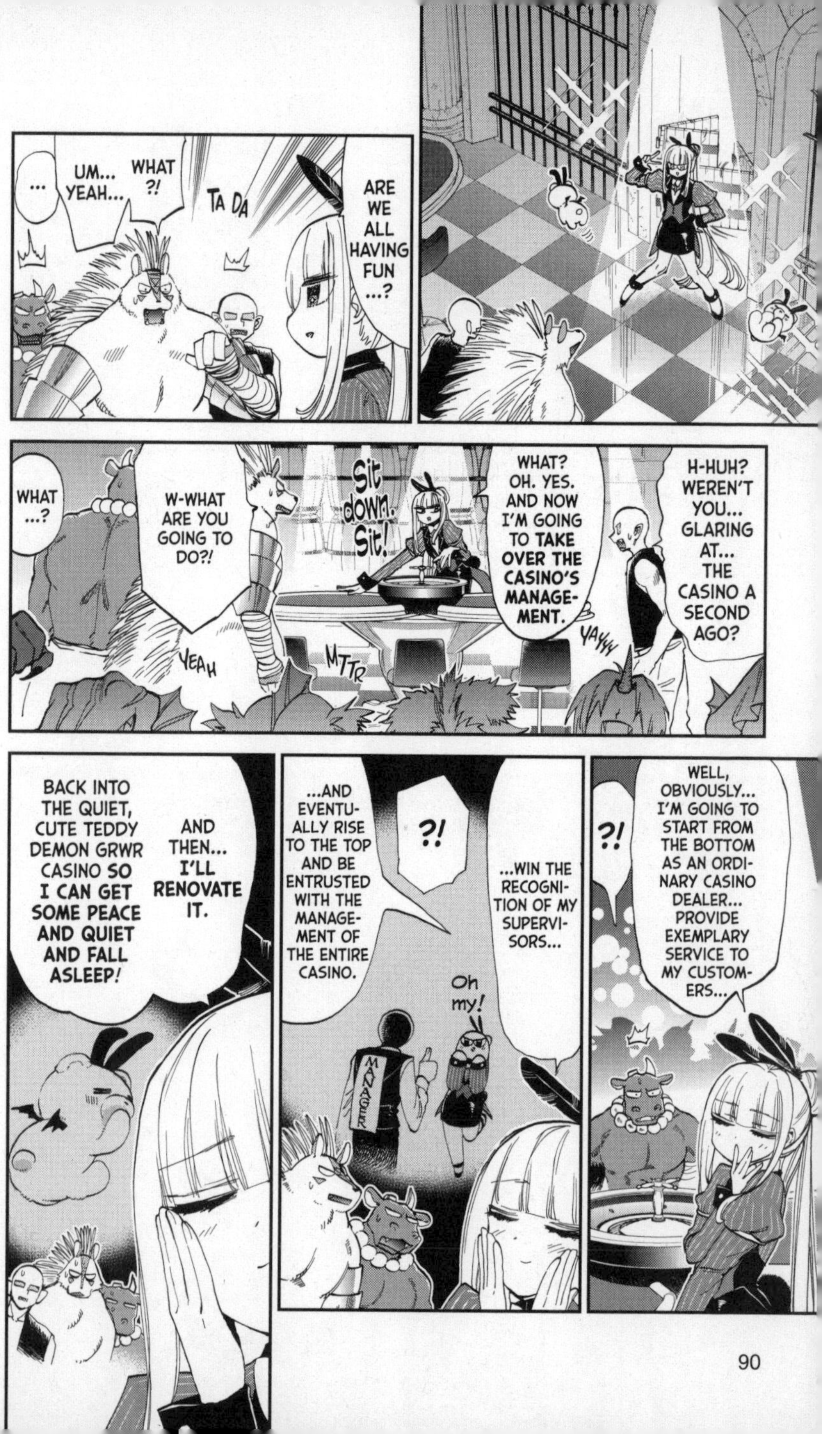
ARE WE ALL HAVING FUN ...?
TA DA
WHAT ?!
UM... YEAH...
...
H-HUH? WEREN'T YOU... GLARING AT... THE CASINO A SECOND AGO?
WHAT? OH. YES. AND NOW I'M GOING TO TAKE OVER THE CASINO'S MANAGEMENT.
Sit down. Sit!
YAYYY
MTTR
W-WHAT ARE YOU GOING TO DO?!
YEAH
WHAT ...?
WELL, OBVIOUSLY... I'M GOING TO START FROM THE BOTTOM AS AN ORDINARY CASINO DEALER... PROVIDE EXEMPLARY SERVICE TO MY CUSTOMERS...
?!
...WIN THE RECOGNITION OF MY SUPERVISORS...
?!
...AND EVENTUALLY RISE TO THE TOP AND BE ENTRUSTED WITH THE MANAGEMENT OF THE ENTIRE CASINO.
Oh my!
MANAGER
AND THEN... I'LL RENOVATE IT.
BACK INTO THE QUIET, CUTE TEDDY DEMON GRWR CASINO SO I CAN GET SOME PEACE AND QUIET AND FALL ASLEEP!

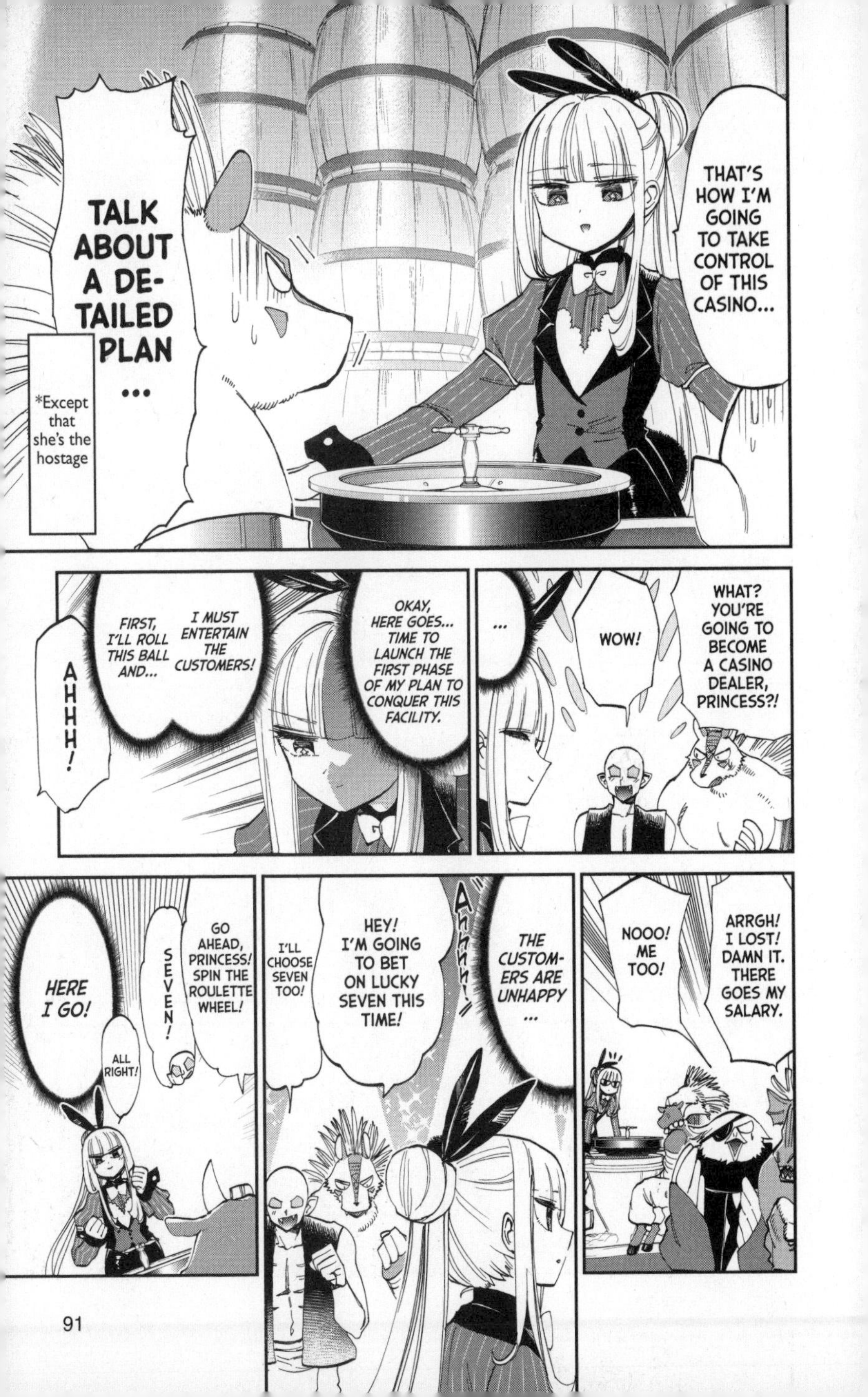
THAT'S HOW I'M GOING TO TAKE CONTROL OF THIS CASINO...
TALK ABOUT A DE-TAILED PLAN...
*Except that she's the hostage
WHAT? YOU'RE GOING TO BECOME A CASINO DEALER, PRINCESS?!
WOW!
...
OKAY, HERE GOES... TIME TO LAUNCH THE FIRST PHASE OF MY PLAN TO CONQUER THIS FACILITY.
I MUST ENTERTAIN THE CUSTOMERS!
FIRST, I'LL ROLL THIS BALL AND...
AHHHH!
ARRGH! I LOST! DAMN IT. THERE GOES MY SALARY.
NOOO! ME TOO!
THE CUSTOM-ERS ARE UNHAPPY...
Ahhhh!
HEY! I'M GOING TO BET ON LUCKY SEVEN THIS TIME!
I'LL CHOOSE SEVEN TOO!
GO AHEAD, PRINCESS! SPIN THE ROULETTE WHEEL!
SEVEN!
ALL RIGHT!
HERE I GO!

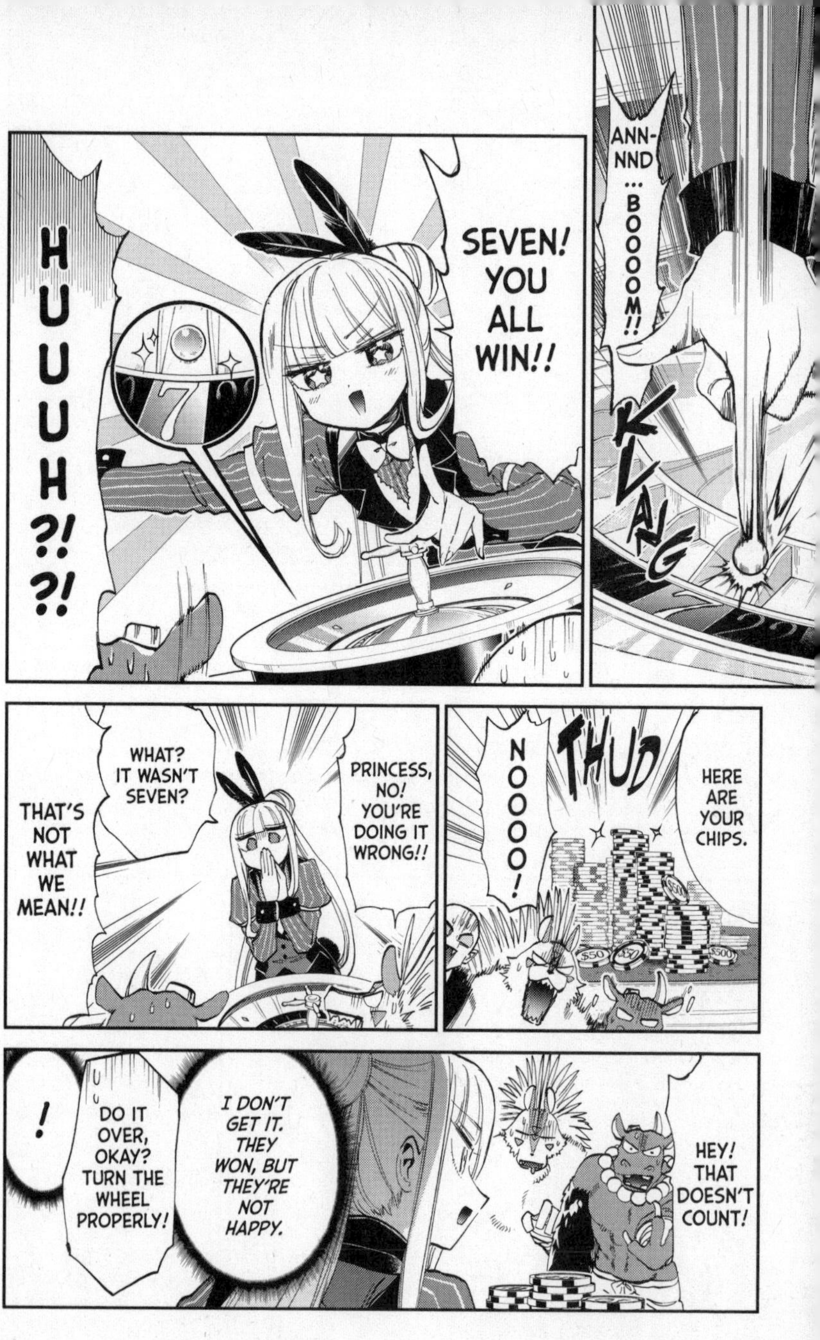
ANN-NND ...BOOOOOM!!
KLANG
SEVEN! YOU ALL WIN!!
HUUUUH?!?!
HERE ARE YOUR CHIPS.
THUD
NOOOOO!
PRINCESS, NO! YOU'RE DOING IT WRONG!!
WHAT? IT WASN'T SEVEN?
THAT'S NOT WHAT WE MEAN!!
HEY! THAT DOESN'T COUNT!
I DON'T GET IT. THEY WON, BUT THEY'RE NOT HAPPY.
DO IT OVER, OKAY? TURN THE WHEEL PROPERLY!
!

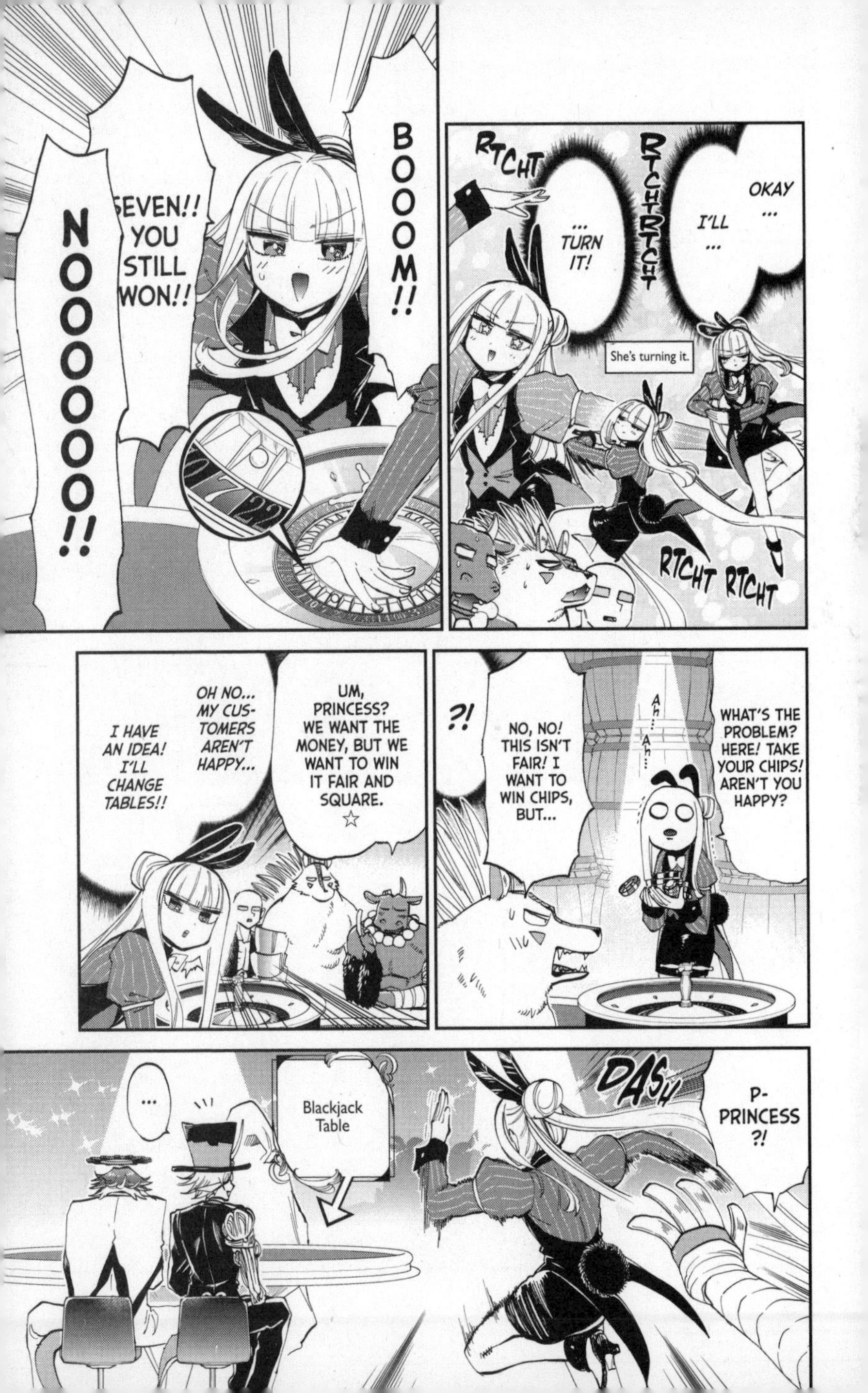
OKAY ...
I'LL ...
RTCHTRTCHTRTCHT
... TURN IT!
RTCHT
She's turning it.
RTCHT RTCHT
BOOOOM!!
SEVEN!! YOU STILL WON!!
NOOOOOOO!!
WHAT'S THE PROBLEM? HERE! TAKE YOUR CHIPS! AREN'T YOU HAPPY?
Ah... Ah...
NO, NO! THIS ISN'T FAIR! I WANT TO WIN CHIPS, BUT...
?!
UM, PRINCESS? WE WANT THE MONEY, BUT WE WANT TO WIN IT FAIR AND SQUARE. ☆
OH NO... MY CUS-TOMERS AREN'T HAPPY...
I HAVE AN IDEA! I'LL CHANGE TABLES!!
P-PRINCESS?!
DASH
Blackjack Table
...

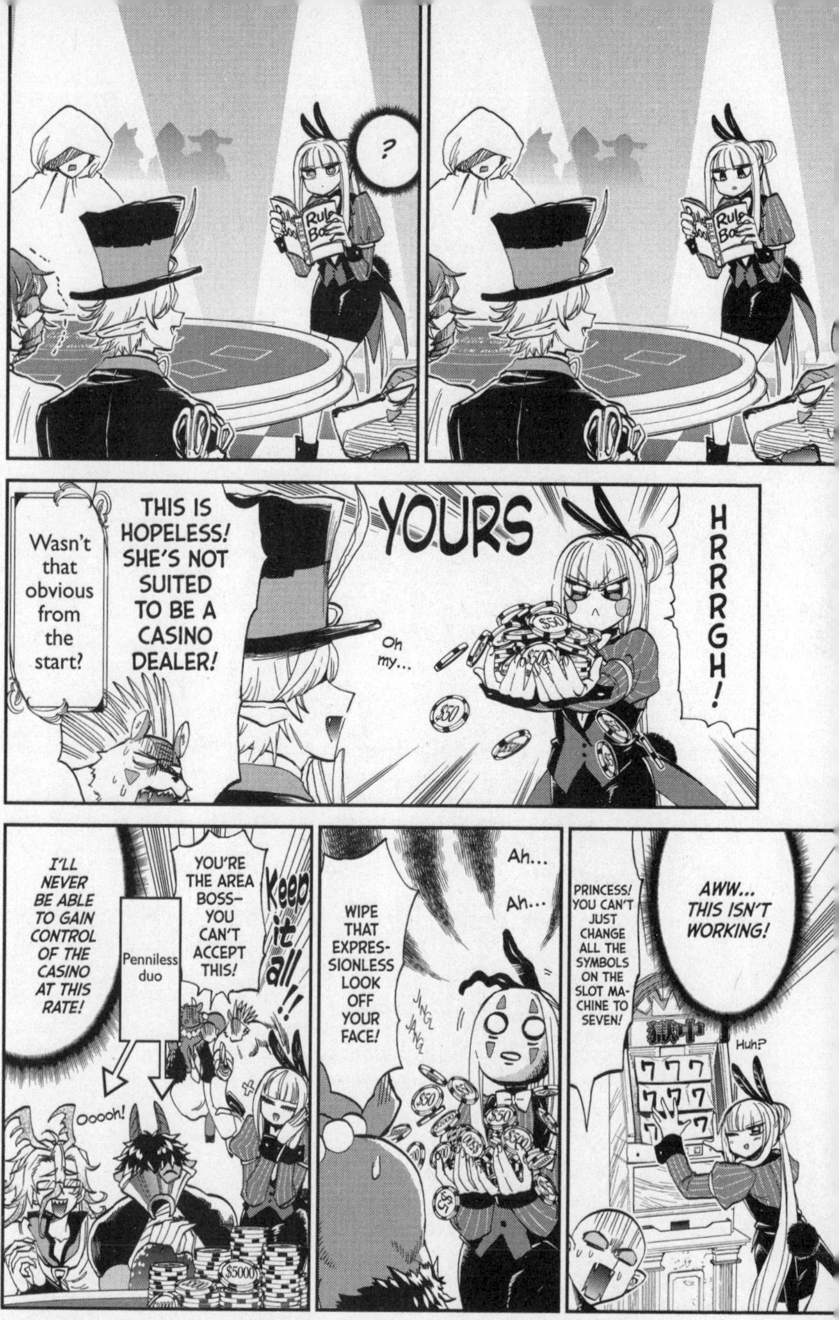
?
HRRRGH!
YOURS
Oh my...
THIS IS HOPELESS! SHE'S NOT SUITED TO BE A CASINO DEALER!
Wasn't that obvious from the start?
AWW... THIS ISN'T WORKING!
Huh?
PRINCESS! YOU CAN'T JUST CHANGE ALL THE SYMBOLS ON THE SLOT MACHINE TO SEVEN!
Ah... Ah...
WIPE THAT EXPRESSIONLESS LOOK OFF YOUR FACE!
JINGL JANGL
Keep it all!!
YOU'RE THE AREA BOSS— YOU CAN'T ACCEPT THIS!
I'LL NEVER BE ABLE TO GAIN CONTROL OF THE CASINO AT THIS RATE!
Penniless duo
Ooooh!

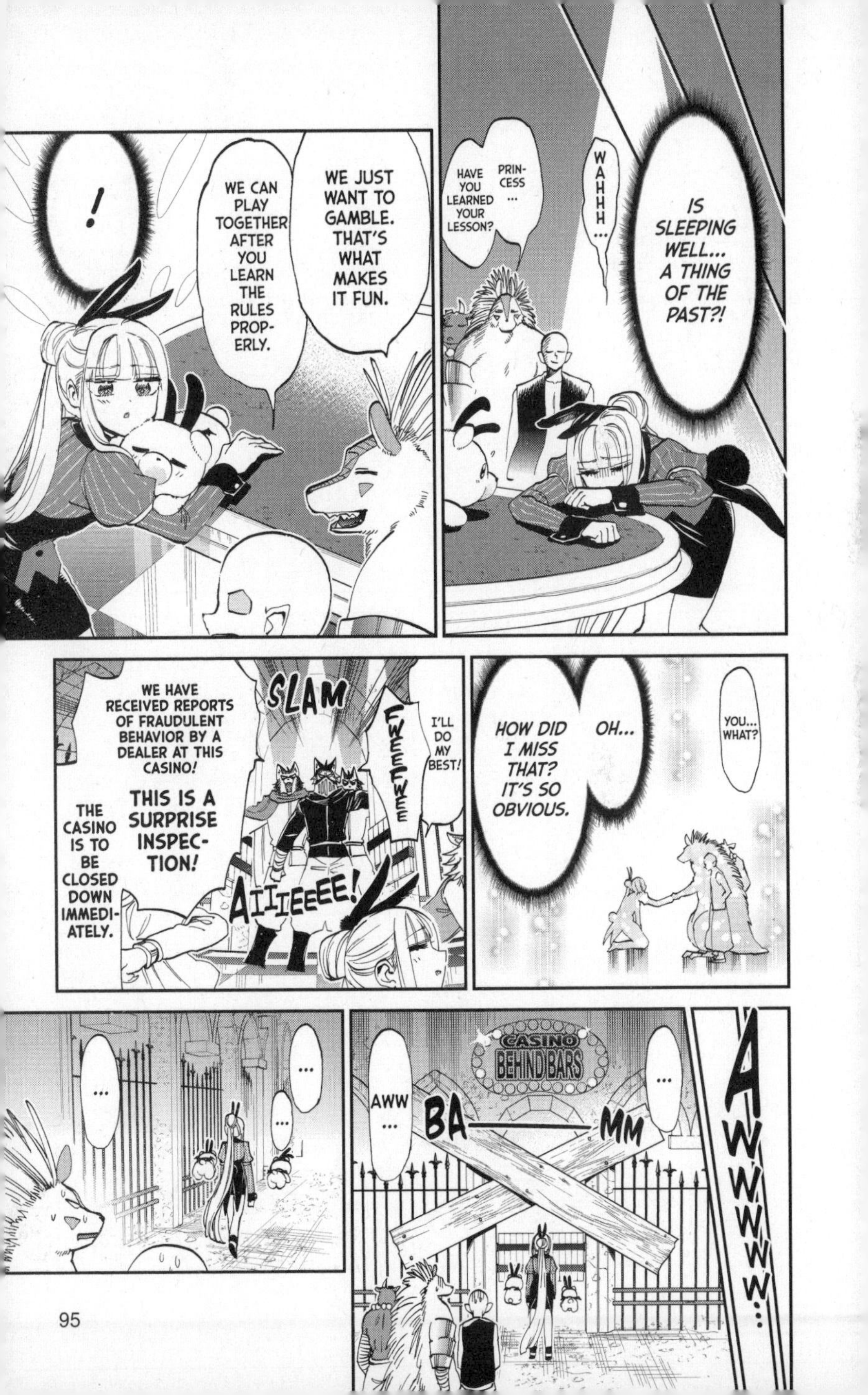

IS SLEEPING WELL... A THING OF THE PAST?!
WAHHH...
PRINCESS...
HAVE YOU LEARNED YOUR LESSON?
WE JUST WANT TO GAMBLE. THAT'S WHAT MAKES IT FUN.
WE CAN PLAY TOGETHER AFTER YOU LEARN THE RULES PROPERLY.
!
YOU... WHAT?
OH...
HOW DID I MISS THAT? IT'S SO OBVIOUS.
I'LL DO MY BEST!
FWEEFWEE
SLAM
WE HAVE RECEIVED REPORTS OF FRAUDULENT BEHAVIOR BY A DEALER AT THIS CASINO!
THIS IS A SURPRISE INSPECTION!
THE CASINO IS TO BE CLOSED DOWN IMMEDIATELY.
AIIIEEEE!
AWWWWWW...
...
CASINO BEHIND BARS
BA——MM
AWW...
...
...
...

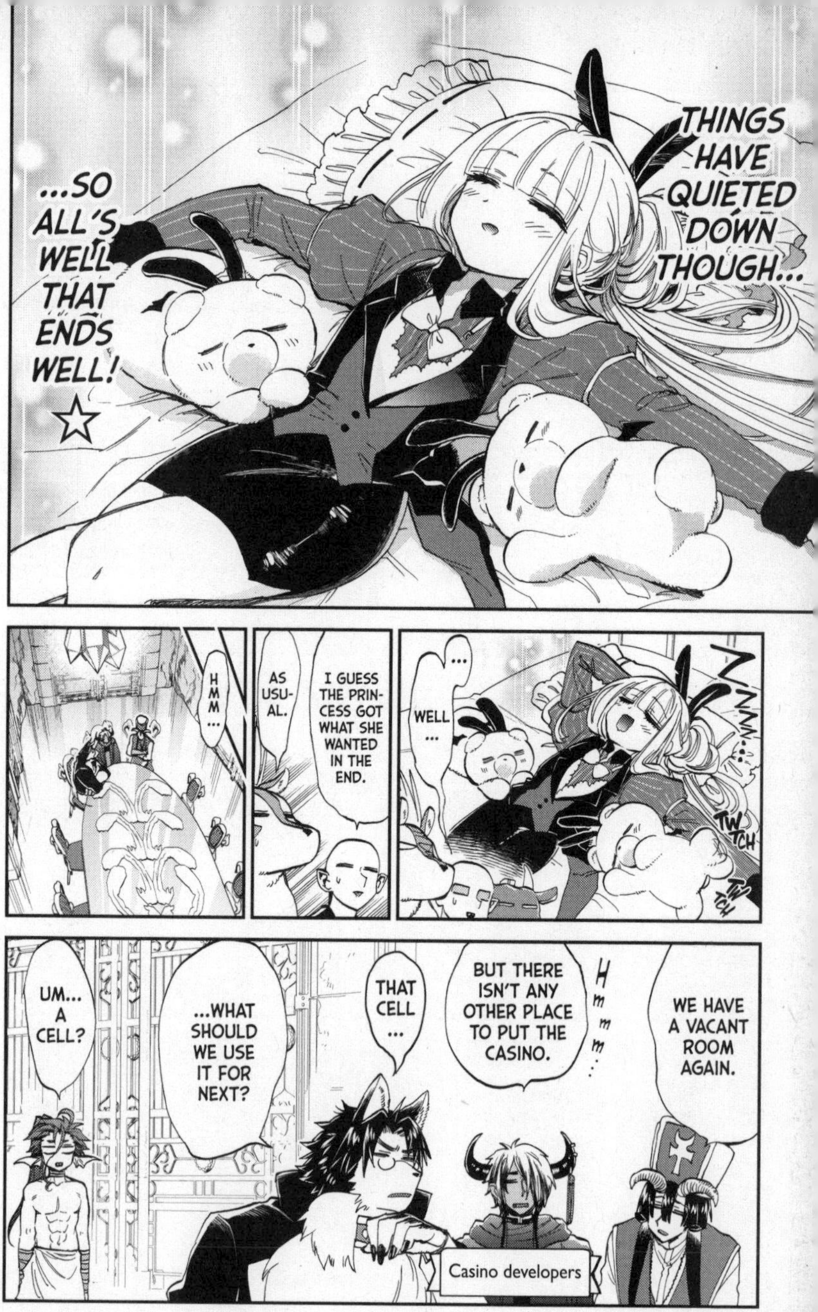
THINGS HAVE QUIETED DOWN THOUGH...
...SO ALL'S WELL THAT ENDS WELL! ☆
ZZZ...
...
WELL ...
TWITCH
TWITCH
I GUESS THE PRINCESS GOT WHAT SHE WANTED IN THE END.
AS USUAL.
HMM...
WE HAVE A VACANT ROOM AGAIN.
Hmmm...
BUT THERE ISN'T ANY OTHER PLACE TO PUT THE CASINO.
THAT CELL ...
...WHAT SHOULD WE USE IT FOR NEXT?
UM... A CELL?
Casino developers

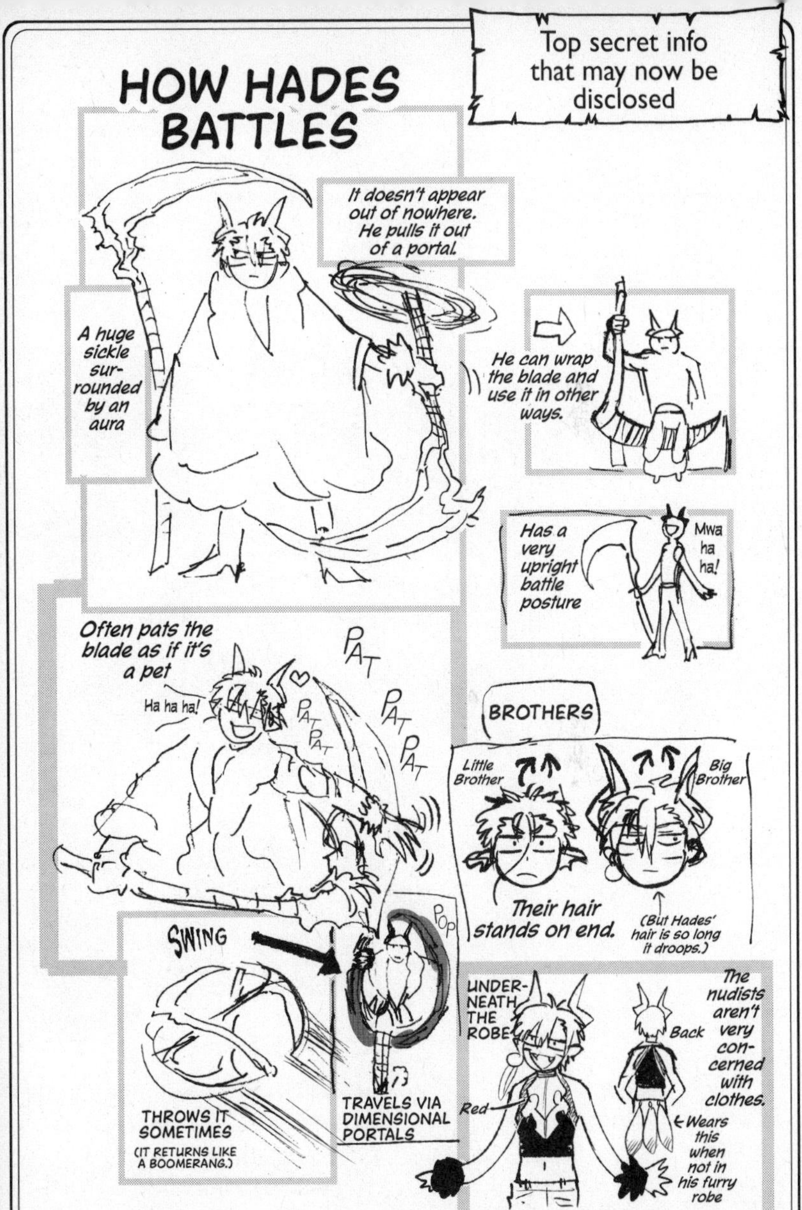

Top secret info that may now be disclosed
HOW HADES BATTLES
It doesn't appear out of nowhere. He pulls it out of a portal.
A huge sickle surrounded by an aura
He can wrap the blade and use it in other ways.
Has a very upright battle posture
Mwa ha ha!
BROTHERS
Big Brother
Little Brother
Their hair stands on end.
(But Hades' hair is so long it droops.)
Often pats the blade as if it's a pet
PAT
PAT
PAT
PAT PAT
Ha ha ha!
The nudists aren't very concerned with clothes.
UNDERNEATH THE ROBE
Back
Red
Wears this when not in his furry robe
POP
TRAVELS VIA DIMENSIONAL PORTALS
SWING
THROWS IT SOMETIMES
(IT RETURNS LIKE A BOOMERANG.)

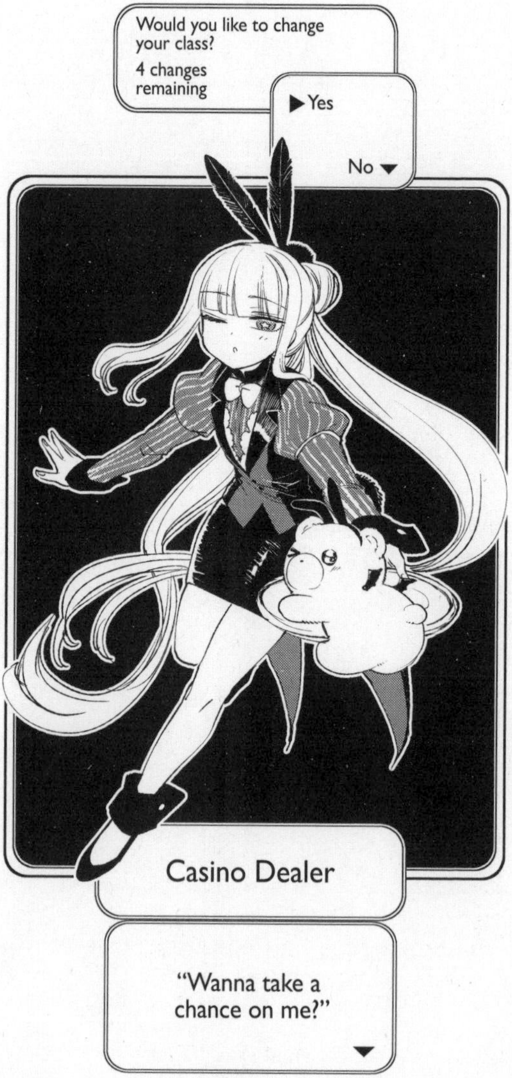
Would you like to change your class?
4 changes remaining
▶Yes
No ▼
Casino Dealer
"Wanna take a chance on me?"

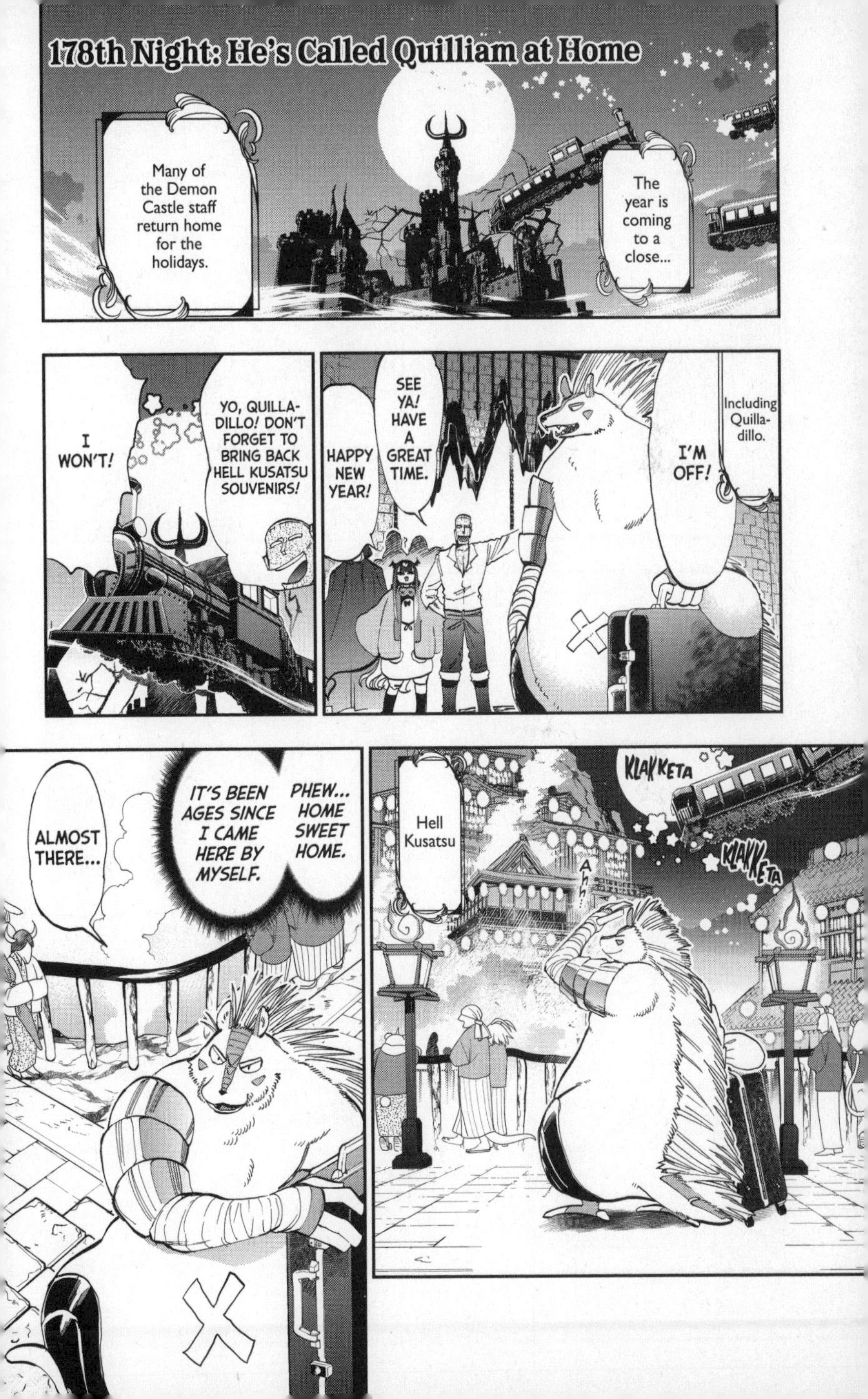
178th Night: He's Called Quilliam at Home
The year is coming to a close...
Many of the Demon Castle staff return home for the holidays.
Including Quilla-dillo.
I'M OFF!
SEE YA! HAVE A GREAT TIME.
HAPPY NEW YEAR!
YO, QUILLA-DILLO! DON'T FORGET TO BRING BACK HELL KUSATSU SOUVENIRS!
I WON'T!
KLAKKETA
Hell Kusatsu
KLAKKETA
Ahh...
PHEW... HOME SWEET HOME.
IT'S BEEN AGES SINCE I CAME HERE BY MYSELF.
ALMOST THERE...

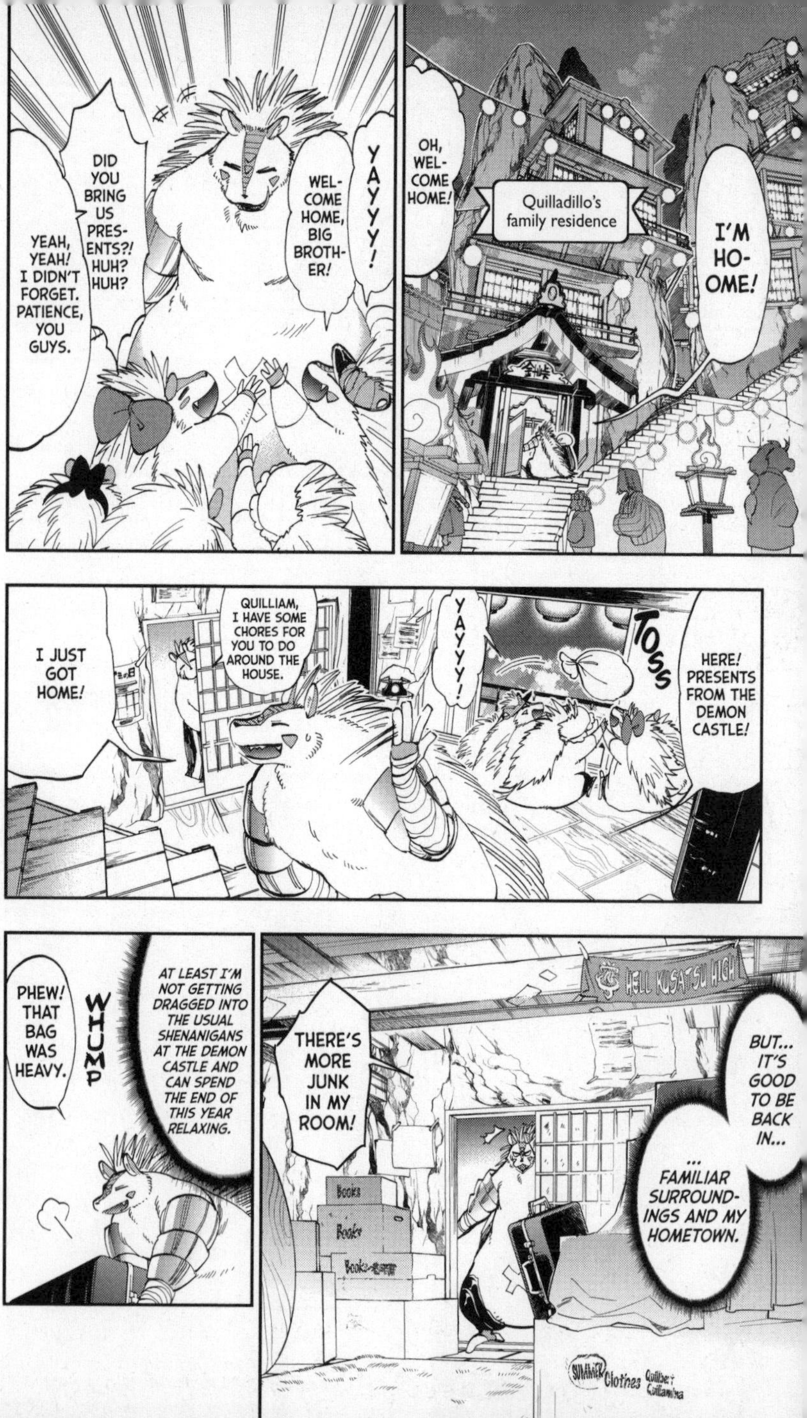
I'M HO-OME!
Quilladillo's family residence
OH, WEL-COME HOME!
YAYYY!
WEL-COME HOME, BIG BROTH-ER!
DID YOU BRING US PRES-ENTS?! HUH? HUH?
YEAH, YEAH! I DIDN'T FORGET. PATIENCE, YOU GUYS.
HERE! PRESENTS FROM THE DEMON CASTLE!
TOSS
YAYYY!
QUILLIAM, I HAVE SOME CHORES FOR YOU TO DO AROUND THE HOUSE.
I JUST GOT HOME!
BUT... IT'S GOOD TO BE BACK IN...
...FAMILIAR SURROUND-INGS AND MY HOMETOWN.
HELL KUSATSU HIGH
THERE'S MORE JUNK IN MY ROOM!
Books
Books
Books
SUMMER Clothes
AT LEAST I'M NOT GETTING DRAGGED INTO THE USUAL SHENANIGANS AT THE DEMON CASTLE AND CAN SPEND THE END OF THIS YEAR RELAXING.
WHUMP
PHEW! THAT BAG WAS HEAVY.

178th Night: He's Called Quilliam at Home

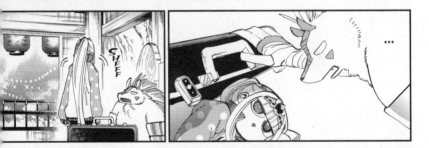

SHFF

...

ARGH!

HEH HEH ...

AHH, HELL KUSAT-SU AT LAST...

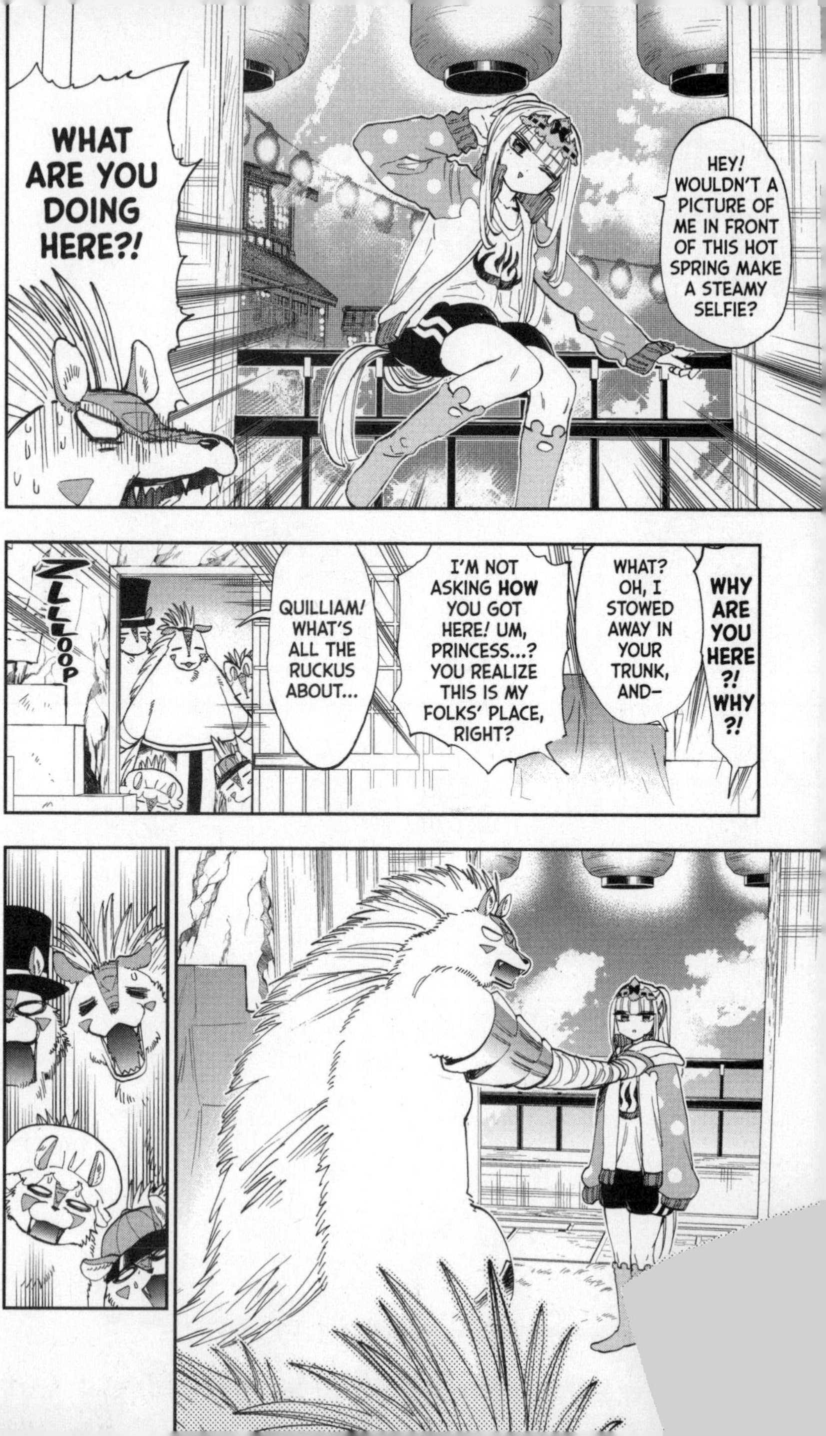
HEY! WOULDN'T A PICTURE OF ME IN FRONT OF THIS HOT SPRING MAKE A STEAMY SELFIE?
WHAT ARE YOU DOING HERE?!
WHY ARE YOU HERE?! WHY?!
WHAT? OH, I STOWED AWAY IN YOUR TRUNK, AND—
I'M NOT ASKING **HOW** YOU GOT HERE! UM, PRINCESS...? YOU REALIZE THIS IS MY FOLKS' PLACE, RIGHT?
QUILLIAM! WHAT'S ALL THE RUCKUS ABOUT...
ZLLLOOP

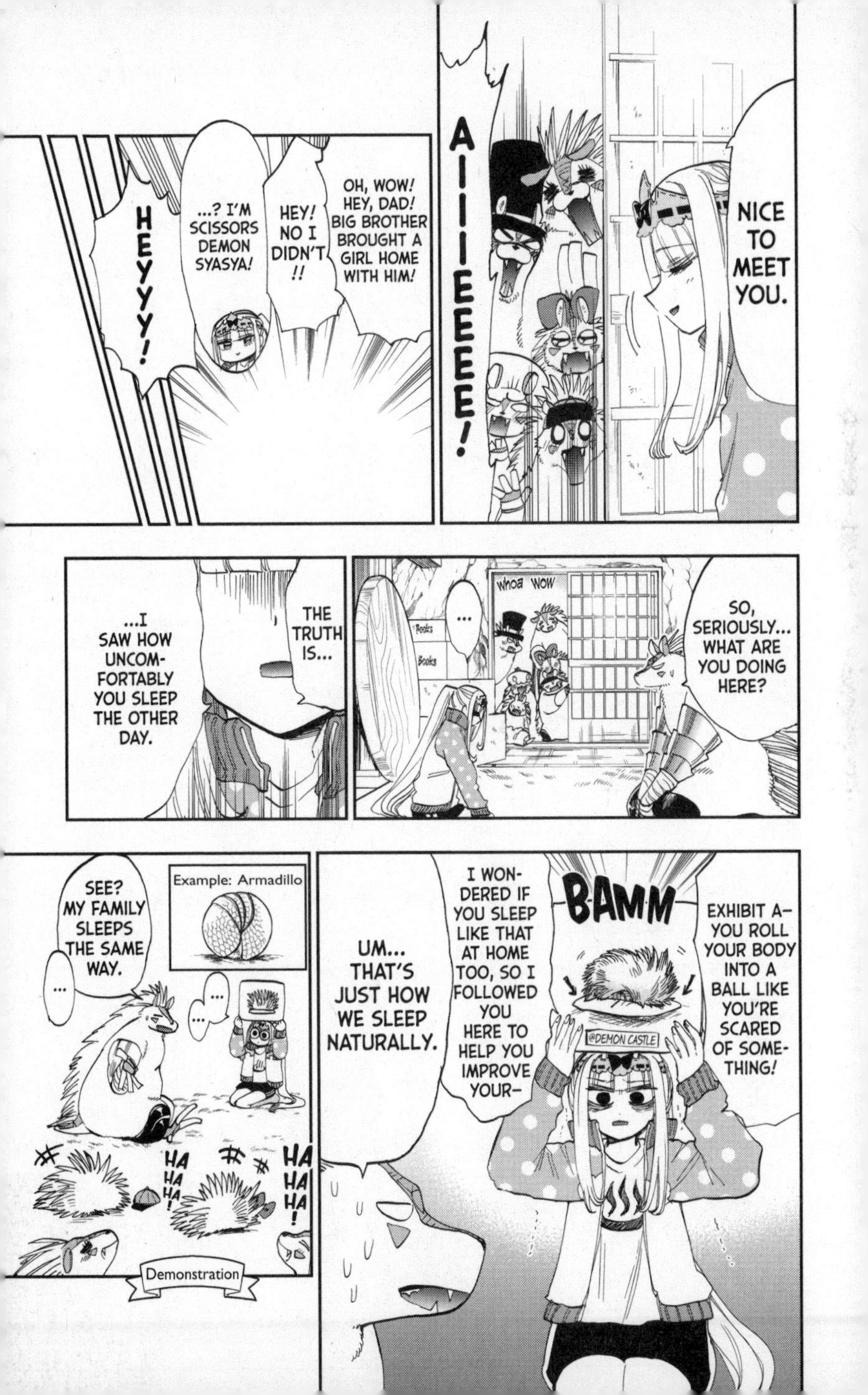
NICE TO MEET YOU.
AIIIEEEEE!
OH, WOW! HEY, DAD! BIG BROTHER BROUGHT A GIRL HOME WITH HIM!
HEY! NO I DIDN'T!!
...? I'M SCISSORS DEMON SYASYA!
HEYYY!
SO, SERIOUSLY... WHAT ARE YOU DOING HERE?
WHOA WOW
BOOKS
BOOKS
...
THE TRUTH IS...
...I SAW HOW UNCOM-FORTABLY YOU SLEEP THE OTHER DAY.
EXHIBIT A– YOU ROLL YOUR BODY INTO A BALL LIKE YOU'RE SCARED OF SOME-THING!
BAMM
@DEMON CASTLE
I WON-DERED IF YOU SLEEP LIKE THAT AT HOME TOO, SO I FOLLOWED YOU HERE TO HELP YOU IMPROVE YOUR–
UM... THAT'S JUST HOW WE SLEEP NATURALLY.
Example: Armadillo
SEE? MY FAMILY SLEEPS THE SAME WAY.
...
...
...
HA HA HA!
HA HA HA!
Demonstration

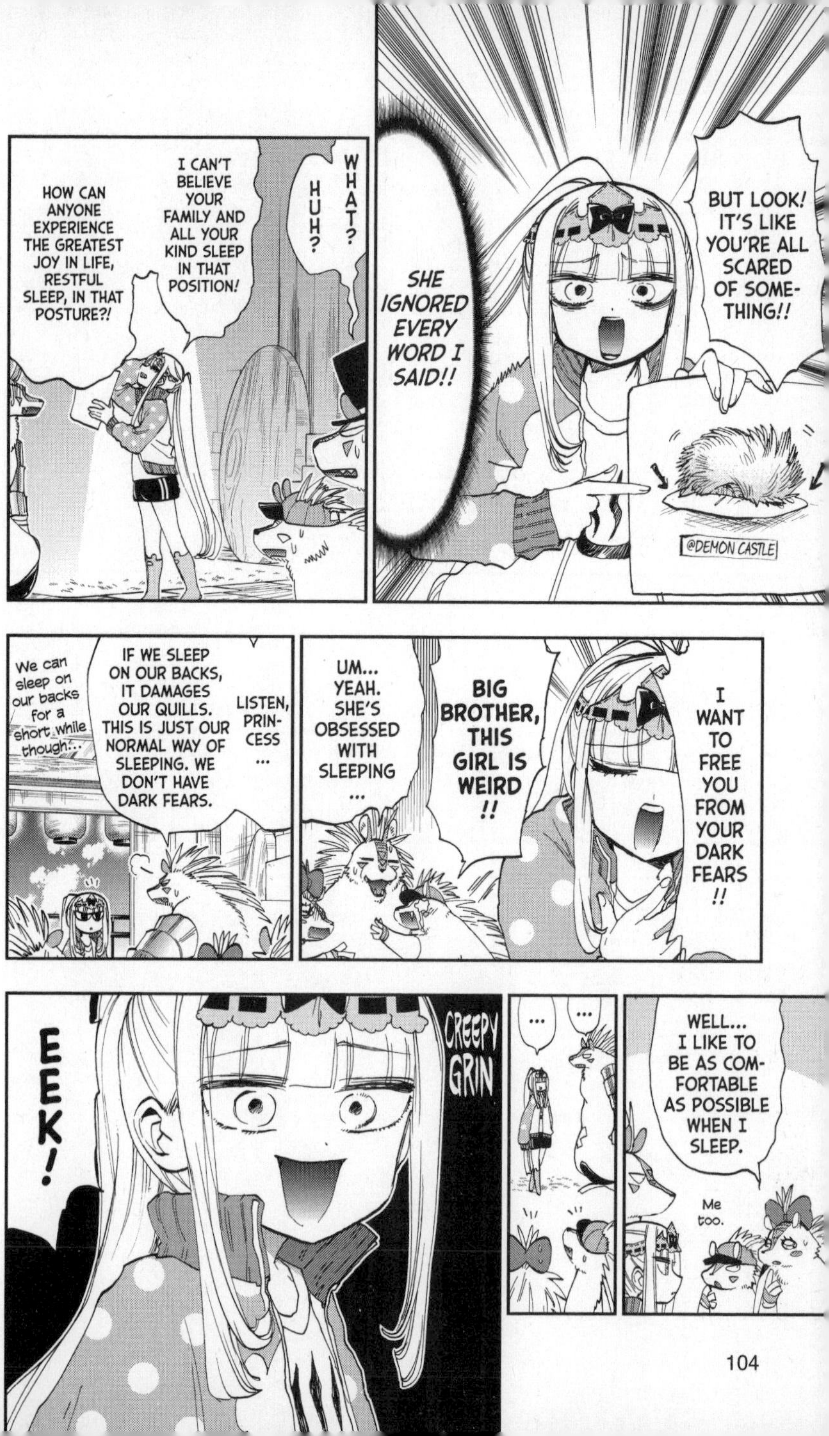
BUT LOOK! IT'S LIKE YOU'RE ALL SCARED OF SOME-THING!!
@DEMON CASTLE
SHE IGNORED EVERY WORD I SAID!!
WHAT?
HUH?
I CAN'T BELIEVE YOUR FAMILY AND ALL YOUR KIND SLEEP IN THAT POSITION!
HOW CAN ANYONE EXPERIENCE THE GREATEST JOY IN LIFE, RESTFUL SLEEP, IN THAT POSTURE?!
I WANT TO FREE YOU FROM YOUR DARK FEARS!!
BIG BROTHER, THIS GIRL IS WEIRD!!
UM... YEAH. SHE'S OBSESSED WITH SLEEPING...
LISTEN, PRIN-CESS...
IF WE SLEEP ON OUR BACKS, IT DAMAGES OUR QUILLS. THIS IS JUST OUR NORMAL WAY OF SLEEPING. WE DON'T HAVE DARK FEARS.
We can sleep on our backs for a short while though...
WELL... I LIKE TO BE AS COM-FORTABLE AS POSSIBLE WHEN I SLEEP.
Me too.
...
...
CREEPY GRIN
EEK!

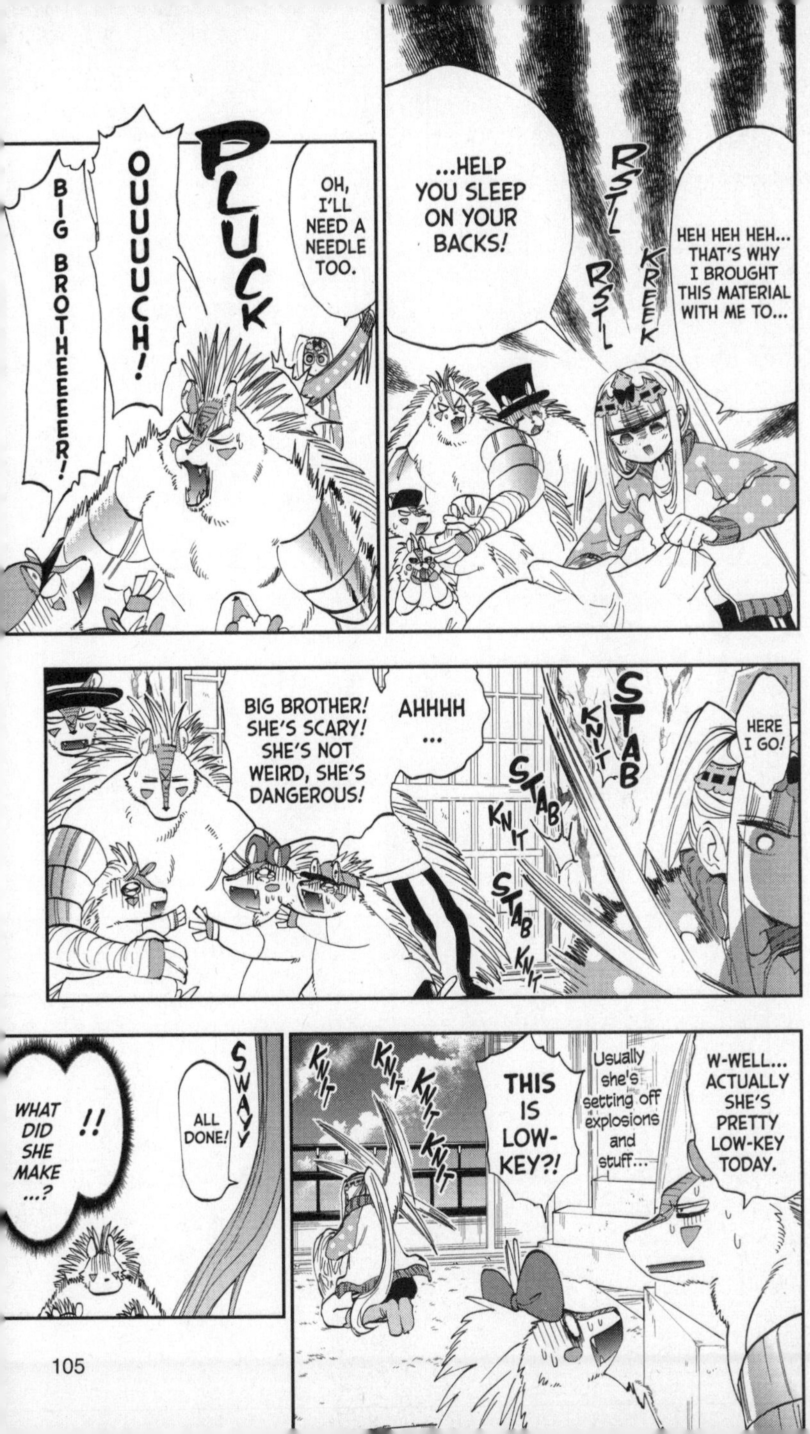
HEH HEH HEH... THAT'S WHY I BROUGHT THIS MATERIAL WITH ME TO...
RSTL
KREEK
RSTL
...HELP YOU SLEEP ON YOUR BACKS!
OH, I'LL NEED A NEEDLE TOO.
PLUCK
OUUUUCH!
BIG BROTHEEEEER!
HERE I GO!
STAB
KNIT
STAB
KNIT
STAB
KNIT
AHHHH ...
BIG BROTHER! SHE'S SCARY! SHE'S NOT WEIRD, SHE'S DANGEROUS!
W-WELL... ACTUALLY SHE'S PRETTY LOW-KEY TODAY.
Usually she's setting off explosions and stuff...
THIS IS LOW-KEY?!
KNIT
KNIT
KNIT
KNIT
KNIT
SWAYY
ALL DONE!
!!
WHAT DID SHE MAKE ...?

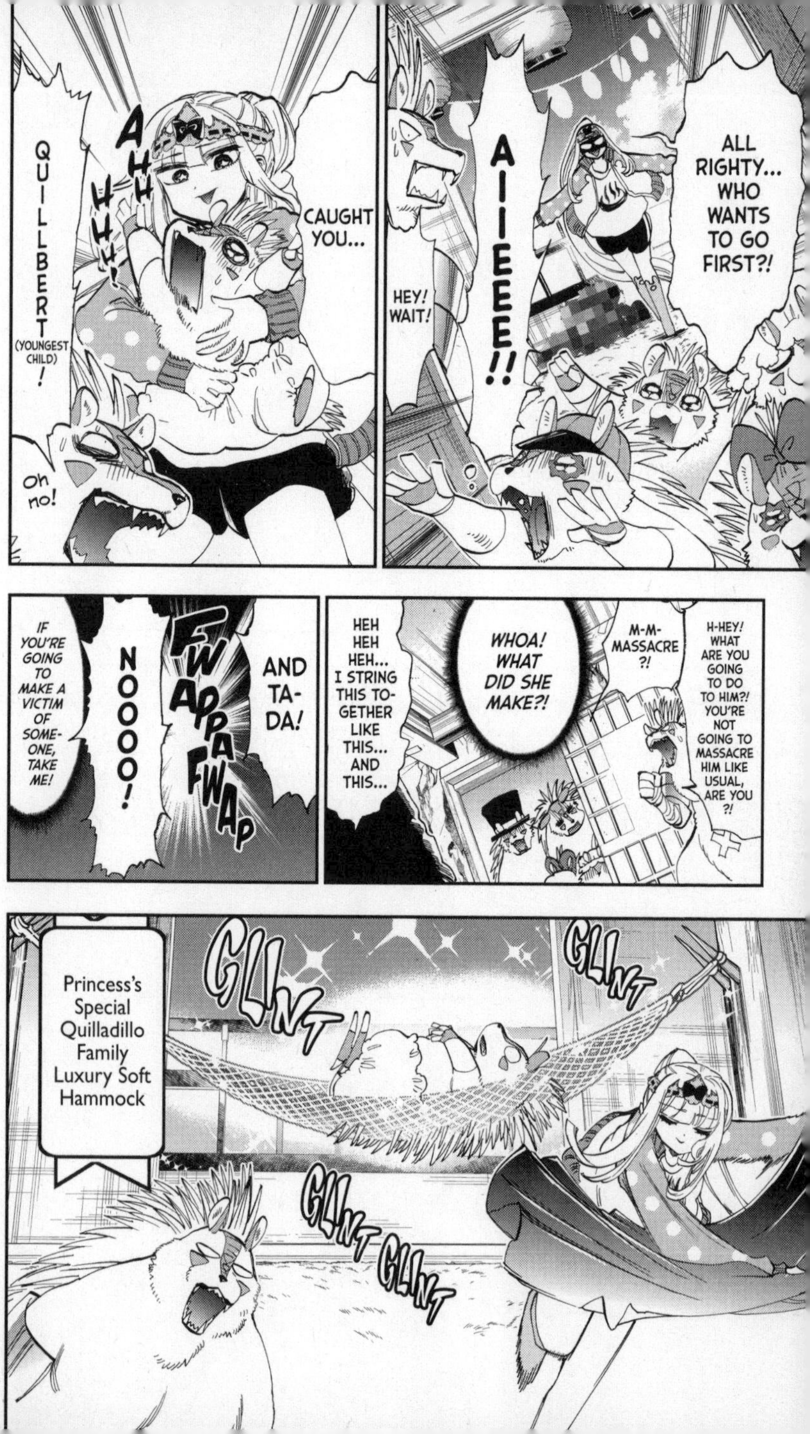
ALL RIGHTY... WHO WANTS TO GO FIRST?!
AIIEEE!!
HEY! WAIT!
CAUGHT YOU...
AHHHHH!
QUILLBERT (YOUNGEST CHILD)!
Oh no!
H-HEY! WHAT ARE YOU GOING TO DO TO HIM?! YOU'RE NOT GOING TO MASSACRE HIM LIKE USUAL, ARE YOU?!
M-M-MASSACRE?!
WHOA! WHAT DID SHE MAKE?!
HEH HEH HEH... I STRING THIS TO-GETHER LIKE THIS... AND THIS...
AND TA-DA!
FWAPPA FWAP
NOOOOO!
IF YOU'RE GOING TO MAKE A VICTIM OF SOME-ONE, TAKE ME!
GLINT
GLINT
Princess's Special Quilladillo Family Luxury Soft Hammock
GLINT GLINT GLINT

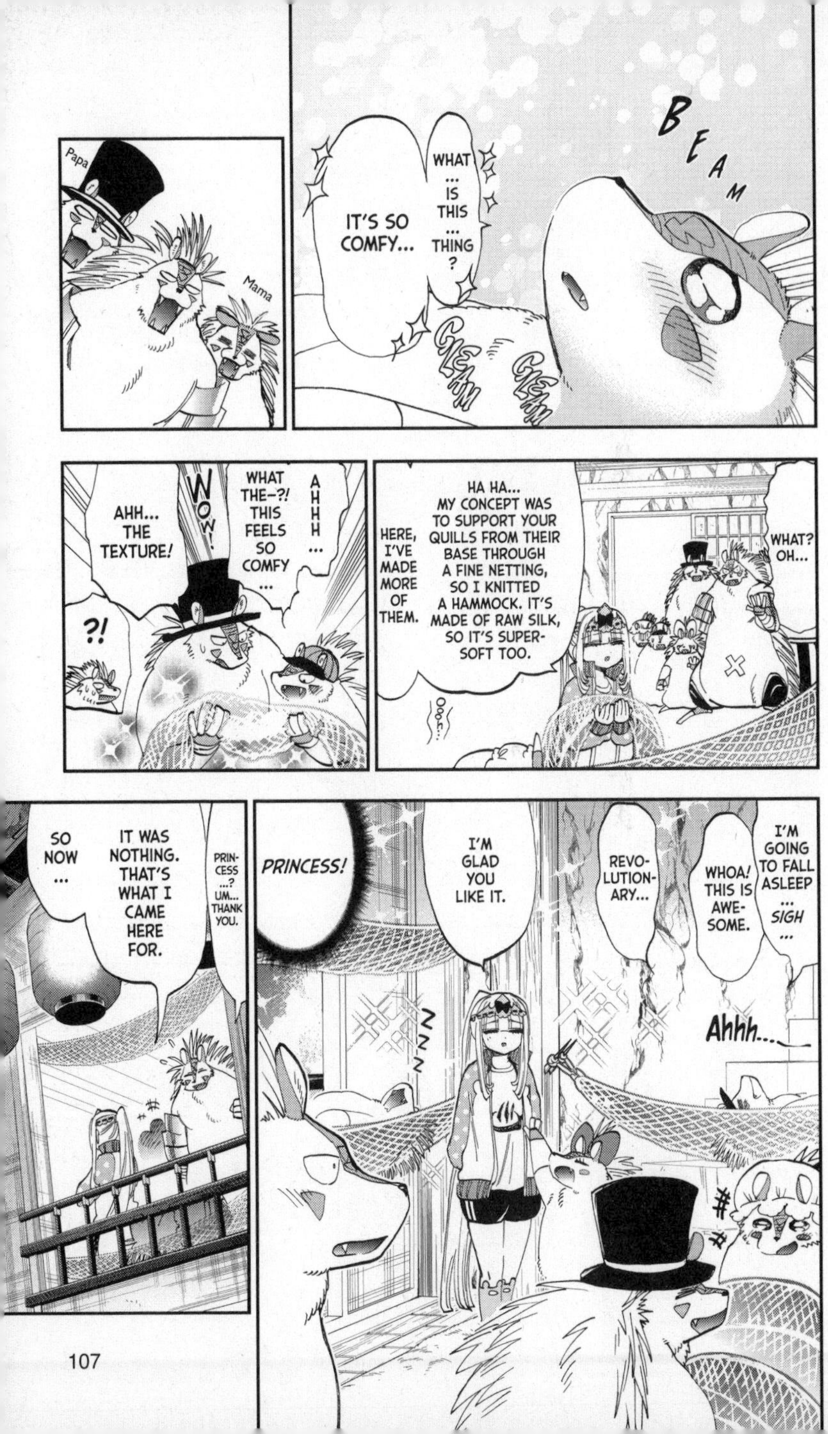
BEAM
WHAT ... IS THIS ... THING?
IT'S SO COMFY...
GLEAM GLEAM
Papa
Mama
WHAT? OH...
HA HA... MY CONCEPT WAS TO SUPPORT YOUR QUILLS FROM THEIR BASE THROUGH A FINE NETTING, SO I KNITTED A HAMMOCK. IT'S MADE OF RAW SILK, SO IT'S SUPER-SOFT TOO.
HERE, I'VE MADE MORE OF THEM.
OOOF...
AHHH...
WHAT THE–?! THIS FEELS SO COMFY...
WOW!
AHH... THE TEXTURE!
?!
I'M GOING TO FALL ASLEEP... SIGH...
WHOA! THIS IS AWESOME.
REVOLUTIONARY...
I'M GLAD YOU LIKE IT.
PRINCESS!
ZZZ
Ahhh...
PRINCESS...? UM... THANK YOU.
IT WAS NOTHING. THAT'S WHAT I CAME HERE FOR.
SO NOW...

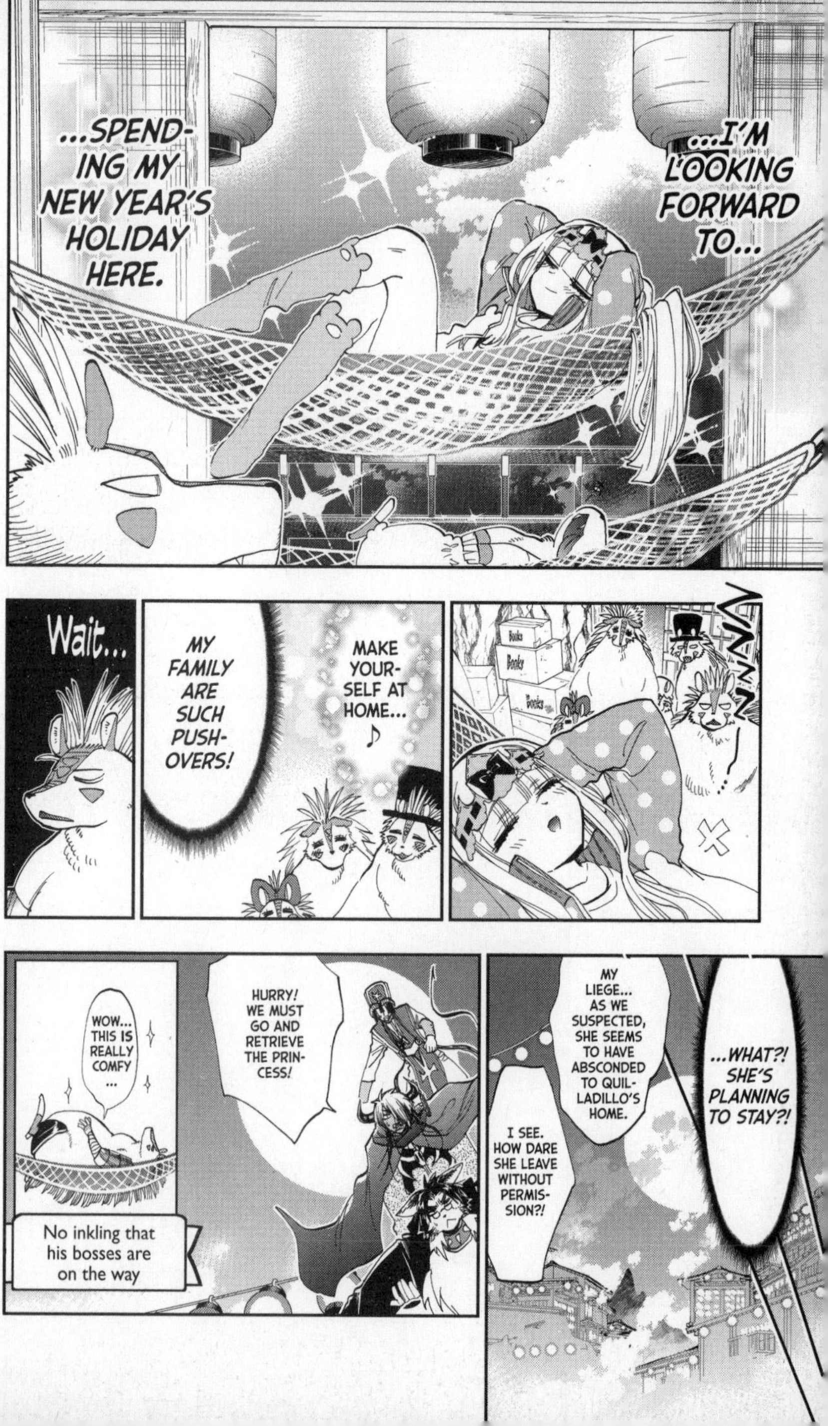

...I'M LOOKING FORWARD TO...
...SPENDING MY NEW YEAR'S HOLIDAY HERE.
MAKE YOURSELF AT HOME... ♪
MY FAMILY ARE SUCH PUSHOVERS!
Wait...
...WHAT?! SHE'S PLANNING TO STAY?!
MY LIEGE... AS WE SUSPECTED, SHE SEEMS TO HAVE ABSCONDED TO QUILLADILLO'S HOME.
I SEE. HOW DARE SHE LEAVE WITHOUT PERMISSION?!
HURRY! WE MUST GO AND RETRIEVE THE PRINCESS!
WOW... THIS IS REALLY COMFY...
No inkling that his bosses are on the way

TEACH ME DEMON CASTLE (QUESTION CORNER)

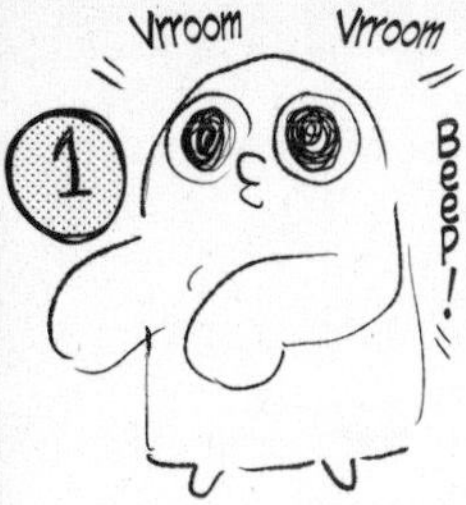
1
Vrroom
Vrroom
Beeep!

This is a corner for me to answer the questions I receive on Twitter.

Letters are fine too.

● Does sushi exist in the world of *Sleepy Princess in the Demon Castle*? I'd love to find out what everyone's favorite sushi is.

A. **Wonderful question!** It does exist, because I love sushi...

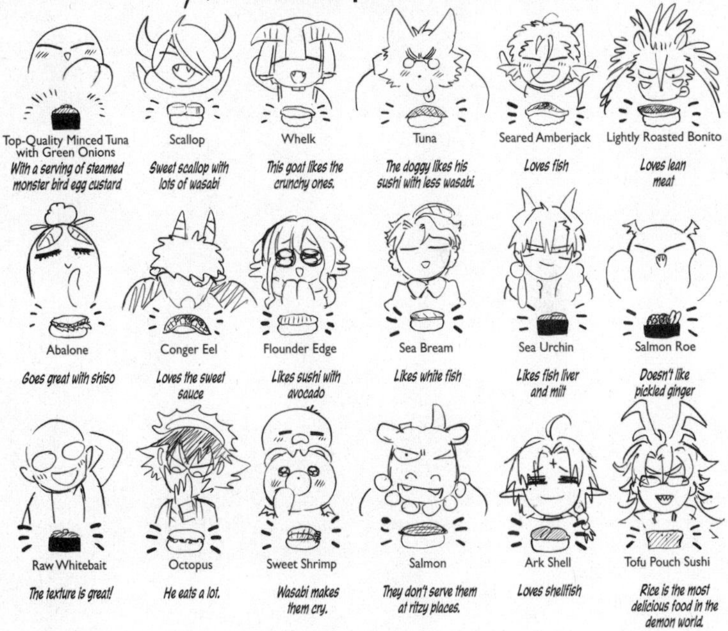
Top-Quality Minced Tuna with Green Onions
With a serving of steamed monster bird egg custard
Scallop
Sweet scallop with lots of wasabi
Whelk
This goat likes the crunchy ones.
Tuna
The doggy likes his sushi with less wasabi.
Seared Amberjack
Loves fish
Lightly Roasted Bonito
Loves lean meat
Abalone
Goes great with shiso
Conger Eel
Loves the sweet sauce
Flounder Edge
Likes sushi with avocado
Sea Bream
Likes white fish
Sea Urchin
Likes fish liver and milt
Salmon Roe
Doesn't like pickled ginger
Raw Whitebait
The texture is great!
Octopus
He eats a lot.
Sweet Shrimp
Wasabi makes them cry.
Salmon
They don't serve them at ritzy places.
Ark Shell
Loves shellfish
Tofu Pouch Sushi
Rice is the most delicious food in the demon world.

● Why didn't Poseidon want to wear underwear when he transformed into his Marine Day form?

A. He doesn't like to wear things that are a different size from his usual clothes.

● Who is Yellow Kosui Pear from the Demon Castle roster?

A. Well, kosui is a type of pear...

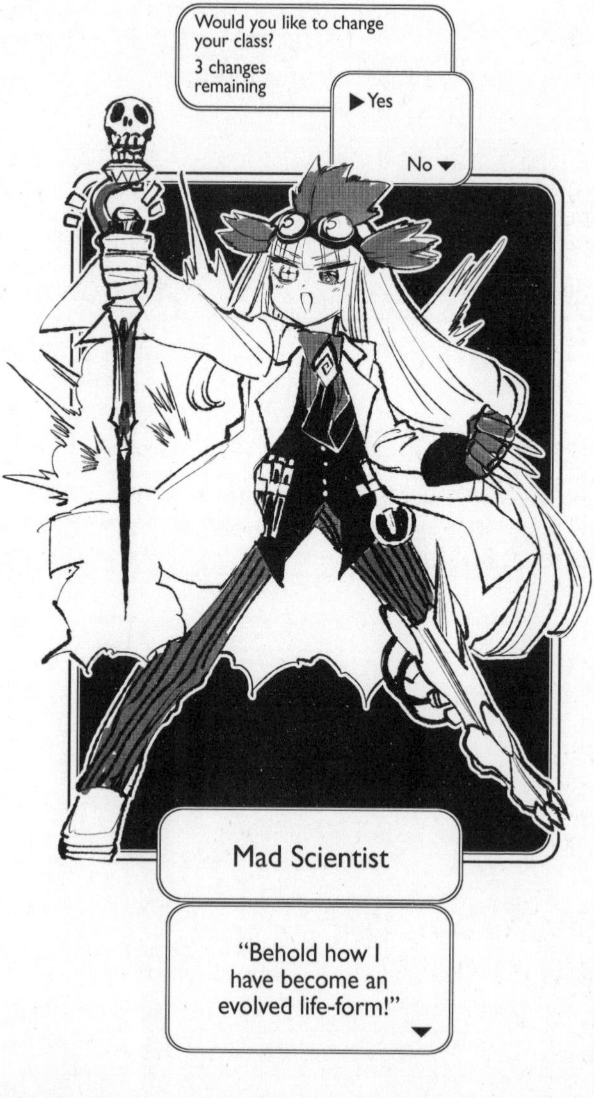
Would you like to change your class?
3 changes remaining
▶Yes
No ▼
Mad Scientist
"Behold how I have become an evolved life-form!"

179th Night: Living the Dream: End-of-the-Year Hot Springs Resort Vacation

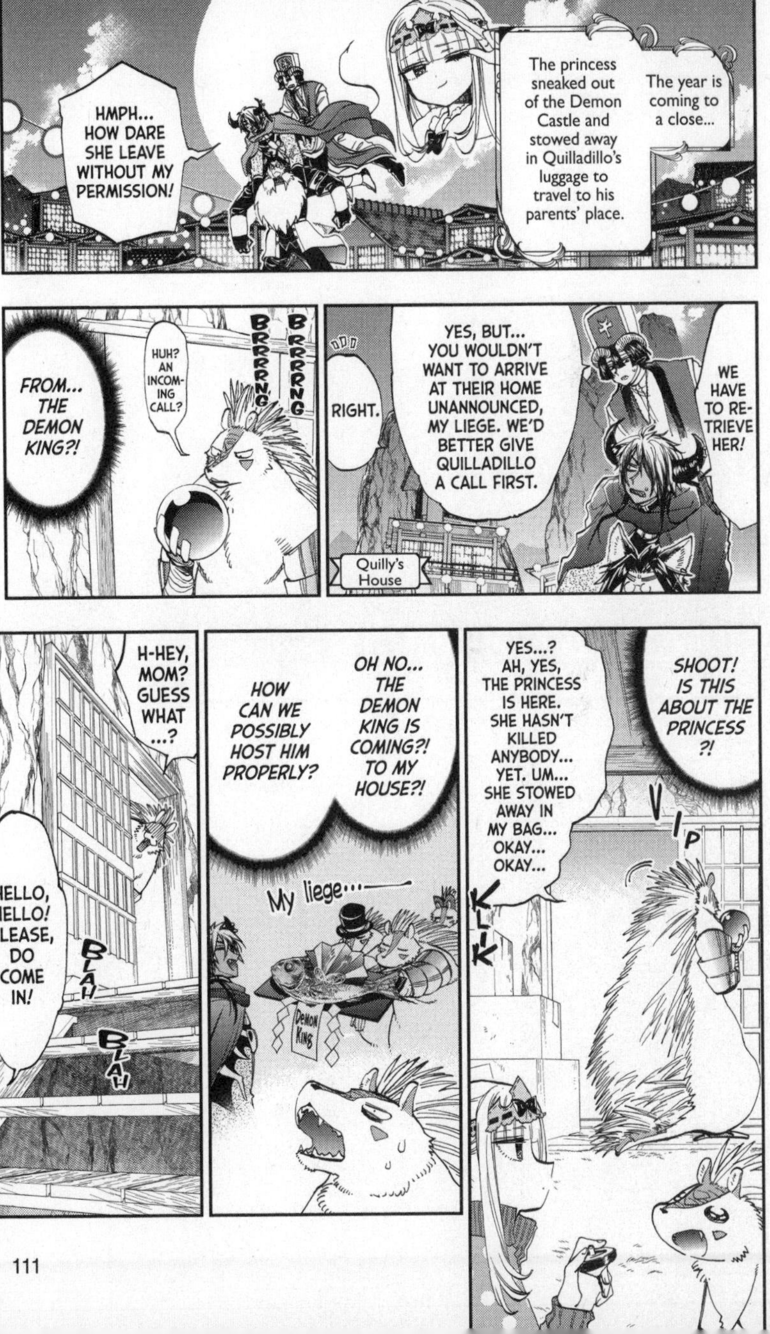

The year is coming to a close...
The princess sneaked out of the Demon Castle and stowed away in Quilladillo's luggage to travel to his parents' place.
HMPH... HOW DARE SHE LEAVE WITHOUT MY PERMISSION!
WE HAVE TO RETRIEVE HER!
YES, BUT... YOU WOULDN'T WANT TO ARRIVE AT THEIR HOME UNANNOUNCED, MY LIEGE. WE'D BETTER GIVE QUILLADILLO A CALL FIRST.
RIGHT.
Quilly's House
BRRRRNG BRRRRNG
HUH? AN INCOMING CALL?
FROM... THE DEMON KING?!
SHOOT! IS THIS ABOUT THE PRINCESS?!
VIP
YES...? AH, YES, THE PRINCESS IS HERE. SHE HASN'T KILLED ANYBODY... YET. UM... SHE STOWED AWAY IN MY BAG... OKAY... OKAY...
KLIK
OH NO... THE DEMON KING IS COMING?! TO MY HOUSE?!
HOW CAN WE POSSIBLY HOST HIM PROPERLY?
My liege...
DEMON KING
H-HEY, MOM? GUESS WHAT...?
HELLO, HELLO! PLEASE, DO COME IN!
BLAH BLAH

179th Night: Living the Dream: End-of-the-Year Hot Springs Resort Vacation

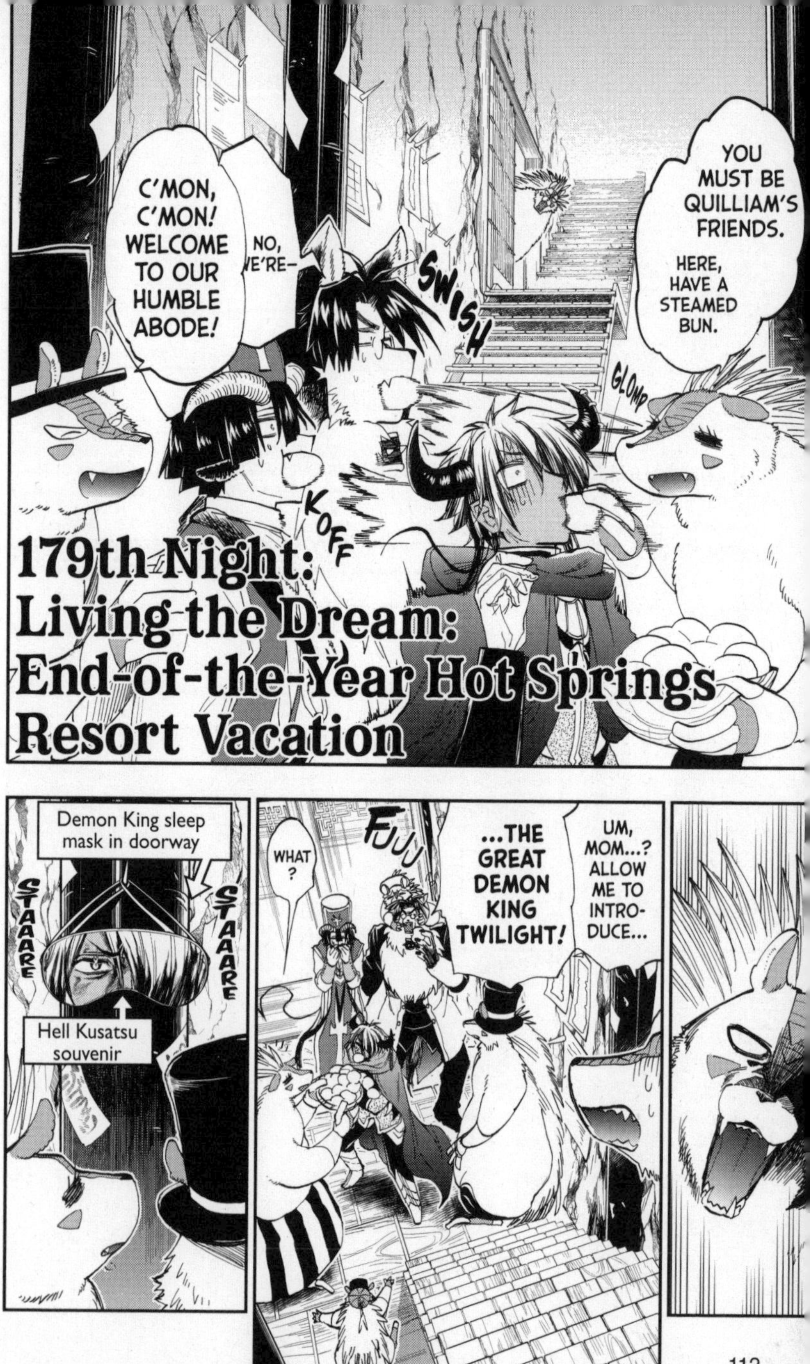
YOU MUST BE QUILLIAM'S FRIENDS.
HERE, HAVE A STEAMED BUN.
GLOMP
SWISH
C'MON, C'MON! WELCOME TO OUR HUMBLE ABODE!
NO, WE'RE—
KOFF
UM, MOM...? ALLOW ME TO INTRO-DUCE...
...THE GREAT DEMON KING TWILIGHT!
FUUU
WHAT?
Demon King sleep mask in doorway
STAAARE
STAAARE
Hell Kusatsu souvenir

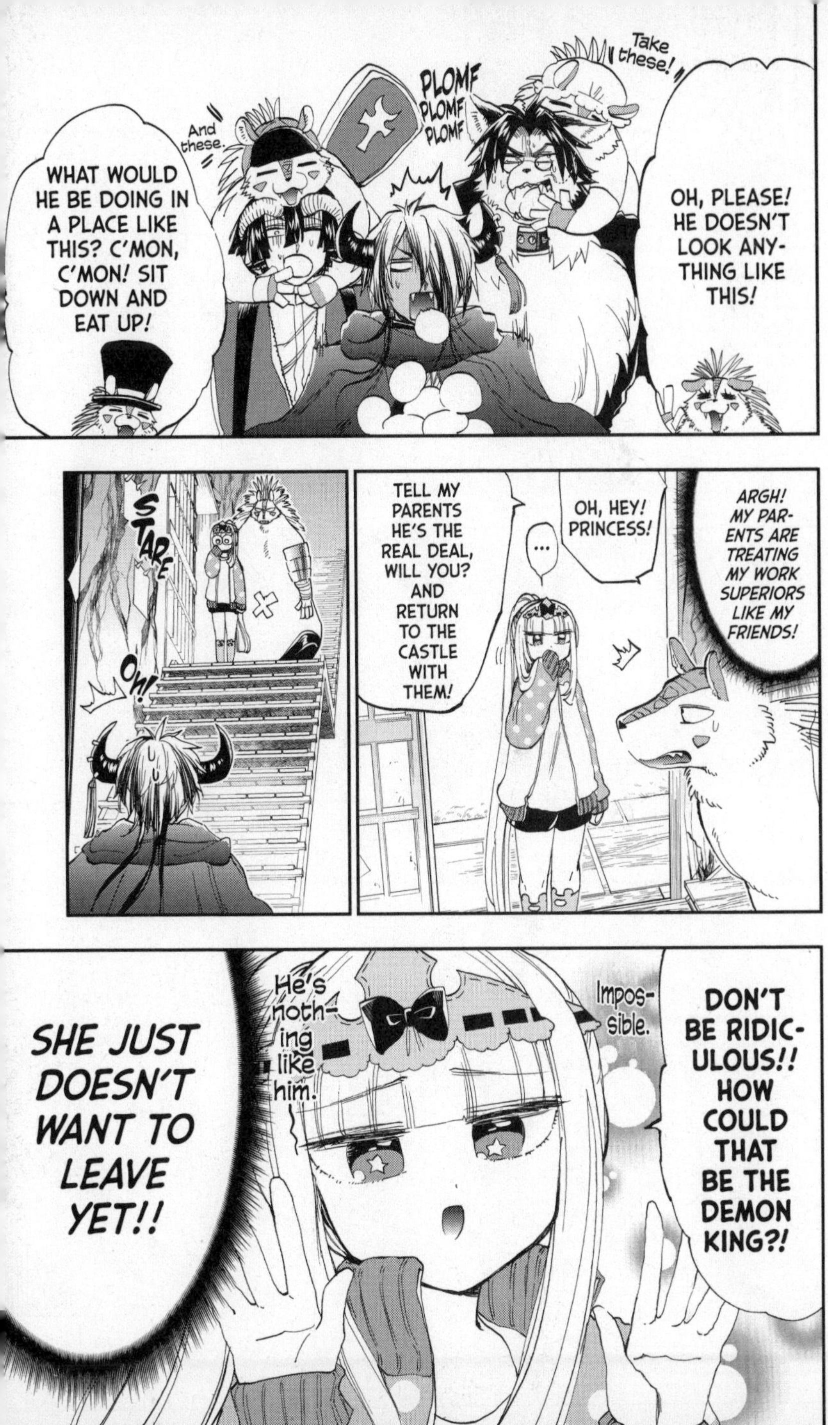
Take these!
OH, PLEASE! HE DOESN'T LOOK ANYTHING LIKE THIS!
PLOMF PLOMF PLOMF
And these.
WHAT WOULD HE BE DOING IN A PLACE LIKE THIS? C'MON, C'MON! SIT DOWN AND EAT UP!
ARGH! MY PARENTS ARE TREATING MY WORK SUPERIORS LIKE MY FRIENDS!
OH, HEY! PRINCESS!
...
TELL MY PARENTS HE'S THE REAL DEAL, WILL YOU? AND RETURN TO THE CASTLE WITH THEM!
STARE
OH!
DON'T BE RIDICULOUS!! HOW COULD THAT BE THE DEMON KING?!
Impossible.
He's nothing like him.
SHE JUST DOESN'T WANT TO LEAVE YET!!

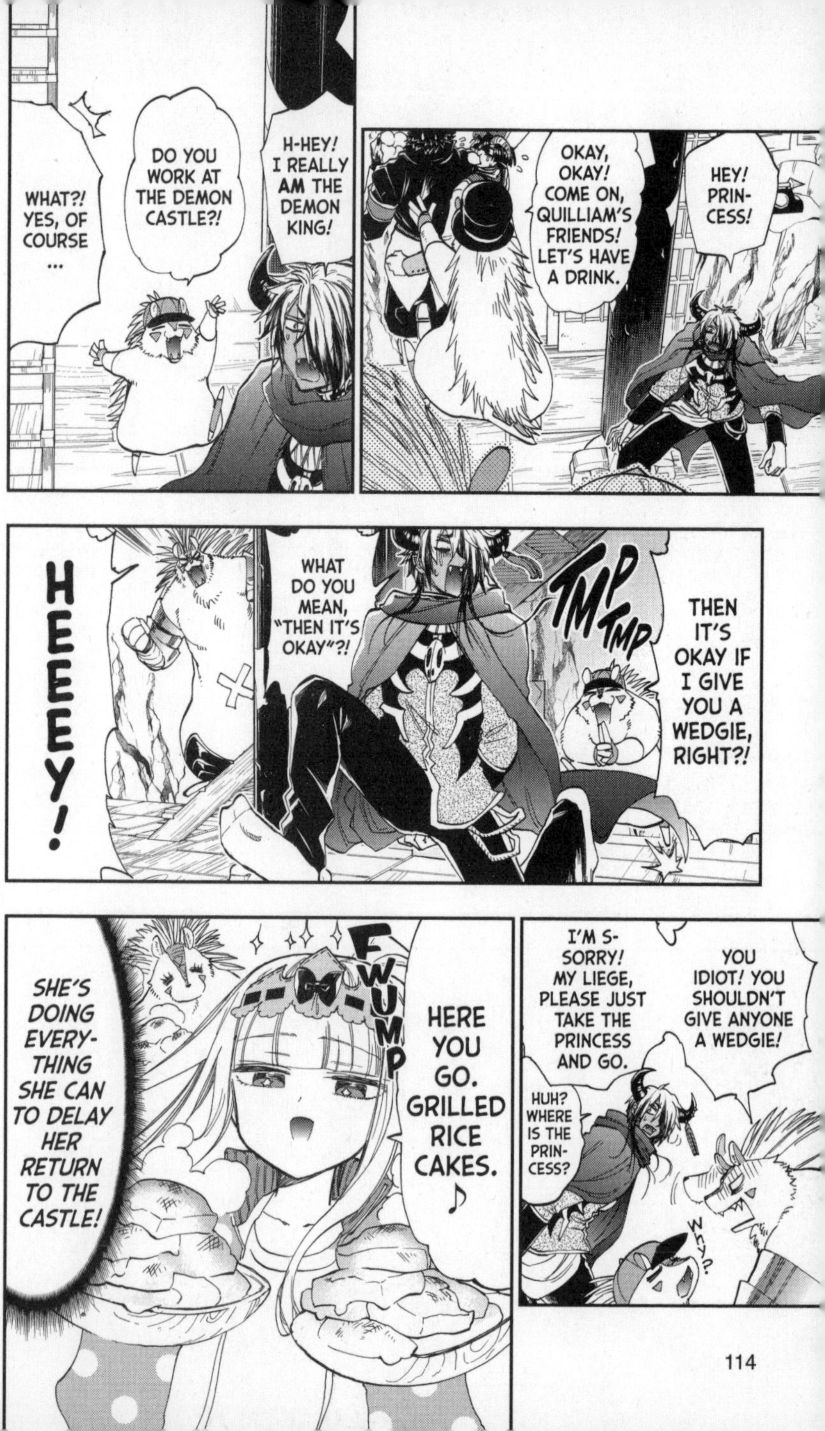
HEY! PRINCESS!
OKAY, OKAY! COME ON, QUILLIAM'S FRIENDS! LET'S HAVE A DRINK.
H-HEY! I REALLY AM THE DEMON KING!
DO YOU WORK AT THE DEMON CASTLE?!
WHAT?! YES, OF COURSE ...
THEN IT'S OKAY IF I GIVE YOU A WEDGIE, RIGHT?!
TMP TMP
WHAT DO YOU MEAN, "THEN IT'S OKAY"?!
HEEEEY!
YOU IDIOT! YOU SHOULDN'T GIVE ANYONE A WEDGIE!
I'M S-SORRY! MY LIEGE, PLEASE JUST TAKE THE PRINCESS AND GO.
HUH? WHERE IS THE PRINCESS?
WHY?
FWUMP
HERE YOU GO. GRILLED RICE CAKES. ♪
SHE'S DOING EVERYTHING SHE CAN TO DELAY HER RETURN TO THE CASTLE!

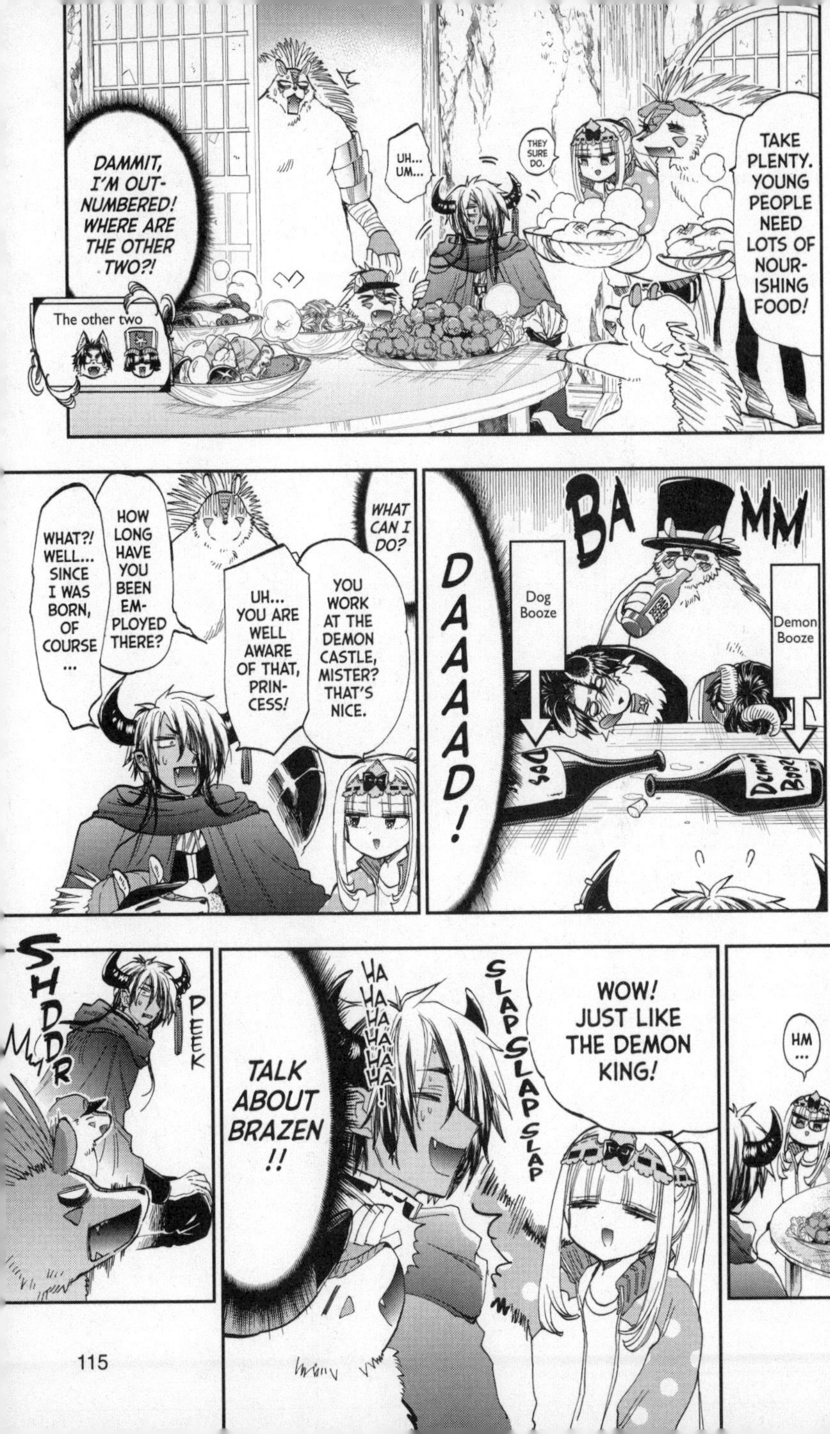
TAKE PLENTY. YOUNG PEOPLE NEED LOTS OF NOURISHING FOOD!
THEY SURE DO.
UH... UM...
DAMMIT, I'M OUTNUMBERED! WHERE ARE THE OTHER TWO?!
The other two
BAMM
Demon Booze
Dog Booze
DAAAAAD!
WHAT CAN I DO?
YOU WORK AT THE DEMON CASTLE, MISTER? THAT'S NICE.
UH... YOU ARE WELL AWARE OF THAT, PRINCESS!
HOW LONG HAVE YOU BEEN EMPLOYED THERE?
WHAT?! WELL... SINCE I WAS BORN, OF COURSE...
HM...
WOW! JUST LIKE THE DEMON KING!
SLAP SLAP SLAP SLAP
HA HA HA HA HA HA!
TALK ABOUT BRAZEN!!
PEEK
SHDDR

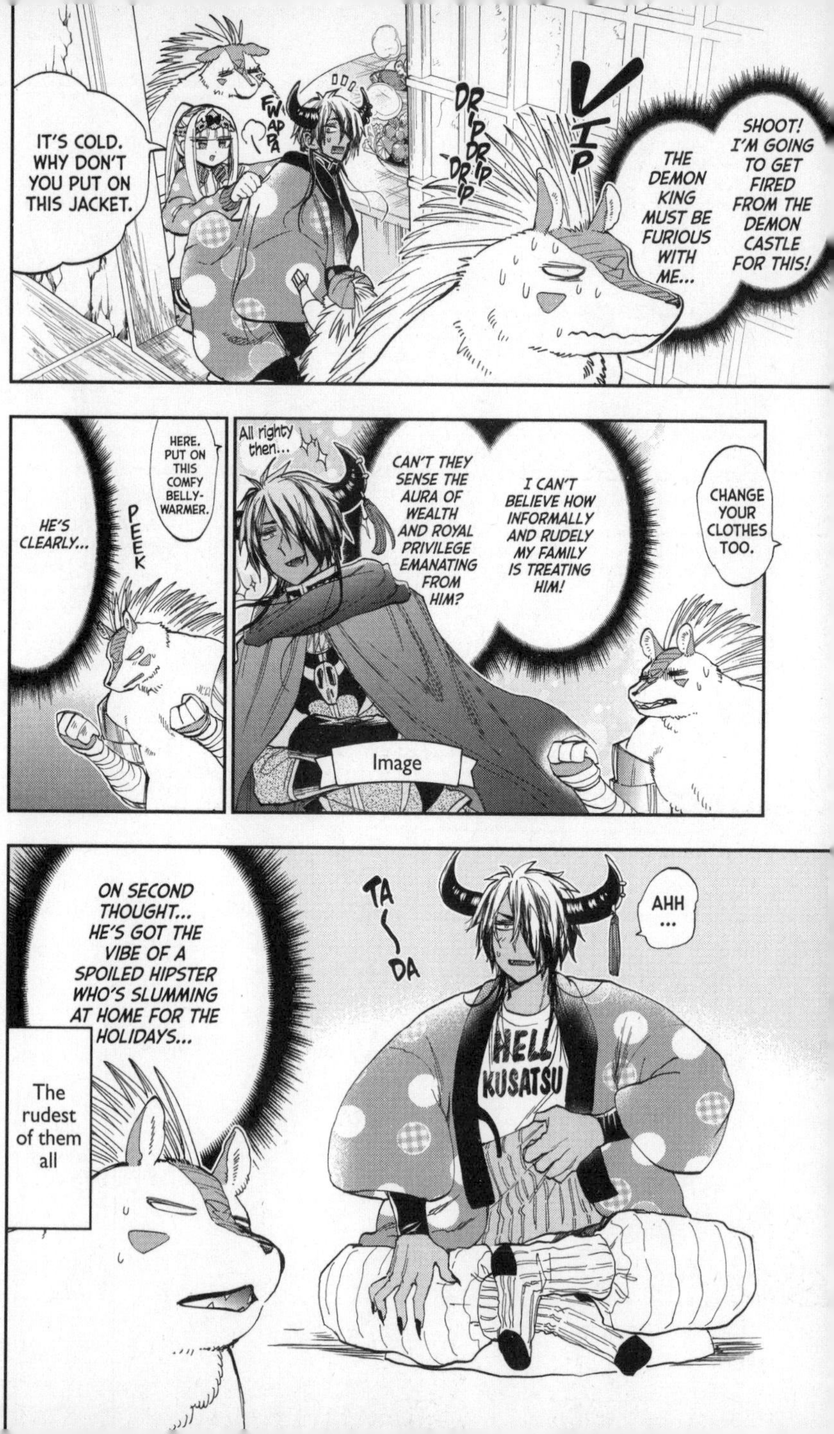
VIP
SHOOT! I'M GOING TO GET FIRED FROM THE DEMON CASTLE FOR THIS!
THE DEMON KING MUST BE FURIOUS WITH ME...
DRIP DRIP DRIP
FWAP PA
IT'S COLD. WHY DON'T YOU PUT ON THIS JACKET.
CHANGE YOUR CLOTHES TOO.
I CAN'T BELIEVE HOW INFORMALLY AND RUDELY MY FAMILY IS TREATING HIM!
CAN'T THEY SENSE THE AURA OF WEALTH AND ROYAL PRIVILEGE EMANATING FROM HIM?
All righty then...
Image
HERE. PUT ON THIS COMFY BELLY-WARMER.
PEEK
HE'S CLEARLY...
AHH ...
TA-DA
ON SECOND THOUGHT... HE'S GOT THE VIBE OF A SPOILED HIPSTER WHO'S SLUMMING AT HOME FOR THE HOLIDAYS...
HELL KUSATSU
The rudest of them all

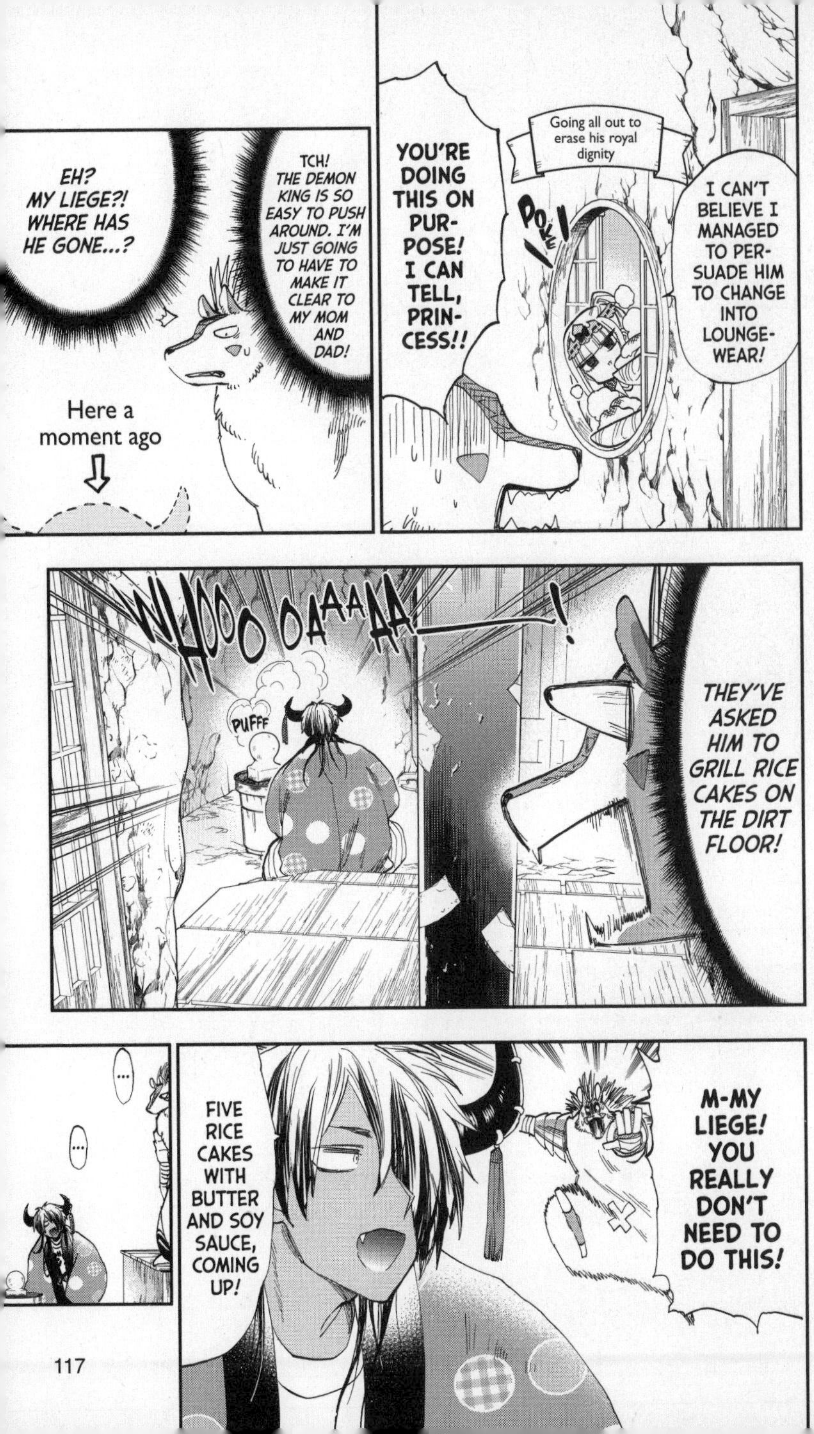
Going all out to erase his royal dignity
I CAN'T BELIEVE I MANAGED TO PERSUADE HIM TO CHANGE INTO LOUNGEWEAR!
POKE
YOU'RE DOING THIS ON PURPOSE! I CAN TELL, PRINCESS!!
TCH! THE DEMON KING IS SO EASY TO PUSH AROUND. I'M JUST GOING TO HAVE TO MAKE IT CLEAR TO MY MOM AND DAD!
EH? MY LIEGE?! WHERE HAS HE GONE...?
Here a moment ago
THEY'VE ASKED HIM TO GRILL RICE CAKES ON THE DIRT FLOOR!
WHOOO OAAAAA—!
PUFFF
M-MY LIEGE! YOU REALLY DON'T NEED TO DO THIS!
FIVE RICE CAKES WITH BUTTER AND SOY SAUCE, COMING UP!
...
...

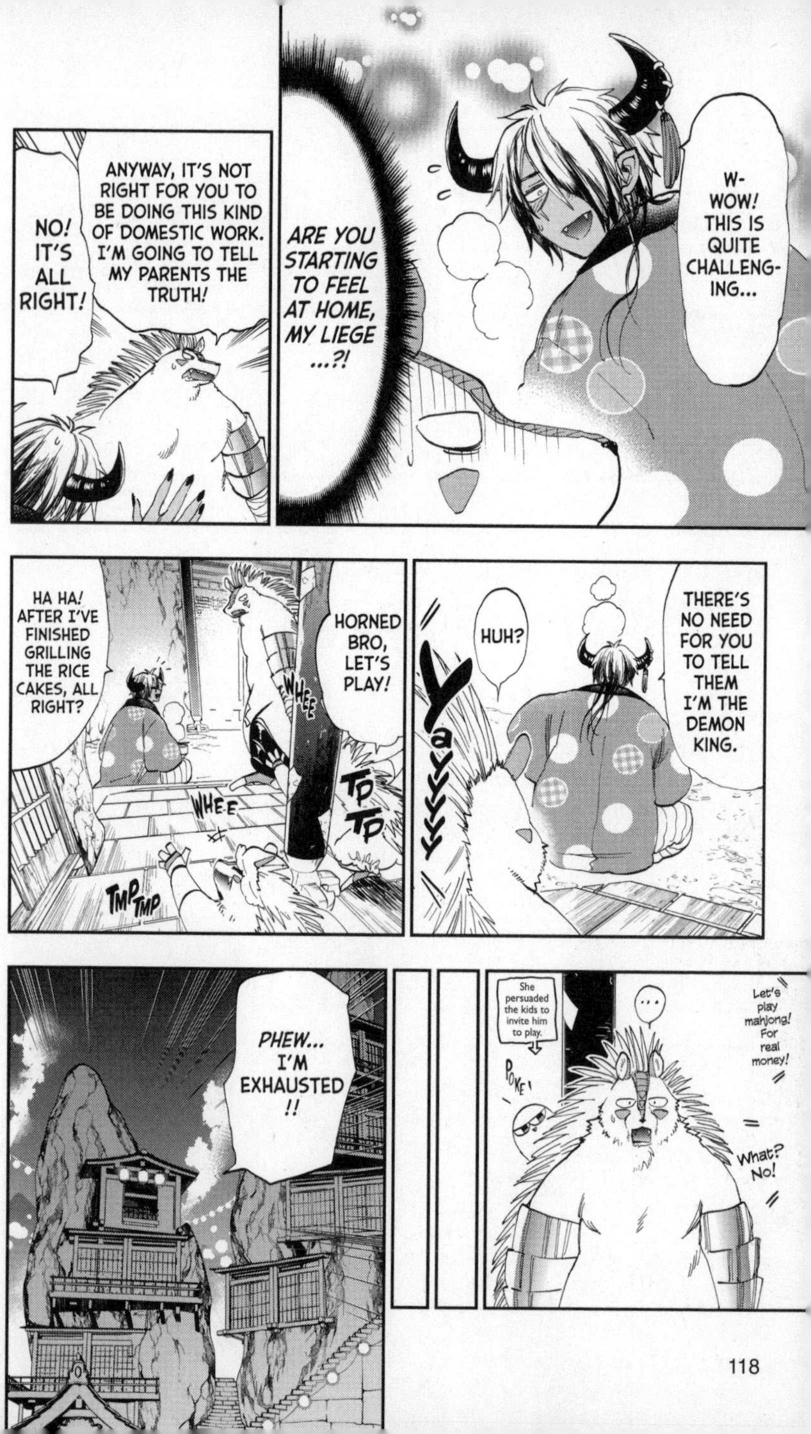
W-WOW! THIS IS QUITE CHALLENGING...
ARE YOU STARTING TO FEEL AT HOME, MY LIEGE ...?!
ANYWAY, IT'S NOT RIGHT FOR YOU TO BE DOING THIS KIND OF DOMESTIC WORK. I'M GOING TO TELL MY PARENTS THE TRUTH!
NO! IT'S ALL RIGHT!
THERE'S NO NEED FOR YOU TO TELL THEM I'M THE DEMON KING.
HUH?
Yaaaaaaa
HORNED BRO, LET'S PLAY!
WHEE
HA HA! AFTER I'VE FINISHED GRILLING THE RICE CAKES, ALL RIGHT?
TP TP
WHEE
TMP TMP
Let's play mahjong! For real money!
...
She persuaded the kids to invite him to play.
POKE
What? No!
PHEW... I'M EXHAUSTED !!

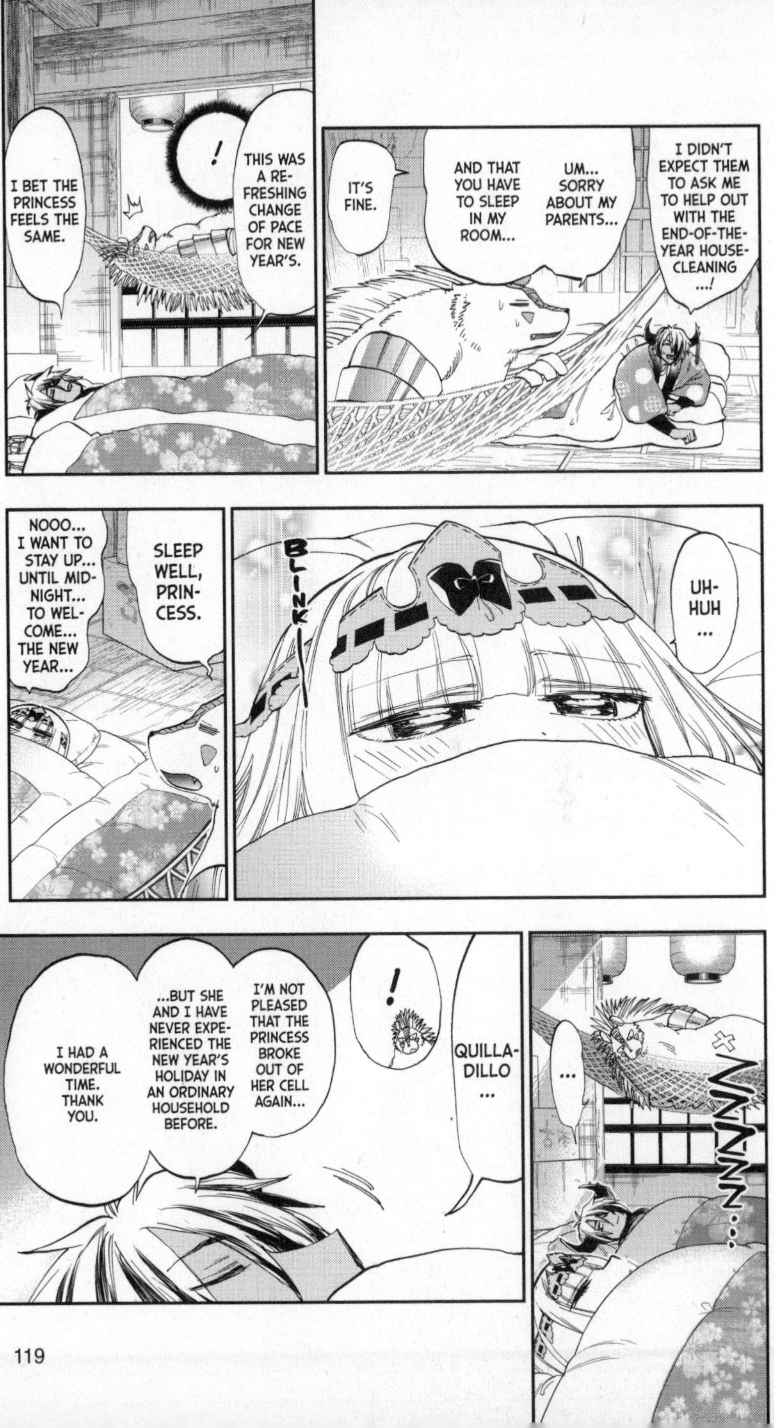
I DIDN'T EXPECT THEM TO ASK ME TO HELP OUT WITH THE END-OF-THE-YEAR HOUSE-CLEANING ...!
UM... SORRY ABOUT MY PARENTS...
AND THAT YOU HAVE TO SLEEP IN MY ROOM...
IT'S FINE.
THIS WAS A REFRESHING CHANGE OF PACE FOR NEW YEAR'S.
!
I BET THE PRINCESS FEELS THE SAME.
UH-HUH ...
BLINK
SLEEP WELL, PRINCESS.
NOOO... I WANT TO STAY UP... UNTIL MIDNIGHT... TO WELCOME... THE NEW YEAR...
ZZZZZ...
...
QUILLADILLO ...
!
I'M NOT PLEASED THAT THE PRINCESS BROKE OUT OF HER CELL AGAIN...
...BUT SHE AND I HAVE NEVER EXPERIENCED THE NEW YEAR'S HOLIDAY IN AN ORDINARY HOUSEHOLD BEFORE.
I HAD A WONDERFUL TIME. THANK YOU.

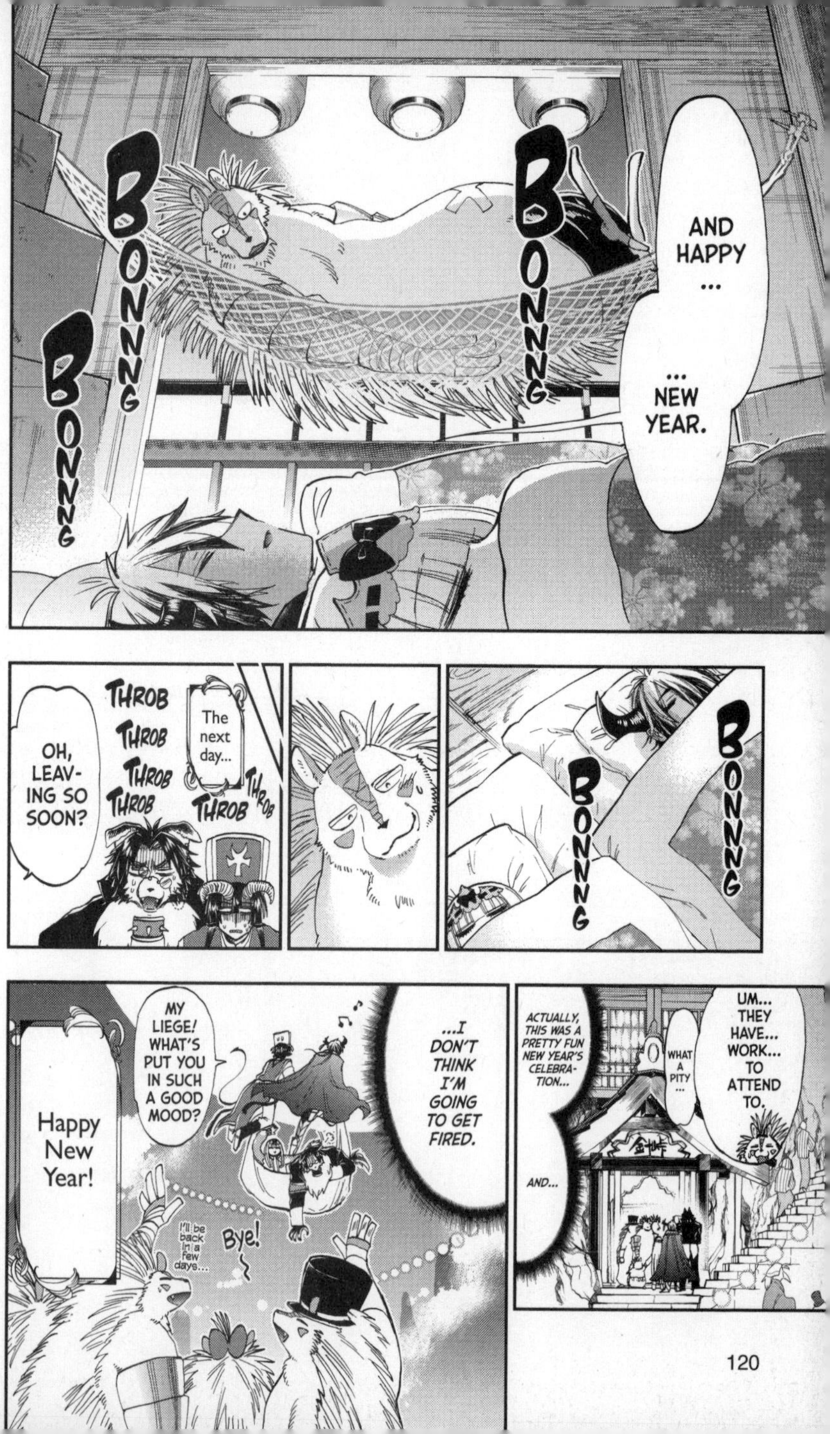
BONNNG
BONNNG
BONNNG
AND HAPPY ...
... NEW YEAR.
BONNNG
BONNNG
The next day...
THROB THROB THROB THROB THROB THROB
OH, LEAV-ING SO SOON?
UM... THEY HAVE... WORK... TO ATTEND TO.
WHAT A PITY ...
ACTUALLY, THIS WAS A PRETTY FUN NEW YEAR'S CELEBRA-TION...
AND...
...I DON'T THINK I'M GOING TO GET FIRED.
MY LIEGE! WHAT'S PUT YOU IN SUCH A GOOD MOOD?
Bye!
I'll be back in a few days...
Happy New Year!

TEACH ME DEMON CASTLE (QUESTION CORNER)

2

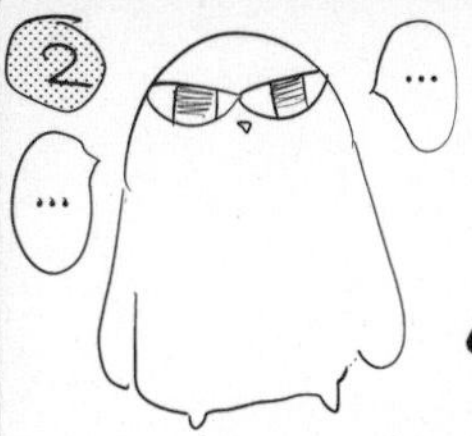
...
...

● The goat took the princess's handmade pillow. What did he do with it?

A He has several of the princess's deluxe pillows and swaps them out.

● A question for Narmie: "I'm curious, do you have a girlfriend, Narmie?"

A My girlfriend is the nation of Goodereste.

● How large can a Monster Bird grow in the human world?

A Before the breeding program was established, there was an incident in which a single Monster Bird filled an entire canyon.

● Both Comolis and Queen Nemlis have royal stars in their eyes. Are those stars something magical that appears in your eyes after you become royalty? Or were the current king and queen already of royal blood and somehow related?

A There are a vast number of human royalty. The king and queen are more distantly related than second cousins.

● Who is Eggplant Seal fonder of, Princess Syalis or Poseidon?

A

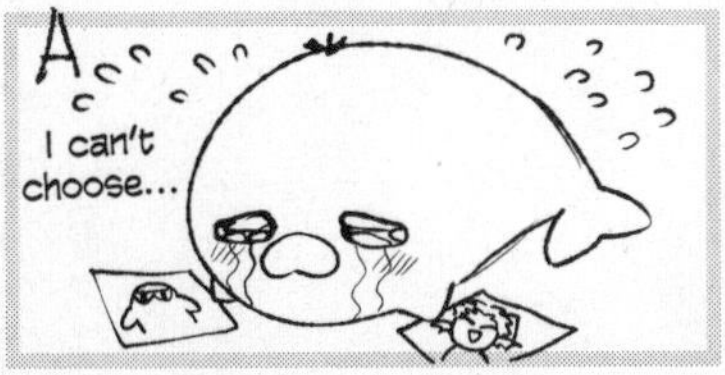
I can't choose...

● Cer, Ber and Rus. Which is which?

A

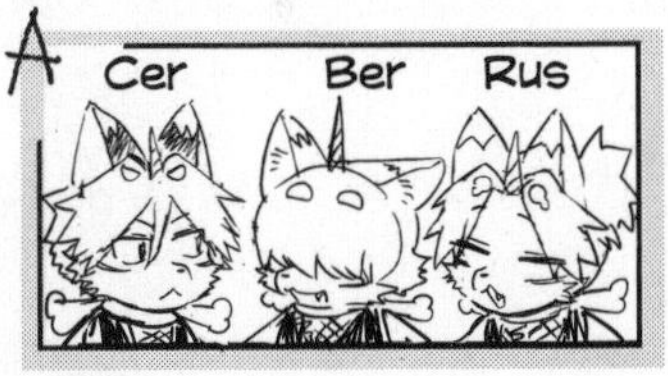
Cer
Ber
Rus

● Is the princess left-handed or ambidextrous?

A Left-handed. Left-handedness is more common in the *Sleepy Princess* world.

● Is the princess still getting herself killed once a week or so?

A Rest assured, she's still getting herself killed.

● Regarding the female troops who appeared in 18th Night, will we meet other members besides Harpy?

A No plans at the moment.

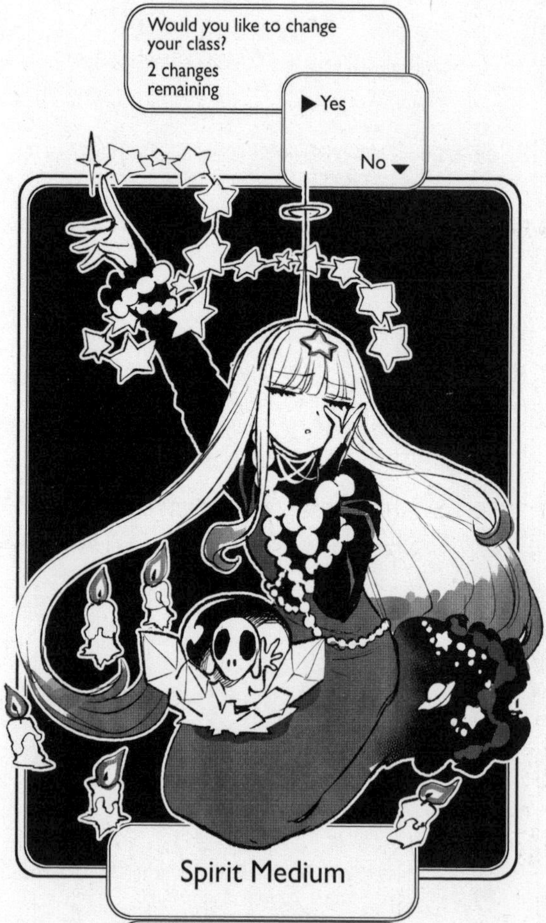
Would you like to change your class?
2 changes remaining
▶ Yes
No
Spirit Medium
"I can hear them... They're talking to me!!"

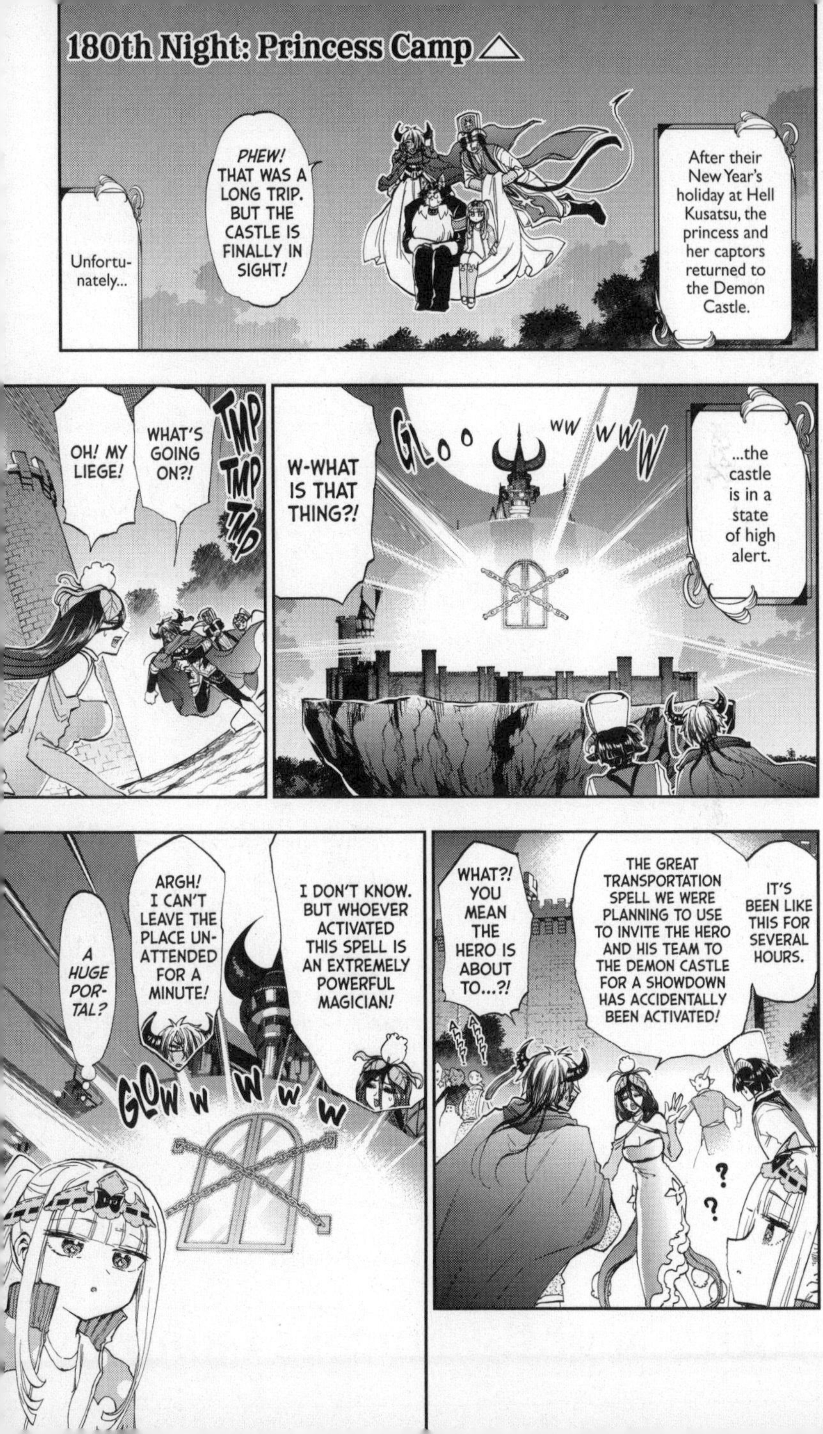
180th Night: Princess Camp △
After their New Year's holiday at Hell Kusatsu, the princess and her captors returned to the Demon Castle.
PHEW! THAT WAS A LONG TRIP. BUT THE CASTLE IS FINALLY IN SIGHT!
Unfortunately...
...the castle is in a state of high alert.
GLOO WW WWW
W-WHAT IS THAT THING?!
TMP TMP TMP
WHAT'S GOING ON?!
OH! MY LIEGE!
IT'S BEEN LIKE THIS FOR SEVERAL HOURS.
THE GREAT TRANSPORTATION SPELL WE WERE PLANNING TO USE TO INVITE THE HERO AND HIS TEAM TO THE DEMON CASTLE FOR A SHOWDOWN HAS ACCIDENTALLY BEEN ACTIVATED!
WHAT?! YOU MEAN THE HERO IS ABOUT TO...?!
I DON'T KNOW. BUT WHOEVER ACTIVATED THIS SPELL IS AN EXTREMELY POWERFUL MAGICIAN!
ARGH! I CAN'T LEAVE THE PLACE UNATTENDED FOR A MINUTE!
A HUGE PORTAL?
GLOW W W W W

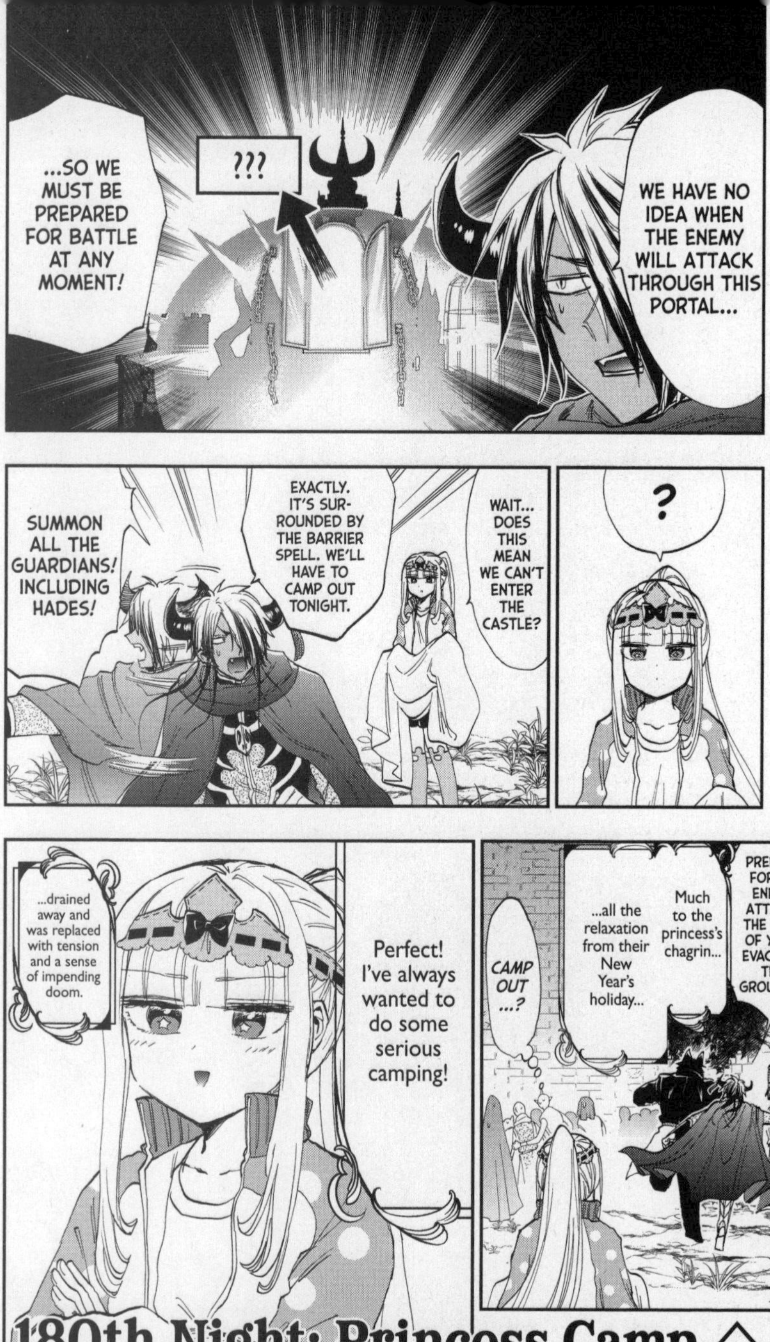
WE HAVE NO IDEA WHEN THE ENEMY WILL ATTACK THROUGH THIS PORTAL...
???
...SO WE MUST BE PREPARED FOR BATTLE AT ANY MOMENT!
?
WAIT... DOES THIS MEAN WE CAN'T ENTER THE CASTLE?
EXACTLY. IT'S SURROUNDED BY THE BARRIER SPELL. WE'LL HAVE TO CAMP OUT TONIGHT.
SUMMON ALL THE GUARDIANS! INCLUDING HADES!
PREPARE FOR AN ENEMY ATTACK! THE REST OF YOU— EVACUATE THE GROUNDS!
Much to the princess's chagrin...
...all the relaxation from their New Year's holiday...
CAMP OUT ...?
...drained away and was replaced with tension and a sense of impending doom.
Perfect! I've always wanted to do some serious camping!

180th Night: Princess Camp △

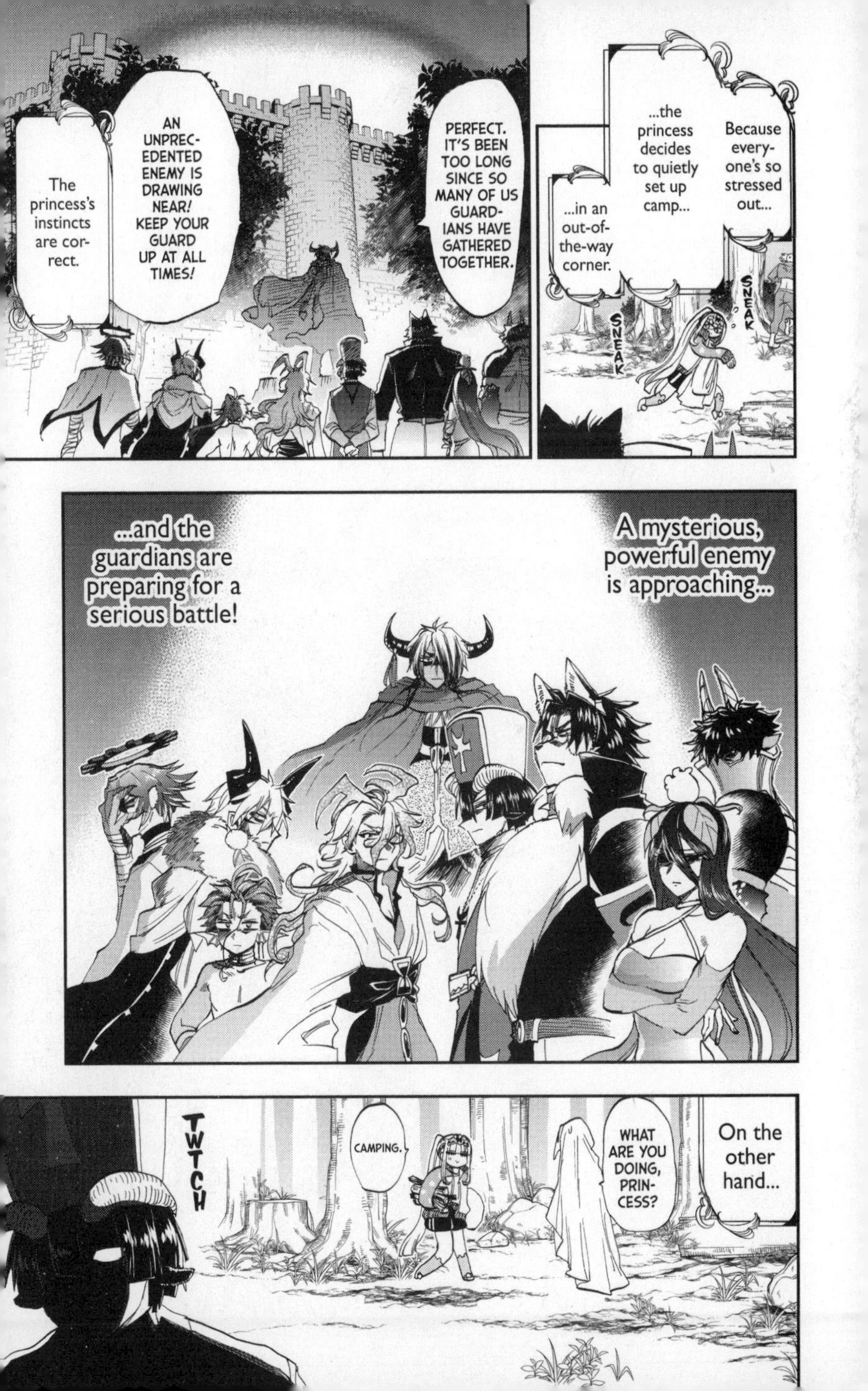
Because everyone's so stressed out...
...the princess decides to quietly set up camp...
...in an out-of-the-way corner.
SNEAK
SNEAK
PERFECT. IT'S BEEN TOO LONG SINCE SO MANY OF US GUARDIANS HAVE GATHERED TOGETHER.
AN UNPRECEDENTED ENEMY IS DRAWING NEAR! KEEP YOUR GUARD UP AT ALL TIMES!
The princess's instincts are correct.
A mysterious, powerful enemy is approaching...
...and the guardians are preparing for a serious battle!
On the other hand...
WHAT ARE YOU DOING, PRINCESS?
CAMPING.
TWTCH

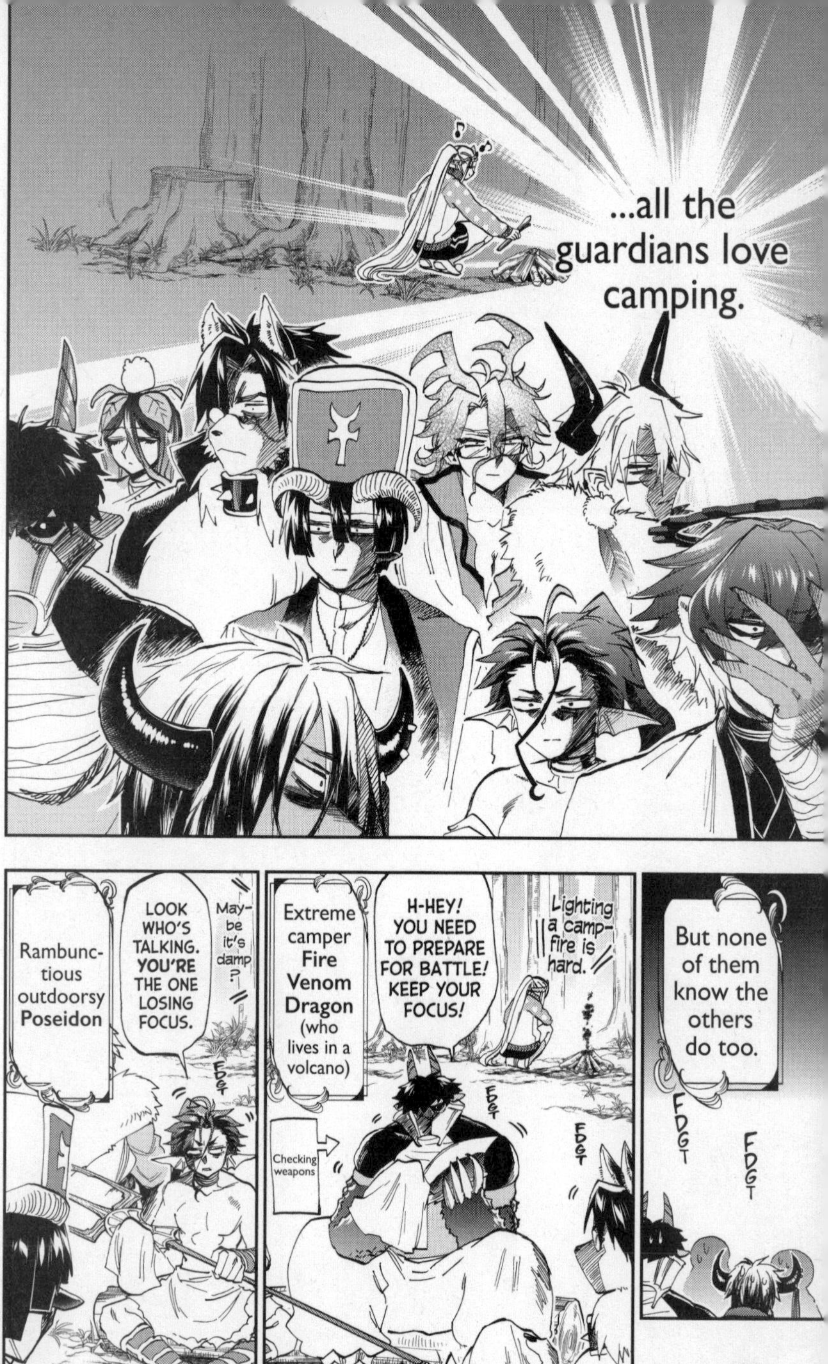
...all the guardians love camping.
But none of them know the others do too.
FDGT
FDGT
Lighting a campfire is hard.
H-HEY! YOU NEED TO PREPARE FOR BATTLE! KEEP YOUR FOCUS!
Extreme camper **Fire Venom Dragon** (who lives in a volcano)
FDGT
FDGT
Checking weapons
Maybe it's damp?
LOOK WHO'S TALKING. **YOU'RE** THE ONE LOSING FOCUS.
Rambunctious outdoorsy **Poseidon**
FDGT

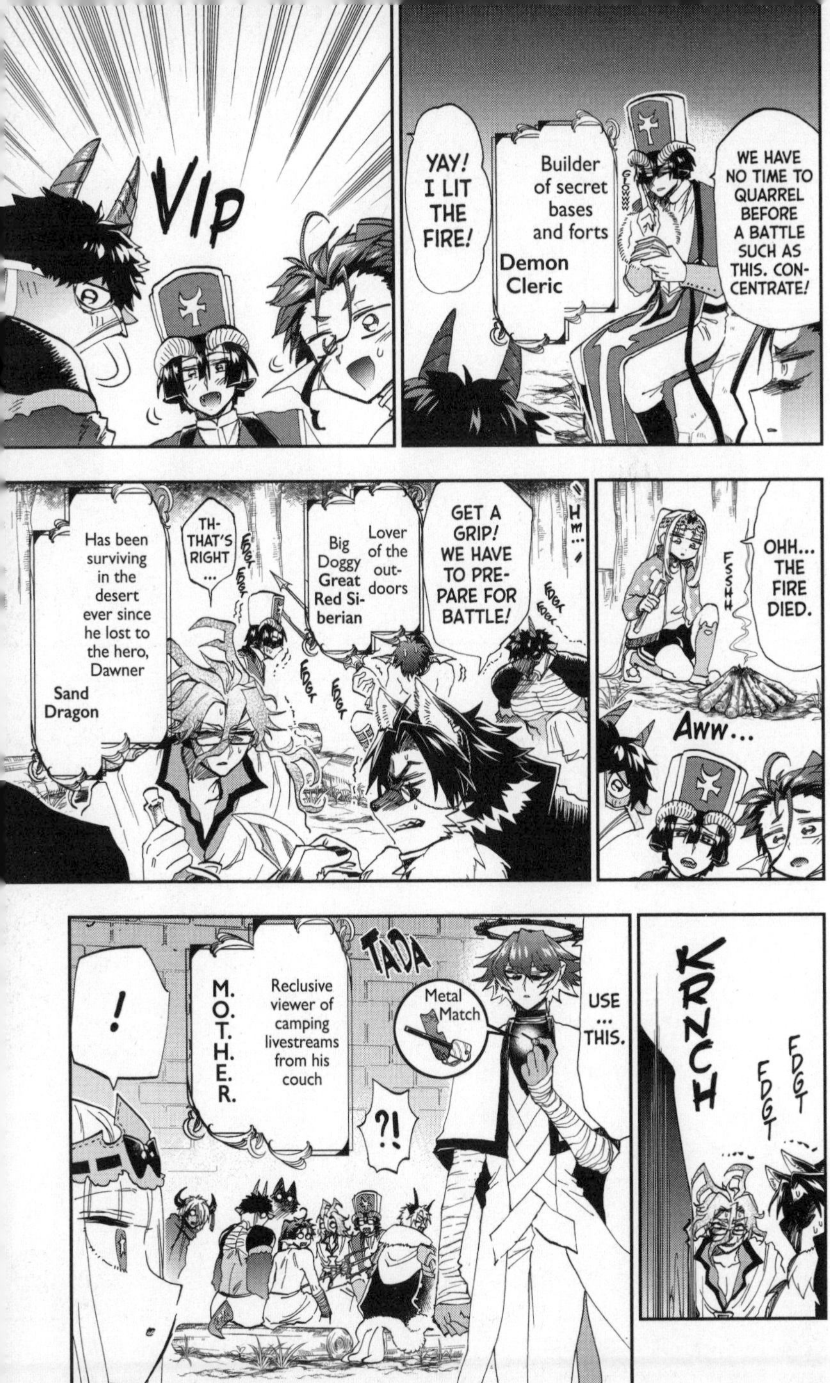
WE HAVE NO TIME TO QUARREL BEFORE A BATTLE SUCH AS THIS. CONCENTRATE!
GLOWWW
Builder of secret bases and forts
Demon Cleric
YAY! I LIT THE FIRE!
VIP
OHH... THE FIRE DIED.
FSSHH
AWW...
HM...
GET A GRIP! WE HAVE TO PREPARE FOR BATTLE!
FDGT FDGT
Lover of the outdoors
Big Doggy Great Red Siberian
FDGT FDGT
FDGT FDGT
TH-THAT'S RIGHT...
Has been surviving in the desert ever since he lost to the hero, Dawner
Sand Dragon
KRNCH
FDGT FDGT
USE... THIS.
TADA
Metal Match
Reclusive viewer of camping livestreams from his couch
M.O.T.H.E.R.
?!
!

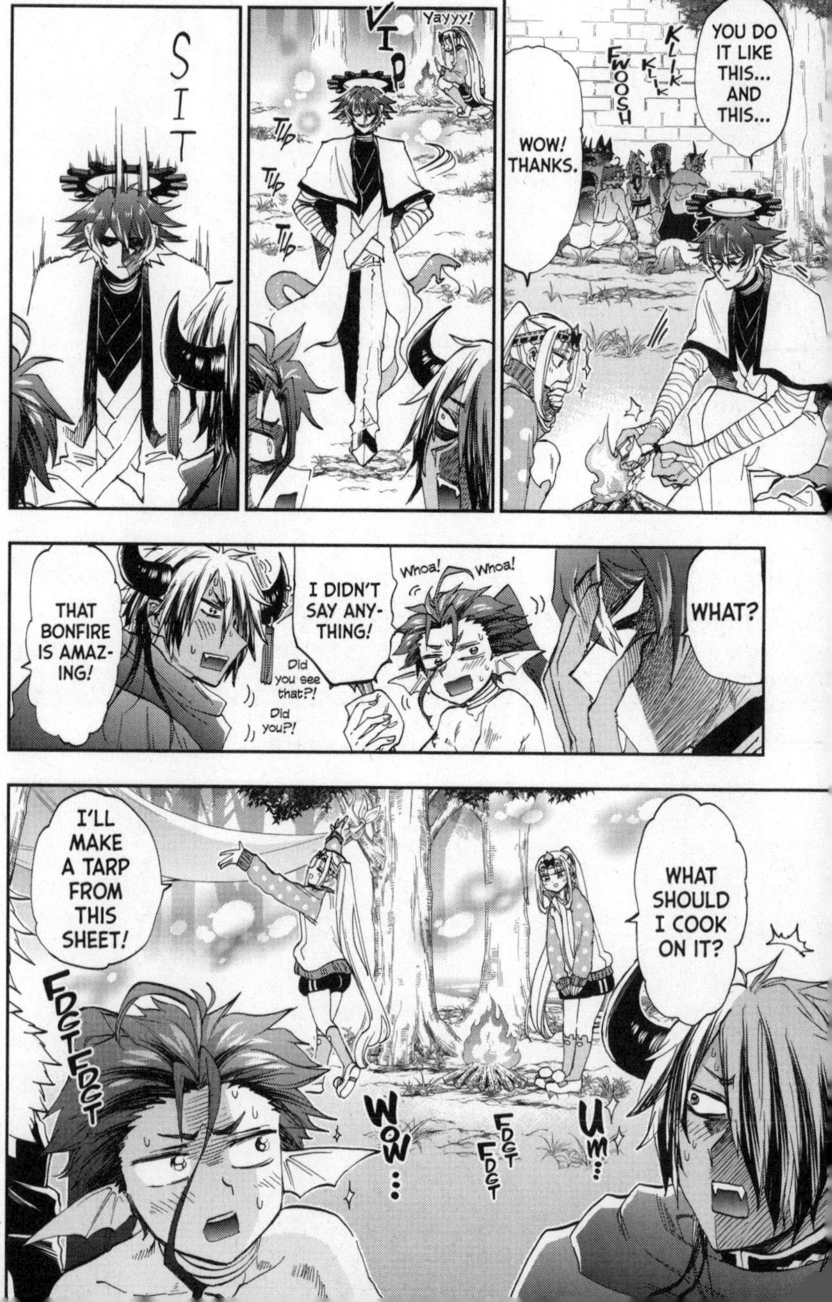
YOU DO IT LIKE THIS... AND THIS...
KLIK
KLIK
FWOOSH
WOW! THANKS.
Yayyy!
VIP
TUP
TUP
TUP
SIT
WHAT?
Whoa!
Whoa!
I DIDN'T SAY ANY-THING!
Did you see that?!
Did you?!
THAT BONFIRE IS AMAZ-ING!
WHAT SHOULD I COOK ON IT?
I'LL MAKE A TARP FROM THIS SHEET!
UM...
FDGT
FDGT
WOW...
FDGTFDGT

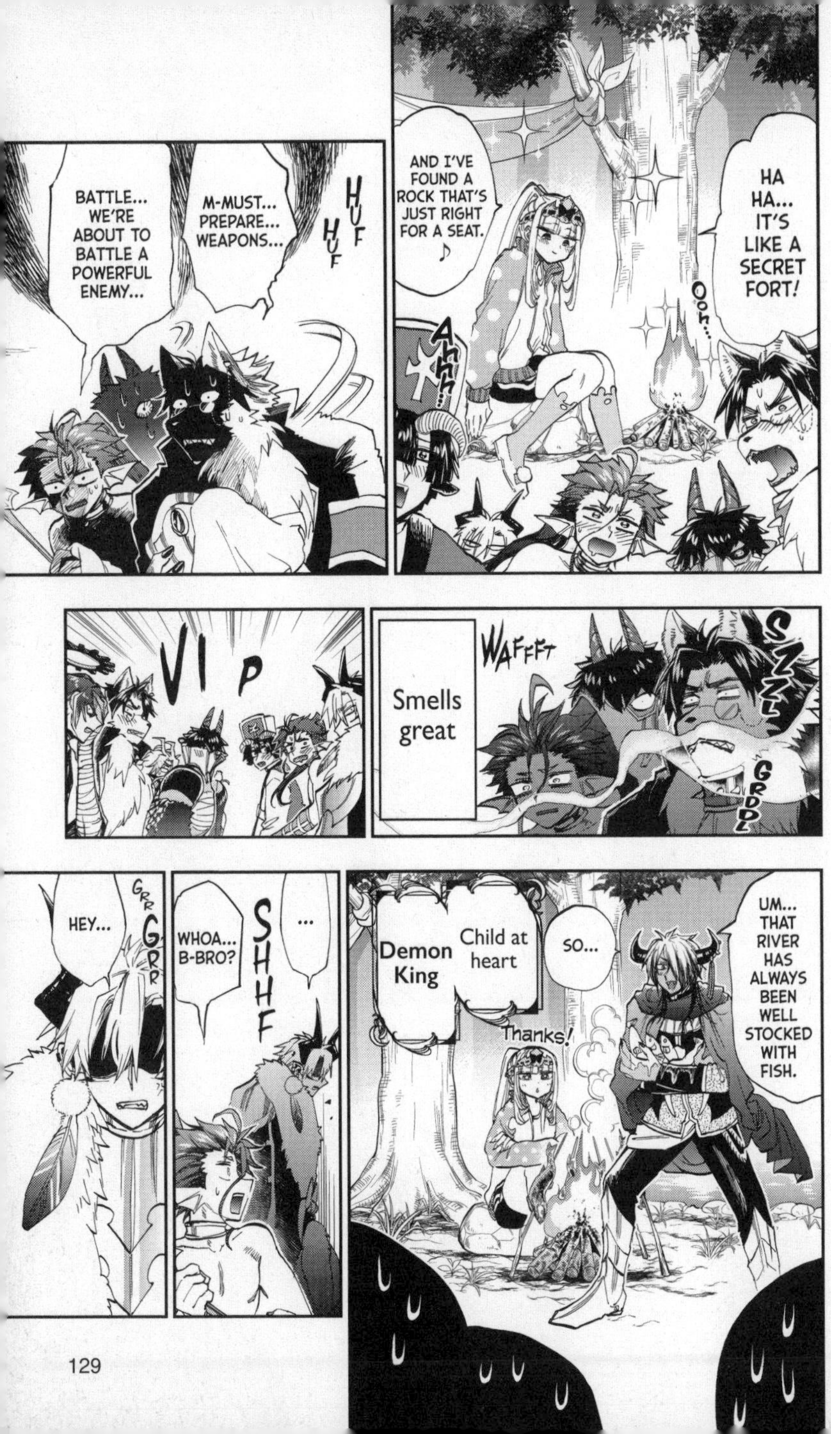
HA HA... IT'S LIKE A SECRET FORT!
Ooh...
AND I'VE FOUND A ROCK THAT'S JUST RIGHT FOR A SEAT. ♪
Ahhh...
M-MUST... PREPARE... WEAPONS...
HUF HUF
BATTLE... WE'RE ABOUT TO BATTLE A POWERFUL ENEMY...
SZZL
WAFFFT
Smells great
GRDDL
VIP
UM... THAT RIVER HAS ALWAYS BEEN WELL STOCKED WITH FISH.
SO...
Thanks!
Child at heart
Demon King
...
SHHF
WHOA... B-BRO?
GRR GRR
HEY...

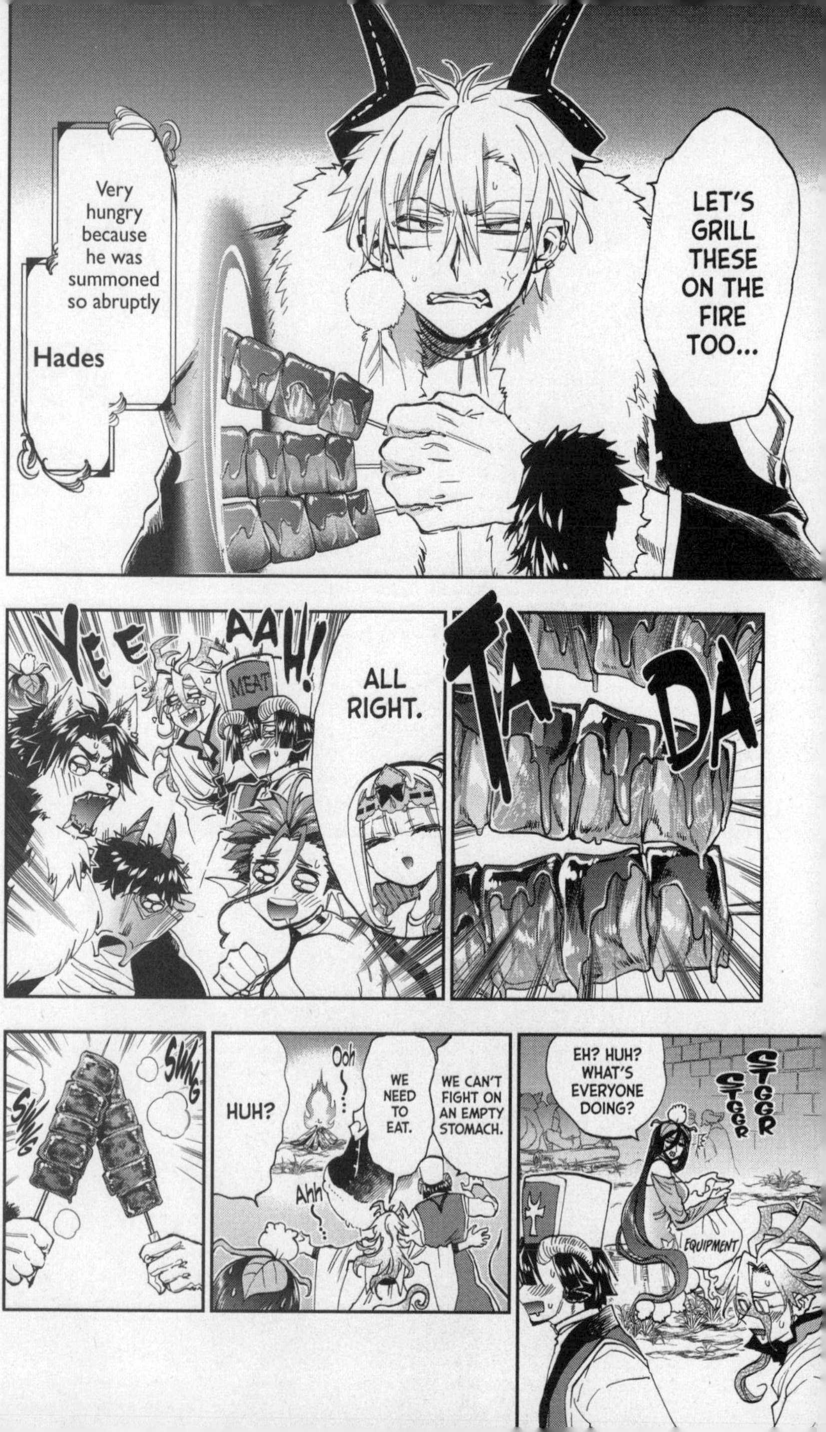
LET'S GRILL THESE ON THE FIRE TOO...
Very hungry because he was summoned so abruptly
Hades
TA DA
ALL RIGHT.
MEAT
YEE AAAH!
EH? HUH? WHAT'S EVERYONE DOING?
STGGR
STGGR
EQUIPMENT
WE CAN'T FIGHT ON AN EMPTY STOMACH.
WE NEED TO EAT.
Ooh...
HUH?
Ahh...
SWING
SWING

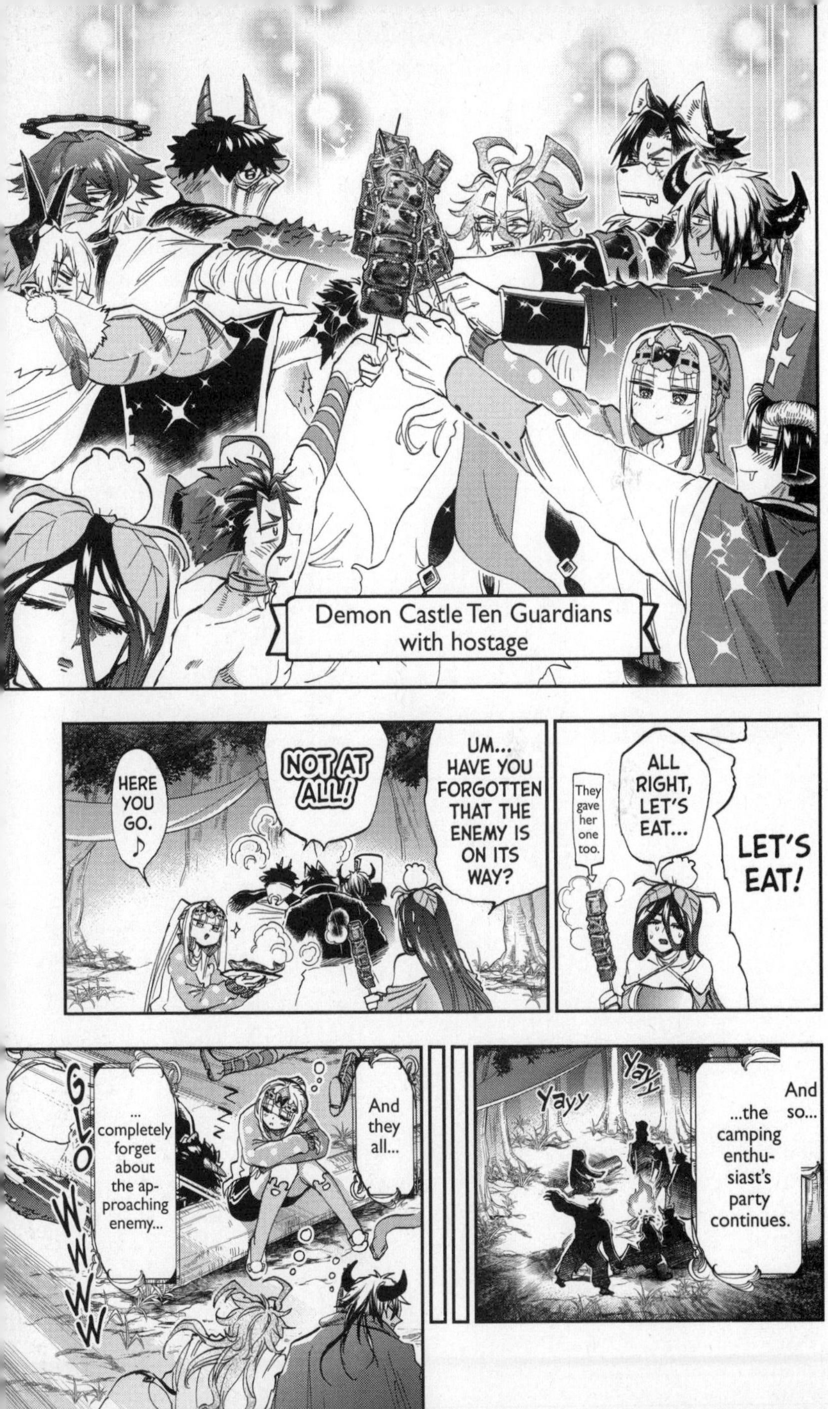
Demon Castle Ten Guardians with hostage
ALL RIGHT, LET'S EAT...
LET'S EAT!
They gave her one too.
UM... HAVE YOU FORGOTTEN THAT THE ENEMY IS ON ITS WAY?
NOT AT ALL!
HERE YOU GO. ♪
And so...
...the camping enthu-siast's party continues.
Yayy
Yayy
And they all...
... completely forget about the ap-proaching enemy...
GLOWWWWW

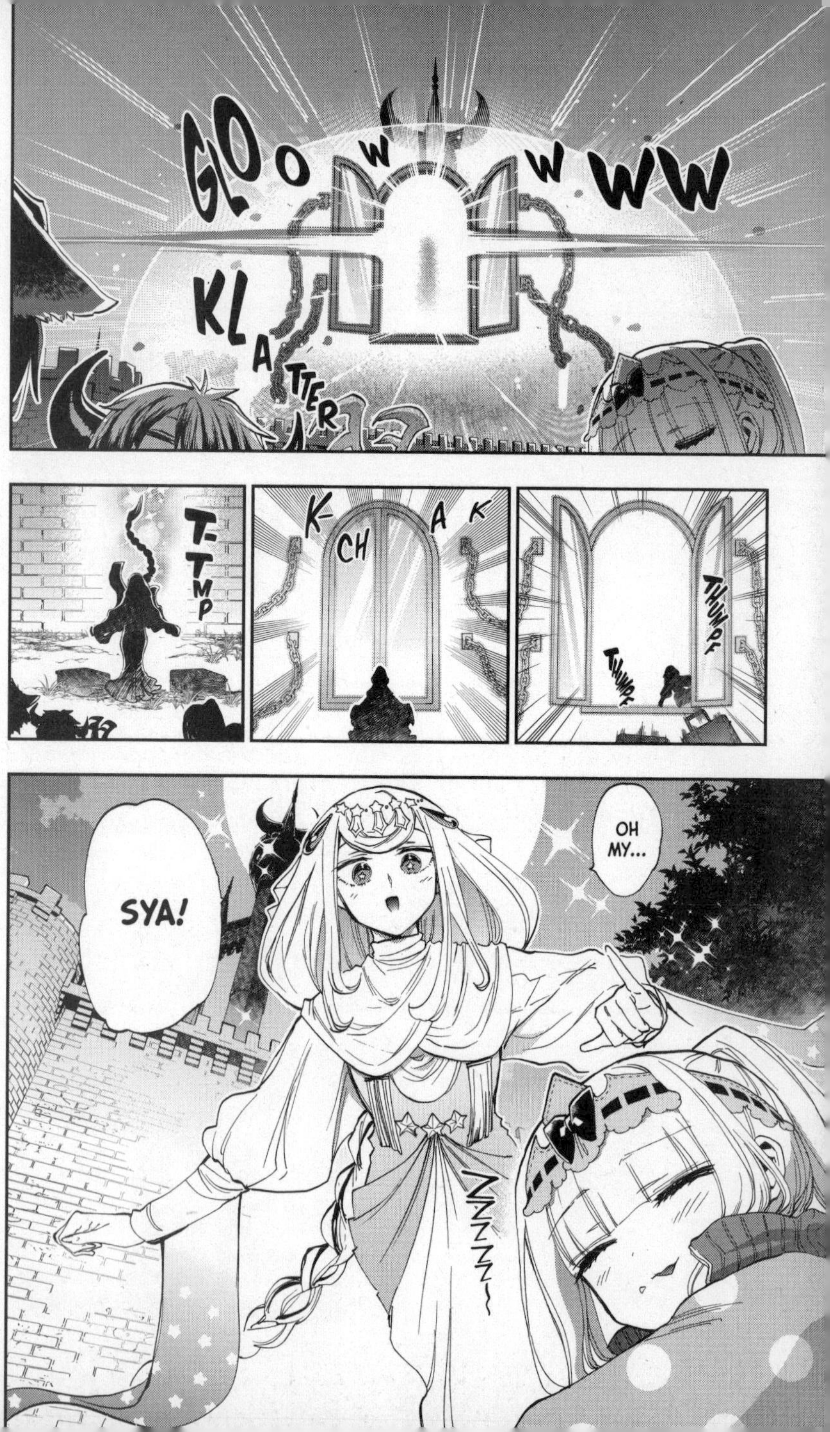
GLOOWWWW
KLATTER
THUMPF
THUMPF
K-CH-AK
T-TTMP
OH MY...
SYA!
ZZZZZ~

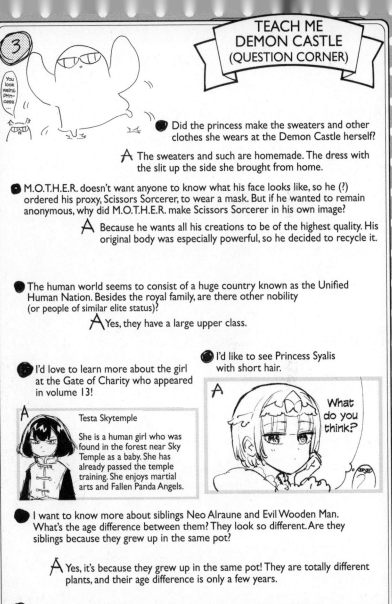

You look weird, Princess...

TEACH ME DEMON CASTLE (QUESTION CORNER)

● Did the princess make the sweaters and other clothes she wears at the Demon Castle herself?

A The sweaters and such are homemade. The dress with the slit up the side she brought from home.

● M.O.T.H.E.R. doesn't want anyone to know what his face looks like, so he (?) ordered his proxy, Scissors Sorcerer, to wear a mask. But if he wanted to remain anonymous, why did M.O.T.H.E.R. make Scissors Sorcerer in his own image?

A Because he wants all his creations to be of the highest quality. His original body was especially powerful, so he decided to recycle it.

● The human world seems to consist of a huge country known as the Unified Human Nation. Besides the royal family, are there other nobility (or people of similar elite status)?

A Yes, they have a large upper class.

● I'd love to learn more about the girl at the Gate of Charity who appeared in volume 13!

A

Testa Skytemple

She is a human girl who was found in the forest near Sky Temple as a baby. She has already passed the temple training. She enjoys martial arts and Fallen Panda Angels.

● I'd like to see Princess Syalis with short hair.

A

What do you think?

● I want to know more about siblings Neo Alraune and Evil Wooden Man. What's the age difference between them? They look so different. Are they siblings because they grew up in the same pot?

A Yes, it's because they grew up in the same pot! They are totally different plants, and their age difference is only a few years.

● What is the black part of the cloth around Hypnos's neck for?

A It's basically the same thing as the red bib the Japanese folklore hero Kintaro wears.

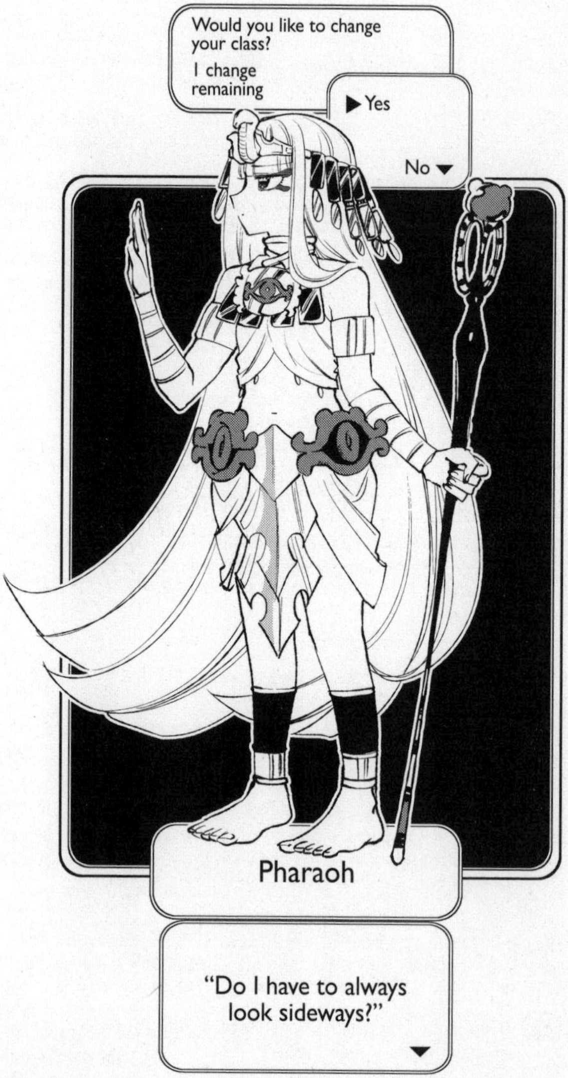
Would you like to change your class?
1 change remaining
▶Yes
No
Pharaoh
"Do I have to always look sideways?"

181st Night: Sleepy Sya Somnambulent Nem

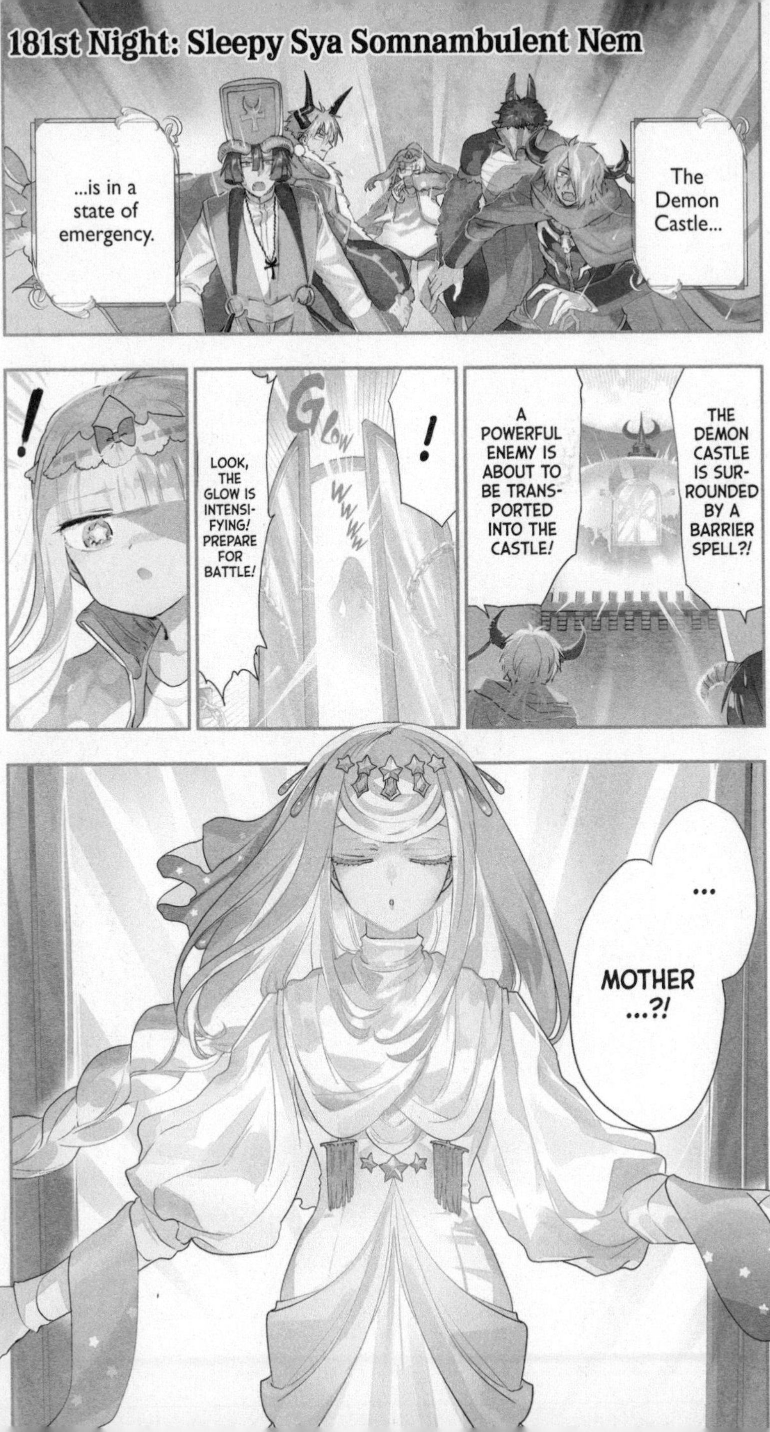
The Demon Castle...
...is in a state of emergency.
THE DEMON CASTLE IS SURROUNDED BY A BARRIER SPELL?!
A POWERFUL ENEMY IS ABOUT TO BE TRANSPORTED INTO THE CASTLE!
!
GLOW WWWW
LOOK, THE GLOW IS INTENSIFYING! PREPARE FOR BATTLE!
!
... MOTHER ...?!

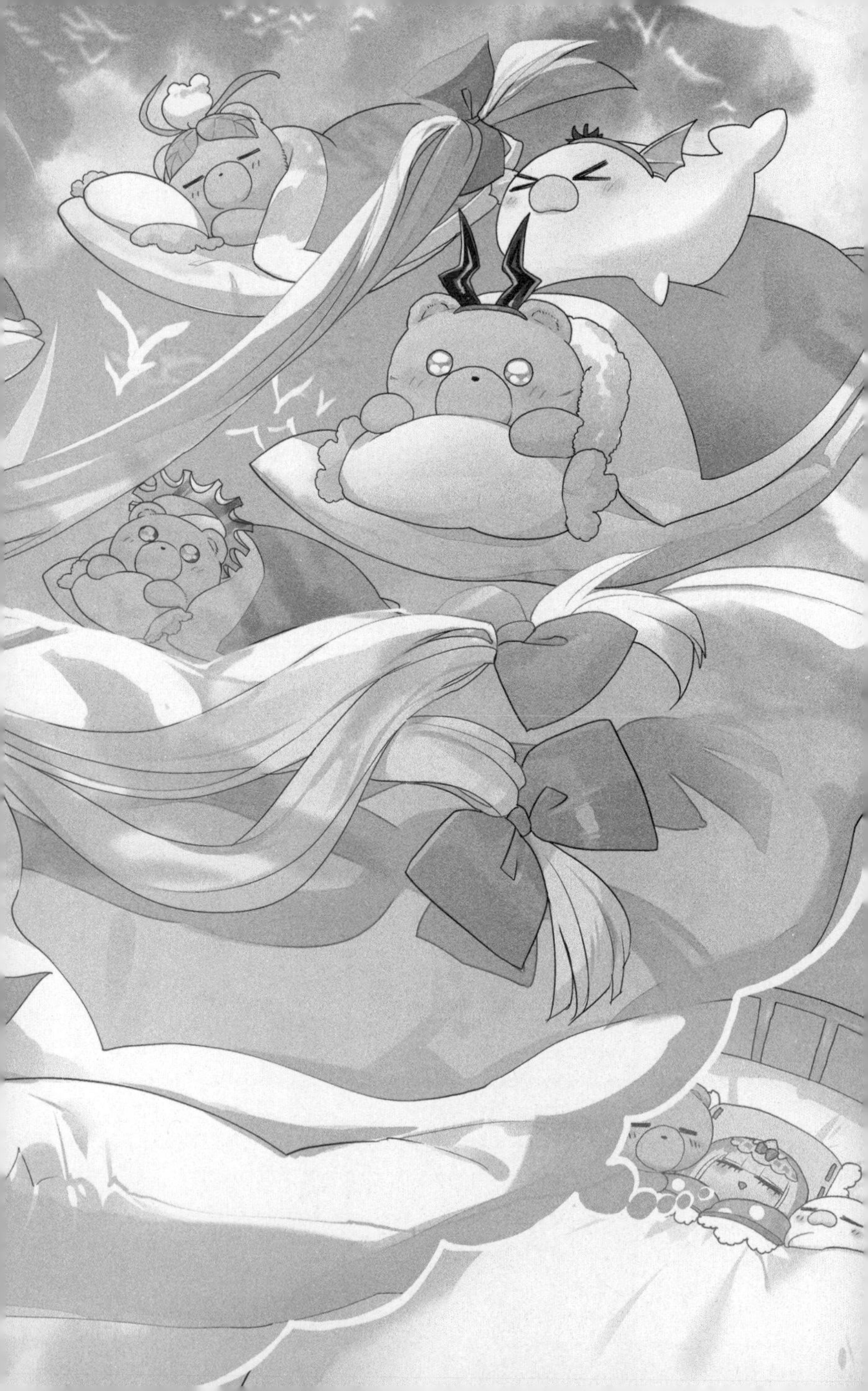

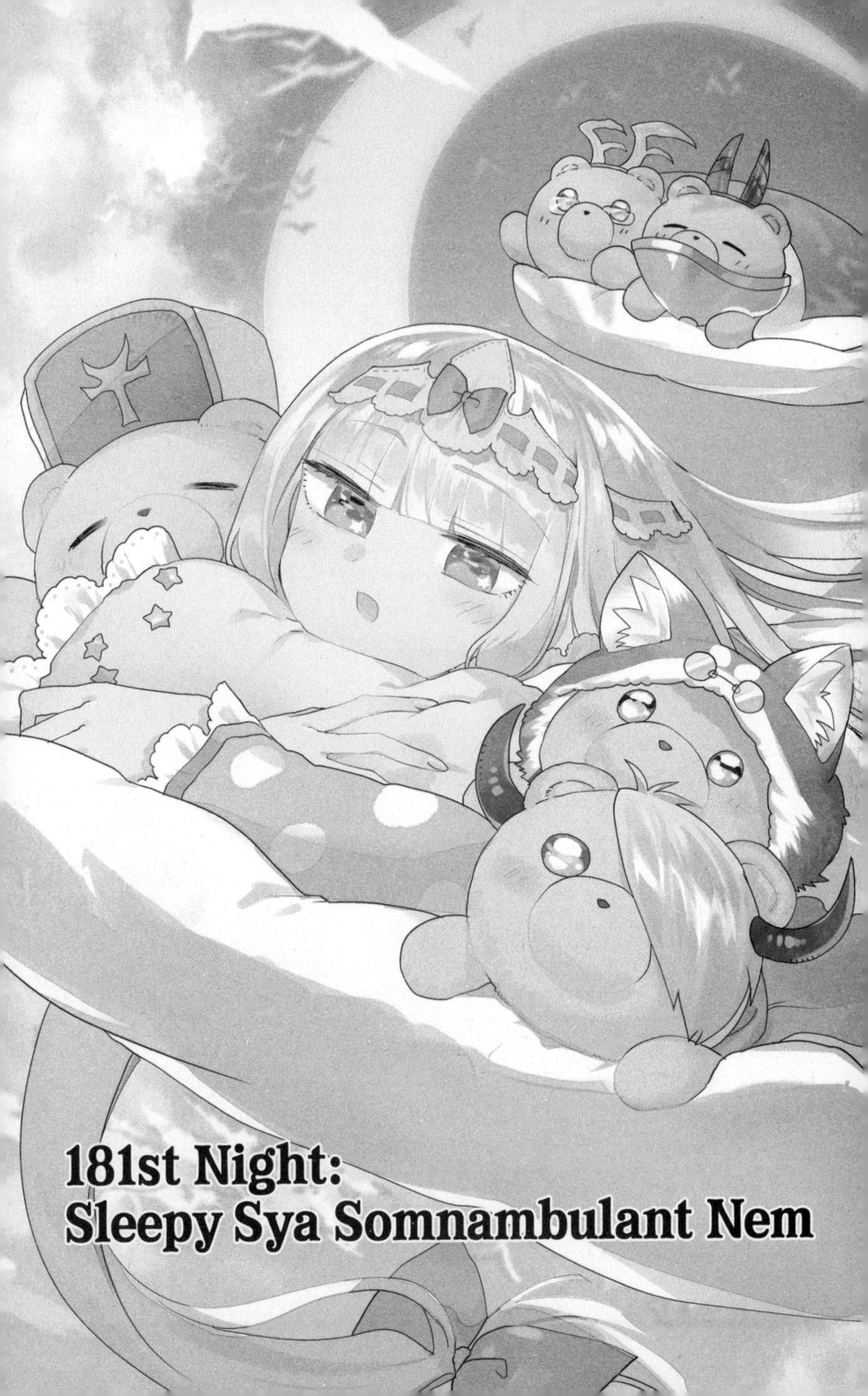
181st Night:
Sleepy Sya Somnambulant Nem

SLEEPY PRINCESS
IN THE
DEMON CASTLE

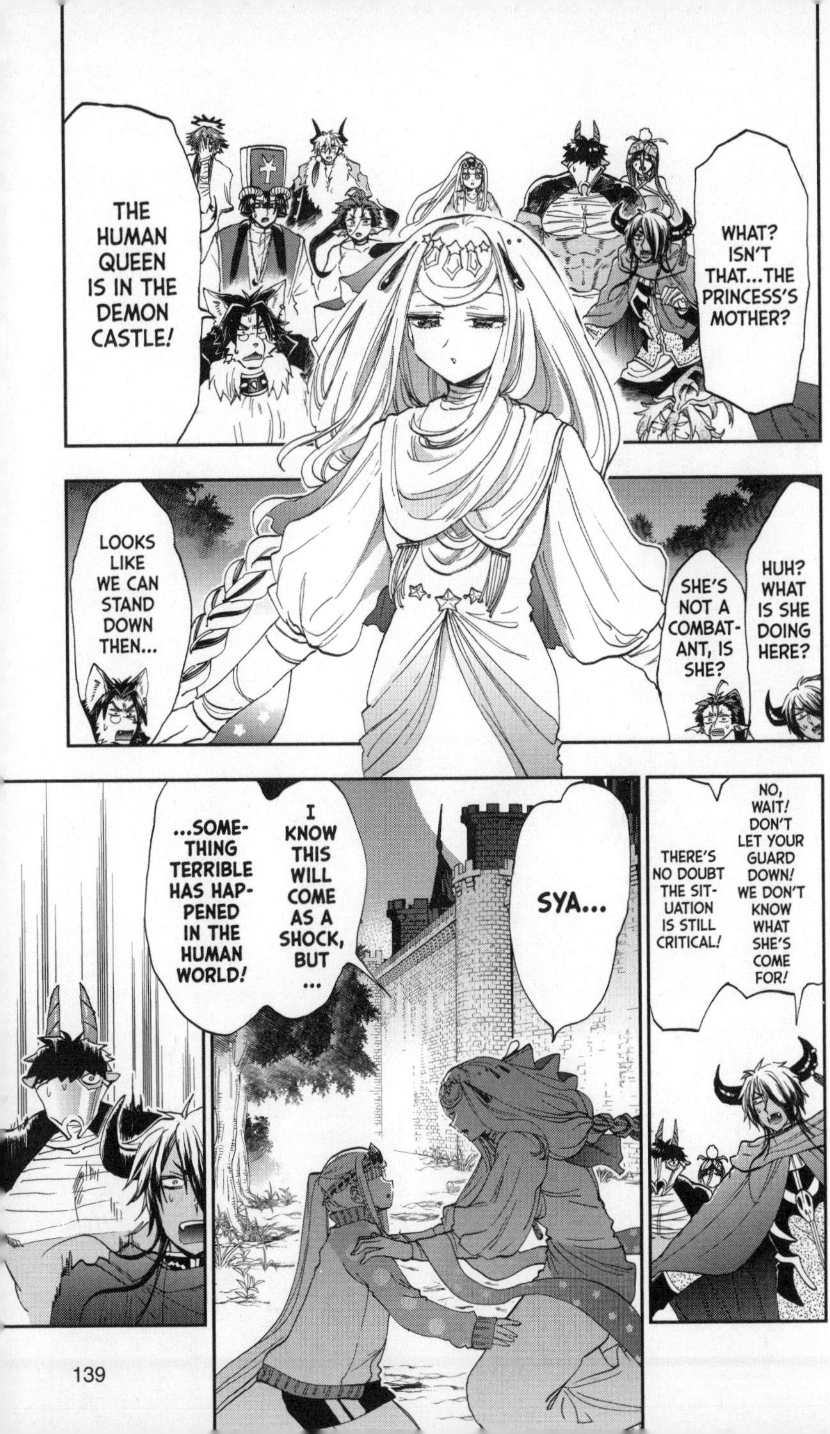
WHAT? ISN'T THAT...THE PRINCESS'S MOTHER?
THE HUMAN QUEEN IS IN THE DEMON CASTLE!
HUH? WHAT IS SHE DOING HERE?
SHE'S NOT A COMBAT-ANT, IS SHE?
LOOKS LIKE WE CAN STAND DOWN THEN...
NO, WAIT! DON'T LET YOUR GUARD DOWN! WE DON'T KNOW WHAT SHE'S COME FOR!
THERE'S NO DOUBT THE SIT-UATION IS STILL CRITICAL!
SYA...
I KNOW THIS WILL COME AS A SHOCK, BUT ...
...SOME-THING TERRIBLE HAS HAP-PENED IN THE HUMAN WORLD!

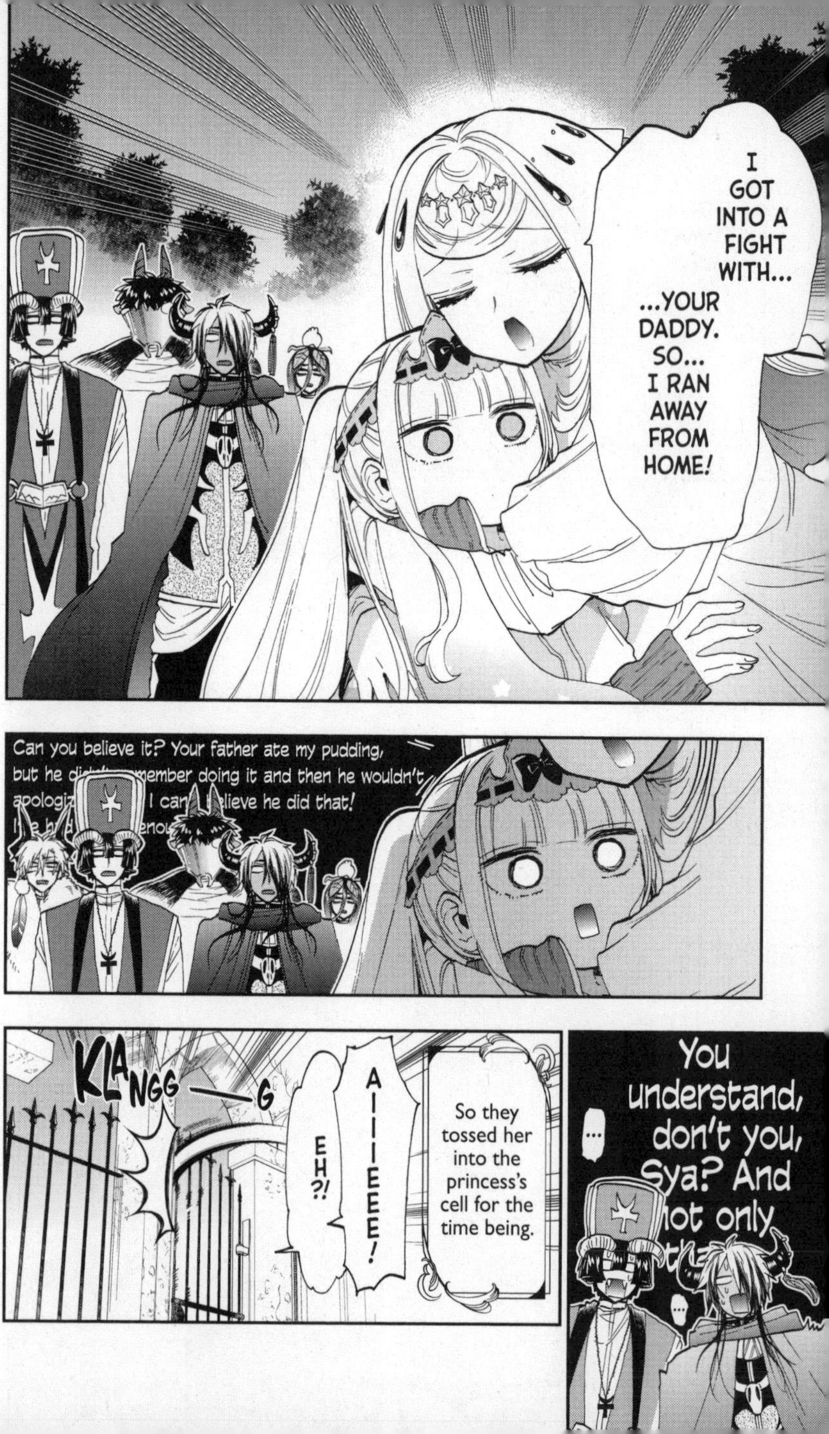
I GOT INTO A FIGHT WITH...
...YOUR DADDY. SO... I RAN AWAY FROM HOME!
Can you believe it? Your father ate my pudding,
but he
member doing it and then he wouldn't
I can
lieve he did that!
You understand, don't you, Sya? And
ot only
...
...
So they tossed her into the princess's cell for the time being.
AIIIEEE!
EH?!
KLANGG—G

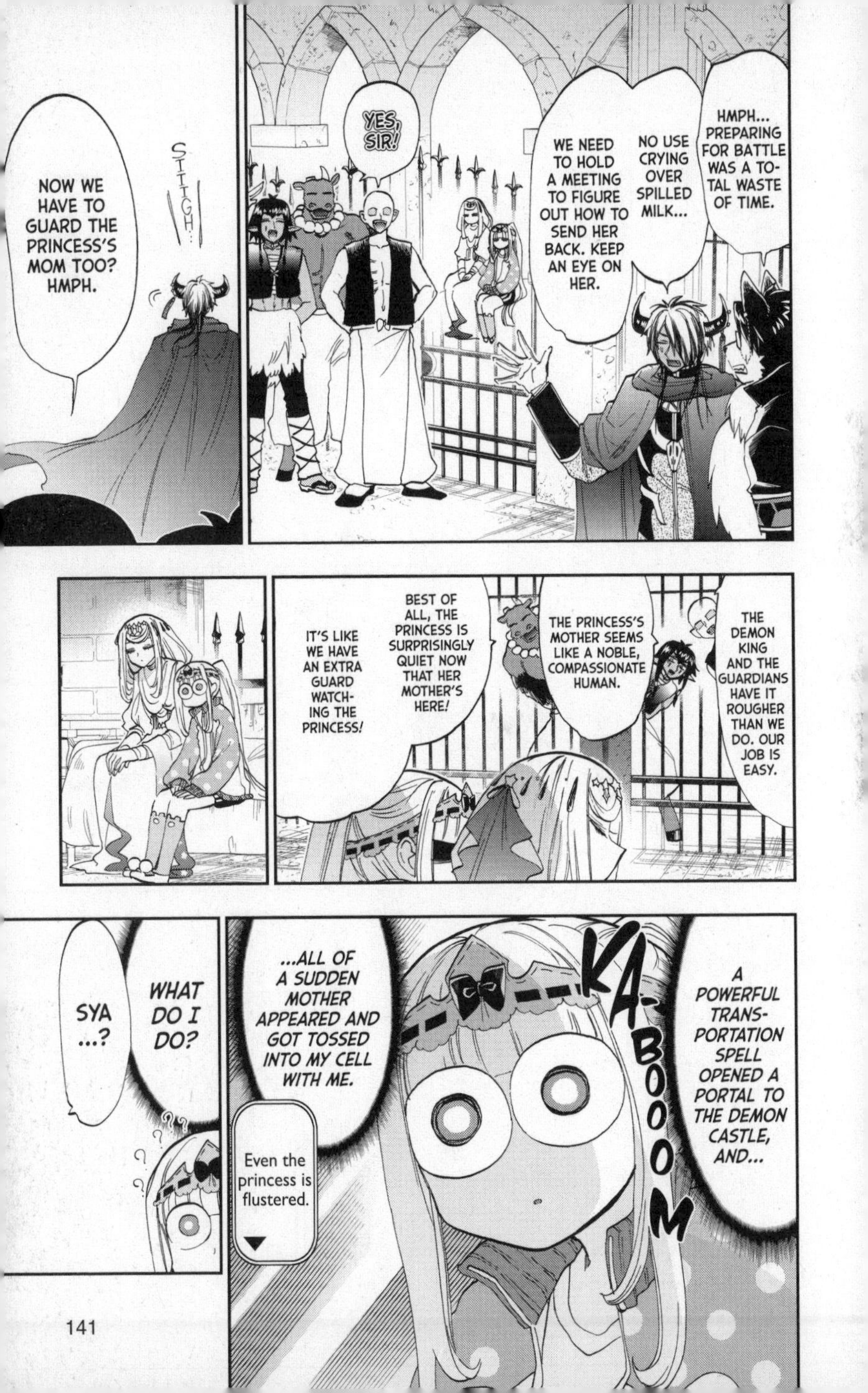
HMPH... PREPARING FOR BATTLE WAS A TO-TAL WASTE OF TIME.
NO USE CRYING OVER SPILLED MILK...
WE NEED TO HOLD A MEETING TO FIGURE OUT HOW TO SEND HER BACK. KEEP AN EYE ON HER.
YES, SIR!
SIIIGH...
NOW WE HAVE TO GUARD THE PRINCESS'S MOM TOO? HMPH.
THE DEMON KING AND THE GUARDIANS HAVE IT ROUGHER THAN WE DO. OUR JOB IS EASY.
THE PRINCESS'S MOTHER SEEMS LIKE A NOBLE, COMPASSIONATE HUMAN.
BEST OF ALL, THE PRINCESS IS SURPRISINGLY QUIET NOW THAT HER MOTHER'S HERE!
IT'S LIKE WE HAVE AN EXTRA GUARD WATCH-ING THE PRINCESS!
A POWERFUL TRANS-PORTATION SPELL OPENED A PORTAL TO THE DEMON CASTLE, AND...
KA-BOOOOOM
...ALL OF A SUDDEN MOTHER APPEARED AND GOT TOSSED INTO MY CELL WITH ME.
Even the princess is flustered.
WHAT DO I DO?
SYA ...?

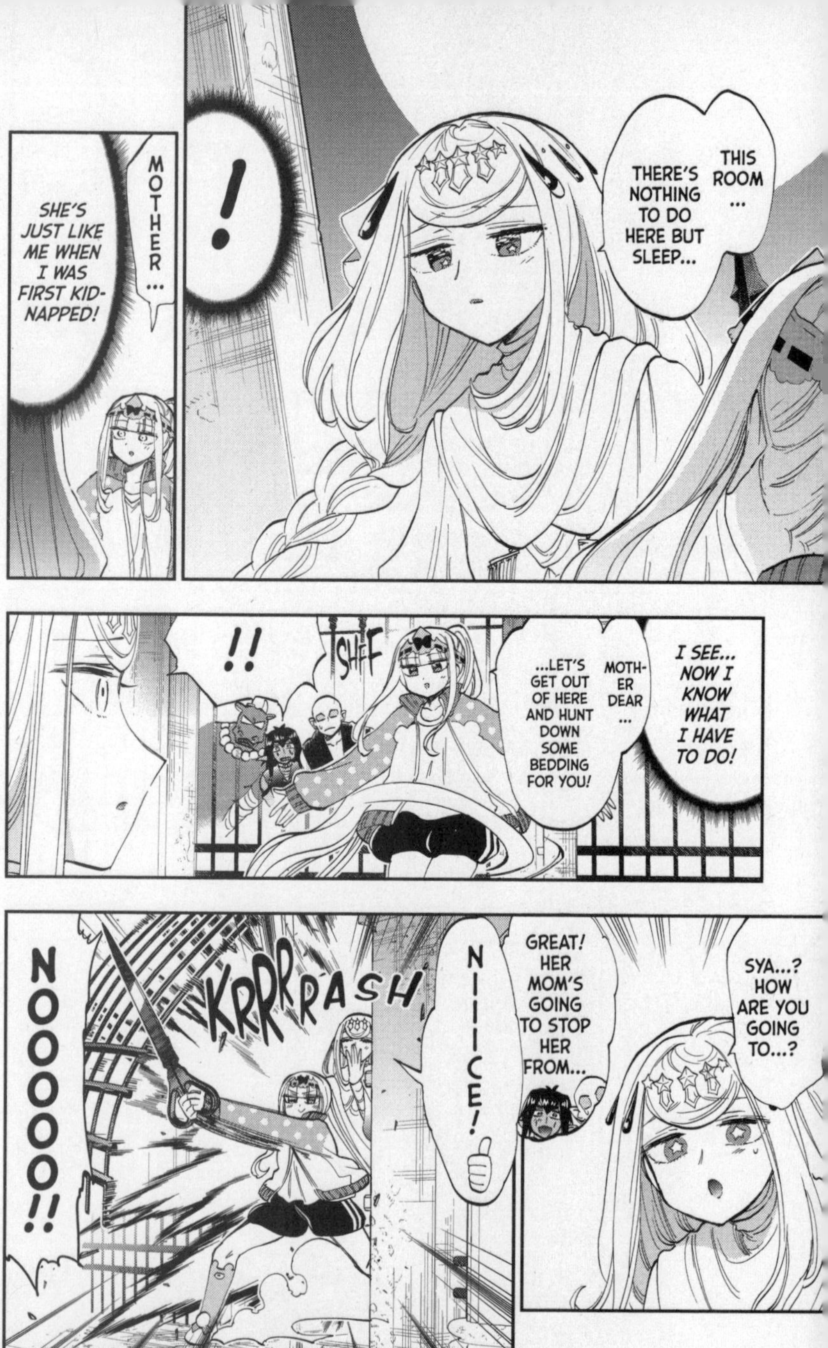

THIS ROOM... THERE'S NOTHING TO DO HERE BUT SLEEP...
!
MOTHER...
SHE'S JUST LIKE ME WHEN I WAS FIRST KID-NAPPED!
I SEE... NOW I KNOW WHAT I HAVE TO DO!
MOTHER DEAR...
...LET'S GET OUT OF HERE AND HUNT DOWN SOME BEDDING FOR YOU!
TSHFF
!!
SYA...? HOW ARE YOU GOING TO...?
GREAT! HER MOM'S GOING TO STOP HER FROM...
NIIICE!
KRRRRASH
NOOOOOO!!

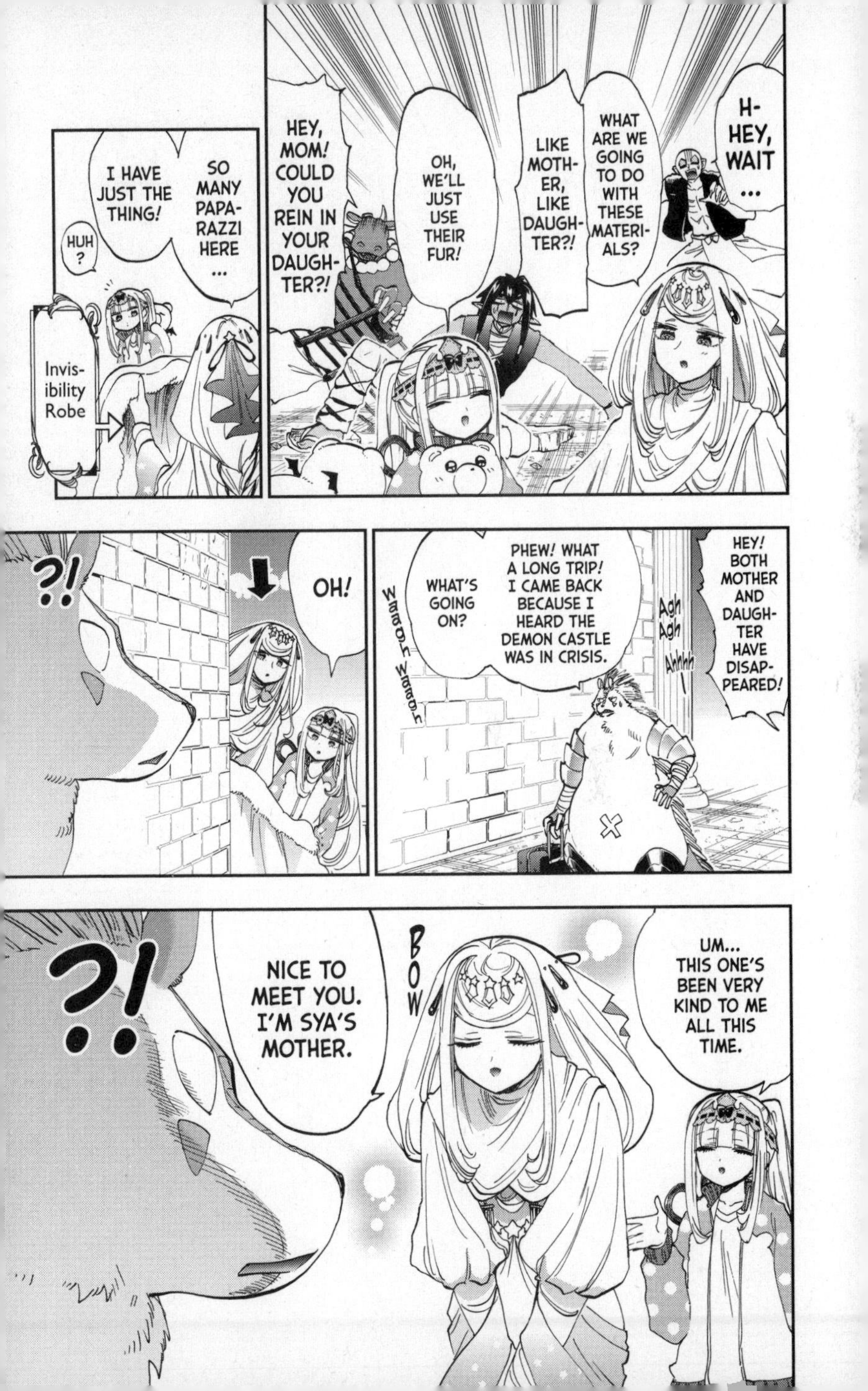

H-HEY, WAIT...
WHAT ARE WE GOING TO DO WITH THESE MATERIALS?
LIKE MOTHER, LIKE DAUGHTER?!
OH, WE'LL JUST USE THEIR FUR!
HEY, MOM! COULD YOU REIN IN YOUR DAUGHTER?!
SO MANY PAPARAZZI HERE...
I HAVE JUST THE THING!
HUH?
Invisibility Robe
HEY! BOTH MOTHER AND DAUGHTER HAVE DISAPPEARED!
Agh Agh Ahhhh
PHEW! WHAT A LONG TRIP! I CAME BACK BECAUSE I HEARD THE DEMON CASTLE WAS IN CRISIS.
WHAT'S GOING ON?
OH!
?!
UM... THIS ONE'S BEEN VERY KIND TO ME ALL THIS TIME.
BOW
NICE TO MEET YOU. I'M SYA'S MOTHER.
?!

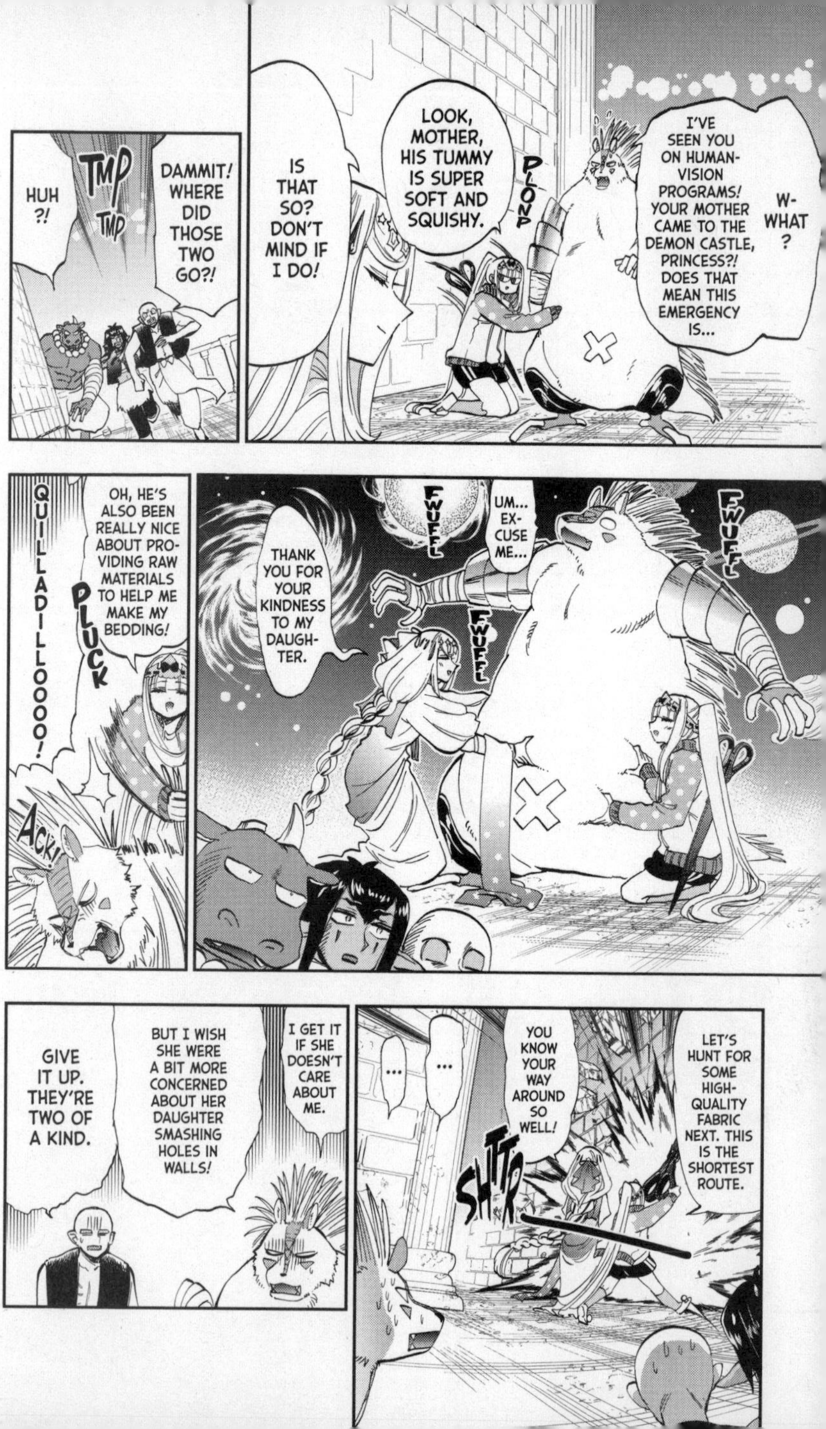
W- WHAT ?
I'VE SEEN YOU ON HUMAN-VISION PROGRAMS! YOUR MOTHER CAME TO THE DEMON CASTLE, PRINCESS?! DOES THAT MEAN THIS EMERGENCY IS...
PLONP
LOOK, MOTHER, HIS TUMMY IS SUPER SOFT AND SQUISHY.
IS THAT SO? DON'T MIND IF I DO!
DAMMIT! WHERE DID THOSE TWO GO?!
TMP
TMP
HUH ?!
FWUFF
UM... EXCUSE ME...
FWUFF
THANK YOU FOR YOUR KINDNESS TO MY DAUGHTER.
FWUFF
QUILLADILLOOOOO!
OH, HE'S ALSO BEEN REALLY NICE ABOUT PROVIDING RAW MATERIALS TO HELP ME MAKE MY BEDDING!
PLUCK
ACK!
LET'S HUNT FOR SOME HIGH-QUALITY FABRIC NEXT. THIS IS THE SHORTEST ROUTE.
YOU KNOW YOUR WAY AROUND SO WELL!
...
...
SHTTR
I GET IT IF SHE DOESN'T CARE ABOUT ME.
BUT I WISH SHE WERE A BIT MORE CONCERNED ABOUT HER DAUGHTER SMASHING HOLES IN WALLS!
GIVE IT UP. THEY'RE TWO OF A KIND.

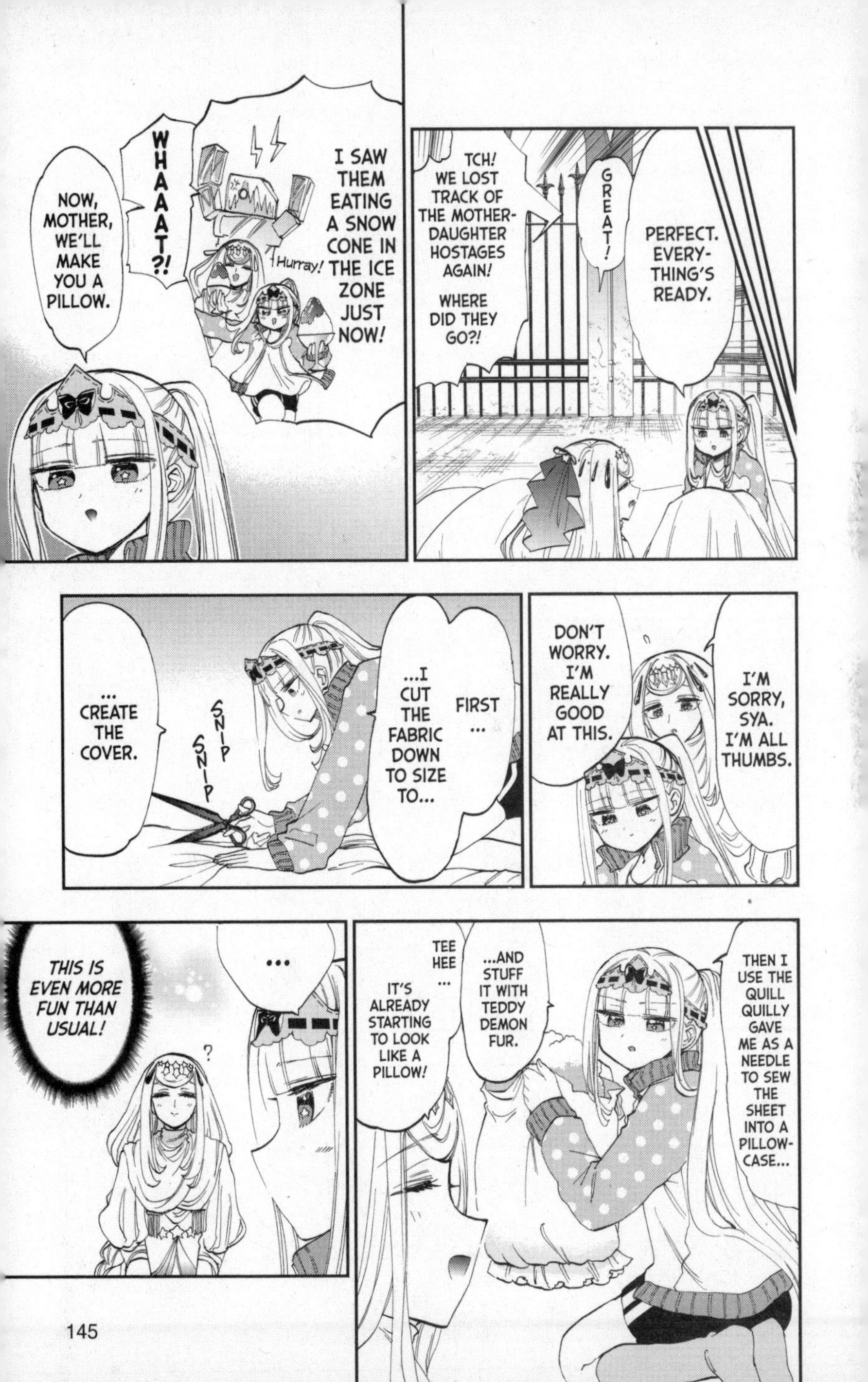
PERFECT. EVERY-THING'S READY.
GREAT!
TCH! WE LOST TRACK OF THE MOTHER-DAUGHTER HOSTAGES AGAIN!
WHERE DID THEY GO?!
I SAW THEM EATING A SNOW CONE IN THE ICE ZONE JUST NOW!
Hurray!
WHAAAAT?!
NOW, MOTHER, WE'LL MAKE YOU A PILLOW.
I'M SORRY, SYA. I'M ALL THUMBS.
DON'T WORRY. I'M REALLY GOOD AT THIS.
FIRST...
...I CUT THE FABRIC DOWN TO SIZE TO...
SNIP SNIP
...CREATE THE COVER.
THEN I USE THE QUILL QUILLY GAVE ME AS A NEEDLE TO SEW THE SHEET INTO A PILLOW-CASE...
...AND STUFF IT WITH TEDDY DEMON FUR.
TEE HEE...
IT'S ALREADY STARTING TO LOOK LIKE A PILLOW!
...
?
THIS IS EVEN MORE FUN THAN USUAL!

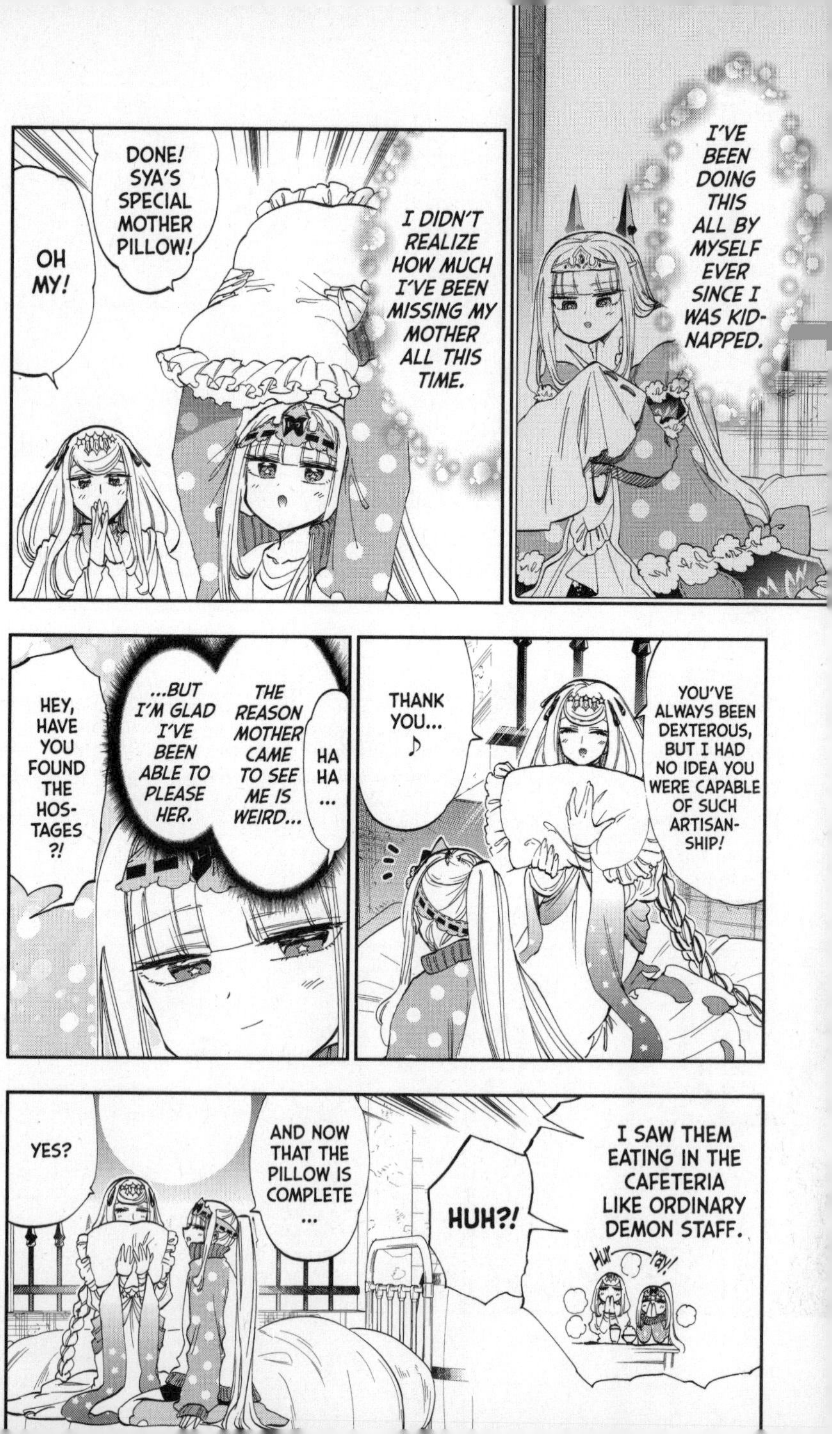
I'VE BEEN DOING THIS ALL BY MYSELF EVER SINCE I WAS KID-NAPPED.
I DIDN'T REALIZE HOW MUCH I'VE BEEN MISSING MY MOTHER ALL THIS TIME.
DONE! SYA'S SPECIAL MOTHER PILLOW!
OH MY!
YOU'VE ALWAYS BEEN DEXTEROUS, BUT I HAD NO IDEA YOU WERE CAPABLE OF SUCH ARTISAN-SHIP!
THANK YOU... ♪
THE REASON MOTHER CAME TO SEE ME IS WEIRD...
HA HA ...
...BUT I'M GLAD I'VE BEEN ABLE TO PLEASE HER.
HEY, HAVE YOU FOUND THE HOS-TAGES ?!
I SAW THEM EATING IN THE CAFETERIA LIKE ORDINARY DEMON STAFF.
HUR-RAY!
HUH?!
AND NOW THAT THE PILLOW IS COMPLETE ...
YES?

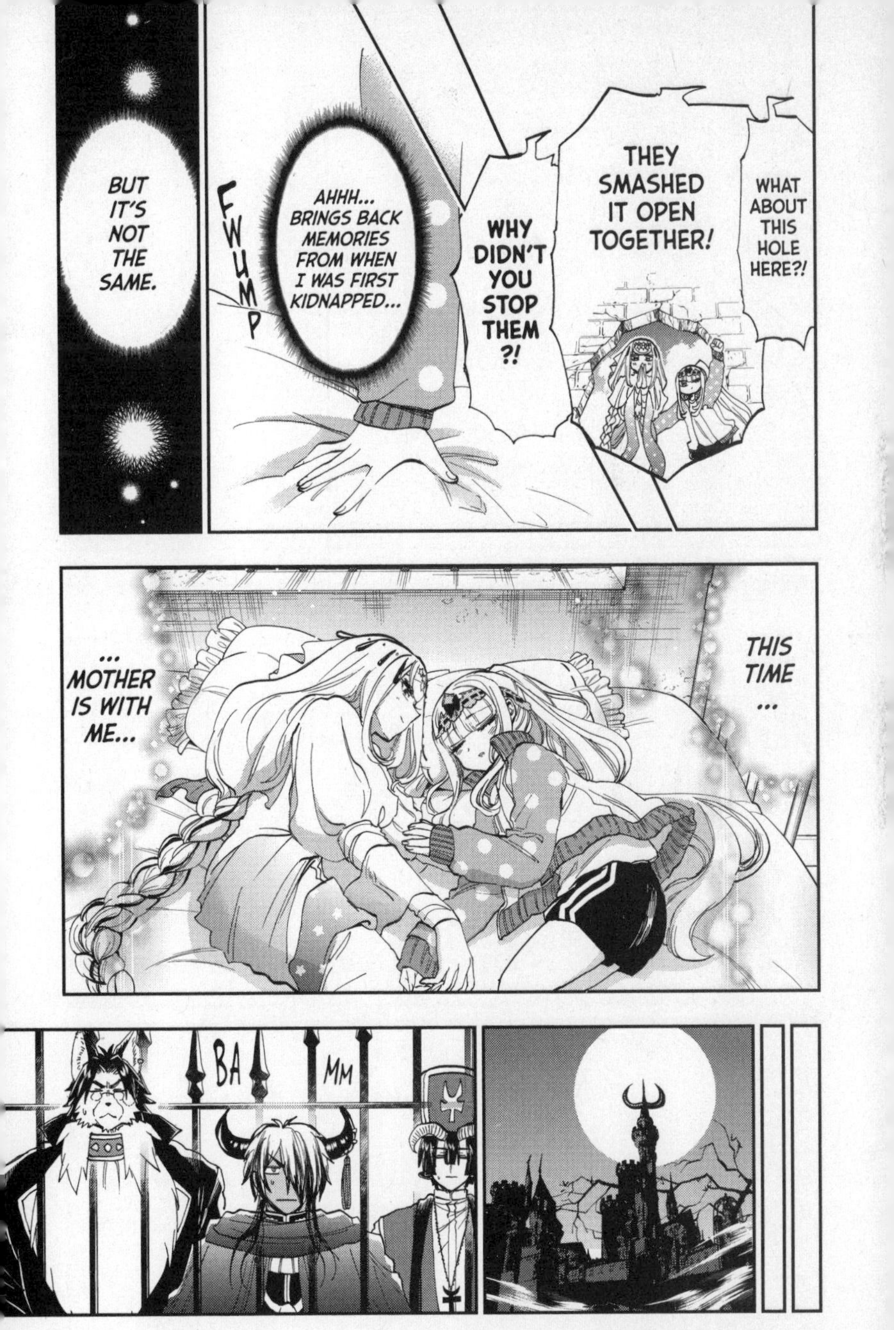
WHAT ABOUT THIS HOLE HERE?!
THEY SMASHED IT OPEN TOGETHER!
WHY DIDN'T YOU STOP THEM ?!
AHHH... BRINGS BACK MEMORIES FROM WHEN I WAS FIRST KIDNAPPED...
FWUMP
BUT IT'S NOT THE SAME.
THIS TIME ...
... MOTHER IS WITH ME...
BAMM

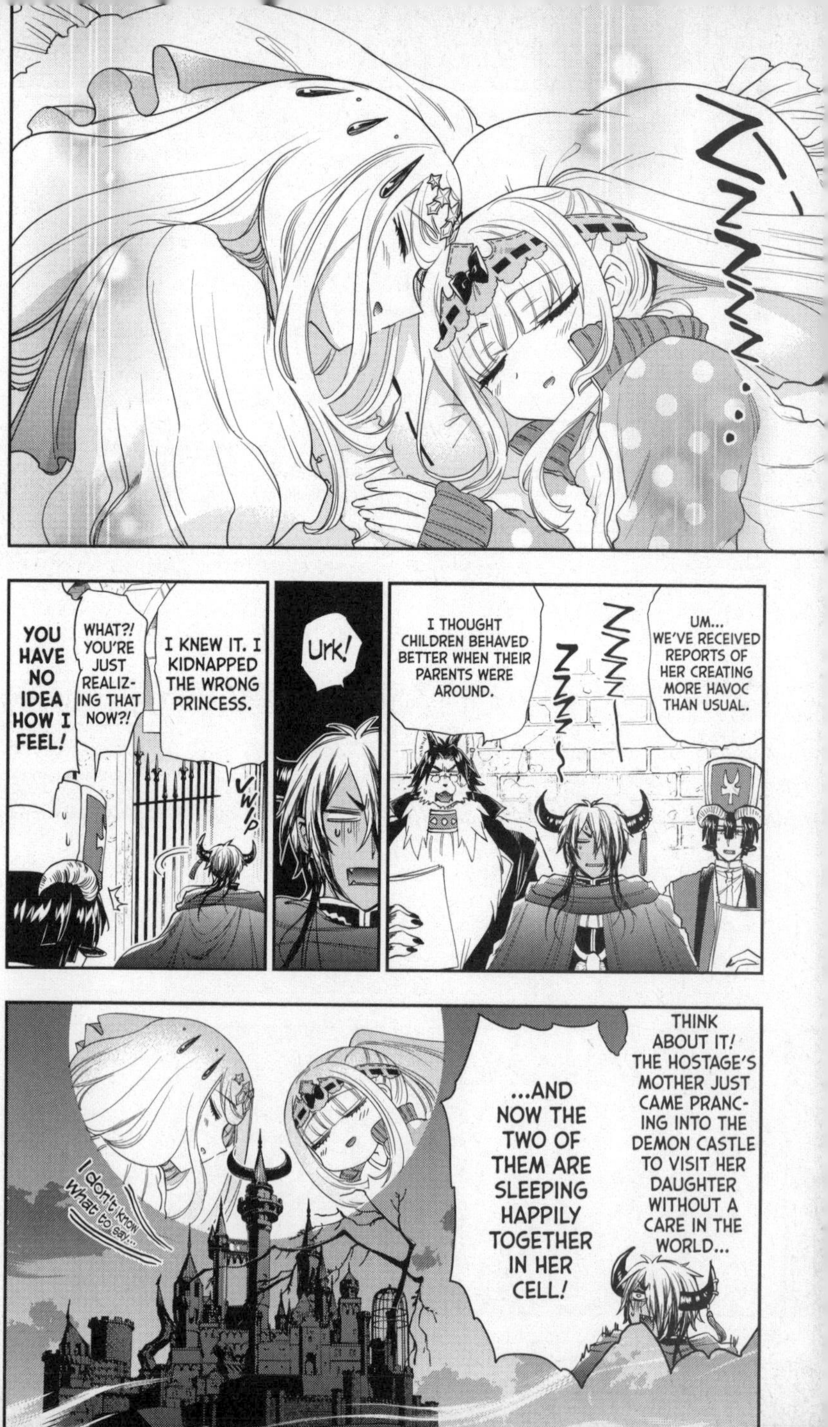

UM... WE'VE RECEIVED REPORTS OF HER CREATING MORE HAVOC THAN USUAL.
I THOUGHT CHILDREN BEHAVED BETTER WHEN THEIR PARENTS WERE AROUND.
Urk!
I KNEW IT. I KIDNAPPED THE WRONG PRINCESS.
VWIP
WHAT?! YOU'RE JUST REALIZING THAT NOW?!
YOU HAVE NO IDEA HOW I FEEL!
THINK ABOUT IT! THE HOSTAGE'S MOTHER JUST CAME PRANCING INTO THE DEMON CASTLE TO VISIT HER DAUGHTER WITHOUT A CARE IN THE WORLD...
...AND NOW THE TWO OF THEM ARE SLEEPING HAPPILY TOGETHER IN HER CELL!
I don't know what to say...

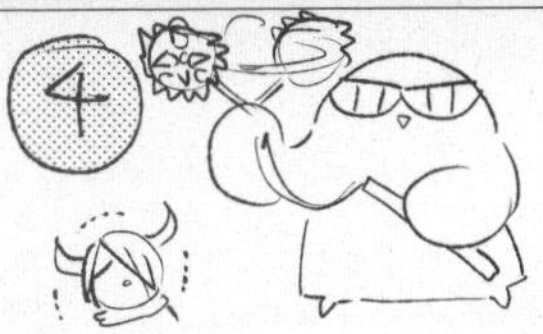
4

TEACH ME DEMON CASTLE (QUESTION CORNER)

● I want to know if the Demon King, Grandpa, Hades and other horned demons roll over in their sleep. I'm worried they'd tear their pillows.

A The Demon King has round, curved horns, which protect the sheets. But he can't roll over on them, so he sometimes uses pillows specially designed for horned demons. The goat is a quiet sleeper, so he doesn't budge at night. Hades has sharp horns and tosses in his sleep a lot, so pillows are disposable items for him.

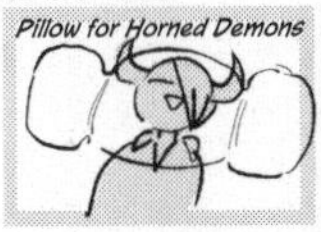
Pillow for Horned Demons

● Did the princess receive gifts from everyone on her birthday?

A Probably not. I don't think they know when her birthday is.

● What happens to Great Red's fur during shedding season?

● I want to see Twilight and Great Red Siberian in a furry scene!

A

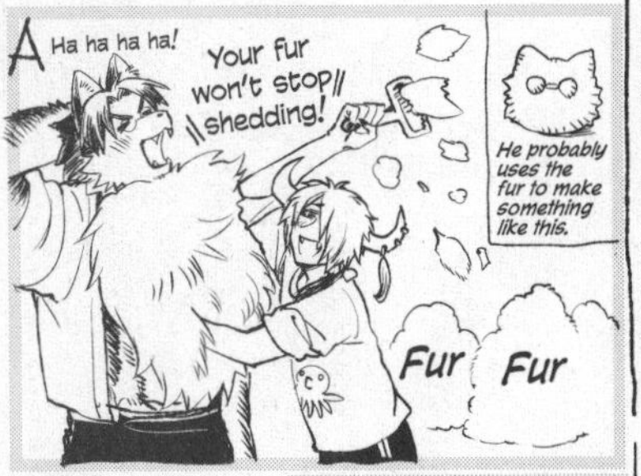
Ha ha ha ha!
Your fur won't stop!! shedding!
He probably uses the fur to make something like this.
Fur
Fur

● I love Fire Venom Dragon, so I'm very interested in his bio data, such as how tall he is and so forth!

● Please tell me the ages of M.O.T.H.E.R., Fire Venom Dragon and Sand Dragon.

A

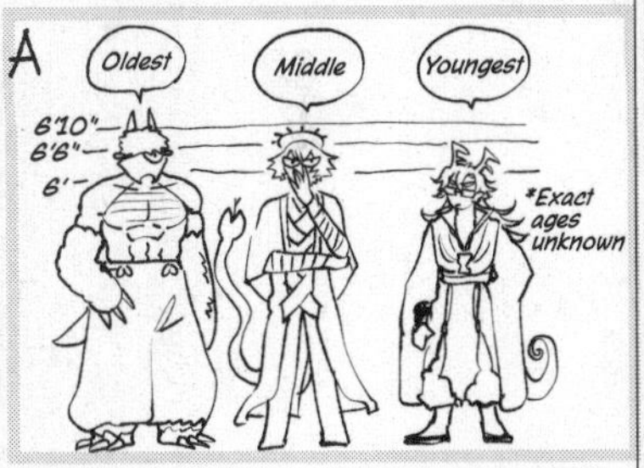
Oldest
Middle
Youngest
6'10"
6'6"
6'
*Exact ages unknown

● What is this demon's name?

A Eagle Samurai.

That's his name. He's friends with Scaly Reindeer and the others.

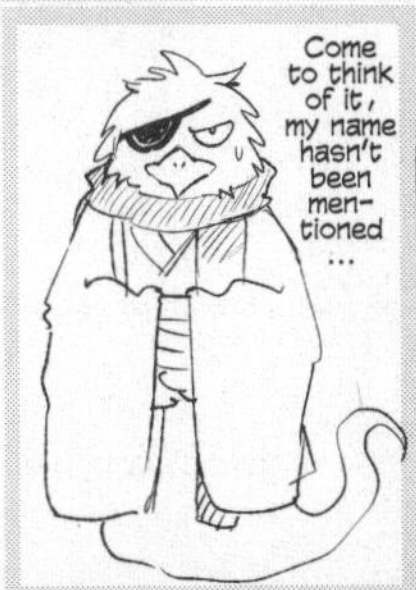
Come to think of it, my name hasn't been mentioned ...

● I want to see the goat as a kid when he lived in Devil's Bridge City.

A He probably looked something like this.

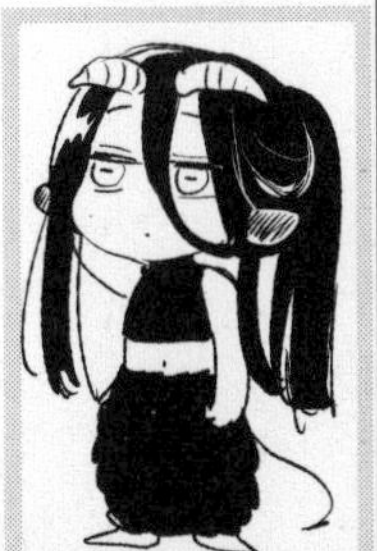

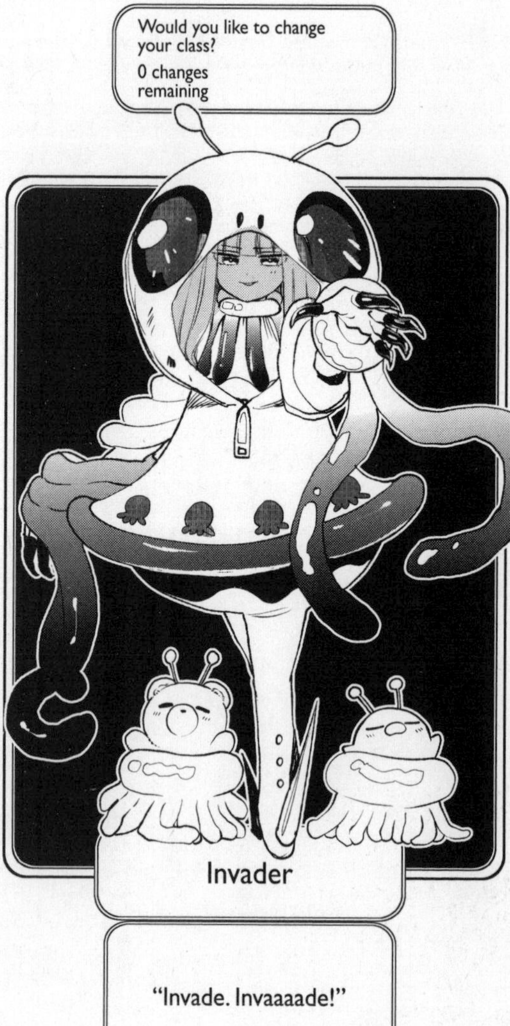
Would you like to change your class?
0 changes remaining
Invader
"Invade. Invaaaade!"

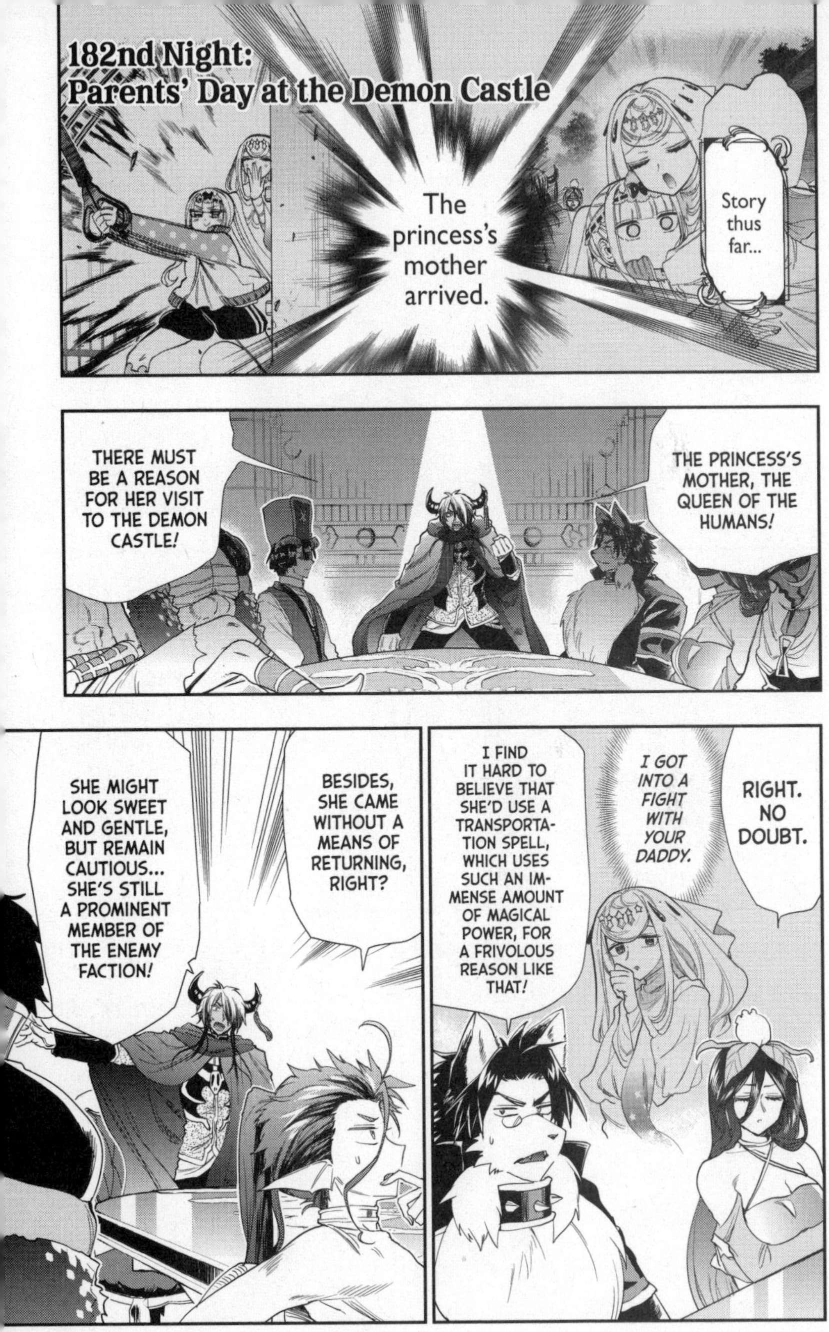
182nd Night:
Parents' Day at the Demon Castle
Story thus far...
The princess's mother arrived.
THE PRINCESS'S MOTHER, THE QUEEN OF THE HUMANS!
THERE MUST BE A REASON FOR HER VISIT TO THE DEMON CASTLE!
RIGHT. NO DOUBT.
I GOT INTO A FIGHT WITH YOUR DADDY.
I FIND IT HARD TO BELIEVE THAT SHE'D USE A TRANSPORTATION SPELL, WHICH USES SUCH AN IMMENSE AMOUNT OF MAGICAL POWER, FOR A FRIVOLOUS REASON LIKE THAT!
BESIDES, SHE CAME WITHOUT A MEANS OF RETURNING, RIGHT?
SHE MIGHT LOOK SWEET AND GENTLE, BUT REMAIN CAUTIOUS... SHE'S STILL A PROMINENT MEMBER OF THE ENEMY FACTION!

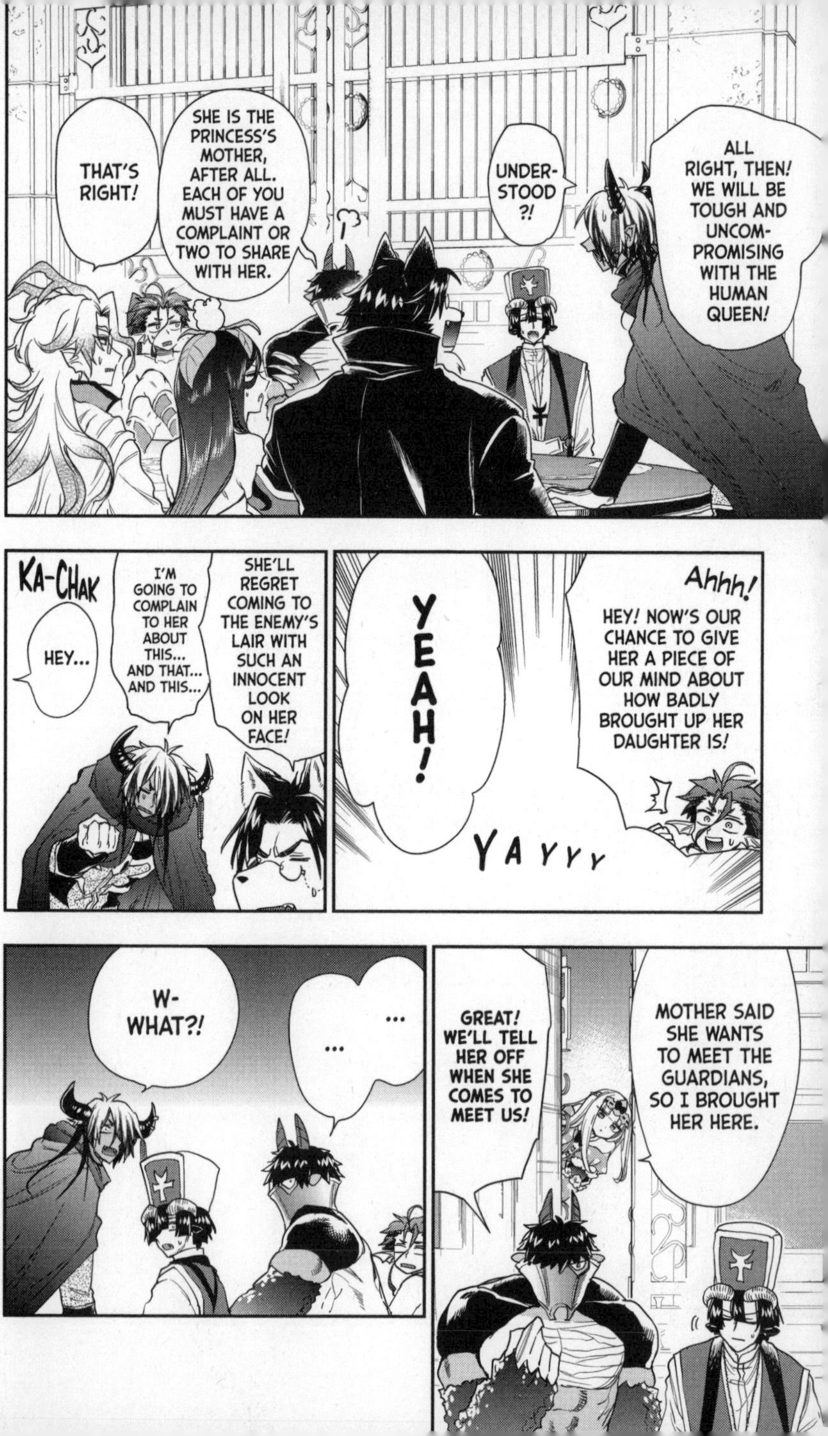
ALL RIGHT, THEN! WE WILL BE TOUGH AND UNCOM-PROMISING WITH THE HUMAN QUEEN!
UNDER-STOOD?!
SHE IS THE PRINCESS'S MOTHER, AFTER ALL. EACH OF YOU MUST HAVE A COMPLAINT OR TWO TO SHARE WITH HER.
THAT'S RIGHT!
Ahhh!
HEY! NOW'S OUR CHANCE TO GIVE HER A PIECE OF OUR MIND ABOUT HOW BADLY BROUGHT UP HER DAUGHTER IS!
YEAH!
YAYYY
SHE'LL REGRET COMING TO THE ENEMY'S LAIR WITH SUCH AN INNOCENT LOOK ON HER FACE!
I'M GOING TO COMPLAIN TO HER ABOUT THIS... AND THAT... AND THIS...
KA-CHAK
HEY...
MOTHER SAID SHE WANTS TO MEET THE GUARDIANS, SO I BROUGHT HER HERE.
GREAT! WE'LL TELL HER OFF WHEN SHE COMES TO MEET US!
... ...
W-WHAT?!

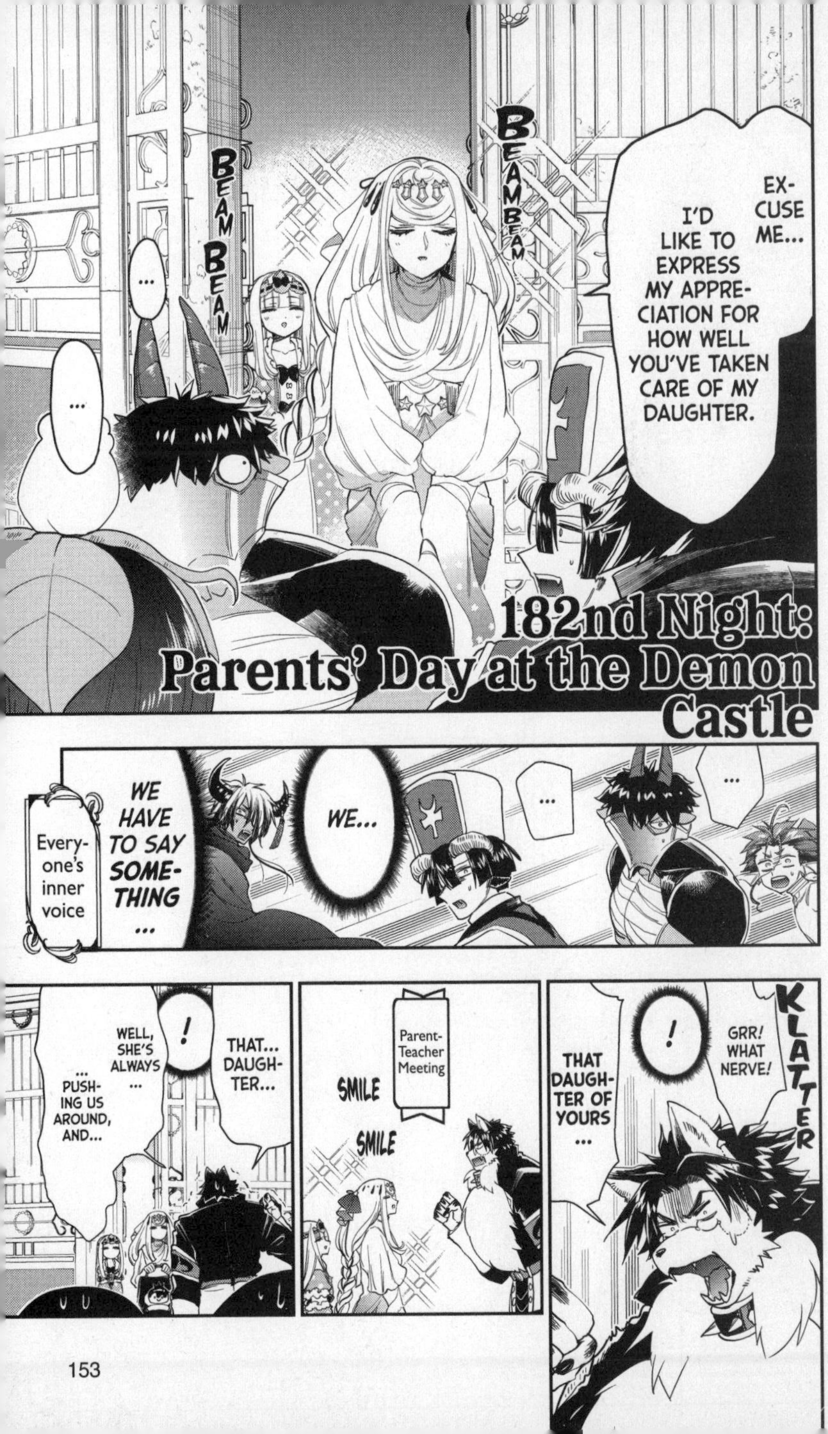
EXCUSE ME... I'D LIKE TO EXPRESS MY APPRECIATION FOR HOW WELL YOU'VE TAKEN CARE OF MY DAUGHTER.
BEAMBEAM
BEAM BEAM
...
...
182nd Night: Parents' Day at the Demon Castle
...
...
WE...
WE HAVE TO SAY SOMETHING...
Everyone's inner voice
KLATTER
GRR! WHAT NERVE!
!
THAT DAUGHTER OF YOURS...
Parent-Teacher Meeting
SMILE
SMILE
THAT... DAUGHTER...
!
WELL, SHE'S ALWAYS...
...PUSHING US AROUND, AND...

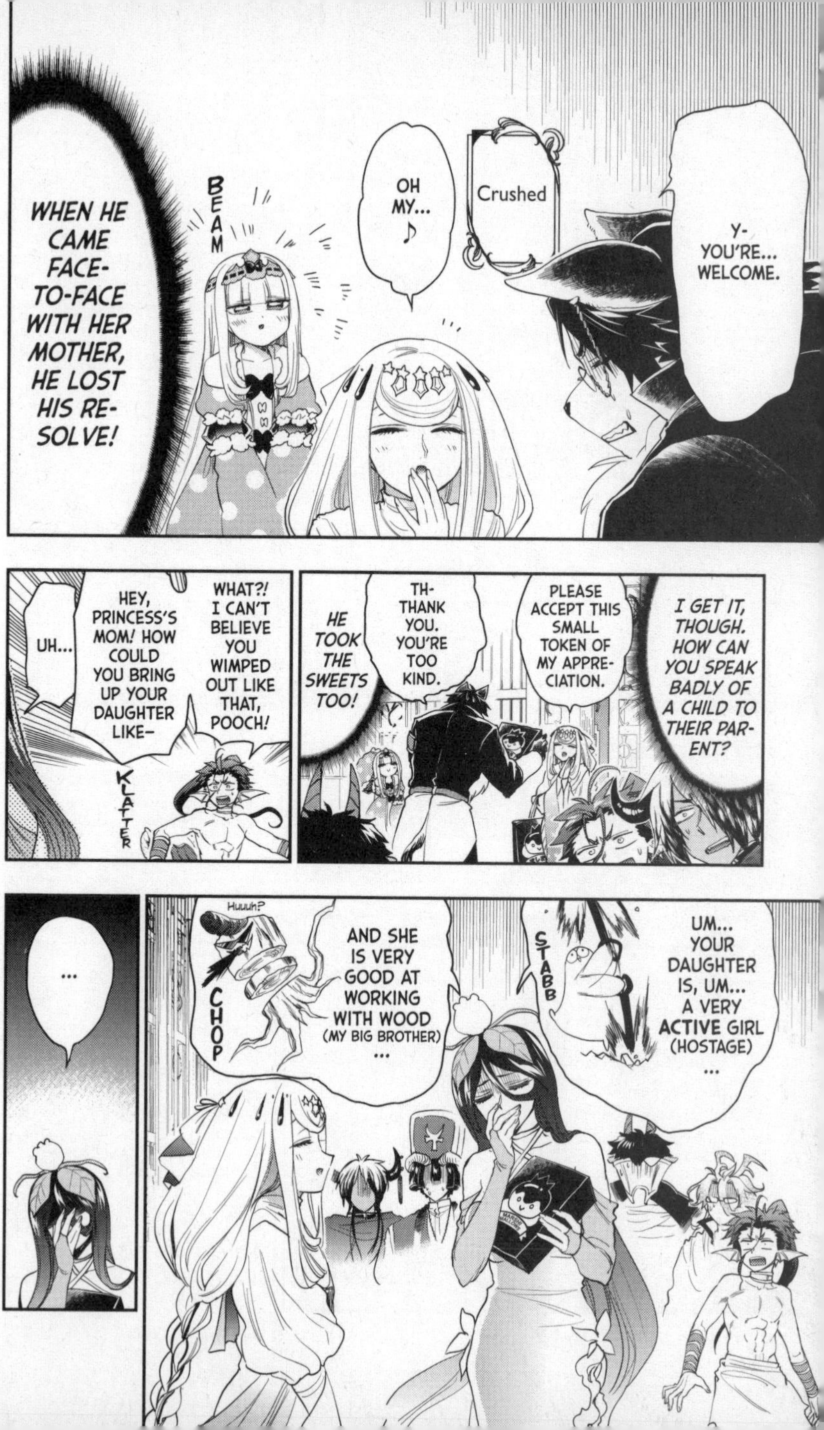
Y- YOU'RE... WELCOME.
Crushed
OH MY... ♪
BEAM
WHEN HE CAME FACE-TO-FACE WITH HER MOTHER, HE LOST HIS RE-SOLVE!
I GET IT, THOUGH. HOW CAN YOU SPEAK BADLY OF A CHILD TO THEIR PAR-ENT?
PLEASE ACCEPT THIS SMALL TOKEN OF MY APPRE-CIATION.
TH-THANK YOU. YOU'RE TOO KIND.
HE TOOK THE SWEETS TOO!
WHAT?! I CAN'T BELIEVE YOU WIMPED OUT LIKE THAT, POOCH!
HEY, PRINCESS'S MOM! HOW COULD YOU BRING UP YOUR DAUGHTER LIKE–
KLATTER
UH...
UM... YOUR DAUGHTER IS, UM... A VERY ACTIVE GIRL (HOSTAGE) ...
STABB
AND SHE IS VERY GOOD AT WORKING WITH WOOD (MY BIG BROTHER) ...
Huuuh?
CHOP
...

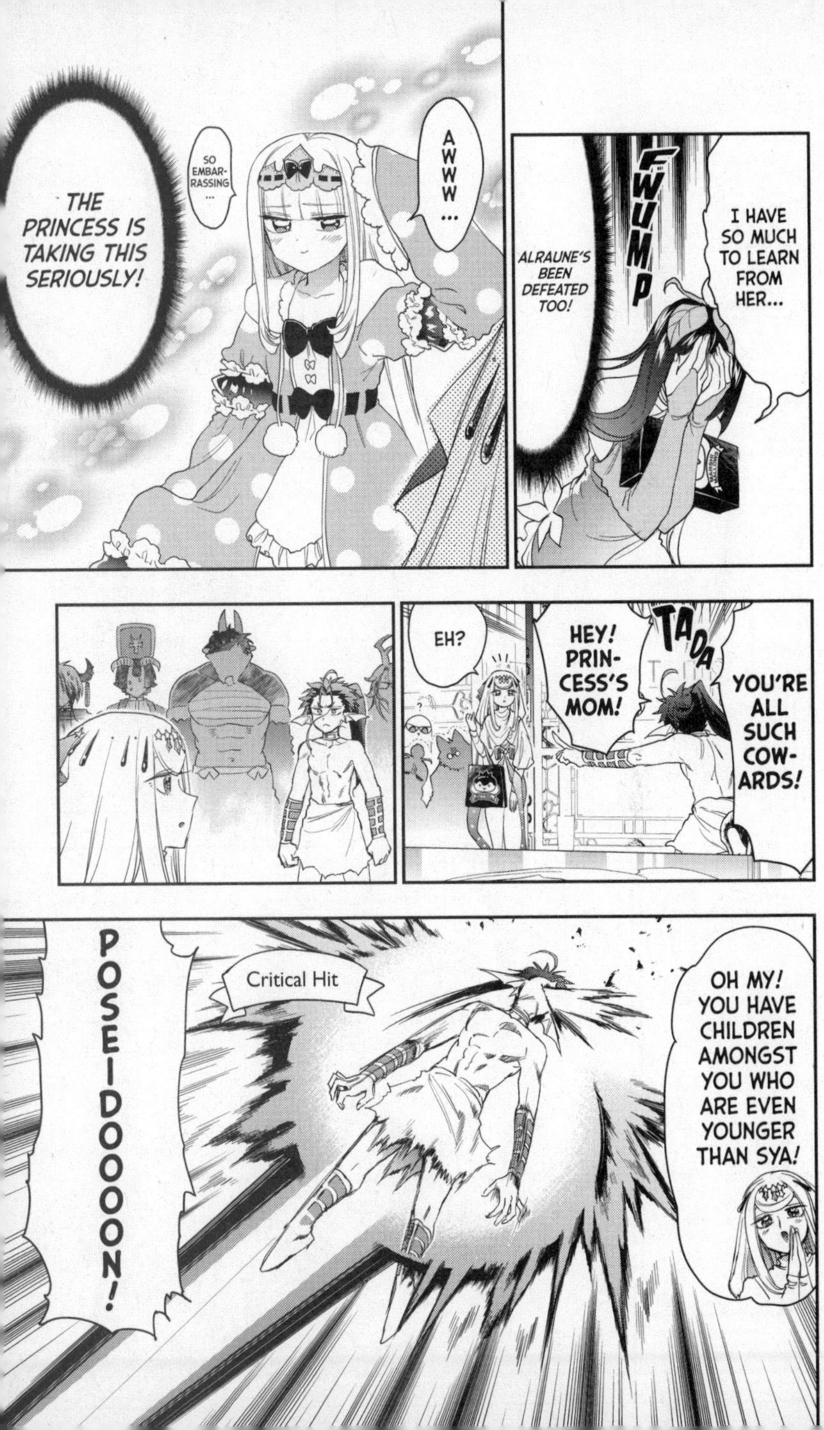
FWUMP
I HAVE SO MUCH TO LEARN FROM HER...
ALRAUNE'S BEEN DEFEATED TOO!
AWWW...
SO EMBARRASSING...
THE PRINCESS IS TAKING THIS SERIOUSLY!
TADA
YOU'RE ALL SUCH COWARDS!
HEY! PRINCESS'S MOM!
EH?
OH MY! YOU HAVE CHILDREN AMONGST YOU WHO ARE EVEN YOUNGER THAN SYA!
Critical Hit
POSEIDOOOOON!

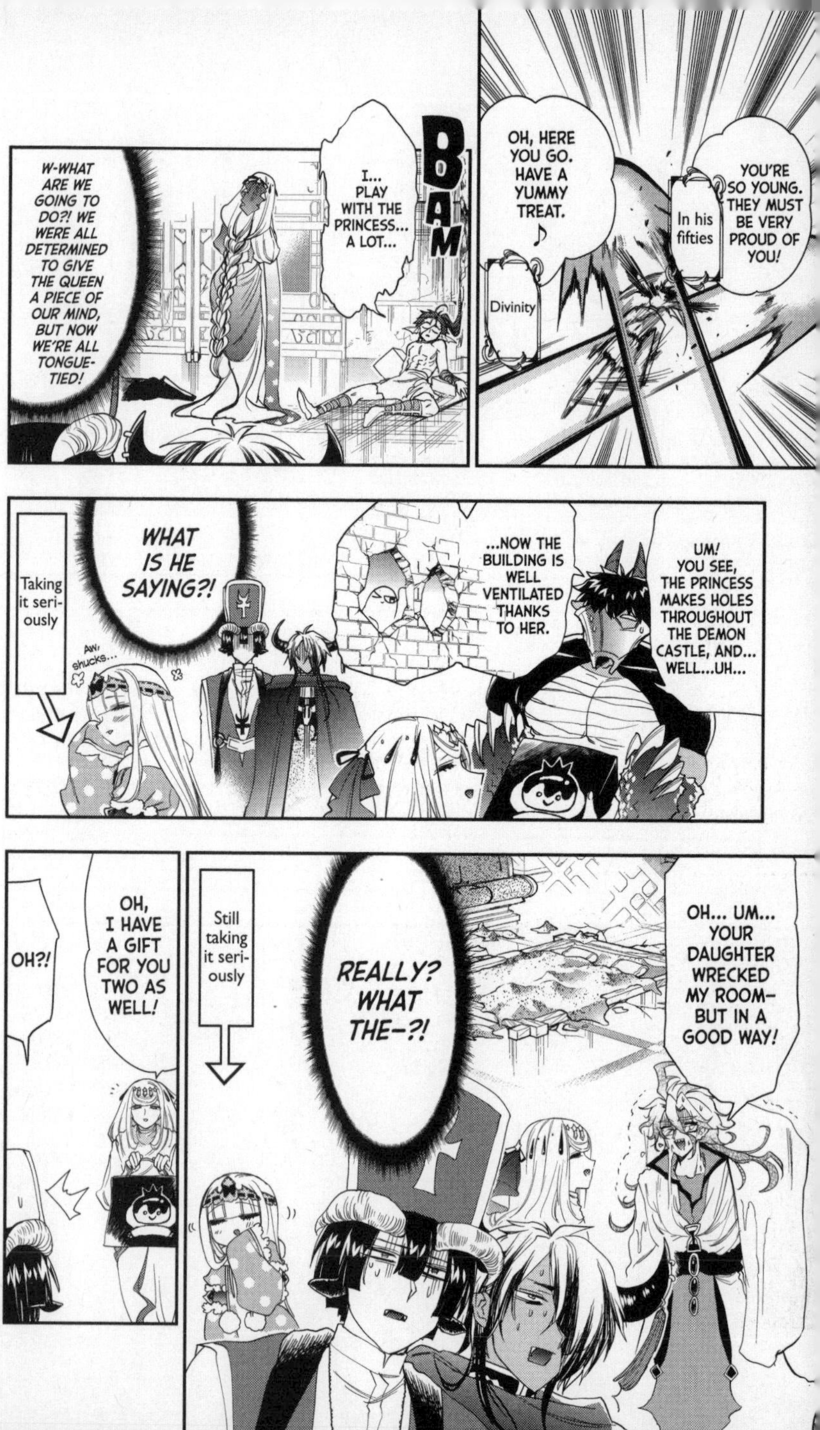
YOU'RE SO YOUNG. THEY MUST BE VERY PROUD OF YOU!
In his fifties
OH, HERE YOU GO. HAVE A YUMMY TREAT. ♪
Divinity
BAM
I... PLAY WITH THE PRINCESS... A LOT...
W-WHAT ARE WE GOING TO DO?! WE WERE ALL DETERMINED TO GIVE THE QUEEN A PIECE OF OUR MIND, BUT NOW WE'RE ALL TONGUE-TIED!
UM! YOU SEE, THE PRINCESS MAKES HOLES THROUGHOUT THE DEMON CASTLE, AND... WELL...UH...
...NOW THE BUILDING IS WELL VENTILATED THANKS TO HER.
WHAT IS HE SAYING?!
Taking it seri-ously
Aw, shucks...
OH... UM... YOUR DAUGHTER WRECKED MY ROOM— BUT IN A GOOD WAY!
REALLY? WHAT THE–?!
Still taking it seri-ously
OH, I HAVE A GIFT FOR YOU TWO AS WELL!
OH?!

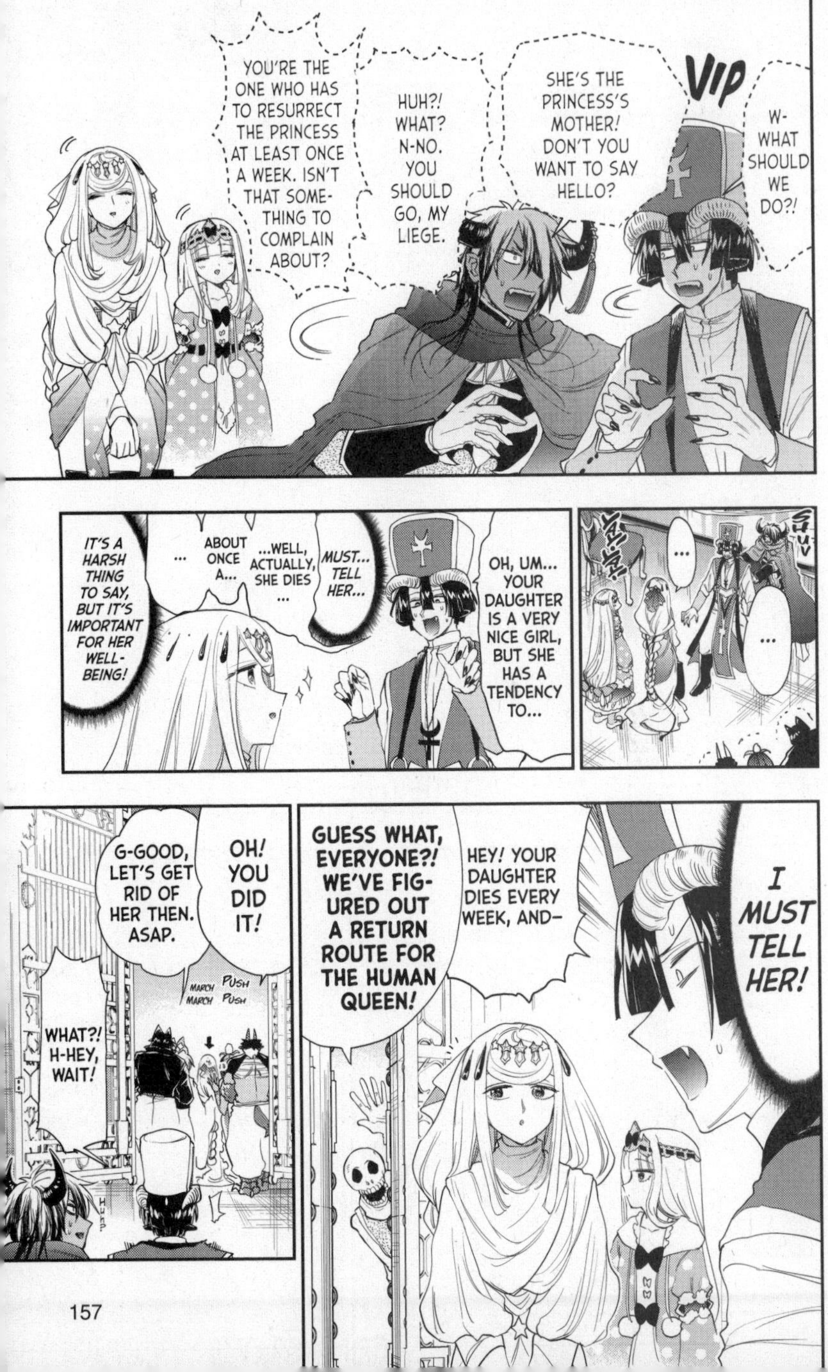
VIP
W-
WHAT SHOULD WE DO?!
SHE'S THE PRINCESS'S MOTHER! DON'T YOU WANT TO SAY HELLO?
HUH?! WHAT? N-NO. YOU SHOULD GO, MY LIEGE.
YOU'RE THE ONE WHO HAS TO RESURRECT THE PRINCESS AT LEAST ONCE A WEEK. ISN'T THAT SOMETHING TO COMPLAIN ABOUT?
SHUV
...
...
OH, UM... YOUR DAUGHTER IS A VERY NICE GIRL, BUT SHE HAS A TENDENCY TO...
MUST... TELL HER...
...WELL, ACTUALLY, SHE DIES ...
ABOUT ONCE A...
...
IT'S A HARSH THING TO SAY, BUT IT'S IMPORTANT FOR HER WELL-BEING!
I MUST TELL HER!
HEY! YOUR DAUGHTER DIES EVERY WEEK, AND—
GUESS WHAT, EVERYONE?! WE'VE FIGURED OUT A RETURN ROUTE FOR THE HUMAN QUEEN!
OH! YOU DID IT!
G-GOOD, LET'S GET RID OF HER THEN. ASAP.
PUSH PUSH
MARCH MARCH
WHAT?! H-HEY, WAIT!

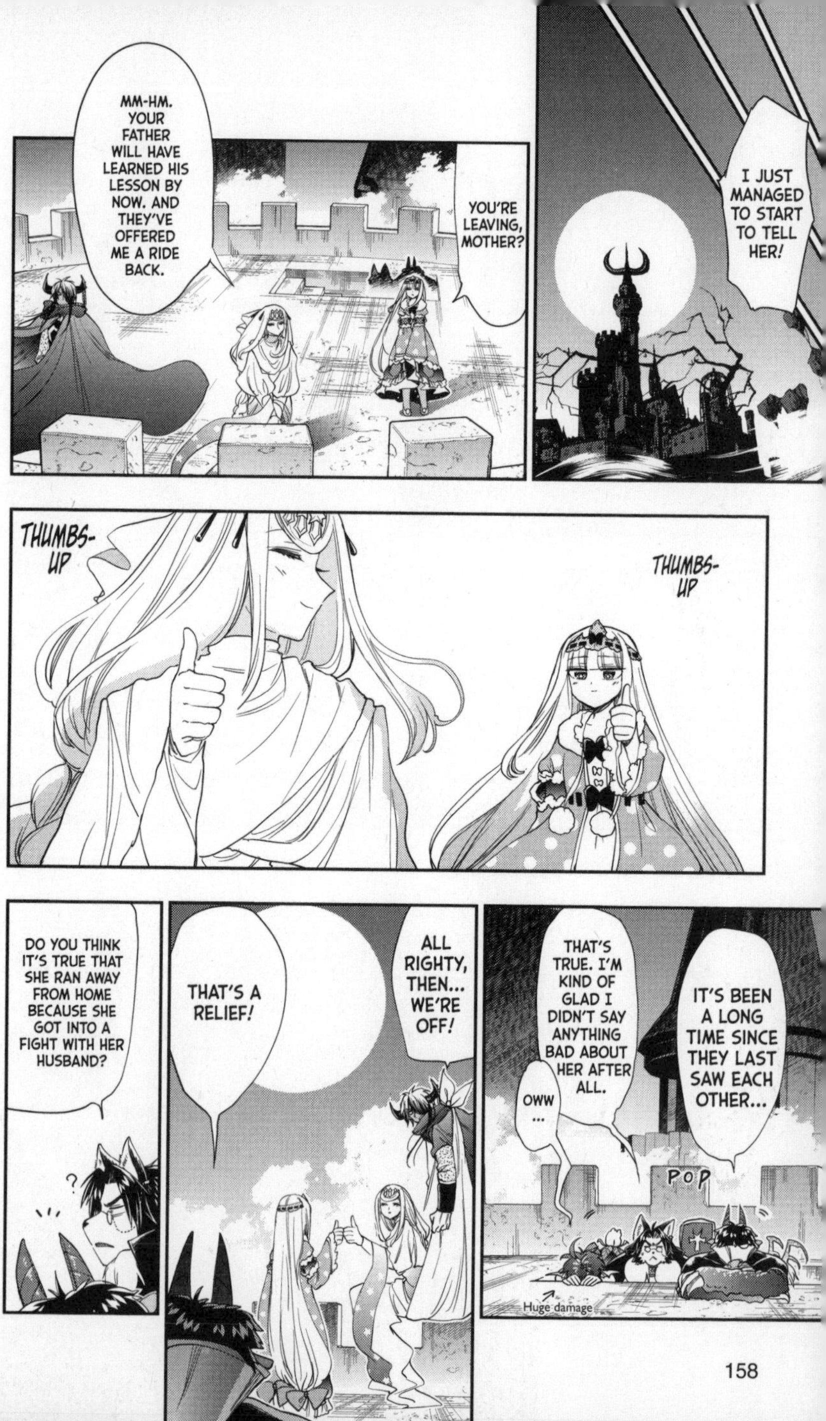
I JUST MANAGED TO START TO TELL HER!
YOU'RE LEAVING, MOTHER?
MM-HM. YOUR FATHER WILL HAVE LEARNED HIS LESSON BY NOW. AND THEY'VE OFFERED ME A RIDE BACK.
THUMBS-UP
THUMBS-UP
IT'S BEEN A LONG TIME SINCE THEY LAST SAW EACH OTHER...
THAT'S TRUE. I'M KIND OF GLAD I DIDN'T SAY ANYTHING BAD ABOUT HER AFTER ALL.
OWW ...
POP
Huge damage
ALL RIGHTY, THEN... WE'RE OFF!
THAT'S A RELIEF!
DO YOU THINK IT'S TRUE THAT SHE RAN AWAY FROM HOME BECAUSE SHE GOT INTO A FIGHT WITH HER HUSBAND?
?

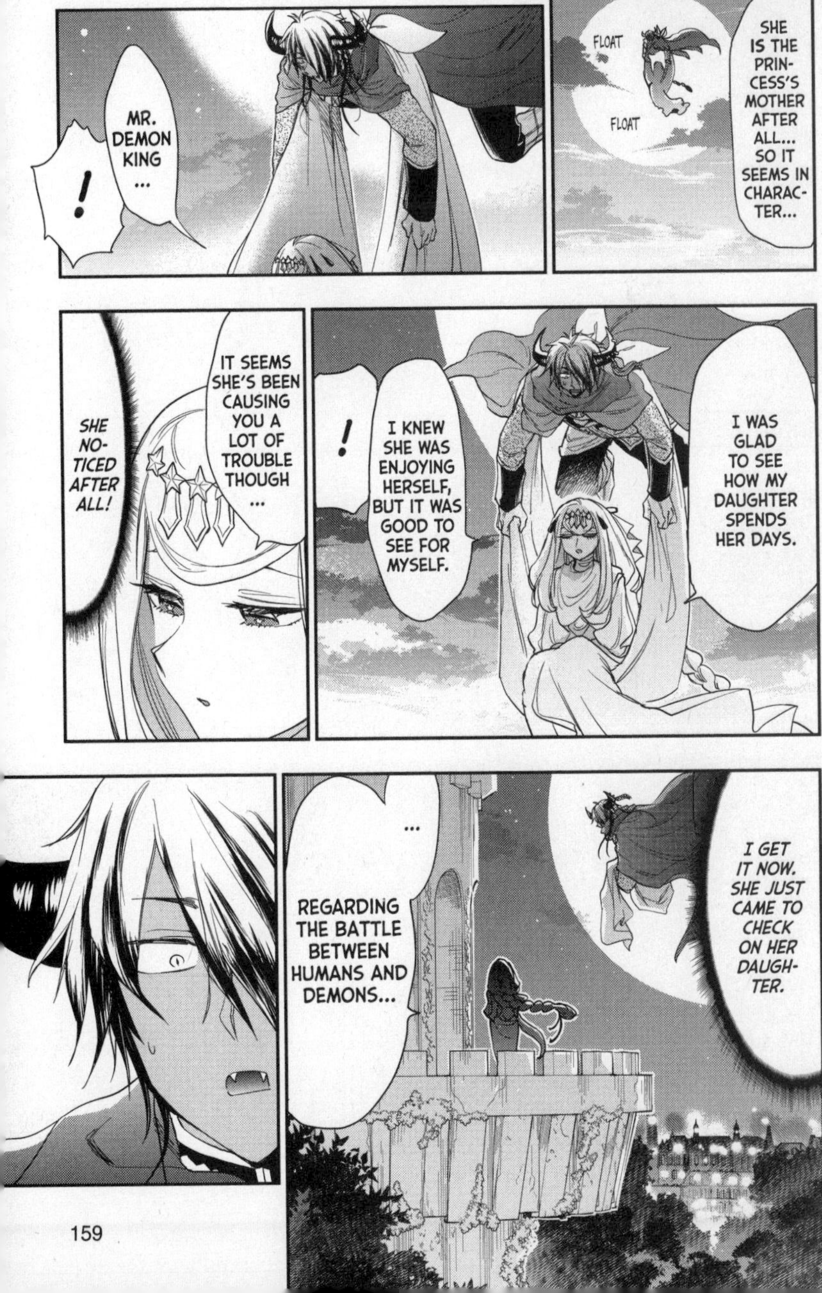
SHE IS THE PRINCESS'S MOTHER AFTER ALL... SO IT SEEMS IN CHARACTER...
FLOAT
FLOAT
MR. DEMON KING ...
!
I WAS GLAD TO SEE HOW MY DAUGHTER SPENDS HER DAYS.
I KNEW SHE WAS ENJOYING HERSELF, BUT IT WAS GOOD TO SEE FOR MYSELF.
!
IT SEEMS SHE'S BEEN CAUSING YOU A LOT OF TROUBLE THOUGH ...
SHE NOTICED AFTER ALL!
I GET IT NOW. SHE JUST CAME TO CHECK ON HER DAUGHTER.
...
REGARDING THE BATTLE BETWEEN HUMANS AND DEMONS...

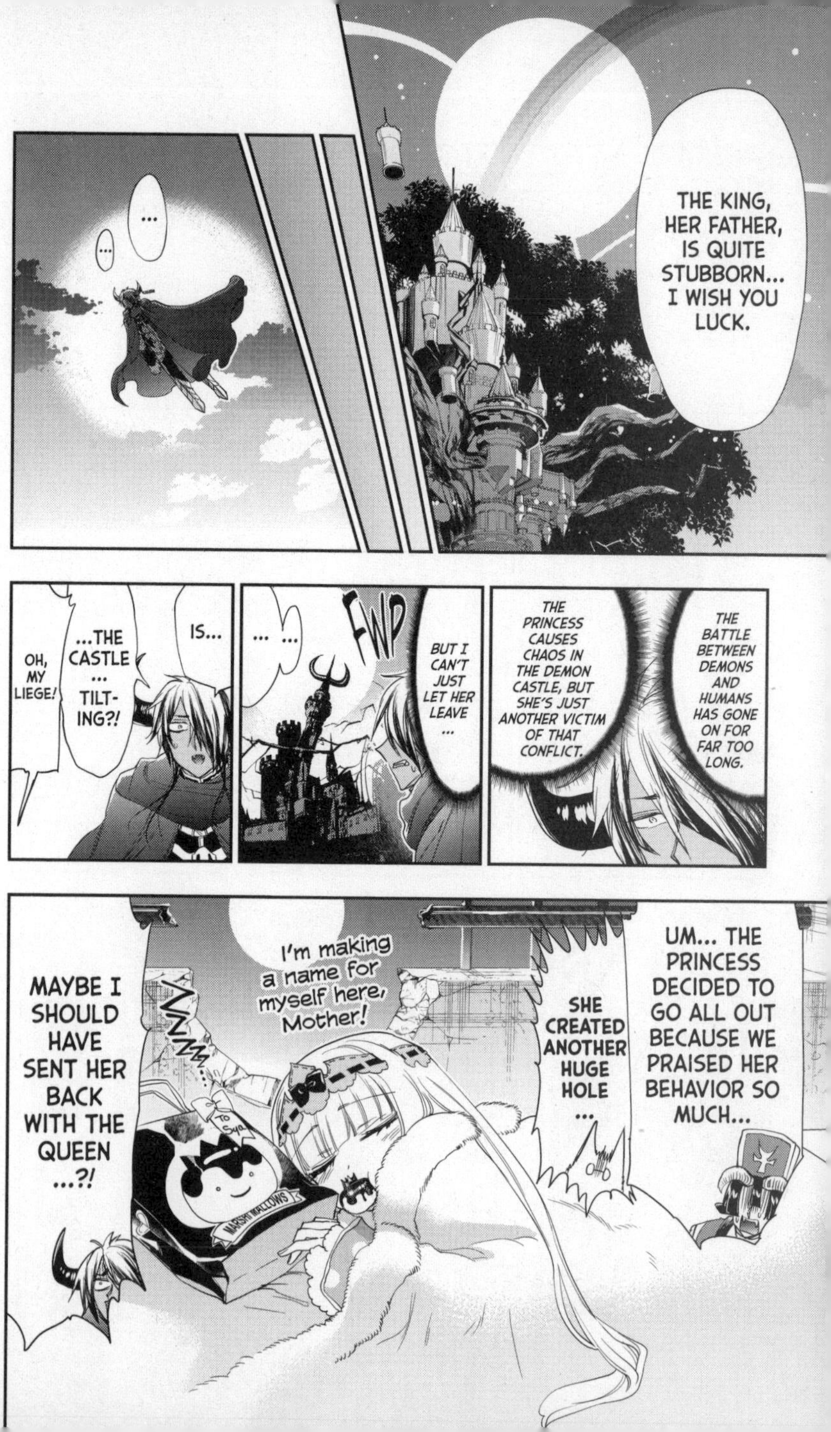
THE KING, HER FATHER, IS QUITE STUBBORN... I WISH YOU LUCK.
...
...
THE BATTLE BETWEEN DEMONS AND HUMANS HAS GONE ON FOR FAR TOO LONG.
THE PRINCESS CAUSES CHAOS IN THE DEMON CASTLE, BUT SHE'S JUST ANOTHER VICTIM OF THAT CONFLICT.
BUT I CAN'T JUST LET HER LEAVE ...
FWP
... ...
IS...
...THE CASTLE ... TILT-ING?!
OH, MY LIEGE!
UM... THE PRINCESS DECIDED TO GO ALL OUT BECAUSE WE PRAISED HER BEHAVIOR SO MUCH...
SHE CREATED ANOTHER HUGE HOLE ...
I'm making a name for myself here, Mother!
ZZZ...
MARSHMALLOWS
MAYBE I SHOULD HAVE SENT HER BACK WITH THE QUEEN ...?!

A Mom's Regret

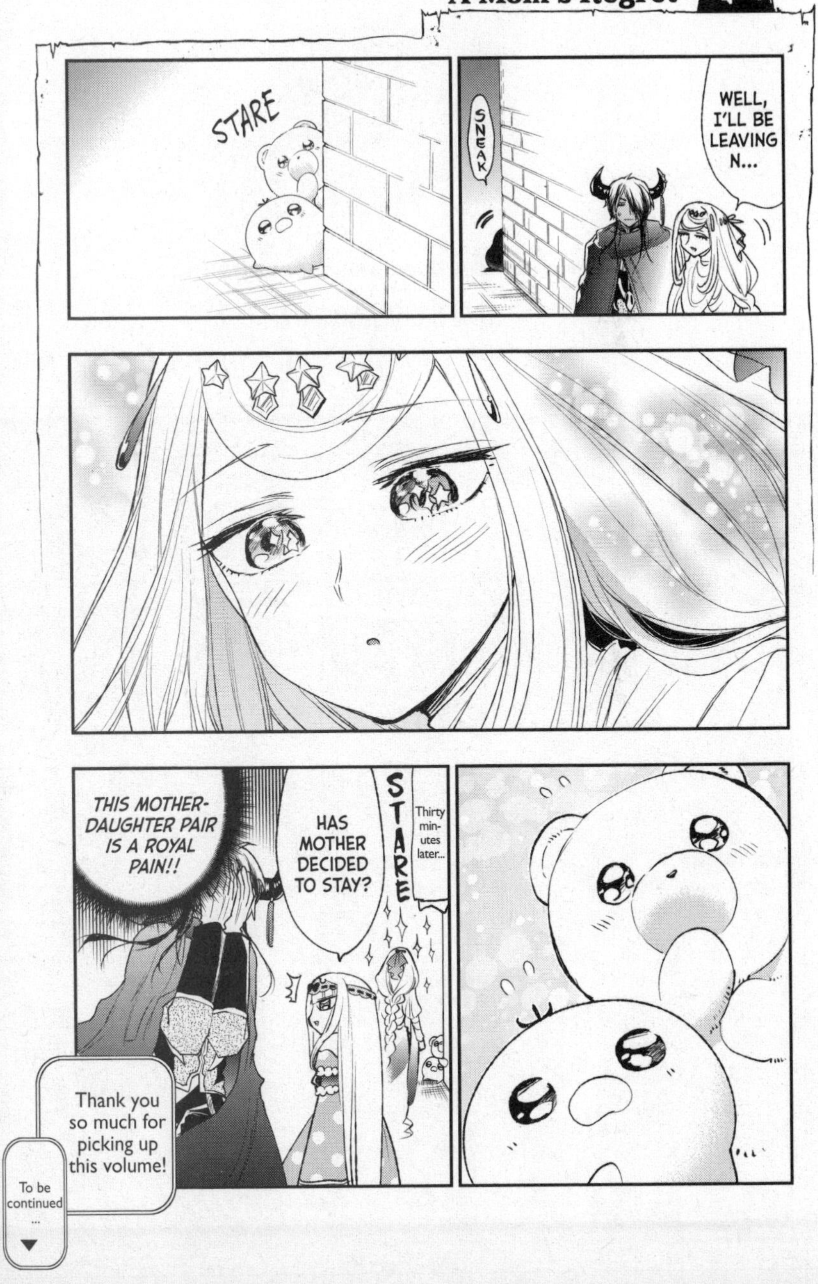
WELL, I'LL BE LEAVING N...
SNEAK
STARE
Thirty min-utes later...
STARE
HAS MOTHER DECIDED TO STAY?
THIS MOTHER-DAUGHTER PAIR IS A ROYAL PAIN!!
Thank you so much for picking up this volume!
To be continued ...

Answering reader questions is so much fun...

— KAGIJI KUMANOMATA

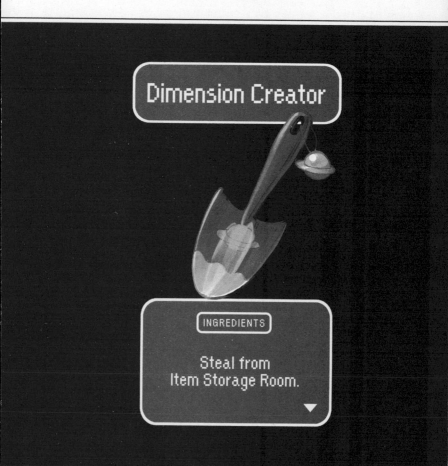

Dimension Creator

INGREDIENTS

Steal from
Item Storage Room.

▼

Those who lurk beneath the cover...

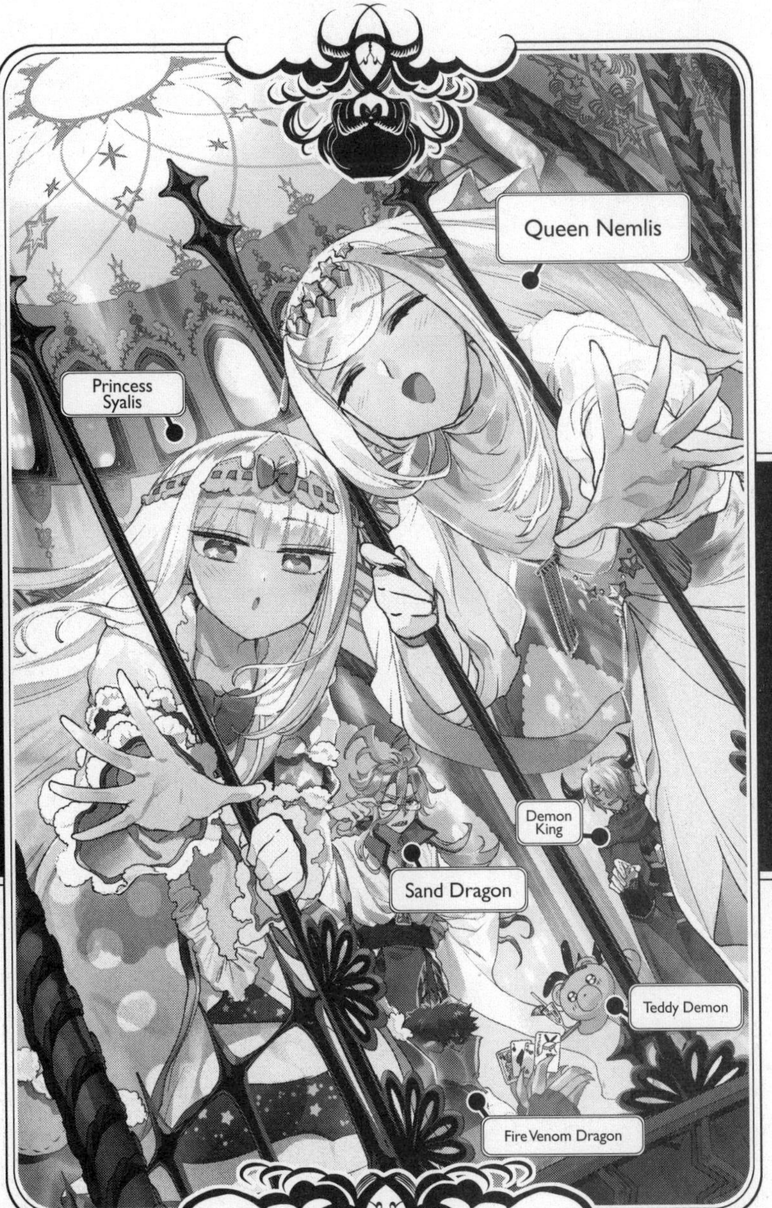
Queen Nemlis
Princess Syalis
Demon King
Sand Dragon
Teddy Demon
Fire Venom Dragon

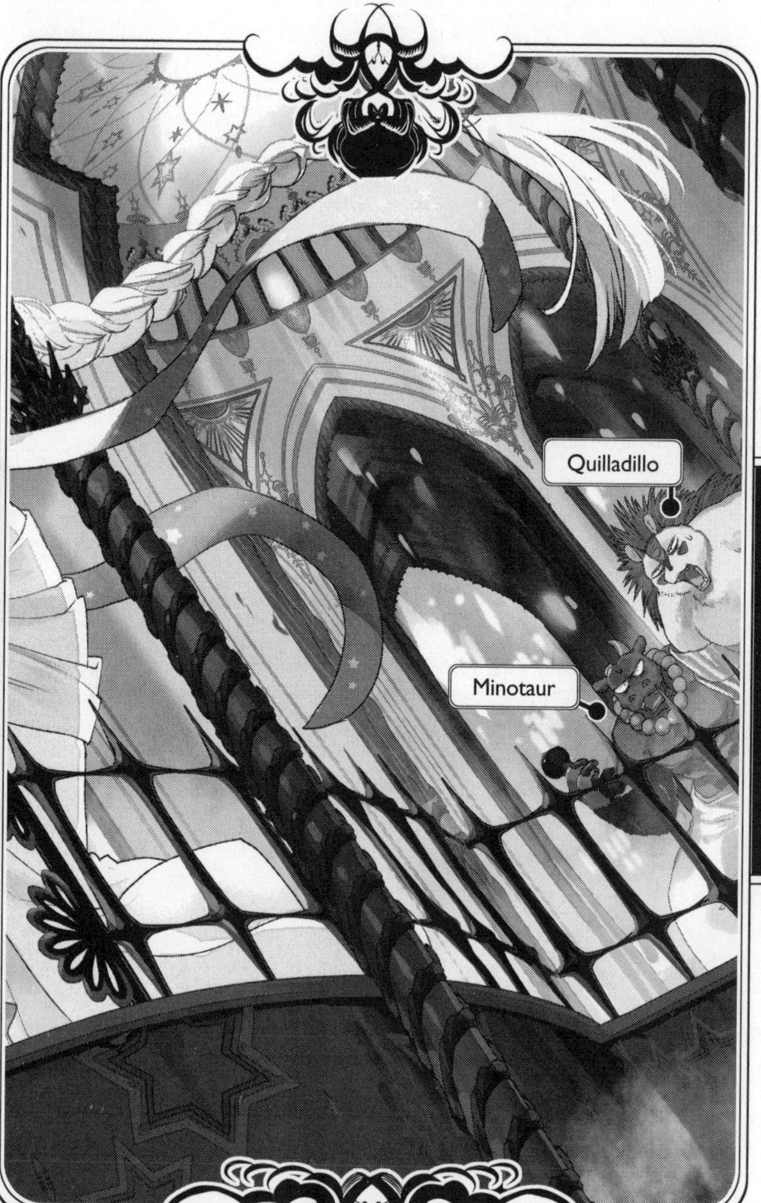
Quilladillo
Minotaur

SLEEPY PRINCESS IN THE DEMON CASTLE

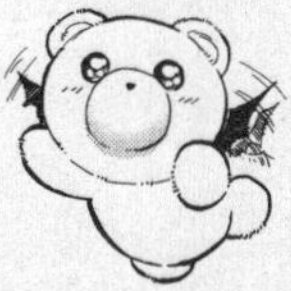

14

Shonen Sunday Edition

STORY AND ART BY

KAGIJI KUMANOMATA

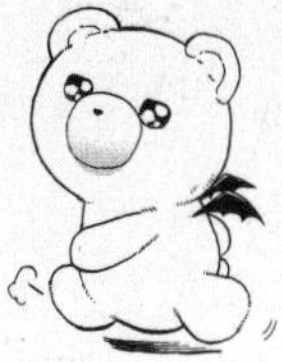

TRANSLATION **TETSUICHIRO MIYAKI**
ENGLISH ADAPTATION **ANNETTE ROMAN**
TOUCH-UP ART & LETTERING **JAMES GAUBATZ**
COVER & INTERIOR DESIGN **ALICE LEWIS**
EDITOR **ANNETTE ROMAN**

Printed in the U.S.A.

Published by VIZ Media, LLC
P.O. Box 77010
San Francisco, CA 94107

10 9 8 7 6 5 4 3 2 1
First printing, April 2021

ratings.viz.com RATED T TEEN

PARENTAL ADVISORY
SLEEPY PRINCESS IN THE DEMON CASTLE is rated T for Teen and is recommended for ages 13 and up. This volume contains fantasy violence.

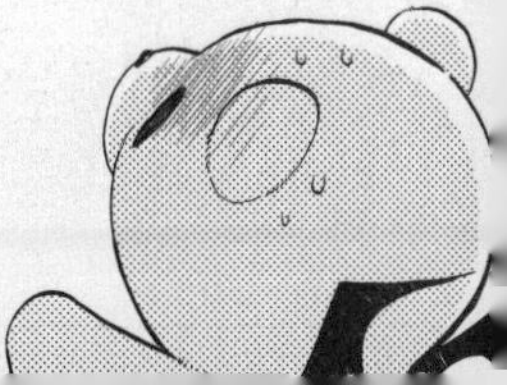

VIZ MEDIA
viz.com

SHONEN SUNDAY
shonensunday.com

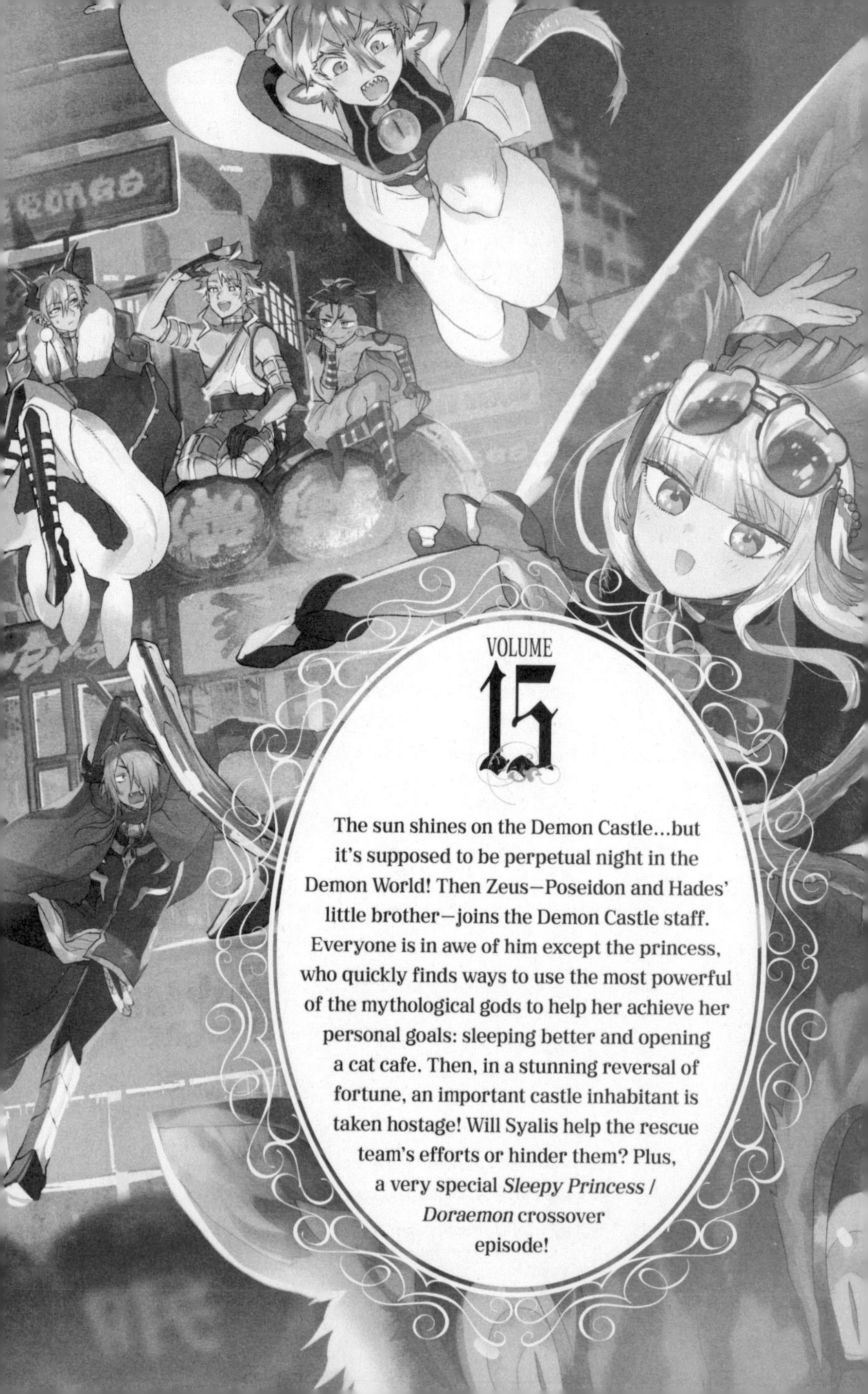

VOLUME

15

The sun shines on the Demon Castle…but it's supposed to be perpetual night in the Demon World! Then Zeus—Poseidon and Hades' little brother—joins the Demon Castle staff. Everyone is in awe of him except the princess, who quickly finds ways to use the most powerful of the mythological gods to help her achieve her personal goals: sleeping better and opening a cat cafe. Then, in a stunning reversal of fortune, an important castle inhabitant is taken hostage! Will Syalis help the rescue team's efforts or hinder them? Plus, a very special *Sleepy Princess / Doraemon* crossover episode!

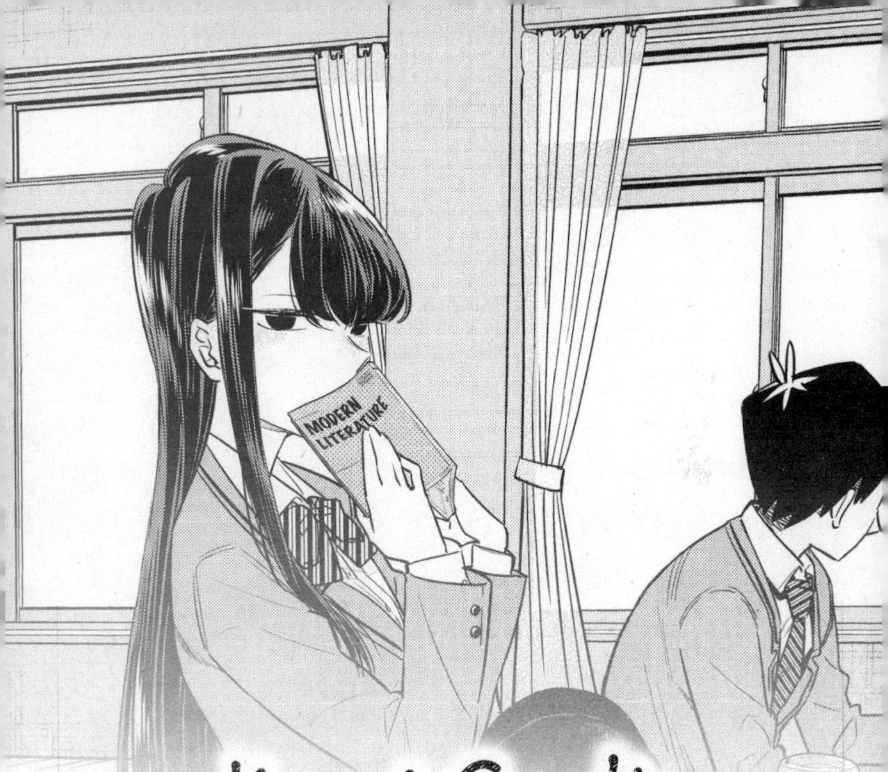
MODERN LITERATURE

Komi Can't Communicate

Story & Art by Tomohito Oda

The journey to a hundred friends begins with a single conversation.

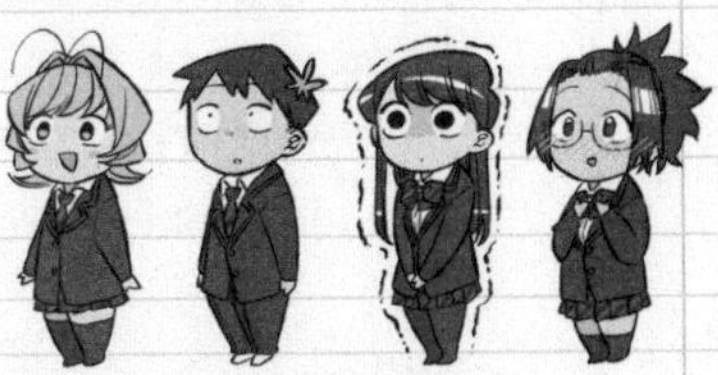

Socially anxious high school student Shoko Komi's greatest dream is to make some friends, but everyone at school mistakes her crippling social anxiety for cool reserve. With the whole student body keeping its distance and Komi unable to utter a single word, friendship might be forever beyond her reach.

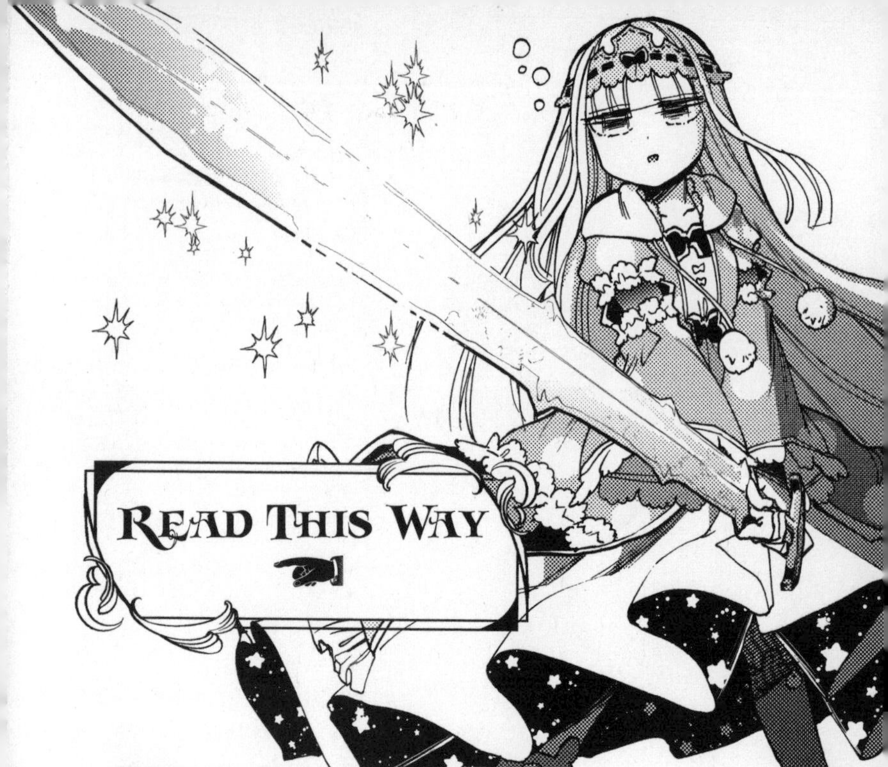
READ THIS WAY

STOP!

You may be reading the wrong way!

In keeping with the original Japanese comic format, this book reads from right to left—so action, sound effects and word balloons are completely reversed to preserve the orientation of the original artwork.

Check out the diagram shown here to get the hang of things, and then turn to the other side of the book to get started!

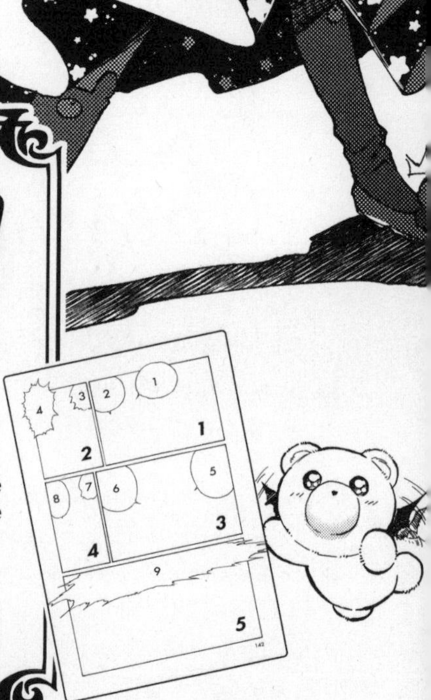